Lecture Notes in Computer Science   8276

Commenced Publication in 1973
Founding and Former Series Editors:
Gerhard Goos, Juris Hartmanis, and Jan van Leeuwen

Gabriel Urzaiz   Sergio F. Ochoa
José Bravo   Liming Luke Chen
Jonice Oliveira (Eds.)

Ubiquitous Computing and Ambient Intelligence

Context-Awareness and Context-Driven Interaction

7th International Conference, UCAmI 2013
Carrillo, Costa Rica, December 2-6, 2013
Proceedings

 Springer

Volume Editors

Gabriel Urzaiz
Universidad Anáhuac Mayab, Mérida, YUC, México
E-mail: gabriel.urzaiz@anahuac.mx

Sergio F. Ochoa
University of Chile, Santiago de Chile, Chile
E-mail: sochoa@dcc.uchile.cl

José Bravo
MAmI Research Lab, Castilla-La Manca University, Ciudad Real, Spain
E-mail: jose.bravo@uclm.es

Liming Luke Chen
University of Ulster, Newtownabbey, County Antrim, UK
E-mail: l.chen@ulster.ac.uk

Jonice Oliveira
Universidade Federal do Rio de Janeiro, Rio de Janeiro, Brazil
E-mail: jonice@dcc.ufrj.br

ISSN 0302-9743   e-ISSN 1611-3349
ISBN 978-3-319-03175-0   e-ISBN 978-3-319-03176-7
DOI 10.1007/978-3-319-03176-7
Springer Cham Heidelberg New York Dordrecht London

CR Subject Classification (1998): H.4, C.2.4, H.3, I.2.11, H.5, D.2, K.4

LNCS Sublibrary: SL 3 – Information Systems and Application, incl. Internet/Web and HCI

Typesetting: Camera-ready by author, data conversion by Scientific Publishing Services, Chennai, India

Printed on acid-free paper

Springer is part of Springer Science+Business Media (www.springer.com)

Preface

This year we are celebrating at Carrillo, Costa Rica a joint event, which includes the 7th International Conference on Ubiquitous Computing and Ambient Intelligence (UCAmI 2013), the 5th International Work Conference on Ambient Assisted Living (IWAAL 2013), the 6th Latin American Conference on Human Computer Interaction (CLIHC 2013), and the Workshop on Urban Applications and Infrastructures (UrbAI 2013). The program of this joint event includes a rich variety of technical sessions to cover the most relevant research topics of each conference. A total number of 116 submissions were received, and the acceptance rate for long papers was 58 percent.

UCAmI 2013 counts on Dr. Julie A. Jacko and Prof. Mariano Alcañiz Raya as prominent keynote speakers. We would like to thank both of them for their participation and contribution to this joint event.

UCAmI 2013 is focused on research topics related to context-awareness and context-driven interaction, including: human interaction in ambient intelligence, solutions to implement smart environments and objects, intelligence for ambient adaptation, internet of things, social web of things, and intelligent transportation systems.

In this seventh edition of UCAmI we received 48 submissions that involved 157 authors from 14 different countries. A total number of 109 reviews were done by 81 reviewers from 20 countries, with an average of 2.27 reviews per paper. We would like to thank all those who submitted papers for consideration and also the reviewers participating in this process.

In this proceedings book, it is a great pleasure for us to also include the 8 articles that were accepted in the workshop UrbAI 2013. This workshop provided a forum to share knowledge and experiences towards the assessment, development, and deployment of ubiquitous computing and ambient intelligence solutions for urban domains.

Finally, we would like to express our deepest thanks to the colleagues who helped to organize the conference, particularly Dr. Luis Guerrero of the University of Costa Rica. We would also like to thank all Program Committee members who have given tirelessly their time to contribute to this event.

December 2013

Gabriel Urzaiz
José Bravo
Sergio F. Ochoa
Liming Luke Chen
Jonice Oliveira

Organization

General Chairs

Jose Bravo   Castilla La Mancha University, Spain
Sergio F. Ochoa   University of Chile, Chile

UCAmI PC Chairs

Gabriel Urzaiz   Universidad Anahuac Mayab, Mexico
Liming Luke Chen   University of Ulster, UK
Jonice Oliveira   Federal University of Rio de Janeiro, Brazil

Workshop Chair

Ramón Hervás   Castilla La Mancha University, Spain

Local Chair

Luis A. Guerrero   Universidad de Costa Rica, Costa Rica

Publicity Chairs

Jesus Fontecha   Castilla La Mancha University, Spain
Vladimir Villarreal   Technological University of Panama, Panama

Program Committee

Hamid Aghajan   Stanford University, USA
Mariano Alcañiz   UPV - i3bh/LabHuman, Spain
Roberto Aldunate   Applied Research Associates, USA
Jan Alexandersson   DFKI GmbH, Germany
Cecilio Angulo   Universitat Politècnica de Catalunya, Spain
Mert Bal   Miami University, USA
Madeline Balaam   Newcastle University, UK
Nelson Baloian   University of Chile, Chile
Denilson Barbosa   University of Alberta, Canada
Sergio Barbosa   Universidade Federal do Rio de Janeiro, Brazil
Jean-Paul Barthes   University of Technology of Compiègne, France
Paolo Bellavesta   University of Bologna, Italy
Marcos Borges   Universidade Federal do Rio de Janeiro, Brazil

Jose Bravo   Castilla La Mancha University, Spain
Ceren Budak   University of California at Santa Barbara, USA
Sophie Chabridon   Institut TELECOM, France
Ranveer Chandra   Microsoft Research, USA
Ignacio Chang   Universidad Tecnológica de Panamá, Panama
Liming Luke Chen   University of Ulster, UK
Diane J. Cook   Washington State University, USA
Geoff Coulson   Lancaster University, UK
Kevin Curran   University of Ulster, UK
Coen De Roover   Vrije Universiteit Brussel, Belgium
Boris De Ruyter   Philips Research, The Netherlands
Anind Dey   Carnegie Mellon University, USA
Simon Dobson   University of St Andrews, UK
Mohamed Fayad   San Jose State University, USA
João M. Fernandes   Universidade do Minho, Portugal
Carlo Ferrari   University of Padua, Italy
Jesús Fontecha   Castilla La Mancha University, Spain
Lidia Fuentes   University of Malaga, Spain
Dan Grigoras   University College Cork, Ireland
Luis Guerrero   Universidad de Chile, Chile
Bin Guo   Northwestern Polytechnical University, China
Chris Guy   University of Reading, UK
Antonio Gómez Skarmeta   Universidad de Murcia, Spain
Ramon Hervas   Castilla La Mancha University, Spain
Jesse Hoey   University of Waterloo, Canada
Bin Hu   Kenan-Flagler Business School, University of
                                  North Carolina, USA
Anne James   Appl. Comput. Res. Centre (ACRC), Coventry
                                  University, UK
Miren Karmele   EHU (Basque Country University), Spain
Jean Christophe Lapayre   Franche-Comte University, France
Erns Leiss   University of Houston, USA
Wenfeng Li   Wuhan University of Technology, China
Tun Lu   Fudan University, China
Juan Carlos López   Castilla La Mancha University, Spain
Diego López-De-Ipiña   University of Deusto, Spain
Ricardo-J. Machado   Universidade do Minho, Portugal
Francisco Moya   Castilla La Mancha University, Spain
Lilia Muñoz   Technological University of Panama, Panama
Andres Neyem   Pontificia Universidad Católica de Chile, Chile
David H. Nguyen   University of California at Irvine, USA
Chris Nugent   University of Ulster, UK

Table of Contents

Session 2
Human Interaction in Ambient Intelligence (2/2)

Session 3
ICT Instrumentation and Middleware Support for Smart Environments and Objects

Session 6
Workshop on Urban Applications and Infrastructures (UrbAI)

Context-Aware Energy Efficiency
in Smart Buildings

María Victoria Moreno Cano, José Santa,
Miguel Angel Zamora, and Antonio F. Skarmeta Gómez

University of Murcia, Department of Information and Communications Egineering
Campus de Espinardo, 30100 Murcia, Spain
{mvmoreno,josesanta,mzamora,skarmeta}@um.es

Abstract. When talking about energy efficiency at global scale, buildings are the cornerstone in terms of power consumption and CO_2 emissions. New communication paradigms, such as Internet of Things, can improve the way sensors and actuators are accessed in smart buildings. Following this approach, we present an energy efficiency subsystem integrated with a building automation solution that makes the most of the energy consumed, considering user preferences, environmental conditions, and presence/identity of occupants. Through a three-stage approach based on behavior-centred mechanisms, the system is able to propose concrete settings on building devices to cope with energy and user comfort restrictions. The proposal has been implemented and deployed on a smart building. A set of tests validates the system when users are correctly located and identified at comfort service points, and first experimental stages already reflect energy saves in heating and cooling about 20%.

Keywords: Smart Buildings, Energy Efficiency, Context Awareness.

1 Introduction

National governments, industries and citizens worldwide have recognized the need for a more efficient and responsible use of the planet's resources, and new energy and climate goals have already been adopted accordingly, for example the EU's 20-20-20 goals[1]. Due to their relevance in the daily life and their impact on worldwide power consumption, buildings are key infrastructures when talking about the synergy between technology advances and energy efficiency. Indoor environments have a direct relation with quality of life and power consumption both at the work and in citizens private life. Thus, future buildings should be capable of providing mechanisms to minimize their energy consumption, and integrate local power sources improving their energy balance.

Last advances on Information and Communication Technologies (ICT) and Internet of Things (IoT) [1] are identified as key enablers for accessing remote sensing units and managing building automation systems. Nevertheless, although

---

[1] www.ec.europa.eu/clima/policies/package/index_en.htm

G. Urzaiz et al. (Eds.): UCAmI 2013, LNCS 8276, pp. 1–8, 2013.

there are already works addressing the problem of energy efficiency in buildings, few of them benefit from the boost provided by IoT capabilities in this environment to optimize energy consumption using real-time information or include individual user data. In this sense, the smart energy management system presented in this paper considers an IoT-based building automation platform that gathers real-time data from a huge variety of sensors, and uses behavior-based techniques to determine appropriate control actions on individual lighting and heat, ventilation, air conditioning (HVAC), in order to satisfy comfort conditions of users while saving energy. Most of our IoT infrastructure is composed of wired and wireless sensors and actuator networks embedded in the environment, but individuals play a fundamental role, since the system is able to consider user comfort needs. Moreover, we also show how despite the relatively short time of operation of our system in a real smart building, energy saving is already achieved thanks to consider accurate user location data and individualized control of appliances, in order to provide environmental comfort at specific target locations.

The rest of the paper is organized as follows: Section 2 places the proposal in the literature by reviewing recent related works. Section 3 describes our proposal for intelligent energy management, integrated in a reference building automation solution. Section 4 details the system deployment carried out in a reference smart building where initial tests have been performed for assessing the system operation. Finally, Section 5 concludes the paper with a set of final remarks and presenting future lines.

2   Literature Review

Most of the previous approaches addressing the problem of energy efficiency of buildings present partial solutions regarding monitoring, data collection from sensors or control actions. In [2] an examination of the main issues in adaptive building management systems is carried out, and as the authors state, there are few works dealing with this problem completely. Regarding building automation systems, there are many works in literature extending the domotics field initially focused only on houses. For instance, a relevant example is the proposal given in [3], where the authors describe an automation system for smart homes on top of a sensor network. The work presented in [4] is also based on a sensor network to cope with the building automation problem, but this time the messages of the routing protocol include monitoring information of the building context. The literature about energy efficiency in buildings using automation platforms is more limited. In [5], for instance, a reference implementation of an energy consumption framework is given to analyze only the efficiency of a ventilation unit. In [6] it is described a deployment of a common client/server architecture focused on monitoring energy consumption but without performing any control action.

In this paper, we present a real and interoperable experience on a general purpose platform for building automation, which addresses the problem of energy efficiency of buildings, comfort services of occupants, environmental monitoring and security issues, among others, by means of a flexible IoT platform, which allows to gather data from a plethora of different sources and to control a wide range of automated parts of the building.

3   Intelligent Management System for Energy Efficiency of Buildings

For a building to be considered energy-efficient it must be able to minimize conventional energy consumption (i.e. non-renewable energy) with the goal of saving energy and using it rationally. Optimizing energy efficiency in buildings is an integrated task that covers the whole lifecycle of the building [5], and during these phases it is necessary to continuously adapt the operation of its subsystems to optimize energy performance indexes. However, this process is a complex task full of variables and constraints. Furthermore, the quality of life of occupants should be ensured through at least three basic factors: thermal comfort, visual comfort and indoor air quality (IAQ). But the definition of these factors is not fixed [7], since they depend on user comfort perception with a high subjective load. Therefore, it is necessary to provide users with increased awareness (mainly concerning the energy they consume), and permit them to be an input more to the underlying processes of the energy efficiency subsystem. Bearing these aspects in mind, below we present the base platform for our proposal of building management system, which is described subsequently.

3.1   Holistic IoT Platform for Smart Buildings

Our base automation platform used for integrating energy efficiency features is based on the CityExplorer solution (formerly called Domosec), whose main components were presented in detail in [8]. CityExplorer gathers information from sensors and actuators deployed in a building following an IoT approach and it is responsible for monitoring environmental parameters, gathering tracking data about occupants, detecting anomalies (such as fire and flooding among others), and it is able to take actions dealing with key efficiency requirements, such as saving power or water consumption. The main components of CityExplorer are the network of Home Automation Modules (HAM) and the SCADA (supervisory control and data acquisition). Each HAM module comprises an embedded system connected to all the appliances, sensors and actuators of various spaces of a building. These devices centralize the intelligence of each space, controlling the configuration of the installed devices. Additionally, the SCADA offers management and monitoring facilities through a connection with HAMs. Thus, all the environmental and location data measured by the deployed sensors are first available in HAMs and then reported to the SCADA, which maintains a global view of the whole infrastructure. Sensors and actuators can be self-configured and controlled remotely through the Internet, enabling a variety of monitoring and control applications.

3.2 Energy Efficiency Subsystem in CityExplorer

Our proposal of intelligent management system has capabilities for adapting the behavior of automated devices deployed in the building in order to meet energy consumption restrictions while maintaining the comfort level of occupants. The system is integrated in the back office part of the CityExplorer solution, using the SCADA as both data source and gateway to control automated devices. This way, the decisions taken by the intelligent management module are reflected on the actuators deployed in the building, such as the heating/cooling units and electric lights. We base our energy performance model on the CEN standard EN 15251 [9], which specifies the design criteria to be used for dimensioning the energy system in buildings, establishing and defining the main input parameters for estimating building energy requirements and evaluating the indoor environment. On the other hand, the comfort management algorithms are based on the models for predicting the comfort response of building occupants described in [10]. Taking into account all these criteria, we define the input data of our system, which are showed in Fig.1.

Our building management system for comfort and energy efficiency uses a combination of techniques based on behavior-centred mechanisms and computational intelligence [11] for auto-adapting its operation. This way, it is necessary to consider the data provided directly by users through their interaction, since they can change the comfort conditions provided automatically by the system and, consequently, the system can learn and auto-adjust according to the changes.

As can be seen in Fig. 1, an important prior issue to be solved is the indoor localization problem, since apart from environmental data, user identification and location data are also required to provide customized indoor services in smart buildings. Therefore, information about the number, location and identity of occupants, and even on their activity levels, are needed to adapt the comfort conditions provided in the spaces where occupants stay. Such comfort adaptation is performed through the individual management of the automated appliances in charge of providing their services in such areas. In this way, it is possible to carry out control decisions and define strategies to minimize the energy consumption of the building depending on user presence. For this reason, we have implemented an indoor localization system that provides positioning data of occupants by using RFID (Radio-Frequency Identification) and IR (Infra-Red) sensors deployed in the building [12]. This system is able to provide all user data mentioned as relevant for our problem.

On the other hand, the smart comfort and energy management system is divided in two main modules (see Fig. 1): the subsystem responsible for assuring the environmental comfort on the basis of the user preferences (*Smart Comfort Prediction*), and the subsystem in charge of estimating the energy wastage associated to such preferences and providing the optimal comfort settings that ensure the energy efficiency of the building (*Efficient Comfort Management*). The first module provides the optimum comfort conditions according to the occupants, their activities and their locations, apart from the individual comfort preferences. Once the comfort conditions for each location of the building have been estimated, the second module is responsible for estimating the optimum operational settings for the involved appliances, which ensure minimum energy consumption of the building while considering the previous estimated comfort conditions. For that, it is taken into account a forecast of environmental parameters and the energy generated by alternative energy sources installed in the building.

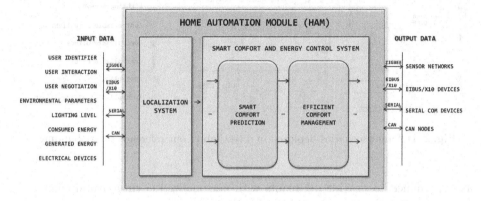

Fig. 1. Schema of the modules composing the management system focused on energy-efficient buildings

4   System Deployment and Tests

The reference building where our smart system has been deployed is the Technology Transfer Centre of the University of Murcia[2], where CityExplorer is already installed and working. All input data involved in our energy and comfort management system are available in real-time through the SCADA access, and the actions for achieving a comfortable and energy-efficient behavior of the building can be performed. All the rooms of the building have been automated (through an HAM unit) to minimize their energy consumption according to the actions suggested by our management system, while user comfort aspects are communicated to the system by user interaction with the system through a control panel or a user restricted access to the SCADA view. In one of the floors of such reference building, we have taken one laboratory as a reference testbed for carrying energy efficiency experiments. In this test lab we have allocated different room spaces, as can be seen in Fig. 2. In these spaces, separate automation functions for managing lighting, HVAC, switches and blinds are provided, where these devices provide comfort services in different regions. Taking into account such service regions, as well as the features of each space in terms of natural lighting, activities to be carried out, and the estimated comfort requirements (for instance, the case of an individual lamp placed on a desk, the user location must

---

[2] www.um.es/otri/?opc=cttfuentealamo

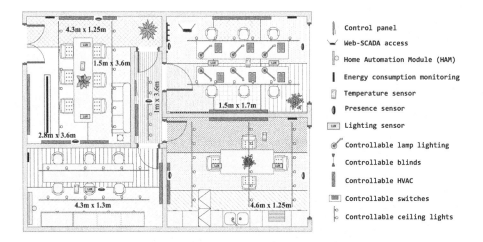

\	Control panel
∨	Web-SCADA access
⌐	Home Automation Module (HAM)
▌	Energy consumption monitoring
▨	Temperature sensor
◖	Presence sensor
⬚LUX	Lighting sensor
◉	Controllable lamp lighting
⥿	Controllable blinds
▌	Controllable HVAC
▦	Controllable switches
⌐	Controllable ceiling lights

Fig. 2. Different scenarios deployed in a test lab of our reference smart building

be determined to provide occupants with personalized environmental comfort. These target regions are showed in Fig. 2.

Comfort and energy efficiency services provided in these scenarios are strongly dependent on the location data provided by the localization system integrated in the HAMs of CityExplorer. This system must be capable of providing user location estimation with a mean error lower than the target service regions showed in Fig. 2. A previous work [12] evaluated in detail the accuracy of such localization system. For our current tests, we analyze its accuracy considering the scenarios showed in Fig.2. For that, different user transitions between the different spaces are tracked by the system. According to the obtained results, it can be safely said that the system is able to track users with enough level of accuracy and precision. More specifically, the mean error obtained in this tracking scenario is 1 m., which is enough to offer individualized comfort services to users. In this sense, for instance, among the target service regions here analyzed, the individual lamp light represents the most restrictive case, with a service region of 1.5 m. x 1.7 m., which represents a restriction in terms of location accuracy higher than the mean error provided by our localization system.

Taking as starting point the suitability of the localization system integrated in the building management proposal, we can now demonstrate the benefits of considering such accurate positioning information (including identification) in terms of energy savings by using comfort services. Depending on the user allocated in each target area and the environmental parameters sensed in the room (temperature and humidity in this case of studio), the intelligent management process is responsible for communicating different settings to the appropriate HVAC appliances. All the information sensed is gathered in real-time and is available through CityExplorer. For the comfort management implemented, different comfort profiles for each user involved in the tests were considered.

Besides, maximum and minimum indoor temperatures were established as control points for ensuring minimal thermal conditions in each scenario. In this way, customized comfort services are provided to users ensuring their quality of life, and the energy consumed is optimized thanks to the individual user location and identification data. Moreover, any energy wastage derived from overestimated or inappropriate thermal settings is avoided.

It is important to highlight that our energy efficiency system needs a long evaluation period to extract relevant figures of merit regarding energy saves. Furthermore, each simplification or adjustment in the system (different input data, rules, locations, comfort conditions, etc.) requires extensive testing and validation with respect to the environment chosen to carry out the evaluation. In addition, the system validation must cover different seasons in order to analyze its behavior with different weather conditions along the year. Despite all these considerations, we can state that the experiment results obtained until now already reflect energy saves in cooling/heating about 20%, attending to the energy consumption in A/C in prior months without considering our energy management system. It is clear that the environmental conditions are hardly repeatable, but the comparison was performed between consecutive months in the winter of 2013 which presented very similar environmental conditions and context features. Specifically, we consider the month of January without energy management, and February enabling intelligent management decisions. At this moment a constant evaluation is being performed day-by-day for providing further evaluations in future works.

5 Conclusions and Future Work

The proliferation of ICT solutions (IoT among them) represents new opportunities for the development of new intelligent services for achieving energy efficiency. In this work we propose a platform which is powered by IoT capabilities and is part of a novel context-and location-aware system that deals with the issues of data collection, intelligent processing for saving energy according to user comfort preferences, and proper actuation features to modify the operation of relevant indoor devices. An essential part of the energy efficiency module of the proposal is the user location and identity, so that customized services can be provided. The applicability of our system proposal has been demonstrated through a real implementation in a concrete smart building, gathering sensor data for monitoring the power consumption and tracking occupants following an IoT approach to access localization sensors. The localization system has been evaluated and an accuracy of about one meter has been obtained, which is considered more than enough to provide personalized environmental comfort to users for saving energy. Furthermore, using this localization system and the whole energy management platform, an overall energy save of 20% has been recently achieved.

As it has been already mentioned, a longer evaluation period to extract more relevant and precise results is needed. In this line, we are carrying out assessments aimed to analyze individual parts of our system. Several years of experimentation and analysis are needed to tune up the system and leave it ready to operate under different conditions, such as different seasons, people, behaviors, etc. Moreover, we are experimenting on mobile crowd-based sensing techniques for gathering data from occupants' devices, since this information will complement the data obtained by our infrastructure-based system.

Acknowledgments. This work has been sponsored by European Commission through the FP7-SMARTIE-609062 EU Project, and the Spanish Seneca Foundation by means of the Excellence Researching Group Program (04552/GERM/06) and the FPI program (grant 15493/FPI/10).

References

1. Atzori, L., Iera, A., Morabito, G.: The internet of things: A survey. Computer Networks 54(15), 2787–2805 (2010)
2. Stunder, M.J., Sebastian, P., Chube, B.A., Koontz, M.D.: Integration of real-time data into building automation systems (No. DOE/OR22674/611-30050-01). Air-Conditioning and Refrigeration Technology Institute, US (2003)
3. Han, D., Lim, J.: Design and implementation of smart home energy management systems based on ZigBee. IEEE Transactions on Consumer Electronics 56, 1417–1425 (2010)
4. Oksa, P., Soini, M., Sydänheimo, L., Kivikoski, M.: Kilavi platform for wireless building automation. Energy and Buildings 40(9), 1721–1730 (2008)
5. Morrissey, E., O'Donnell, J., Keane, M., Bazjanac, V.: Specification and implementation of IFC based performance metrics to support building life cycle assessment of hybrid energy systems (2004)
6. Escrivá-Escrivá, G., Álvarez-Bel, C., Peñalvo-López, E.: New indices to assess building energy efficiency at the use stage. Energy and Buildings 43(2), 476–484 (2011)
7. Handbook, A. S. H. R. A. E.: Fundamentals. American Society of Heating, Refrigerating and Air Conditioning Engineers, Atlanta (2001)
8. Zamora-Izquierdo, M.A., Santa, J., Gómez-Skarmeta, A.F.: An Integral and Networked Home Automation Solution for Indoor Ambient Intelligence. IEEE Pervasive Computing 9, 66–77 (2010)
9. Centre Europeen de Normalisation: Indoor Environmental Input Parameters for Design and Assesment of Energy Performance of Buildings - Addressing Indoor Air Quality, Thermal Environment, Lighting and Acoustics. EN 15251 (2006)
10. Berglund, L.: Mathematical models for predicting the thermal comfort response of building occupants. ASHRAE Transactions 84(1), 1848–1858 (1978)
11. Callaghan, V., et al.: Inhabited intelligent environments. BT Technology Journal 22(3), 233–247 (2004)
12. Moreno-Cano, M.V., Zamora-Izquierdo, M.A., Santa, J., Skarmeta, A.F.: An indoor localization system based on artificial neural networks and particle filters applied to intelligent buildings. Neurocomputing (2013)

Magnetic-Field Feature Extraction for Indoor Location Estimation

Carlos Eric Galván-Tejada, Juan Pablo García-Vázquez, and Ramón Brena

Instituto Tecnológico y de Estudios Superiores de Monterrey,
Monterrey, Nuevo León, México
Autonomous Agents in Ambient Intelligence
ericgalvan@uaz.edu.mx, {ramon.brena,jpablo.garcia}@itesm.mx

Abstract. User indoor positioning has been under constant improvement especially with the availability of new sensors integrated into the
modern mobile devices. These sensory devices allow us to exploit not only
infrastructures made for every day use, such as Wi-Fi, but also natural
infrastructure, as is the case of natural magnetic fields. From our experience working with mobile devices and Magnetic-Field based location
systems, we identify some issues that should be addressed to improve
the performance of a Magnetic-Field based system, such as a reduction
of the data to be analyzed to estimate an individual location. In this
paper we propose a feature extraction process that uses magnetic-field
temporal and spectral features to acquire a classification model using the
capabilities of mobile phones. Finally, we present a comparison against
well known spectral classification algorithms with the aim to ensure the
reliability of the feature extraction process.

Keywords: Magnetic Field Measurements, Magnetometers, Location,
Indoor Positioning, Location Estimation, Feature Extraction.

1 Introduction

User positioning has been the focus of many research groups around the globe.
Several approaches have been proposed to estimate the location of an individual.
For instance RFID, Wi-Fi and Bluetooth, which provide evidence of their ability
to locate an individual indoors [1–3]. However, they require a dedicated infrastructure, and thus system scalability can be expensive, as it requires adding
devices. Therefore new approaches have been proposed to avoid those issues;
these new approaches are based on the reuse of the technologies that we use
everyday (i.e. mobile devices) and using the signals already available in the indoor environment. An example of those approaches is indoor positioning systems
based on Magnetic-fields [4].

The use of magnetic fields for indoor location systems has been explored
in some pioneer works such as [5, 6]. Their idea is to use the irregularities of
the earth's natural magnetic field induced by building's structures and other

G. Urzaiz et al. (Eds.): UCAmI 2013, LNCS 8276, pp. 9–16, 2013.
© Springer International Publishing Switzerland 2013

elements common in indoor environments, and detect these irregularities as clues for finding the user's location, with the help of a magnetometer such as those available in smartphones. Such approaches involve the previous mapping of a given indoor environment, measuring at each point the magnitude and direction of the magnetic field, and then, using this magnetic map for location purposes, finding the most similar place in the magnetic map to the one detected at a given point. ana

In our approach, the goal is to identify the "room" in which the user is at a certain moment, not to give exact coordinates, like some other methods do. In this setting, the precision is the percentage or times the system gives the correct room, not a measure in centimeters or other length measures. But in most practical situations, to know in which room the user is located, is exactly the type of information he/she needs, not to have a vector of coordinates.

Further, we developed an original method in which there is no need of constructing a detailed magnetic map, which is a grid of magnetic measures for each point in the building, as other approaches do, but just to store a kind of "signature" taken from a random walk inside a given room, which takes as an essential component the frequency spectrum of the magnetic signal, obtained from the Fourier transform of that signal. This method has been shown to be independent of the exact path used when picking the magnetic signal, thus giving it a very desirable robustness.

From our experience working with Magnetic-Field based location systems, we identify some issues that should be addressed to improve a Magnetic-Field based system. In particular, we guess that clever feature extraction from the magnetic field signal would reduce the amount of data required to estimate the location of an individual. We have the hypothesis that this feature extraction process improves the accuracy and the robustness of the system, and reduce the computational cost, enabling the system to be executed on a mobile device.

The aim of this work is to present a temporal and spectral feature extraction process, exploiting the statistical parameters to summarize the behavior of the signal. Further, we intend to obtain a classification model from temporal and spectral features of the magnetic field using a magnetic sensor included in a conventional mobile device.

This paper is organized as follows. A description of related works for location estimation that uses the magnetic-field is given in Section 2. A description of spectral and statistical features is presented in Section 3. Experimental procedures are described in Section 4. Section 5 shows the experimental results obtained after running the classification model. Finally conclusions and future work are presented in Section 6.

2   Related Work

Indoor positioning technologies can be classified into three categories: technologies based on signals-of opportunity (signals that are not intended for positioning and navigation), technologies based on pre-deployed infrastructure (such as positioning systems using infrared, ultrasound and ultra wide band) and others [7]. Coverage using technologies based on signals-of opportunity often is very limited, however, many attempts has been done using different technologies i.e., Bluetooth, Wi-Fi[1–3]. Nevertheless the magnetic field could be categorized as a signals-of opportunity approach, but without the coverage constrain because the magnetic disturbances are present in any environment.

Some approaches show that using the magnetic field like a complementary sensor can improve the location precision results. For instance, [8] improves a SLAM algorithm adding a magnetometer as a new sensor to locate a robot in a building hallway. At some point, the robot is hijacked to an unknown place in the same hallway, and continues to run. They demonstrate that the use of the magnetic filed data can improve the localization of the robot on the existing map after a hijacking.

Location fingerprinting schemes are feasible solutions for indoor positioning as described in [9] and [10]. In [7] many tests are done in order to determine how feasible is the use of magnetic field alone for indoor positioning. The results of the tests show that the indoor geomagnetic field is stable, just with small changes when furniture is moved or small objects are near to the magnetometer used to sense the magnetic field, concluding that applying the figerprinting scheme for positioning is possible, but they propose to improve the estimation of the position by adding extra information to complement the magnetic field measurements. In this sense, others are exploring to add additional characteristics to the magnetic field magnitude, in [11] they propose the use of two timestamp additionally to the magnetic field samples. They presents an alternative leader-follower form of waypoint- navigation system; magnetometer readings are compared to a pre-recorded magnetic "leader" trace containing magnetic data collected along a route and annotated with waypoint information. Each sample was given a timestamp from the Android system associated with its time of collection by the phone. A second timestamp was generated by the sensor unit and consists of an integer that is incremented at each sample. Timestamps allow dropped packets to be detected, and enable the individual sensor results to be aligned with each other, improving the proposed indoor navigation system.

The present work enhances the proposal presented in [4] through feature extraction to reduce the information used to achieve indoor positioning with less computational cost, since one of the objectives is to use the method in mobile devices.

3 Spectral and Statistical Features Extraction

The feature extraction is a process that consists in performing efficient data reduction while preserving the appropriate amount of information of the signal [12]. Given the similarity between a magnetic field signal and an audio waveform, (variation of a disturbance with time), audio analysis techniques can be applied to the magnetic-field-based signature to the temporal and spectral evolution.

Features can be classified into three categories:

- *Temporal Shape*: features (global or instantaneous) computed from the waveform. From the temporal shape were extracted the following 16 features, chosen because of the statistical potential to summarize the behavior of the signal: Kurtosis, Mean, Median, Standard Deviation, Variance, Trimmed Mean, Coefficient of Variation, Inverse Coefficient of Variation and 1,5,25,50,75,95 and 99 percentile.
- *Spectral Shape*: Features computed from the Fast Fourier Transform of the signal. From the spectral shape were extracted the following 20 features; they were also chosen because of the statistical potential to summarize the spectral shape: Shannon Entropy, Slope, Spectral Flatness, Spectral Centroid, Coefficient of Variation, Skewness, Kurtosis, Mean, Median, Standard Deviation, Variance, Trimmed Mean, Inverse Coefficient of Variation and 1,5,25,50,75,95 and 99 percentile.
- *Energy Features*: Features (instantaneous) referring to energy content of the signal. From the energy features were extracted the first 10 frequencies, because the majority of the energy is concentrated in them.

4   Experimentation

4.1   Collecting Device

To avoid specialized sensors, the collecting device consists of an Acer A500 tablet with a built-in three-axis sensor with appropriate software applications to collect magnetic data.

The application is implemented in Java and makes use of Google libraries to obtain a link to the magnetic sensor of the device. The application collects data of the three physical axis x, y, and z of the magnetic field and stores them in the device for later processing.

4.2   Collecting Procedures

Experiments were performed at the ground floor of a residential home shown in figure 1a. The open spaces in rooms were completely mapped in a period of time of about 10 seconds, and were independent of the walking patterns. Every room has different kinds of furniture and distributions allowing us to have different magnetic signatures.

The experiments were performed in 4 rooms: kitchen, living room, bathroom and dining room, collecting the field strengths walking around the room during 10 seconds with the tablet at the waist with an average walking speed of 3.0 kilometers per hour. All the rooms are close to each other as it is shown in figure 1b. For each room, a total of thirteen signatures were collected, number of signatures calculated with the equation 1 presented in [13], where x is the number of experiments, and N is the number of variables. In this experimentation N is equal to 2,000 considering 1,000 from temporal signal and 1,000 from spectal signal; from the equation we obtain 11.97 adding 1 more to increase the training set.

$$x = log_2(N) + 1. \tag{1}$$

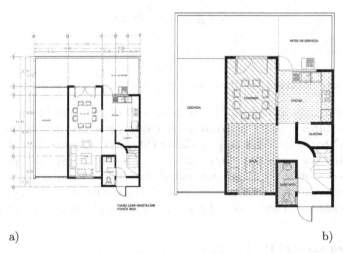

a)   b)

Fig. 1. a) First floor house plans with furniture. b)Location of different rooms to be used for experimentation. Living room (Blue), Dining room (Red), Kitchen (Green), Bathroom (Pink).

Given the fact that magnetic fields are time invariant [14], i.e., they remain constant over long periods of time [7, 14] and the ambient geomagnetic field strength B can be modeled as a vector of three components $Bx, By,$ and Bz [5], we can compute the magnitude of the field as described in Eq. 2, where $Mx, My,$ and Mz are the three physical axes along $x, y,$ and z respectively.

$$|M| = \sqrt{Mx^2 + My^2 + Mz^2} \tag{2}$$

Each signature has 1000 readings, i.e., 100 readings per second. Then the magnitude was calculated for each reading using the equation 2.

After the signature has been precisely recorded, we eliminate spatial scaling and shifting by normalizing each signature using equation 3, where $z_{i,d}$ is the normalized reading, $r_{i,d}$ refers to the ith observation of the signature in dimension d μ_d is the mean value of the signature for dimension d and σ_d is the standard deviation of the signature for dimension d.

$$\forall i \in m : z_{i,d} = \frac{r_{i,d} - \mu_d}{\sigma_d} \tag{3}$$

Equation 3 is applied for all dimensions in R^d

To extract spectral features, the spectral signal is acquired by performing a P-point Fast Fourier Transform (FFT) [15] to each signature, as shown in Eq. 4, where ES_i is the ith energy signature of the normalized magnetic field, and NS_i is the ith normalized magnetic field signature.

$$\forall i \in n : ES_i = FFT(NS_i) \qquad (4)$$

.

4.3 Feature Extraction Process

Each signature was loaded as a vector composed of 1,000 data points; then the temporal features were extracted to the signatures and stored in a table. A FFT was applied to every signature, obtaining the spectra, stored in a 1,000 data points vector per signature. Once the spectra was obtained, the spectral and energy features were extracted and stored in a table. Finally the tables were combined to create one with the 46 features. The feature extraction process was done programming a script in *R Project for Statistical Computing* software.

4.4 Experimental Procedures

The feature extraction process was applied to a data set composed by 52 magnetic-field signatures. 46 features were obtained for each signature, 30 of them from the spectral signal and 16 from the temporal signal. After the feature extraction process a percentile rank score is calculated for all features to keep every values between 0 to 1. The data set was divided into 2 sets, 32 signatures in the training set, and 20 in the test set. A random forest composed of 5000 trees was trained in order to obtain a prediction model. The Random Forest algorithm was chosen because it is an ensemble supervised machine learning technique and is based on bagging and random feature selection [16].

5   Experimental Results

Table 1 shows the confusion matrix acquired from the classification model of the random forest using the training set applied to the test set. The obtained model can classify correctly 86 percent of test set even when the walking pattern is totally different and the signatures are composed by a vector of 46 features instead of a 2,000 data point vector (1,000 from temporal signal, and 1,000 from the spectral signal).

The obtained model using the random forest approach is compared against other commonly used spectral classification algorithms, able to deal with non-linear relations, insensitive to missing values and capable of handling numerical and categorical inputs [17, 18], and against our proposal Magnetic-Field-Based FFT Signature [4], as it is shown in Table 2.

Table 1. Signatures Classification For Different Locations

	Living Room	Dining Room	Kitchen	Bathroom
Living Room	4	0	0	1
Dining Room	0	5	0	0
Kitchen	0	0	5	0
Bathroom	0	1	0	4

Table 2. Comparison of Different Approaches

Approach	Classification Rate (in percentage)
Spectral Correlation Mapper	70
Magnetic-Field-Based FFT Signature	75.4
Our Approach	86.1

6 Conclusions and Future Work

In this paper we propose feature extraction from a magnetic-field signatures to use it as a localization technique that can be used to identify rooms inside a building using a mobile device which include a magnetic sensor. This is an improvement in our basic approach, which builds a magnetic "signature" of rooms by taking in consideration the frequency spectrum of the magnetic signal registered in a random path inside the room.

The obtained classification model outperformed the 2 methods with which it was compared, even when the other 2 methods use the complete signal data (2,000 data points) instead the 46 vector of features.

Future work consists in improving the feature extraction to avoid incurring into the so called curse of dimensionality and use different methods of regression to improve the performance of the classification model.

References

1. Almaula, V., Cheng, D.: Bluetooth Triangulator. Technical report, Department of Computer Science and Engineering, University of California, San Diego (2006)
2. Altini, M., Brunelli, D., Farella, E., Benini, L.: Bluetooth indoor localization with multiple neural networks. In: 2010 5th IEEE International Symposium on Wireless Pervasive Computing (ISWPC), pp. 295–300 (2010)
3. Fernandez, T., Rodas, J., Escudero, C., Iglesia, D.: Bluetooth Sensor Network Positioning System with Dynamic Calibration. In: 4th International Symposium on Wireless Communication Systems (ISWCS 2007), pp. 45–49 (2007)
4. Galvn-Tejada, C.E., Carrasco-Jimenez, J.C., Brena, R.: Location Identification Using a Magnetic-field-based FFT Signature. Procedia Computer Science 19, 533–539 (2013)
5. Storms, W., Shockley, J., Raquet, J.: Magnetic field navigation in an indoor environment. In: Ubiquitous Positioning Indoor Navigation and Location Based Service (UPINLBS), pp. 1–10 (October 2010)

6. Chung, J., Donahoe, M., Schmandt, C., Kim, I.J., Razavai, P., Wiseman, M.: Indoor location sensing using geo-magnetism. In: Proceedings of the 9th International Conference on Mobile Systems, Applications, and Services (MobiSys 2011), pp. 141–154. ACM, New York (2011)

7. Li, B., Gallagher, T., Dempster, A., Rizos, C.: How feasible is the use of magnetic field alone for indoor positioning? In: 2012 International Conference on Indoor Positioning and Indoor Navigation (IPIN), pp. 1–9 (2012)

8. Zhang, H., Martin, F.: Robotic mapping assisted by local magnetic field anomalies. In: 2011 IEEE Conference on Technologies for Practical Robot Applications (TePRA), pp. 25–30 (2011)

9. Bargh, M.S., de Groote, R.: Indoor localization based on response rate of bluetooth inquiries. In: Proceedings of the first ACM International Workshop on Mobile Entity Localization and Tracking in GPS-Less Environments (MELT 2008), pp. 49–54. ACM, New York (2008)

10. Machaj, J., Brida, P., Tatarova, B.: Impact of the number of access points in indoor fingerprinting localization. In: 2010 20th International Conference on Radioelektronika (RADIOELEKTRONIKA), pp. 1–4 (2010)

11. Riehle, T., Anderson, S., Lichter, P., Condon, J., Sheikh, S., Hedin, D.: Indoor waypoint navigation via magnetic anomalies. In: 2011 Annual International Conference of the IEEE Engineering in Medicine and Biology Society (EMBC), pp. 5315–5318 (2011)

12. Agostini, G., Longari, M., Pollastri, E.: Musical instrument timbres classification with spectral features. In: 2001 IEEE Fourth Workshop on Multimedia Signal Processing, pp. 97–102 (2001)

13. Eberhardt, F., Glymour, C., Scheines, R.: On the number of experiments sufficient and in the worst case necessary to identify all causal relations among n variables. arXiv preprint arXiv:1207.1389 (2012)

14. Bancroft, J., Lachapelle, G.: Use of magnetic quasi static field (QSF) updates for pedestrian navigation. In: 2012 IEEE/ION Position Location and Navigation Symposium (PLANS), pp. 605–612 (April 2012)

15. Tsai, W.H., Tu, Y.M., Ma, C.H.: An FFT-based fast melody comparison method for query-by-singing/humming systems. Pattern Recognition Letters 33(16), 2285–2291 (2012)

16. Kulkarni, V., Sinha, P.: Pruning of Random Forest classifiers: A survey and future directions. In: 2012 International Conference on Data Science Engineering (ICDSE), pp. 64–68 (2012)

17. De Carvalho, O., Meneses, P.R.: Spectral correlation mapper (SCM): An improvement on the spectral angle mapper (SAM). In: 2000 Workshop Proceedings of the Airborne Visible/Infrared Imaging Spectrometer (AVIRIS), Pasadena (2000)

18. Kuching, S.: The performance of maximum likelihood, spectral angle mapper, neural network and decision tree classifiers in hyperspectral image analysis. Journal of Computer Science 3(6), 419–423 (2007)

A Safe Kitchen for Cognitive Impaired People

Antonio Coronato and Giovanni Paragliola

ICAR- CNR Naples, Italy, via P. Castellino 111
{antonio.coronato,giovanni.paragliola}@na.icar.cnr.it

Abstract. Cognitive diseases such as Alzheimer, Parkinson, Autism, etc. affect millions of people around the world and they reduce the quality of life for the patient and their relatives. An impaired patient may show irrationally behaviors which could led him to perform abnormal and/or dangerous actions for his safety. This paper presents an approach for modeling and detecting of anomalous and dangerous situations. The proposed method adopts the Situation-awareness paradigm for the detection of anomalous situations in a kitchen environment. Test performed in laboratory and theoretic results show the validity of the approach. Future work will develop a smart kitchen able to detect risks for the patient.

Keywords: Situation-Awareness, Ambient Assisted Living, Intelligent Artificial, Detection.

1 Introduction

Cognitive diseases such as Alzheimer, Parkinson, Autism are a category of mental health disorders which primarily affect learning, memory, perception, and problem solving, and include amnesia, dementia, and delirium. Patients with such diseases require daily monitoring by clinicians and caregivers [1]. In particular, cognitive impaired patients need constant monitoring of their daily activities living in order to guarantee their safety. Our research aims to detect anomalous situations which could put patient in dangerous. The paper also provides a classification of possible anomalous situations and a definition of intelligent prolog agents for detecting them. The Situation-Awareness paradigm is used to reach our scope [2]. Our approach is based on anomalous situations classification and runtime verification of correctness properties. It adopts *Situation Calculus* [3] for defining correctness properties and *Golog* for realizing intelligent agents for the detection.

The rest of paper is structured in the following paragraphs. Section 2 presents related work. Section 3 focuses on Situation Awareness. Section 4 presents the proposed approach. Section 5 describes conclusion, future works and limits.

2 Related Work

Human behaviors monitoring is an active research topic. In the last years several research projects have been developed with the aim to provide enabling technologies for smart home and Ambient Assisted living (AAL): The Microsoft's

G. Urzaiz et al. (Eds.): UCAmI 2013, LNCS 8276, pp. 17–25, 2013.

EasyLiving project [4] , the iterative room iRoom [5] and the CASAS smart home project [6] are some examples of published project. The understand human behavior relies on the system's ability to recognize actions and activities performed in a living environment. The literature proposes a lot of works about activity recognition. [7] Describes a kinect-based solution for monitoring and recognizing cooking activities in a kitchen. [8] models complex activities like cooking into sequence of atomic actions; segmentation and tracking are applied to video stream in order to recognize the correct sequence of actions. Compare these related works with our solution we have used different kinds of sensors such as cameras, accelerometers and virtual sensors in order to get as more events as possible from the domain. All such events are sent to intelligent agents which reason in order to detect possible anomalies. Supporting by activity recognition, we can introduce a more complex topic: behavior recognition that aims to model and detect human behaviors in a living environment. Many works have been proposed to address this issue. [9] adopts neural networks to recognize more complex activities, a network sensors is used for modeling resident activities in the environment, as a sequence of sensor events. This approach strongly depends to training phase of the neural networks differently our solution does not need it. [10] and [11] model human behavior by means of Hidden Markov Model (HMM) [12]. This approach is efficient when we model behaviors which follow well-defined and predictable patterns. However, a drawback come out when this solution is applied to patient with cognitive diseases. Patient with Alzheimer's disease shows bizarre and unpredictable behaviors, therefore an approach based on HMMs would be very complex due to large set of transitions of the all possible future actions performable by the patient. An examples is while a patient with Alzheimer's disease takes an inflammable object in his hands. In this scenario, the patient could decide to put the object on a table, or put it on the floor and soon on as well as he could decide to put it on a heater, this scenario arises a dangerous situation; if we model all these cases by means of HMM then we will spent a lot of resources in terms of states and transitions. Our paper defines a new method for saving resources and avoiding over-costs in terms of states and transitions, it suggests to use a different approach based on the definition and run-time verification of correctness properties. When a violation of one of these correctness properties is detected an abnormal or dangerous situation is involved. The main advantage of this approach is the independence from the previous actions done by the patient.

3   Situation Awareness

Data gathered from ambient by means of sensors networks should be processed in a smart environment within different semantic levels. Situation-Awareness (SA) provides the methodologies to process them. As suggested by [2], we should distinguish between Context and Situation-Awareness. Authors propose the following definitions: Primary context is the full set of data acquired by real and virtual sensors; Secondary context concerns with information inferred and/or derived from several data streams (primary contexts); *Situation* is, instead, an abstract state of affairs of interest for designers and applications, which is derived from context and hypothesis about how observed context relates to factors of interest. Although events processed by our proposal solution are generated by emulator of the upcoming smart home environments, this does not weak the validation of our work. [13] and [14] show that the developing of smart kitchen technologies are taken in attention by research community. The situation model has been described by using Situation Calculus (SC).

The SC is a first-order logic language proposed by John Mc-Carthy [3]. it has been adopted for modeling dynamic worlds. A dynamic world is modeled through a series of situations as a result of actions being performed within the world. It is important to note that a situation is not a state of the world, but just a history of a finite sequence of actions. The constant S_0 denotes the initial situation; whereas, do(a,S) indicates the situation resulting from the execution of the action a in situation S. The mainly concepts of SC are *action, situation* and *fluents*. These are the three fundamental *sort* for programming logic. In this context *sort* means like data type in a programming language such as java. **Action** is a *sort* of the domain. It defines all possible actions performable in the domain and can be quantified. An example, *moveOn(Objecet, Device)* defines an action that allows to move an object on a device. A special predicate *Poss(moveOn(Objecet, Device),S)* indicates when the action *moveOn(Objecet, Device)* is executable in the situation S. **Situation** is a first order term which represents a sequence of occurred actions. It embodies the history of the system. An example, *do(moveOn(Object,Device), s0)*, denotes the situation S that has been obtained performing the action *moveOn(Objecet, Device)* in the initial situation *s0*. **Fluents**, all relations functions whose values change from situation to situation are called *fluent*. They are denoted by predicate symbols whose last argument is a situation term. Relation Fluents denote what is true or false in the current situation. An example, *isPlacedOn(Object,Device,do(moveOn(Object,Device), s0))* denotes that in the situation *do(moveOn(Object,Device), s0))* , the entity *object* is placed on the entity *Device*. A basic action theory is a set of axioms including the initial world axioms, unique names axioms, actions precondition, and successor state axioms, that describe a dynamically changing world [15]. In this paper we use intelligent prolog agents that exploit the situation-awareness paradigm to reason in order to detect anomalous situations in the kitchen environment and generate opportune alarms when an anomaly is arisen.

4   Proposed Approach

In our approach, situation-awareness is the enabling paradigm that allows to define correctness properties. We define a set of axioms which model the properties of all entities into the environment, an example is axioms 2, it models the properties of objects to be inflammable. We use these axioms to define fluents which model relations amongst all entities. Fluents and properties are used for defining more complex axioms able to detect anomalous iterations amongst entities.

These axioms are used for detecting anomalous situations. We use as working scenario the kitchen environment. We show a sub-set of possible activities that a cognitive impaired can perform in a kitchen. First, we have to define the initial world axioms. Axioms [1 - 11] define some entities of interest in the the kitchen and their properties.

$$\mathbf{isObject(X)} \equiv X \in \{dish, knife, book\}; \quad Objects\ locate\ in\ the\ kitchen \quad (1)$$

$$\mathbf{isInflammable(X)} \equiv X \in \{dish\}; Inflammable\ objects \quad (2)$$

$$\mathbf{isMetallic(X)} \equiv X \in \{knife\}; Metallic\ objects \quad (3)$$

$$\mathbf{isDevice(X)} \equiv X \in \{oven, refrigerator, microwave\}; Device\ locate\ in\ the\ kitchen \quad (4)$$

$$\mathbf{hasSurface(X)} \equiv X \in \{oven\}; Surfaced\ device \quad (5)$$

$$\mathbf{isMovable(X)} \equiv X \in \{dish, fork, knife\}; Movable\ objects \quad (6)$$

$$\mathbf{isSwitchable(X)} \equiv X \in \{oven, refrigerator, microwave\}; Objects\ can\ be\ switched \quad (7)$$

$$\mathbf{isHeater(X)} \equiv X \in \{oven\}; Devices\ are\ heater \quad (8)$$

$$\mathbf{isMicrowave(X)} \equiv X \in \{microwave\}; microwave\ device \quad (9)$$

$$\mathbf{isFood(X)} \equiv X \in \{fish, pasta, meat\}; Food\ located\ in\ the\ kitchen \quad (10)$$

$$\mathbf{isSwitchable\_state(X)} \equiv X \in \{on, off\}; powed\ state\ On/Off \quad (11)$$

Axiom [12] describes a sub-set of actions performable in the kitchen by the patient. We can distinguish between *Endogenous* actions and *Exogenous* actions. Endogenous actions exclusively can be perform by software agents for technical reasons, an example *resetCount* resets a counter. Exogenous actions are performed by the patient (e.g. *pickup(obj)*).

$$a \in \{\mathbf{pickup(obj), placeOn(obj, sur), placeIn(obj, con)},$$
$$\mathbf{switch(dev, state)},$$
$$\mathbf{eat(food), stopEating(food), resetCount()}\} \quad (12)$$

In order to recognize activities several classes of anomalous behaviors have been defined:

Location Class, Duration Class, Frequency Class and *Time Class*.

Each class models an anomalous behavior by means of SC. For readable reasons we show only sub-set of properties and fluents for each class.

4.1   Anomalous Classification

Location Class. The location class aims to detect anomalous situations arisen by objects misplacement. [16] describes some sources of dangers which can occur in an ambient living. An Example of dangerous object misplacement is when the patient puts on inflammable object in contact with an heater (e.g. a plastic plate into the oven). We define fluents able to trigger when such situation happens. For the sake of brevity, we show a sub-set of all fluents. Axiom 13 defines under which condition *placeOn(obj,Dev)* can be executed. Axiom 14 is a functional fluent, it model the powered state (*On / Off*) of devices into the environment. Axiom 15 is a relational fluent, its values is true whenever an object is placed on a surfaced device. We want to focus on axioms 16 that triggers when an inflammable object is placed on a switched heater on.

$$\mathbf{Poss(placeOn(Obj, Dev), S)} \equiv \qquad (13)$$
$$\{isMovable(obj) \land isDevice(dev) \land hasSurface(dev) \land \neg isPlaced(Obj, Dev, S)\}$$

$$\mathbf{state(dev, power, do(a, S))} \equiv \qquad (14)$$
$$\{(a = switch(dev, value) \land$$
$$isSwitchabe\_state(value) \land isSwitchable(dev) \land$$
$$value = on)- > power = value \lor$$
$$state(dev, value, do(a, S))\}$$

$$\mathbf{isPlacedOn(obj, sur, do(a, S))} \equiv \qquad (15)$$
$$\{a = placeOn(obj, sur) \land isObject(obj) \lor$$
$$isPlacedOn(obj, sur, S) \land (a \neq pickup(obj))\}$$

$$\mathbf{isAnomalousObjectPlacement(obj, dev, do(a, S))} \equiv \qquad (16)$$
$$\{(a = placeOn(obj, dev) \land isHeater(dev) \land$$
$$state(dev, on, S) \land isInflammable(obj))$$
$$a = switch(dev, on) \land isPlacedOn(obj, dev, S)$$
$$isHeater(dev) \land isInflammable(obj)\} \lor$$
$$isAnomalousObjectPlacement(obj, dev, S) \land$$
$$\neg\{(a = pickup(obj) \land (isPlacedOn(obj, dev, S)) \lor$$
$$isAnomalousObjectPlacement(obj, dev, S) \land$$
$$\neg(a = switch(Dev, Off) \land isPlacedOn(obj, dev, S))\}$$

Our approach allows to ignore all possible actions that can be performed between switching the device and placing the object.

Duration Class. The duration class models all such anomalous situations entailed by actions whose duration time is recognized as abnormal. Axiom 17 changes its truth value whenever a cooking activity is performed. Axiom 18 triggers when anomalous cooking duration is detected.

T_startCooking and T_currentTime are temporal parameters. They are used by the reasoner for monitoring the cooking time. The duration time $(T_{startCooking} - T_{currentTime})$ is compered with an opportune threshold, whenever it's over-limit, an alert is generated. Δ_{food} is a parameter customized for each kind of foods.

$$\mathbf{isCooking(food, dev, do(a, S))} \equiv \qquad (17)$$
$$\{(a = placeOn(food, dev) \land isFood(food)$$
$$isHeater(dev) \land state(dev, on, S)) \lor$$
$$isCooking(food, sur, S) \land \neg(a = pickup(obj) \lor a = switch(dev, off))\}$$

$$\mathbf{isAbnormalCookingDuration(food, dev, do(a, S))} \equiv \qquad (18)$$
$$\{(a = checkDuration(\Delta_{food}) \land isCooking(food, dev, S) \land$$
$$(T_{startCooking} - T_{currentTime}) > \Delta_{food})\} \lor$$
$$(isAbnormalCookingDuration(food, dev, S)) \land$$
$$\neg\{a = pickup(food) \lor a = switch(dev, off))\}$$

Frequency Class. Anomalous behaviors such as eating disorders may fall into these class. The frequency class models all these situations wherein it recognizes abnormal occurrences times of an action. An example, taking in attention eating disorders, a sane person usually eats 3-4 times by day, a patient be affected by eating disorders can show disease as over-nutrition(more then 6 time by day) or under-nutrition(less then 2 times by day). Axiom 19 describes the eating activity in a generic situation S. we focus on axioms 20, it triggers whenever the current meals counter exceed a threshold.

$$\mathbf{isEaiting(food, do(a, S))} \equiv \tag{19}$$
$$\{(a = eat(food) \wedge isFood(food)) \vee$$
$$isEating(food, S) \wedge \neg(a = stopEating(S))\}$$

$$\mathbf{isAbnormalOverEating(food, do(a, S))} \equiv \tag{20}$$
$$\{(a = checkCountingMeal \wedge isEating(food, S) \wedge$$
$$(\gamma_{DeilyMeals} > \gamma_{alert}) \vee$$
$$(isAbnormalEating(food, S)) \wedge$$
$$\neg(a = resetCount))\}$$

Timing Class. The timing class describes anomalous behaviors whenever actions such as eating, cooking are performed in abnormal period of day. A meal consumed at 4 A.M. is strange. The axioms 21 models such anomaly, it becomes true as soon as the patient starts eating outside the windows time, $T_{StartEating}$ is the started eating time, T_{min} and T_{max} are time thresholds which mark a reasonable windows eating time for consuming a meal.

$$\mathbf{isAbnormalTimeEating(food, do(a, S))} \equiv \tag{21}$$
$$\{(a = eat(food) \wedge (T_{StartEating} \notin [T_{min}, T_{max}]) \vee$$
$$(isAbnormalTimeEating(food, S)) \wedge$$
$$\neg(a = reset))\}$$

4.2   System Architecture

A logical view of the architecture that we are developing is presented in Fig. 1. It consists of two main components : the *primary context* component and the *secondary context* component. The *primary context* component is still under developing, it provides services for recognizing activities and generating events. *Activity Recognition* functionality is provided using *sensors* embedded in the environment or deployed on patient's body. Embedded sensors are RGB-D cameras can detected activities like walking as well as RGB-D cameras give the ability to perform object recognition activities. Body sensors are deployed on patient'body, examples of that technological are accelerometers used for recognizing activities such as taking an object, eating. The module *Activity Recognition* is still developing.

The *secondary context* component implements our proposal approach, it includes the prolog agents and the behaviors detector(BD). The prolog agents are developed by means of *Golog*, the prolog interpret for *Situayion Calculus*.

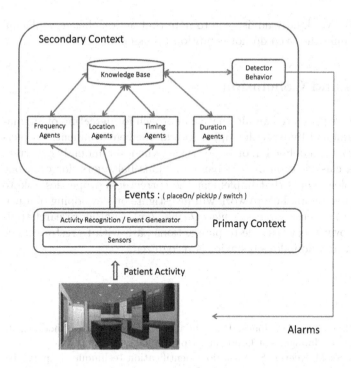

Fig. 1. Monitoring System Architecture

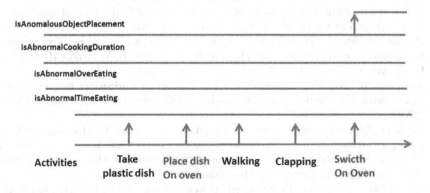

Fig. 2. Object Misplacement Scenario

The Prolog engine used for developing agents is Eclipse [17], a reasoner that supports logic programming. The BD monitors the current situation by means of values of agents, when a anomaly is arisen opportune alarms is generated. The *anomalous agents* monitors truth values of fluents belonged to affinity class (e.g. anomalous frequency agents monitor fluents belonging to frequency class). The Fig. 2 shows a object misplacement scenario generated by events emulator. The agent *isAnomalousObjectPlacement* becomes true as soon as the correctness property is violated. We kindly advise you to note that actions between placing the dish and switching the oven do not condition the agents.

5   Discussion and Conclusion

In this paper we have presented an alternative approach for detecting of anomalous behaviors in ambient living with emphasis on kitchen environment. Correctness properties have been defined in order to trigger whenever anomaly occurred. We also provide a classification of possible anomalous behaviors, for each one we have define prolog agents that implement the correctness properties able to detect anomalous behaviors. Future work will investigate on developing of a primary context able to generate events as *placeOn(obj,dev)*. Another research topis will designed a recovery services able to plan actions path with to restore a safe situation whenever an anomalous behavior is recognized.

References

1. Segal-Gidan, F., Cherry, D., Jones, R., Williams, B., Hewett, L., Chodosh, J.: Alzheimers Disease Management Guideline: Update 2008 (2011)
2. Ye, J., Dobson, S., McKeever, S.: Situation identification techniques in pervasive computing: A review. In: Pervasive and Mobile Computing (2011) (in press, Corrected Proof),
   http://www.sciencedirect.com/science/article/pii/S1574119211000253
3. McCarthy, J.: Situations, actions, and causal laws. Stanford Artificial Intelligence Project, Stanford University, Tech. Rep. Memo 2 (1963)
4. Brumitt, B., Meyers, B., Krumm, J., Kern, A., Shafer, S.: Easyliving: Technologies for intelligent environments. In: Thomas, P., Gellersen, H.-W. (eds.) HUC 2000. LNCS, vol. 1927, pp. 12–29. Springer, Heidelberg (2000)
5. Johanson, B., Fox, O., Winograd, T.: The interactive workspaces project: Experiences with ubiquitous computing rooms. IEEE Pervasive Computing 1, 67–74 (2002)
6. Cook, D., Schmitter-Edgecombe, M., Crandall, A., Sanders, C., Thomas, B.: Collecting and disseminating smart home sensor data in the casas project. In: Proc. of CHI 2009 Workshop on Developing Shared Home Behavior Datasets to Advance HCI and Ubiquitous Computing Research (2009)
7. Lei, J., Ren, X., Fox, D.: Fine-grained kitchen activity recognition using rgb-d. In: Proceedings of the 2012 ACM Conference on Ubiquitous Computing, UbiComp 2012, pp. 208–211. ACM, New York (2012),
   http://doi.acm.org/10.1145/2370216.2370248
8. Tran, Q.T., Calcaterra, G., Mynatt, E.D.: Cooks collage: Dj vu display for a home kitchen. In: Proceedings of HOIT: Home-Oriented Informatics and Telematics 2005, pp. 15–32 (2005)
9. Mozer, M.C., Dodier, R.H., Anderson, M., Vidmar, L., Iii, R.F.C., Miller, D.: The neural network house: An overview (1995)
10. Monekosso, D., Remagnino, P.: Behavior analysis for assisted living. IEEE Transactions on Automation Science and Engineering 7(4), 879–886 (2010)

11. Gehrig, D., Krauthausen, P., Rybok, L., Kuehne, H., Hanebeck, U., Schultz, T., Stiefelhagen, R.: Combined intention, activity, and motion recognition for a humanoid household robot. In: 2011 IEEE/RSJ International Conference on Intelligent Robots and Systems (IROS), pp. 4819–4825 (2011)
12. Rabiner, L., Juang, B.-H.: An introduction to Midden Markov Models. IEEE ASSP Magazine 3(1), 4–16 (1986)
13. Tenorth, M., Bandouch, J., Beetz, M.: The tum kitchen data set of everyday manipulation activities for motion tracking and action recognition. In: IEEE 12th International Conference on Computer Vision Workshops (ICCV Workshops), pp. 1089–1096 (2009)
14. Rybok, L., Friedberger, S., Hanebeck, U.D., Stiefelhagen, R.: The KIT Robo-Kitchen Data set for the Evaluation of View-based Activity Recognition Systems. In: IEEE-RAS International Conference on Humanoid Robots (2011)
15. Reiter, R.: Knowledge in Action: Logical Foundations for Specifying and Implementing Dynamical Systems. The MIT Press, Massachusetts (2001)
16. Anna-Karin Lindberg, S.O.H.: Accident prevention through experience feedback from the rescue services - a study of incident reports in sweden. Safety Science Monitor 16 (2012)
17. Eclipse prolog, http://eclipseclp.org

Breaking the Pattern:
Study on Stereoscopic Web Perception

Diego González-Zúñiga, Alexey Chistyakov, Pilar Orero, and Jordi Carrabina

Universitat Autònoma de Barcelona, Bellaterra, 08193, Spain
diekus@acm.org, alexey.chistyakov@e-campus.uab.cat,
{pilar.orero,jordi.carrabina}@uab.cat

Abstract. With this paper we document an experiment that is defined to test to what extent stereoscopic depth may control a user's gaze pattern while performing a search task. The experiment consisted in displaying a search engine result page created in a 2D and 3D side by side format, and a questionnaire that gathers information about participants' opinion towards a stereoscopic 3D experience. While this experiment is a first pilot and more research is needed, it is indicative of user behavior. In this paper we describe preparations for the study, hardware and software tools used to carry out the experiment, and results analysis.

Keywords: 3D, stereoscopic, stereoscopic 3D, web, web page, interface, search engine, user interface, human factors.

1   Introduction

Depth changes the way we perceive content [1]. From movies to video games the level of engagement and enjoyment is known to vary, and gaze patterns become more disperse while observing in 3D [2]. Stereoscopy has changed the way feature films are shot, edited and created [3], causing at the same time an evolution of the tools and techniques [4] present in the process.

Accordingly, hardware required for stereoscopic enjoyment by users has also evolved. Stereoscopic 3D (S3D) has become a standard feature on television displays instead of a novelty selling point, and passive 3D glasses are now thinner and lighter. The market offers a wide selection of passive or active TV sets, and with the introduction of ultra-high resolution (4K) and autostereoscopic displays, the trend of rising numbers on S3D capable devices is expected to continue [5]. The International 3D Society states that by the year 2020 3D content will be serviced from blu-ray discs, applications and the cloud [6]. The full deployment of HbbTV 2.0 will also offer 3D options.

While the number of S3D enabled devices is clearly rising, there seems to be a lack of quality content available for these devices that will support S3D depth. New hardware like 3D smartphones and tablets present an opportunity to create innovative and engaging experiences for users in different areas like education and content retrieval

G. Urzaiz et al. (Eds.): UCAmI 2013, LNCS 8276, pp. 26–33, 2013.

[7], nonetheless the introduction of S3D depth in applications has yet to be explored. This is the main interest of this article.

Nowadays, application development is shifting towards 'new' platforms. Fueled by the development of HTML5, one of these 'new' rising platforms is the web. But in terms of S3D, apart from a few examples like HERE maps' anaglyph version [8] (using WebGL) and several games created with plug-ins like Stereoskopix FOV2GO, this platform is still unexplored. While novel 3D applications and hardware development are a clear trend, little is known about user interaction with the new 3D platforms and contents. On this vein, we proposed an experiment in which an eye tracker (ET) is used to test participants' reaction to the addition of depth into a traditional search engine result page (SERP) in the hierarchic structure of the results.

2   Previous Related Work

Understanding how a user visualizes search results is important because gaze data can show patterns which can then be used to improve the layout of information or work with the placement of relevant content. For example, ocular information can provide a more accurate interpretation of implicit feedback such as "click-through" [9] and "Google's golden triangle" [10] and the "F-shaped pattern" [11] provide information on the way in which users scan the information on a web site, and thus on how content should be positioned.

Also, Cutrell and Guan have conducted experiments varying the size of the contextual snippet provided as an informative aid in search results [12]. This has led to some interesting conclusions which attempt to balance the amount of information displayed to best suit the range of searches performed.

Finally, combining S3D and ET, Wang [13] and Hanhela [14] focus on the development of a technique to estimate gaze depth in a S3D environment.

3   Experiment

Having examined some relevant research being conducted in the fields of ET, SERPs and S3D, our main objective is to analyze the introduction of depth to a SERP UI. Will it change a user's gaze pattern compared with the same interface in 2D? Will this variation also affect the dwell time for different hierarchical (semantic) elements?

The experiment consisted in displaying a search engine result page and giving the user a task to simulate everyday use. A search query was defined and a SERP was created in a 2D and 3D side by side format. Then, participants would see the stimulus and answer some questions, while their eye movements were logged using an eye tracker.

3.1   Stimuli

Having in mind that the main focus of the experiment was to use existing UIs to trigger familiarity with the task, we based the creation of the web page on real screenshots of the search result pages for a specific term. This term would be associated with a task. This implies that the prototypes are not dynamic, which allows us to maintain controlled information and that they comply with the familiarity we are looking for and our depth allocation. We developed two stimuli: 'F' and 'S': they mimic a Google SERP showing results on a "Costa Rica hotels" search query. 'F' is a standard 'flat' web page and 'S' has the same content with S3D depth applied on some elements. Both stimuli were built in strict correspondence with World Wide Web Consortium (W3C) HTML recommendations and contains valid HTML and CSS code.

The ruling for depth allocation in the stimuli was based on the semantic weight of each result on the page: the results that are considered by the search engine's algorithm as more relevant appear on a higher position than the ones ranked lower. At the same time 'S' has the same semantic structure, but additionally highlighted with 3D depth: the results that are considered more relevant stays closer to the user while the results considered less relevant closer to screen plane. The elements were distributed amongst 3D depth and limited to the 3 percent "depth budget" as defined by Sky3D technical guideline [15]. In order to build 'S' we created a 2D-to-3D HTML conversion algorithm and developed a jQuery based framework preliminary called 3DSjQ. The framework exploits this algorithm to achieve S3D depth illusion.

3.2   Participants

We passed 31 participants of the academic community of the university (students and staff) between the ages of 19 and 57 into our research lab (The average age for test subjects was 28 years). Several were discarded because of the ET's inability to track due to eyeglasses or other reason. The chosen users were 20 participants, which were split in half for each stimulus (2D/3D) visualized. We chose participants in a way in which each group would have a similar age and gender distribution. None of them was a frequent consumer of 3D content. The majority of participants (58%) needed to wear their eye glasses during the experiment for proper 3D viewing.

3.3   Hardware

The hardware configuration for this experiment consisted on data collection and data display equipment. To collect data from the users, an SMI RED infrared eye tracker was used. This includes the eye tracker and a workstation with data analysis software. On the displaying side, a passive-polarized 47 inch LG 3D TV was used. An external computer was used as a source for the TV, since the ET workstation was not equipped with a modern browser capable of running a web page coded with HTML5.

3.4 Questionnaire

After participants were exposed to 'S' they were given a questionnaire to get their opinion towards the stimuli and the level of comfort they experienced during the experiment. The questionnaire consisted of two sections. The first identified if the participant was familiar with the GUI and to see if they experienced any problems understanding the purpose of the page. The second gathered the opinion of the participant towards 3D hardware, perception of S3D used on the web page, and level of comfort experienced during the experiment.

4 Results

Two areas of interest (AOI) were defined in order to aggregate data obtained from the participant's saccades and fixations (see Figure 1). These are 'results' (R) and 'ads' (A). A third AOI contains everything outside the two AOIs and can be considered as `white space' (W).

Fig. 1. Areas of interest. Indigo (R) represents 'result AOI', turquoise (A) 'ads AOI'.

We now present the results from the data recorded by the eye tracker. From the different variables logged, we selected dwell time. The definition, according to the SMI BeGaze manual [16] is the "average in ms, which is equal to the sum of all fixations and saccades within an AOI for all selected subjects divided by the number of selected subjects." Other specific data as sequence (order of gaze hits into an AOI), entry time (average duration for the first fixation into the AOI), revisits and hit ratio (how many participants have entered the defined area) to the AOI are compared to reinforce the former data.

The observed results were segmented by time. Since we are interested in studying the gaze pattern and attention to the UI itself, we split the stimuli and look at the data at 5, 10 and 20 seconds. This allows us to compare how the attention is dispersed across time in both stimuli. The following table shows the selected key performance indicators.

Table 1. Dwell Time indicators in results (R) and ads (A)

Stimuli	5s ads	5s results	10s ads	10s results	20s ads	20s results
'F'	352ms (7%)	2375ms (47%)	1604ms (16%)	4526ms (45%)	3340ms (17%)	10330ms (52%)
'S'	141ms (3%)	2847ms (57%)	631ms (6%)	6439ms (64%)	1752ms (9%)	12953ms (65%)

The first five seconds exhibit a difference in sequence and hit ratio. In 'F', sequence starts in the white space, followed by the results and finishing in the ads. Hit ratio is similar in ads and results (around 80 percent). On the other hand, 'S' exposes a different behavior: Sequence starts in the results and finishes in the ads while hit ratio for the results accounts for 100 percent of the participants, in contrast with only 20 percent for the ads.

On the 10 second mark, hit ratio on the ads AOI reaches 100 percent in 'F', but does not surpass 30 percent in 'S'. Therefore, it could be considered that stereoscopic depth is distracting the participant away from the flat ad AOI in 'S'.

Upon ending the 20 seconds, we can observe that the sequence is different between 'F' and 'S': The 2D ('F') stimulus shows a sequence of 'results', 'ads' and finally 'white space', while in the 3D ('S') stereoscopic stimulus, 'white space' precedes 'ads'. Also, 'S' only got 70 percent hit ratio on the ads AOI, which implies that not all participants looked at this AOI during the whole experiment.

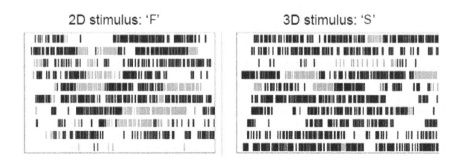

Fig. 2. AOI Sequence charts. Each row in the Y axis represents a user. X axis time (0-20s). Indigo ('R') results and turquoise ('A') ads.

4.1   General Observations

It is noticeable that dwell time in ads on 'F' and 'S' are similar in all time lapses, participants looked in the right ads twice as much in 'F' than in 'S'.

4.2   Questionnaire Results

All the users were able to identify the page purpose and intention. This ensured that the task was obvious and the GUI was familiar to all the participants. They were generally excited with the experience; 23 percent said that they didn't like the experience and 20 percent were indifferent to it.

While being exposed to the stimuli, 30 percent of the participants felt no discomfort at all. Twenty percent felt slightly discomfort only during the first couple of seconds (typical focus, vergence and accommodation issues). A 37 percent reported feeling a little discomfort, stating "difficulties focusing all the time" or "annoyed by the 3D glasses". Only 10 percent of the participants actually felt uncomfortable during the experience. The rest of the participants found it hard to tell how they felt.

Nonetheless, the majority of participants said that they would consider using 3D websites for browsing through any type content browsing only pages containing media content; 27 percent of the participants said that they would not use 3D for web browsing at all and 10 percent of the participants said that they would consider using 3D web if no glasses were required.

The overwhelming majority of the participants answered that 3D influenced the content on the page; 60 percent thought it was a positive influence. On the other hand, 10 percent said that 3D influence was a negative one, making the text hard to scan or read. Twenty-three percent said that 3D did not influenced the content on the page in any way. The rest of the participants found it hard to tell if 3D influenced the content or not.

5   Discussion

This experiment had as primary objective to see if the same semantic hierarchy that exists in 2D SERPs could be reproduced in a familiar web interface with 3D applied. We wanted to know if the introduction of depth would change a user's gaze pattern. This does not mean that we believe the current layout and experience (nor the one we created) is optimal for depth. Interaction, content manipulation and commands are topics that must be studied further.

In order to find out if depth influences the common pattern of web perception, we tested stimulus that represent SERPs using only textual content. The perception of media content (videos and images) in 3D has to be studied more carefully. Participants were pretty clear that while the effect attracts their attention, they want to see it applied to other types of media.

Finally, a more detailed research with a larger amount of participants, along with the exploitation of state-of-the-art eye tracking or other equipment would confirm our findings. This research sets a ground floor for more elaborate studies based on user interfaces in stereoscopic environments. Also, it must be noticed that the element of novelty has a lot to do in the seen gaze patterns.

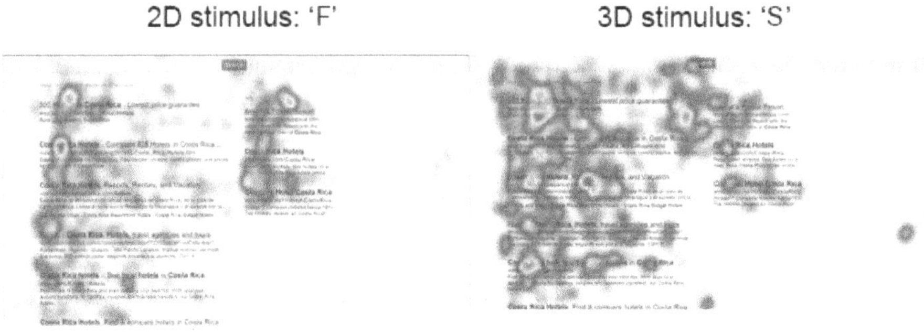

2D stimulus: 'F'   3D stimulus: 'S'

Fig. 3. Heat maps at 20 second mark

6   Conclusion

Does the introduction of depth in a SERP UI change a user's gaze pattern compared with the same interface in 2D? It does. During the experiment we observed that the existing scanning pattern of the webpage [11] was indeed modified. Also, sequence and hit ratio were different between both stimuli. As seen on the heatmaps (Fig. 3) along with the other published data described in hereby paper, it is shown that the attention distribution has clearly distinguishable differences between web pages with and without stereoscopic 3D depth applied. Dwell time in flat areas did not vary, and in comparison to the 3D stimulus, it does increase, all this aligned with what was expressed by users, of needing more time to focus on the 3D areas.

Acknowledgements. This research is supported by the Spanish Ministry of Finance and Competivity (project no. IPT-2012-0630-020000 and grant no. FFI2012-39056-C02-01 Subtitling for the deaf and hard of hearing and audio description: new formats), and also by the Catalan Government funds 2009SGR700. It is also funded by the Catalan Government scholarship 2012FI_B677.

References

1. Sacks, O.: The Mind's Eye. Knopf Doubleday Publishing Group (2010)
2. Hakkinen, J., Kawai, T., Takatalo, J., Mitsuya, R., Nyman, G.: What do people look at when they watch stereoscopic movies? 75240E–75240E10 (2010)
3. Mendiburu, B.: 3D Movie Making. Stereoscopic Digital Cinema from Script to Screen. Focal Press (2009)
4. Bowman, D., Coquillart, S., Froehlich, B., Hirose, M., Kitamura, Y., Kiyokawa, K., Stuerzlinger, W.: 3d user interfaces: New directions and perspectives. IEEE Computer Graphics and Applications 28(6), 20–36 (2008)
5. Research and Markets: 3d-enabled tv sets on the rise worldwide. Technical report, Research and Markets (2011)
6. Chabin, J.: 3dna: 2020 vision (2013),
   http://www.3dathome.org/images/pdf/3dna_april_final2013.pdf

7. Bamford, A.: The 3d in education white paper. Technical report, International Research Agency (2011)
8. Nokia: Navteq + nokia maps = here (2013), http://maps.nokia.com/webgl/
9. Granka, L.A., Joachims, T., Gay, G.: Eye-tracking analysis of user behavior in www search. In: Proceedings of the 27th Annual International ACM SIGIR Conference on Research and Development in Information Retrieval, SIGIR 2004, pp. 478–479. ACM, New York (2004)
10. Eyetools: Google search's golden triangle. Technical report, Eyetools
11. Nielsen, J.: F-shaped pattern for reading web content. Technical report, Nielsen Norman Group (2006)
12. Cutrell, E., Guan, Z.: What are you looking for?: an eye-tracking study of information usage in web search. In: Proceedings of the SIGCHI Conference on Human Factors in Computing Systems, CHI 2007, pp. 407–416. ACM, New York (2007)
13. Wang, R., Pelfrey, B., Duchowski, A., House, D.: Online gaze disparity via bioncular eye tracking on stereoscopic displays. In: 2012 Second International Conference on 3D Imaging, Modeling, Processing,Visualization and Transmission (3DIMPVT), pp. 184–191 (2012)
14. Hanhela, M., Boev, A., Gotchev, A., Hannuteela, M.: Fusion of eye-tracking data from multiple observers for increased 3d gaze tracking precision. In: 2012 Proceedings of the 20th European Signal Processing Conference (EUSIPCO), pp. 420–424 (2012)
15. Sky3D: Bskyb technical guidelines for plano stereoscopic (3d) programme content. Technical report, BSkyB
16. SMI: Begaze 2 manual, http://www.cs.rit.edu/rlc/research/eyetracking/smi/begaze2.pdf

Multiple Views for Supporting Lifelong, Highly Contextual and Ubiquitous Social Learning

Francisco Gutierrez[1], Gustavo Zurita[2], and Nelson Baloian[1]

[1] Computer Science Department, Universidad de Chile
Av. Blanco Encalada 2120, 3rd Floor, Santiago, Chile
[2] Management Control and Information Systems Department, Universidad de Chile
{Frgutier,nbaloian}@dcc.uchile.cl

Abstract. Current social networking services provide ways to access to huge amounts of information in different contexts. However, these applications are still not oriented to managing knowledge or facilitating learning processes. Aiming to help users to access, create, validate and distribute their knowledge, we propose the design of a prototype combining multiple views to support highly contextual learning. This prototype consists on a mobile application based on diverse functionalities and interaction mechanisms currently used in social networking services. With this application, users will be able to register elements from their surrounding environment in form of micronotes, concepts, images, or other media. These knowledge blocks can be processed and rendered in different views (text, map, calendar, concept map, timeline), and augmented with information related to their space, time, and reference contextual information.

1   Introduction

One of the promises of the ubiquitous computing paradigm is to help organize and mediate social interactions wherever and whenever these situations might occur. In fact, its evolution has recently been accelerated by improved wireless telecommunications capabilities, open networks, continued increases in computing power, improved battery technology, and the emergence of flexible software architectures [14]. However, social implications of these technologies are acknowledged, but are rarely considered carefully [8].

Typically, people when are faced to learning situations (either in formal or informal scenarios), tend to involve in communities, which embody beliefs and behaviors to be acquired [17]. The integration of one-to-one computer-to-learner models of technology enhanced by wireless mobile computing and position technologies may provide new ways to integrate indoor and outdoor learning [18].

Considering the current popularity of social software applications including communication and interactive tools for capturing, storing and processing multimedia and localized content (e.g. *Facebook*, *Twitter*, *Foursquare*, *Flickr*, etc.), we are interested on taking advantage of these interaction patterns for generating meaningful

G. Urzaiz et al. (Eds.): UCAmI 2013, LNCS 8276, pp. 34–41, 2013.

experiences in order to support life-long, contextual and social ubiquitous learning. In fact, none of these popular social software applications provide an appropriate context for organizing and adapting this content in order to be useful in either formal or informal learning scenarios. In other words, these services are still not focused to support knowledge management (i.e. knowledge access, creation, validation and distribution), nor facilitating learning processes. Despite the fact that current social applications facilitate the access to huge amounts of information (either structured or not), we still do not have mechanisms that allow users to process or navigate through their own knowledge acquired during their lives in formal or informal scenarios.

In this paper we propose the design of a prototype based on learning theories and patterns of social networking services, which provides multiple views to users for facilitating the access, creation, validation and distribution of his/her knowledge, and therefore facilitating learning in different topics of his/her interest. This acquisition is adapted to the user context (which can be real/virtual, synchronous/asynchronous, co-located/remote), to where this knowledge is acquired or used, lifelong, and supported by recent mobile technologies. The views offered by the application are automatically generated when registering personal notes, and they are augmented with information generated by other users (i.e. in a social context), with real-time information flows (e.g. *Twitter* trending topics or formal media coverage), and with bibliographical content taken from *Wikipedia*.

2   Related Work

This section first introduces a set of models that aim to explain how people learn and in which scenarios. We then present usage patterns in social networking services, indicating why people use these software platforms in general, and in the particular case of *Facebook*, *Twitter*, and *Foursquare*.

Learning is a process that leads to change, which occurs as a result of experience and increases the potential for improved performance and future learning [1]. Moreover, learning is omnipresent in our daily activities, as it does not necessarily depend on instructors, books, self-study programs, or coaching [6]. There are several theories that aim to understand how people learn and which strategies can be used to enhance knowledge acquisition in different scenarios. In this subsection we will briefly review four of them: (1) seamless learning, (2) situated learning, (3) rhizomatic learning, and (4) lifelong learning.

According to Chan et al., the term *seamless learning* refers to activities marked by continuous learning experiences across different contexts, and supported by mobile and ubiquitous technologies [4]. Seamless learning environments bridge private and public learning spaces where learning happens as both individual and collective efforts and across different contexts. There is a need on enabling learners to learn whenever they are curious and seamlessly switch between different contexts. Therefore, there is a need to extend the social spaces in which learners interact [13].

Brown et al. first proposed the concept of *situated learning* [3], in which they claim that meaningful learning will only take place if it is embedded in the social and physical context within which it will be used. Lave and Wenger define situated learning as a model of learning in a community of practice [11].

Seen as a model for the construction of knowledge, **rhizomatic** processes suggest the interconnectedness of ideas as well as boundless exploration across many fronts from different starting points. For the educator, supporting rhizomatic learning requires the creation of a context within which members of a learning community construct knowledge and which can be reshaped in a dynamic manner in response to environmental conditions. The learning experience may build on social, conversational processes, as well as personal knowledge creation, linked into unbounded personal learning networks that merge formal and informal media [5].

Finally, **lifelong learning** is the ongoing, voluntary, and self-motivated pursuit of knowledge for either personal or professional reasons. Therefore, learning can no longer be divided into a place and time to acquire knowledge and a place and time to apply the knowledge acquired [7]. For this reason, learning can be supported by ubiquitous technologies, since it can be seen as something that takes place on an on-going basis from our daily interactions with others and with the world around us. Figure 1 summarizes the main characteristics (context, continuity, mobility and not bounded) that sustain these four learning theories: *lifelong learning* theory is "not bounded" to anything in particular, has a constant "continuity" in its process, and is strongly boosted by "mobility". For both *situated learning* and *rhizomatic* theories, an important aspect is the "context" in which learning situations occur.

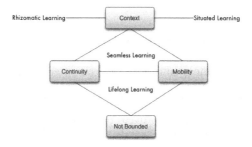

Fig. 1. Main concepts derived from learning theories

Maslow's hierarchy of needs model describes human motivation. However, despite the popularity of this model, insights from the use and adoption of current social networking services show that this model fails at considering current trends of social connection and how social media impacts over the original pyramid [16].

Brandtzaeg and Heim conducted a survey in order to find out why people use social networking services. Among the stated reasons, the most important are: (1) seeking new relations and meeting new people; (2) maintaining contacts with both close friends and acquaintances; and (3) sharing experiences, and commenting [2].

With the uprising popularity of Twitter and microblogging services, Java et al. studied the main uses of these platforms. They found out these are: talk about current events or about what people are currently doing, reply to other users' short messages, share useful information, and report news [9]. Regarding the reasons that motivate users to become members and participate in Facebook. Nadkarni et al. propose a model that suggests that its users have two main needs: belonging and self-presentation [15]. Joinson also studied the different activities that Facebook users perform: contact friends and acquaintances, get to virtually know new people, communicate, and share and comment pictures [10]. Lindqvist et al. conducted a study to understand how and why people use location-sharing applications (e.g. Foursquare), as well as how they manage their privacy [12]. They found out that privacy concerns have not kept users from adopting these services.

3   Prototype Design for Supporting Ubiquitous Social Learning

The prototype runs over a mobile telephone or tablet, since it gives support to note taking on the go. As of the software platform, it relays on a client-server architecture and an integration with social networking services for giving support to social connections. Figure 2 gives an overview of the proposed architecture.

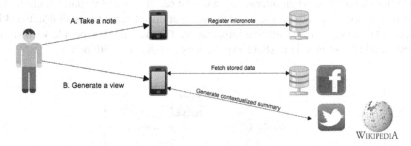

Fig. 2. Proposed architecture of the prototype

Users can interact in two ways with the application: (A) taking a note, by using the mobile interface to register text, pictures, audio, video, or geographical coordinates; and (B) generate a view with the information stored in his/her profile, augmenting it with the relevant notes registered by his/her friends (taken from *Facebook*), and contextualized summaries taken from what is trending in *Twitter* and bibliographical elements from *Wikipedia*. That way, users can benefit from a personalized view that is relevant to them and highly contextual. Users can also navigate through their different notes, thus allowing the access, creation, validation and distribution of his/her knowledge, and facilitating learning in different topics of his/her interest. Figure 3 gives an overview of the user interface design for the proposed prototype. There are two main ways users can interact with the prototype, as shown in Figure 3: (A) registering a note in the field (see the screenshot on the left), and (B) consulting an automatically-generated view from existing notes (see the screenshot on the right, where a view of Figure 4 can be displayed). In the first case, users can either type a message, record an audio or video file, take a picture with the telephone built-in camera, tag a location, or tag other users. It is also possible to set the visibility of each note (i.e. personal, public under a defined perimeter, or public to all users).

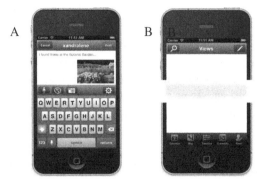

Fig. 3. User interface design of the proposed prototype

The second interface offers five ways to display the information related to the set of notes handled by the user. Moreover, the views are rendered with dynamic information regarding the users' friends and declared acquaintances, thus enhancing a social interaction value when interacting with the registered and visualized notes. This social interaction responds to the typical uses that are observed in social networking services: (1) looking for and sharing information, (2) meeting new people with similar interests, and (3) being able to share experiences and discuss with others.

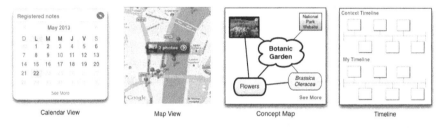

Fig. 4. Supported views for displaying augmented notes

Regarding the views of the second interface, they aim to display the content registered in the different notes, and providing an additional layer of information serving as a bibliographical and social context. That way, users can ease the management of their knowledge by accessing, creating, validating, and distributing their acquired knowledge over time and space. The display of the views is adapted to how the user is actually interacting with the application, by processing his/her habits using cognitive profiling. Figure 4 shows an overview of the different views.

The supported views integrate the main characteristics that are derived from the learning theories reviewed in section 2.1 and summarized in Figure 1: *context*, *continuity*, *mobility*, and *not bounded*. Therefore, there is a particular stress in enhancing the context dimension in each view proposed (calendar, map, timeline, concept map, and feed), supporting *mobility* and *continuity* in the note acquisition, processing, validation and distribution of information, anytime and anywhere, with the support of mobile devices. We expect that users learn about any topic they are interested in; i.e., *not bounded*. The specific elements covered in each view are:

- **Calendar view:** For specifying the *temporal context* in which users register their notes, and how these are related between them as events in specific dates;
- **Map view:** For specifying the *geographical context* of the different notes, represented with a pin over a map;
- **Timeline:** For grouping in time different notes according to the *temporal context* in which they were registered with blocks of events in two dimensions: one related to the notes generated by the user at a specific time, and another that includes *contextual information* to the elements described in the user timeline;
- **Concept map:** For displaying a broad view of how the information registered in the different notes is related to the others by joining concepts, notes, and blocks of external information, providing a scenario for establishing new relations among people who want to exchange notes, concepts, or information in general; and
- **Feed:** For showing a full text-based list of the notes registered by a user.

4   Prototype Evaluation

In order to get a first insight on user's expectations and needs with the proposal, we carried out a *paper prototyping* evaluation with a group of 8 end users (5 men and 3 women, aged between 20 and 32 years old). All of these evaluators stated they use quite often social mobile applications. We used this technique because it is quite useful when evaluating early prototypes, as users feel more comfortable being critical because the prototype is typically not developed at this stage. We printed out a high-resolution set of mock-ups to compensate for the poorer quality of printing, and to make it easier for the observer to see what the users were pointing at. The evaluation was conducted by showing the main user interface to each tester, and we asked them to first comment on their general impression, then to point to any element that they thought they could interact with and tell us what they expected would happen.

This simple method provided us with feedback indicating that the designed views are pertinent when trying to access the registered notes in different contexts. However, it was somewhat difficult for the evaluators to understand at a first glance why the proposal could be useful in a real case scenario (e.g. when going to a museum, or walking along a street, or traveling in any kind of vehicle, etc.). This indicates that the interaction design of our prototype needs to be enhanced, and that further evaluation in the field with end users is required to assess the perceived usefulness and perceived ease of use of the prototype in real use-scenarios. At a second stage, we carried out a survey to assess the perceived usefulness of each one of the views specified in the design of the prototype. The evaluators had to fill a 5-point Likert scale. We also added an open space at the end of the survey for general comments and suggestions. Figure 5 shows the median value given by the evaluators for the perceived usefulness of each view.

Regarding the perception of the different views embedded in the application, the group of users considered the map view and the timeline as the most useful. In fact, open comments showed that the timeline view indicated not only which notes are relevant, but also this view is useful for remembering and putting in context the different notes when they were registered. Concerning the calendar view, however, its usage is rather limited since it is not as expressive as the other proposed views. The feed view (i.e. just a list of all the registered notes in text-form) was evaluated with a median value of 3 out of 5. This result can be linked to the added value that users might have found in different ways of visualizing the same set of notes.

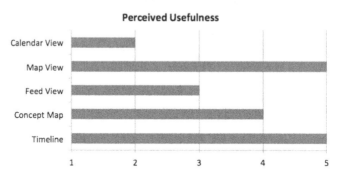

Fig. 5. Survey results: perceived usefulness of the proposed views

Finally, concerning the main concepts derived from the learning theories presented in Figure 1, we can state that mobility and continuity are indeed important elements when defining the contextualized views. In fact, by acquiring pieces of knowledge from the surrounding environment, the user will be able to put in context his/her own previous registered notes, thus being able to organize his/her knowledge.

5   Conclusions and Future Work

In this paper we proposed the design of a prototype based on learning theories, which provides multiple views to users for facilitating the access, creation, validation and distribution of his/her knowledge, and therefore facilitating learning in different topics of his/her interest. Users interact with the application in two ways: (1) by registering personal notes in form of text, pictures, audio, video, and geographical coordinates; and (2), by accessing views that are automatically generated with the registered personal notes, and they are augmented with information generated by other users, with real-time information flows, and with bibliographical content taken from *Wikipedia*. The registered knowledge is adapted to the user context (real/virtual, synchronous/asynchronous, co-located/remote), to where this knowledge is acquired or used, is lifelong, and supported by recent technologies.

Even if it is still quite early to strongly conclude about the pertinence of our proposal, a first end-user evaluation of the prototype proved us right that there is a need for a mobile application that integrates social elements and allows knowledge management. However, in the specific case of the proposed prototype, it is still needed to enhance the interaction design elements, for example by including speech recognition and/or speech synthesis in order to allow audio-based input/outputs.

References

1. Ambrose, S.A., Bridges, M.W., DiPietro, M., Lovett, M.C., Norman, M.K.: How Learning Works. Jossey-Bass, San Francisco (2010)
2. Brandtzaeg, P.B., Heim, J.: Why People Use Social Networking Sites. In: Ozok, A.A., Zaphiris, P. (eds.) OCSC 2009. LNCS, vol. 5621, pp. 143–152. Springer, Heidelberg (2009)
3. Brown, J.S., Collins, A., Duguid, P.: Situated Cognition and the Culture of Learning. Educational Researcher 18(1), 32–42 (1989)
4. Chan, T.-W., Roschelle, J., His, S., Kinshuk, S.M., et al.: One-to-One Technology-Enhanced Learning: An Opportunity for Global Research Collaboration. Research and Practice in Technology Enhanced Learning 1(1), 3–29 (2006)
5. Cormier, D.: Rhizomatic Education: Community as Curriculum. Journal of Online Education 4(5) (2008)
6. Cross, J.: Informal Learning: Rediscovering the Natural Pathways that Inspire Innovation and Performance. Pfeiffer, San Francisco (2006)
7. Fischer, G.: Lifelong Learning – More than Training. Journal of Interactive Learning Research 11(3/4), 265–294 (2000)
8. Grudin, J.: Group Dynamics and Ubiquitous Computing. Communications of the ACM 45(12), 74–78 (2002)
9. Java, A., Song, X., Finin, T., Tseng, B.: Why We Twitter: Understanding Microblogging Usage and Communities. In: Zhang, H., Spiliopoulou, M., Mobasher, B., Giles, C.L., McCallum, A., Nasraoui, O., Srivastava, J., Yen, J. (eds.) WebKDD 2007. LNCS, vol. 5439, pp. 118–138. Springer, Heidelberg (2009)
10. Joinson, A.N.: 'Looking At', 'Looking Up' or 'Keeping Up' With People? Motives and Uses of Facebook. In: Proceedings of the 26th SIGCHI Conference on Human Factors in Computing Systems (CHI 2008), Florence, Italy (2008)
11. Lave, J., Wenger, E.: Situated Learning: Legitimate Peripheral Participation. Cambridge University Press, Cambridge (1991)
12. Lindqvist, J., Cranshaw, J., Wiese, J., Hong, J., Zimmerman, J.: I'm the Mayor of my House: Examining Why People Use Foursquare – A Social-Driven Location Sharing Application. In: Proceedings of the 29th SIGCHI Conference on Human Factors in Computing Systems (CHI 2011), Vancouver, Canada (2011)
13. Looi, C.K., Seow, P., Zhang, B., So, H.J., Chen, W.-L., Wong, L.H.: Leveraging Mobile Technology for Sustainable Seamless Learning: A Research Agenda. British Journal of Educational Technology 41(2), 154–169 (2010)
14. Lyytinen, K., Yoo, Y.: Issues and Challenges in Ubiquitous Computing. Communications of the ACM 45(12), 63–65 (2002)
15. Nadkarni, A., Hofmann, S.G.: Why do People Use Facebook? Personality and Individual Differences 52(3), 243–249 (2012)
16. Rutledge, P.: Social Networks: What Maslow Misses, http://www.psychologytoday.com/blog/positively-media/201111/social-networks-what-maslow-misses-0 (retrieved, last visited May 23, 2013)
17. Wenger, E.: Communities of Practice and Social Learning Systems. Organization 7(2), 225–246 (2000)
18. Zurita, G., Baloian, N.: Context, Patterns and Geo-collaboration to Support Situated Learning. In: Bravo, J., López-de-Ipiña, D., Moya, F. (eds.) UCAmI 2012. LNCS, vol. 7656, pp. 503–511. Springer, Heidelberg (2012)

Boosting Dependable Ubiquitous Computing: A Case Study

Christian Fernández-Campusano, Roberto Cortiñas, and Mikel Larrea

University of the Basque Country UPV/EHU, Spain
{christianrobert.fernandez,roberto.cortinas,mikel.larrea}@ehu.es

Abstract. Ubiquitous computing has inherent features, e.g., a number of elements in the system with restricted communication and computation capabilities, which make harder to achieve dependability. In this work we explore this research line through the study of TrustedPals, a smartcard-based framework which allows implementing security policies in ubiquitous systems and applications in a decentralized way. The current architecture of TrustedPals uses a consensus algorithm adapted to the omission failure model. In this work, we propose to alternatively use the Paxos algorithm, in order to address more ubiquitous environments.

1 Introduction

Dependability is composed of several aspects, such as availability and reliability, which imply fault-tolerance. In this regard, reaching agreement is a key topic to achieve dependability. Consensus [1] is one of the most important problems in fault-tolerant distributed computing, and constitutes a paradigm that represents a family of agreement problems. Roughly speaking, in consensus processes propose an initial value and have to decide on one of the proposed values.

Although many solutions have been proposed to solve consensus in synchronous systems, Fischer et al. [2] showed that it is impossible to solve consensus deterministically in asynchronous systems where at least one process may crash. In order to circumvent this impossibility, Chandra and Toueg [3] proposed the failure detector abstraction. Roughly speaking, a failure detector is an abstract module located at each process of the system that provides information about (the operational state of) other processes in the system. Failure detectors offer a modular approach that allows other applications such as consensus to use them as a building block. Additionally, the failure detector abstraction allows to encapsulate the synchrony assumptions of the system, so applications that make use of failure detectors can be designed as if they run in an asynchronous system.

Recently, Cortiñas et al. [4] proposed a modular architecture which combines failure detectors with a tamper-proof smartcard-based secure platform named *TrustedPals* [5] in order to solve consensus in a partially synchronous system prone to Byzantine failures. They also showed how to solve a security problem called *Secure Multiparty Computation* [6] through consensus. Secure Multiparty Computation is a general security problem that can be used to solve various real-life problems such as distributed voting, private bidding and online auctions.

G. Urzaiz et al. (Eds.): UCAmI 2013, LNCS 8276, pp. 42–45, 2013.

2   Current and Proposed Architecture

Figure 1 (left) presents the current architecture of TrustedPals [4], which is composed of the following elements:

- The TrustedPals platform allows to transform every failure into a process crash or a message omission, which implies that the initial Byzantine failure model is turned into a more benign one, namely the omission failure model.
- An Eventually Perfect ($\Diamond\mathcal{P}$) failure detector adapted to the omission failure model ($\Diamond\mathcal{P}_{om}$) allows to detect *well connected* processes, i.e., processes that can actively participate in the consensus.
- Finally, a consensus algorithm adapted from [3] allows to reach agreement by using the previous $\Diamond\mathcal{P}_{om}$ failure detector.

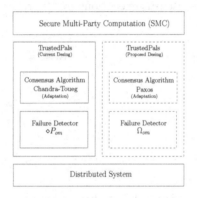

Fig. 1. Current architecture (left) vs proposed one (right)

Although the proposed solution is suitable in the security context presented of [4], it presents some drawbacks that could be improved in order to be applied in other scenarios. For example, it does not consider processes which crash and later recover. Also, the consensus algorithm requires a high degree of reliability on communication, i.e., non-omissive processes and quasi-reliable channels.

Figure 1 (right) presents the architecture we propose in this work. Note that it keeps the modular approach of the previous one, but with two main differences:

- The previous consensus algorithm is replaced by the Paxos algorithm [7].
- The failure detector class considered now is Ω [8].

The combination of those two new elements in the architecture provides the system with several interesting features. On the one side, Paxos allows to reach consensus tolerating a high degree of omissive behaviour (loss of messages at processes or channels). Also, Paxos allows to cope with processes which crash and later recover. On the other hand, the Omega failure detector, Ω, provides Paxos with the eventually stable leader required to guarantee termination.

3   Experimental Results

We have performed a practical comparison of the two architectures for Trust-edPals presented in the previous section. To do so, we have implemented both approaches by using the JBotSim [9] simulator. In this work, we are interested in analysing the latency of the consensus algorithms, defined as the time elapsed between the beginning of the algorithm and the instant at which the first process decides. Note that this definition of latency (also known as *early* latency) is a reasonable performance measure from the point of view of applications relying on TrustedPals (e.g., fault-tolerant ubiquitous services implemented by active replication), which usually will wait until the first reply is returned.

We have measured the latency in three different scenarios, namely (1) failure-free, (2) crash of the first coordinator/leader process, and (3) omissions by the first coordinator/leader process. We have conducted simulations consisting in several sequences of 40 consensus executions by 12 processes.

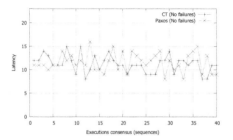

Fig. 2. Failure-free scenario

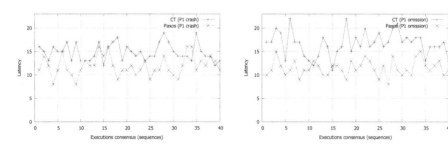

Fig. 3. Crash scenario   **Fig. 4.** Omission scenario

Figures 2, 3 and 4 present the latency of 40 consecutive consensus for the three scenarios. Table 1 presents the average latency. Observe that the results from the current architecture (CT+$\diamond P_{om}$) show a performance overhead of 32% and 48% for the crash and omission scenarios compared to the failure-free scenario, respectively. On the other hand, results from the architecture based on Paxos exhibit a similar latency in the three scenarios. The reason is that the current

Table 1. Average latency of $CT+\Diamond P_{om}$ vs $Paxos+\Omega_{om}$

Scenario	$CT+\Diamond P_{om}$	$Paxos+\Omega_{om}$	Improvement
Failure-free	11.23	11.58	-3%
Crash	14.85	11.90	20%
Omission	16.68	11.48	31%

consensus relies on the rotating coordinator paradigm, while Paxos relies on a leader election mechanism.

4 Conclusions and Future Work

In this short communication we have shown a brief highlight about the suitability of using the Paxos algorithm in order to cope with the more general scenarios we can find in dependable ubiquitous computing. In this sense, although in this work we have focused on the early latency as performance measure, we are working on a Paxos-based proposal which allows to deal with more restricted scenarios in terms of communication and computation capabilities.

Acknowledgement. Research supported by the Spanish Research Council (grant TIN2010-17170), the Basque Government (grants IT395-10 and S-PE12UN109), and the University of the Basque Country UPV/EHU (grant UFI11/45).

References

1. Pease, M.C., Shostak, R.E., Lamport, L.: Reaching agreement in the presence of faults. J. ACM 27(2), 228–234 (1980)
2. Fischer, M.J., Lynch, N.A., Paterson, M.: Impossibility of distributed consensus with one faulty process. J. ACM 32(2), 374–382 (1985)
3. Chandra, T.D., Toueg, S.: Unreliable failure detectors for reliable distributed systems. J. ACM 43(2), 225–267 (1996)
4. Cortiñas, R., Freiling, F.C., Ghajar-Azadanlou, M., Lafuente, A., Larrea, M., Penso, L.D., Soraluze, I.: Secure failure detection and consensus in trustedpals. IEEE Trans. Dependable Sec. Comput. 9(4), 610–625 (2012)
5. Fort, M., Freiling, F.C., Penso, L.D., Benenson, Z., Kesdogan, D.: Trustedpals: Secure multiparty computation implemented with smart cards. In: Gollmann, D., Meier, J., Sabelfeld, A. (eds.) ESORICS 2006. LNCS, vol. 4189, pp. 34–48. Springer, Heidelberg (2006)
6. Yao, A.C.C.: Protocols for secure computations (extended abstract). In: FOCS, pp. 160–164. IEEE Computer Society (1982)
7. Lamport, L.: The part-time parliament. ACM Trans. Comput. Syst. 16(2), 133–169 (1998)
8. Chandra, T.D., Hadzilacos, V., Toueg, S.: The weakest failure detector for solving consensus. Journal of the ACM 43(4), 685–722 (1996)
9. Casteigts, A.: The JBotSim library. CoRR abs/1001.1435 (2010)

Context-Aware Self-adaptations: From Requirements Specification to Code Generation

Tomás Ruiz-López[1], Carlos Rodríguez-Domínguez[1], María José Rodríguez[1],
Sergio F. Ochoa[2], and José Luis Garrido[1]

[1] Department of Software Engineering, University of Granada
Periodista Daniel Saucedo Aranda s/n, 18.071 Granada Spain
{tomruiz,carlosrodriguez,mjfortiz,jgarrido}@ugr.es
[2] Department of Computer Science, University of Chile
sochoa@dcc.uchile.cl

Abstract. Embedding context-aware self-adaptation mechanisms in pervasive systems is key to improve their acceptance by the users. These mechanisms involve a precise definition of the software structures that enable adding, removing or replacing components of the system to perform the adaptations. Typically the definition of these mechanisms is a complex and time consuming task. This paper presents a model-driven engineering approach to generate these context-aware self-adaptation mechanisms. The use of models transformations to define these mechanisms helps to reduce the complexity and effort required to define them. In order to illustrate the usefulness of the proposed approach, this paper reports its application to the development of a context-aware notification service.

Keywords: context-awareness, self-adaptation, model-driven engineering, software engineering.

1 Introduction

Context-awareness is a key feature of pervasive systems, which allows them to sense, reason and react to environmental changes (i.e. context changes). From a software engineering point of view, it oftentimes involves the self-adaptation of the system components (e.g. adding, removing or replacing services), in order to address the new situation and consequently to fulfill the specific goals of the system.

Although there is an extensive research work on context-awareness to support the development of pervasive systems [14], there are no clear guidelines about how to design (structure and behavior) pervasive systems guaranteeing their context adaptation capability. This situation put developers of pervasive systems in an uncomfortable position, since they have to address a complex and transversal design feature (i.e. the context-aware self-adaptation capability) using ad hoc solutions. The literature reports that employ ad hoc solutions usually increase the development effort and complexity, and this reduces the project success rate. Moreover, the technological evolution affecting these systems and the

G. Urzaiz et al. (Eds.): UCAmI 2013, LNCS 8276, pp. 46–53, 2013.

Fig. 1. Different context situations where the notification service makes use of the appropriate mechanism for delivering information

heterogeneity of the devices involved on these solutions [10], demands counting on design guidelines and models to embrace different platform-specific implementations, with the minimum impact for developers; i.e., the development process of pervasive systems should ideally be done in an automatic or semi-automatic way.

This paper presents a model-driven engineering (MDE) approach to support the development of pervasive systems. The proposal stems from the combination of two engineering methods, REUBI [10] and SCUBI [11], which were intended to address respectively the requirements specification and the design phase of this kind of systems. The proposed approach leads to improve the development process using model transformation techniques to automatically derive the specific design models, from the requirements specification (i.e. requirement model) of a pervasive system. Then, the source code of the application is automatically generated applying transformations to the design models. The aim of this proposal is to help developers to specify the system adaptations at a high level of abstraction and, after applying the proposed transformations, derive the appropriate structure and behavior of the system at design and implementation levels.

The rest of this paper is structured as follows. Section 2 describes the proposed approach, explaining how a model-driven strategy is applied to generate a context-aware self-adaptive system. Section 3 indicates the technology used to implement the models and the transformations. Section 4 presents the related work. Finally, the main results from this approach are summarized and the future work is outlined in Section 5.

2   Context-Aware Self-adaptations in Pervasive Systems

This section introduces the proposed development approach, which is complementary to the use of a regular software process. The usefulness of this approach is illustrated through its application in the development of a context-aware notification service.

As depicted in Figure 1, this service provides notifications to users using different mechanisms; for instance, when the user is watching TV, notifications are shown on the screen; when s/he is doing the housework, notifications are delivered using a voice synthesizer; and when the user is sleeping, the service does not deliver notifications not to disturb the user. In the following subsections, the requirements of this system are modeled following the REUBI notation [10], and also the corresponding transformations used to automatically obtain the system design and code are presented.

2.1 Requirements Specification

Several mechanisms can be used to deliver notifications to a user, however their suitability depends on the user context. Therefore the notification mechanism to be used in the system should be carefully chosen in order to maximize the user acceptance. This is a well-known problem that can be solved applying the *Context-sensitive I/O* pattern [12]. This pattern states that each input/output mechanism that is going to be embedded into a service, is related to the context situations where this service will be used.

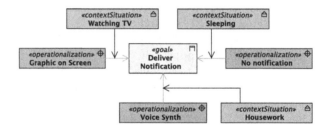

Fig. 2. Notification service requirements in REUBI notation

Thus, as depicted in Figure 2, the three notification mechanisms (i.e., displaying a graphic on the screen, playing a synthesized voice, and silencing the notifications) were considered to reach such a goal. Each mechanism will be used in a particular situation; e.g. when the user is watching TV, doing housework or sleeping, respectively. These situations need to be characterized through their attributes (context variables) in order to distinguish changes among them. This requirements specification is a model that represents the context-aware notification service at a high abstraction level.

2.2 Transforming Requirements into Design

Once the requirements have been modeled, the first model transformation is applied. In order to define these transformations, a metamodel-based approach has been followed [2]. This approach relates elements between the source (i.e., requirements) and target (i.e., design) metamodels in order to describe the transformation to be performed. Table 1 describes the correspondences between the

Table 1. Correspondence between REUBI and SCUBI elements in the transformations between models

Source element	Target Element	Description
Goal	*Functional Interface*	It captures the abstract functionality that enables the goal achivement. In the notification service, it contains methods to perform the delivery of notifications.
	Manager Component	It is in charge of forwarding the requests to an appropriate mechanism in order to fulfill a goal. It acts as a proxy between the service consumers and the components that implement the notification strategies.
	Control Component	It is in charge of fine-tuning the behavior of the manager component. It indicates the manager which of the notification alternatives should be applied at a given moment.
Operationalization	*Component*	It implements the actual behavior of the abstract functionality to fulfill a goal. In the example, each of the three alternatives correspond to a component that provide notifications in a different way.
Context Situation	*Context Consumer*	It is a component that listens to the relevant events that can trigger an adaptation.
	Adaptation Rules	It contains information about the conditions where an adaptation should occur, and which are the components that must change.
	Adaptation Component	It contains the adaptation rules and runs the reasoning procedure to determine if the service adaptation must be applied or not.

elements in the REUBI and SCUBI metamodels, and also the rationale behind these relationships.

Figure 3 depicts the results of applying this model transformation. In the obtained design we can identify different components, each one with specific concerns. These components are responsible of responding to the requests, managing which one of them is in charge of responding and receiving the relevant events, when the system triggers a self-adaptation process during runtime.

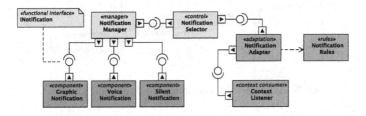

Fig. 3. Notification service design in SCUBI notation

It is important to note that the modification of the requirement model only affects to certain parts of the design model. Thus, if new notification mechanisms are introduced, the system design is able to admit them as new components that implement the desired functionality. Similarly, if new context situations are introduced, or the existing ones are modified, only the components dealing with context sensing and the adaptation rules are subject to changes. Therefore, the resulting system design can be modified with an almost minimal effort.

2.3   Generating Code from the Design

In order to obtain an implementation of the notification service, a code genera-tion strategy has been devised. The strategy considers mapping each element of the design metamodel, to a component template that contains the source code that implements such an element. Multiple template files can be created for dif-ferent programming languages. Also, different file formats can be used to store the adaptation rules.

Figure 4 depicts the code generated, based on the described template-based approach, for a particular component and also for the interface it provides. These templates are filled with data from each entity, such as their name, method signatures, attributes and (in some cases) methods to instantiate and manage them.

Fig. 4. Code generation example for a component and its interface

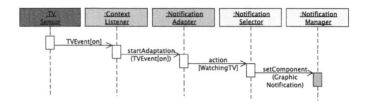

Fig. 5. Example of a runtime self-adaptation process

The generated code has been devised to perform a runtime adaptation process as depicted in Figure 5. For instance, if the user sits to watch TV, an event is triggered notifying the system that TV is on. The context listener receives this event and, since it is interesting to the notification service, decides to trigger an adaptation process. This event triggers the execution of the rule corresponding to the situation *watching TV*. Thus, the adaptation component sends a message to the selector telling it to apply the corresponding action to the situation. As the result of the adaptation process, the selector sends a message to the notification manager setting the graphic notification component as the result of the adaptation process.

3 Implementation Aspects of the Proposal

In order to test the proposal, it has been implemented using the model transformation facilities provided by different Eclipse plugins. The metamodels have been described using the *Eclipse Modeling Framework* (EMF). Models conform to them are described in an XMI file, using a textual notation.

The *Atlas Transformation Language* (ATL) has been used to describe the model transformations. This language aims to follow the *Query-View-Transformation* (QVT)[8] standard. It provides mechanisms to specify declarative rules, but also provides mechanisms to incorporate imperative blocks in some transformations. The ATL file uses the metamodels described in EMF and defines the correspondence between their elements. Then, the ATL file is provided with the source model in XMI format as input, and outputs another XMI file as a result.

Regarding the code generation, the *Acceleo* plugin has been chosen. It follows the *Model to Text* (MOFM2T)[7] standard, consisting of the definition of template files which are filled with information from an XMI file. In this case, we have created templates for code generation in the Java programming language. Also, in order to store the adaptation rules, an XML file is generated.

The process is started with an input requirements model that is created conforming the REUBI metamodel. Then, an ATL transformation is performed and, as a result, a design model conforming the SCUBI metamodel is generated. Finally, this model is used as input for the Acceleo plugin and different Java files are generated with the resulting code[1].

4 Related Work

Several research works that have applied the principles of model-driven engineering (MDE) applied to the development of pervasive system can be found in the bibliography. Some of them are focused on specific aspects of the development. For instance, Cirilo et al. [1] present an approach to provide transformations oriented to interface adaptations based on context changes. Similarly,

---

[1] For the sake of clarity and conciseness, implementation details have been ommitted from the paper, but all the files can be found in:
http://www.ugr.es/~tomruiz/MDAContext.zip

MDE techniques have been applied to hide the management of low-level components to developers, when they have to use wireless sensor networks [9] to implement pervasive systems. Harrington et al. [3] provide a MDE approach focused on planning and optimization algorithms for pervasive environments. Although these approaches are useful, they are not general. Therefore they are not reusable in different development contexts.

On the other hand, Lu et al. [5] present a formal methodology, based on Petri Nets, to systematically assess the design of context-aware systems. However, this work does not provide guidelines to implement the system once it is formally modeled.

There are some other proposals that try to provide wide perspective of the pervasive systems design. Seridi et al. [13] provide a metamodel and a tool for context specification. Similarly, Serral et al. [14] provide mechanisms to represent and manage the context information. They also provide a code generation mechanism to obtain an implementation of the system. Their focus is on context management, rather than in how the software should be structured to ease the self-adaptation process.

Finally, the most similar approach to the presented proposal can be found in [4]. A component-based design method is applied to perform self-adaptations based on context changes. However, our proposal aims to raise the abstraction level and it considers the specification of the self-adaptations at the requirements level.

5   Conclusions and Future Work

This paper proposes and describes a complete methodological approach to support the development of pervasive systems, especially focused on addressing context-aware self-adaptations. The proposal follows a MDE approach to: (1) derive a system design that meets specific requirements, and (2) generate code that implements such a design. The usefulness of the proposed approach has been illustrated through the development of a context-aware notification service.

The proposal aims to raise the abstraction level in which it is possible to specify the self-adaptations of a pervasive system. In the proposed approach these adaptations are specified at the requirements level, and then they are transformed into design and code using automatic models transformations. This strategy speeds up the development process, since the software engineers do not need to focus on certain aspects that can be (semi-)automatically addressed. It also provides more reliable software, since this task is automatized. The methodology needs to be validated and applied to some more projects in order to know which are its strengths and limitations.

The next steps also consider developing a graphical modeling tool that helps developers to implement requirements models, and understand the design models obtained after applying the transformations. Moreover, more transformations between elements will be explored in order to address more complex situations.

Acknowledgements. This research work is funded by the Spanish Ministry of Economy and Competitiveness through the project TIN2012-38600, the Innovation Office from the Andalusian Government through project TIN-6600, and The Spanish Ministry of Education, Culture and Sports through the FPU Scholarship.

References

1. Cirilo, C.E., do Prado, A.F., de Souza, W.L., Zaina, L.A.: Model driven RichUbi: a model driven process for building rich interfaces of context-sensitive ubiquitous applications. In: Proceedings of the 28th ACM International Conference on Design of Communication, pp. 207–214 (2010)
2. Czarnecki, K., Helsen, S.: Classification of model transformation approaches. In: Proceedings of the 2nd OOPSLA Workshop on Generative Techniques in the Context of the Model Driven Architecture, vol. 45(3), pp. 1–17 (2003)
3. Harrington, A., Cahill, V.: Model-driven engineering of planning and optimisation algorithms for pervasive computing environments. Pervasive and Mobile Computing 7(6), 705–726 (2011)
4. Hussein, M., Han, J., Colman, A.: An approach to model-based development of context-aware adaptive systems. In: IEEE 35th Annual Conference Computer Software and Applications (COMPSAC), pp. 205–214 (2011)
5. Lu, T., Bao, J.: A Systematic Approach to Context Aware Service Design. Journal of Computers 7(1), 207–217 (2012)
6. Object Management Group, Model Driven Architecture (2003), http://www.omg.org/mda/
7. Object Management Group, MOF Model To Text Transformation (2008), http://www.omg.org/spec/MOFM2T/
8. Object Management Group, Meta Object Facility 2.0 Query/View/ Transformation, QVT (2011), http://www.omg.org/spec/QVT/
9. Rodrigues, T., Dantas, P., Delicato, F.C., Pires, P.F., Miceli, C., Pirmez, L., Huang, G., Zomaya, A.Y.: A Model-Based Approach for Building Ubiquitous Applications Based on Wireless Sensor Network. In: Sénac, P., Ott, M., Seneviratne, A. (eds.) MobiQuitous 2010. LNICST, vol. 73, pp. 350–352. Springer, Heidelberg (2012)
10. Ruiz-López, T., Noguera, M., Rodríguez, M.J., Garrido, J.L., Chung, L.: REUBI: a Requirements Engineering Method for Ubiquitous Systems. Science of Computer Programming (2012) (in press)
11. Ruiz-López, T., Rodríguez-Domínguez, C., Noguera, M., Rodríguez, M.J., Garrido, J.L.: Towards a Component-based Design of Adaptive, Context-sensitive Services for Ubiquitous Systems. In: Proceedings of the 8th Workshop on Artificial Intelligence Techniques for Ambient Intelligence (AITAmI 2013) (2013)
12. Ruiz-López, T., Noguera, M., Rodríguez, M.J., Garrido, J.L.: Requirements Systematization through Pattern Application in Ubiquitous Systems. In: Ambient Intelligence-Software and Applications, pp. 17–24 (2013)
13. Seridi, H., Bouacha, I., Benselim, M.S.: Development of context-aware web services using the MDA approach. International Journal of Web Science 1(3), 224–241 (2012)
14. Serral, E., Valderas, P., Pelechano, V.: Towards the model driven development of context-aware pervasive systems. Pervasive and Mobile Computing 6(2), 254–280 (2010)

Intelligent Information System to Tracking Patients in Intensive Care Units

Fernando Marins[1], Luciana Cardoso[1], Filipe Portela[2], Manuel Santos[2], António Abelha[1], and José Machado[1,*]

[1] Minho University, CCTC, Departament of Informatics, Braga, Portugal
[2] Minho University, Algoritmi, Departament of Information Systems, Guimarães, Portugal
{f.abreu.marins,lucianacardoso05}@gmail.com,
{cfp,mfs}@dsi.uminho.pt,
{abelha,jmac}@di.uminho.pt

Abstract. With the increasing expansion of health information systems, there is a need to create an interface: human, machine and the surrounding environment. This interface is called Ambient Intelligence and it has been increasing in the healthcare area. In this paper it is presented the Ambient Intelligence system implemented in the Intensive Care Unit of Centro Hospitalar do Porto, a hospital in the north of Portugal. This Ambient Intelligence is consisted by INTCare system, which the main goal is monitoring the patients' vital signs, PaLMS system, responsible for the patient's localisation and identification and AIDA, the platform that guarantees the interoperability from all information systems in the hospital. Furthermore, an usability evaluation was performed, described in this article, to find out what can be improved.

Keywords: Ambient Intelligence, Monitoring System, Interoperability.

1 Introduction

In the last decades, healthcare information systems have been growing but the tools for data processing are not sufficient and new technologies should support a new way of envisaging the future hospital. There is the need to enrich the environment with technology, mainly sensors and network-connected devices, building a system to take decisions that benefit the users of that environment based on real-time information gathered and historical data accumulated, make use of Ambient Intelligence (*AmI*). *AmI* is considered a new paradigm that supports the design of the next generation of intelligent systems and introduces novel means of communication between human, machine, and the surrounding environment [1].

Indeed, *AmI* is a perfect candidate to the healthcare industry, where the demand for new technologies, contributing to a better quality of treatment of

---

* Corresponding author.

G. Urzaiz et al. (Eds.): UCAmI 2013, LNCS 8276, pp. 54–61, 2013.

patients, is constant . In this scenario, both researchers from the University of Minho (Braga, Portugal) and Centro Hospitalar do Porto - CHP (a hospital in Oporto, Portugal) developed INTCare [2], an intelligent decision support system (IDSS) aiming the real-time monitoring of patients in the Intensive Care Unit (ICU) [3].

Whenever a patient leaves the bed, going to another unit to make an exam for instance, INTCare system fails for the recognition of the patient absence, therefore continues to monitor redundant data, store and analyse it, spending unnecessary computational resources. Besides, sound alerts are sent to medical staff due to the monitoring values out of range in some empty bed. A process of automatic identification of the patient is required. PaLMS, a Patient Localization and Management System, is a system being developed and tested in the ICU of CHP. The main goal is to detect the patients' presence in the bed through the Radio-Frequency Identification (RFID) technology, optimizing the INTCare system. RFID is an emerging technology in the healthcare industry, amongst others industries, that can facilitate safe and accurate patient identification, tracking, and processing of important health related information in health care sector, therefore a contributing technology to the implementation of *AmI* scenarios in hospitals [4].

The main goal of this article is to expose the *AmI* present in the CHP's ICU and a usability evaluation of the systems that comprise this environment..

2 AIDA - Agency for Interoperation Diffusion and Archieve of Medical Information

Gathering all patient information and present it in a readable way to physicians it's an interesting task. However, information sources are distributed, ubiquitous, heterogeneous, large and complex and the Hospital Information Systems need to communicate in order to share information and to make it available at any place at any time. So it was developed the AIDA – Agency for Interoperation, diffusion and Archive of Medical Information. AIDA, bringing to the healthcare arena new methodologies for problem solving and knowledge representation, computational models, technologies and tools, which will enable ambient intelligence or ubiquitous computing based practices at the healthcare facilities [5].

AIDA is an agency that supplies intelligent electronic workers called proactive agents, in charge of some tasks. This platform imbues many different integration features, using mainly Service Oriented Architectures (SOA) and MultiAgent Systems (MAS) to implement interoperation in a distributed, specific and conform to a standard manner, comprising all the service providers within the healthcare institution [5, 6].

3 INTCare

INTCare is a Pervasive Intelligent Decision Support System (PIDSS) [3] developed to Intensive Care Unit (ICU) with the main goal to predict the patient organ failure (cardiovascular, hepatic, renal, respiratory, neurologic, coagulation) and patient outcome (discharge condition) for the next 24 hours. This system also alerts the medical staff when vital signs of the patients are out of the normal range. It changed the ICU information system. It modified the data acquisition system, now all the data is acquired, processed and stored automatically and in real-time. Then using online-learning a set of procedures and tasks are executed in order to create new knowledge essential to the decision making process. INTCare is able to provide automatically and in real-time four different types of knowledge anywhere and any-time:

- Probability of occur an organ failure;
- Probability of patient die;
- Tracking critical events;
- Medical Scores results (SAP, SOFA, MEWS, TISS 28, Glasgow).

In order to have correct patient identification it was used an RFID system to identify which patient is in a specific bed. The RFID system is associated to bedside monitors and using some procedures is able to correctly identify the patient in the HL7 message (messages which contains vital signs and patient identification (PID)). When the gateway receives the vital signs from the monitors, it sends a HL7 message [7] to the vital signs acquisition agent and it parses the information. Then the RFID system sends the patient identification (d1, d2) present in the Bed (v1) to be stored in the message. With this option is possible have a perfect match between the PID and vital signs values collected (OBR and OBX). Next, there is a sample of a HL7 message:

```
MSH|^~\&|DHV |h2|h3|h4|||ORU^R01|h1|P|2.3.1
PID|1||d1||d2
PV1|1|U|v1
OBR|1|||DHV|||r1|
OBX|x2|NM|x3^x4^^^x5||x6|x7|||||R|||x1^ v1||
```

Table 1 explains the variables in the exchange of messages between the agents.

Table 1. Variables in the exchange of messages between the agents

h1	Version ID	x1	Producer's ID
h2	Sending Facility	x2	Value Type
h3	Receiving Application	x3	Observation Identifier (cod)
h4	Receiving Facility	x4	Observation Identifier (cod2)
d1	Patient ID (Internal ID)	x5	Observation Identifier (descp)
d2	Patient Name	x6	Observation Value
v1	Assigned Patient Location (BED)	x7	Units
r1	Observation Date/Time	x1	

4   PaLMS - Patient Localisation and Monitoring System

PaLMS is an event-based monitoring system developed using HL7 standard messages embedded in a multi-agent programming ambient. The MAS implemented is endowed with modularity, scalability and adaptability which makes this system possess a huge potential towards interoperability in healthcare information systems [8].

When a patient leaves the ICU for an exam, or for the operating room or any other place while technically he has not discharged the unit, the INTCare alert system indicates a warning state because it reads patient's vital signs as nulls but actually, no patient is in the bed. In these cases, the analysis of vital signs is made, information is stored, but this data is simply redundant. To prevent these situations it was created an intelligent ambient based on RFID tags and theirs antennas that is able to identify if the patient is or not in the bed.

PaLMS includes a Multi-Agent System based on events which react differently according various events. These events are triggered by a bed monitoring system that associates each RFID antenna with the respective bed. The PaLMS must be able to exchange messages between entities, receiving and reacting accordingly to the characteristic of the message, the intelligent agents' behaviour capabilities enable them to have different reactions according the message received. Few steps were already been achieved by some investigators in description of the receiving and sending of HL7 messages within intelligent agents behaviour [9].

4.1   RFID Events

The six most common events associated with the patient cycle in the ICU can be easily associated to HL7 events through trigger-events [10] using ADT messages provided by standard HL7:

1. Admission Event (AE) ↔ ADT_A01 message;
2. Transfer Event (TE) ↔ ADT_A02 message;
3. Discharge Event (DE) ↔ ADT_A03 message;
4. Leave of Absence Event (LoAE) ↔ ADT_A21 message;
5. Return from Leave of Absence Event (RLoAE) ↔ ADT_A22 message;
6. Warning Event (WE) ↔ ADT_A20 message.

In this way, the process of exchanging messages between PMS (Patient Management System) and PaLMS, INTCare and Alert modules (that are incorporate in the AIDA platform) can be easily implemented using HL7 instead of the usual ACL (Agent Communication Language) message.

4.2   MAS in PaLMS

As figure 1 shows, five agents were created for the MAS with the aim to identify and monitoring the patient and to guarantee the interoperability amongst others hospital information systems.

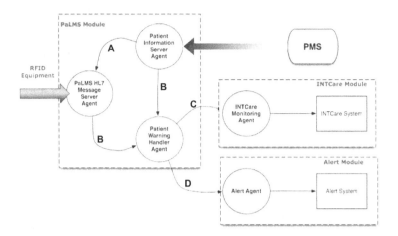

Fig. 1. A - exchanging information about patient's admission, discharges, transfers, leave and return of absences. B - exchanging information about start or stop of the readings or turn on or off de alert system C - receive instructions to start or stop the readings of the patient's vital signs. D - receive instructions to turn on or off the alarm system.

4.3   Implementation

In order to implement the PaLMS system it was necessary to realize a study and to experiment several alternatives to decide how many and where to place the RFID antennas in the ICU facilities of the CHP. The main goals of this study were to test the reliability of the readings and to verify if it exists interference with medical devices. After analyse all the dimensions of an ICU room, it was made four different tests. Two of them using one or two antennas near the wall, 0.95 meters high from the bed (the top of the bed is against the wall). The other two tests using one or two antennas suspended above the bed in the central axis, near the area where the patient's arm is resting (once the bracelet with the RFID tag was placed in the patient's wrist).

The tests using one or two antennas near the wall failed the readings in some situations, especially when the patient was in an abnormal position. On the other hand, the tests using one or two antennas suspended above the bed had success in the readings. No interferences were detected in any test neither a wrong reading from another bed. For the purpose of saving resources, the test with one antenna suspended above the bed was chosen to be implemented.

5   Usability

The International Standards Organization (ISO) refers that usability is the extend to which a system can be used by specific users to achieve specified goals with effectiveness, efficiency and satisfaction in a specified context of use. Although none product, system or service is itself usable or unusable, it has attributes which will determine the usability for a particularly user, task and environment [11, 12]. This aspect led the focus of the evaluation in product development from product assurance testing to integrated product design and development. With this, the term usability arises and gains a lot of importance as more and more people depend of technical devices to carry out their tasks at work or home [12].

Today, hundreds of ICT systems are used in healthcare organizations to serve physicians and other professionals in their daily work with patients. The healthcare community and the medical technology industry are aware that medical equipment needs to have higher usability. Know the usability of healthcare systems is crucial to achieve success, as well as guaranteeing a high level of safe and effective level of patient care. It can decrease the number of errors, leading to improved patient safety, in addition to better efficiency, enabling clinicians to spend more time with their patients [12].

6 Methods - Usability

To appraise the usability of the systems along with AIDA and the monitoring system (INTCare), two different types of usability evaluations were performed.

The first one was a usability inquire method, more precisely a survey. The preference for a survey was grounded, as it is a very well known method to obtain a straight response from participants. With this, it was feasible to the usability evaluators to acquire information about users likes, dislikes, needs and understanding of the system by letting them answer questions in a written form. So, the main propose of this evaluation was to cognize what physicians as well as nurses think of the system. The survey was formed by twelve questions, where eleven of them were of multiple choices. The head one was to identify the working group of who was answering the survey: a physician or a nurse. At the total, 300 surveys were distributed at different services of the hospital for physicians and nurses respond [12].

The second usability evaluation performed was a heuristic walkthrough, an usability inspection method. The first step taken to perform this evaluation was to assembled the evaluation team. This team should be formed by a group of three to five evaluators with knowledge both in usability and in the field in which the system will be used, in this case in healthcare work area. However, finding evaluators who have both usability and clinical expertise prove to be an extremely hard mission. The solution was to bring together two groups of evaluators: usability and clinical experts. This way was made to ensure that the evaluation team had usability and clinical knowledge, crucial to the success of the evaluation. The evaluators have a set of questions to guide their exploration of the interface as well as a set of common user tasks [12]. After completing the first pass, task-focused, evaluators proceed to second step of the evaluation, completing a free form evaluation. During this phase, the evaluators use usability heuristics to assess problems associated with the interface. In other words, they compare the system against an establish set of usability heuristics defined by Jakob Nielsen [13].

7   Results - Usability

As two distinctive methodologies were made, it is essential to analyse the acquired outcomes independently. Regarding the usability surveys were obtained a total of 167 responses: 63 by physicians and 104 by nurses. It was possible to note that all the physicians think they lost too much time in entry data. The great majority also thinks that the time spent to consult information about the patient is excessive. Another finding that it was possible to see concerns about the design of the system. The physicians classified the design of the system with 30 percent of satisfaction. In the other hand the nurses do not think like physicians, they reported that do not lose so much time with data. Moreover, the nurses classified the design of the system with 70 percent of satisfaction.

The heuristic walkthrough evaluation, performed by the evaluators, allowed the identification of some usability issues. The main issue identified concerns about the visibility of the system. When users perform an action that requires some processing, there is not a clear feedback on what is happening. In these situations, a notification should appear. This notification could be a single hourglass where the user is informed that has to wait, but the ideal was that a message appears informing the progress of the action, the time remaining to perform the action and information about what kind of processing was happening. No more issues were found related to the visibility of system status.

8   Conclusion

In this paper we presented a complex system involving the CHP's interoperability platform (AIDA), the INTCare and the PaLMS using the HL7 standard for the information exchange. We conclude that a system for the detection of the patient's presence in a bed is possible with RFID as well as its integration in the AIDA. We consider PaLMS a functional project for the goals proposed, optimizing the medical assistance and the quality of the information acquired, more specifically, the patient's vital signs in the INTCare system. The using of HL7 in message exchange has so far brought no disadvantages nor problems in the process, and provides interoperability for all systems.

Also in this paper it was presented an usability evaluation to the system (AIDA and the monitoring systems PaLMS and INTCare). Two different methods were chosen: inquiry method (survey) followed by an inspection method (heuristic walkthrough). They proved to be very cheap methods and easy to perform, which provided immediate results about the usability of the system. Those evaluations made possible to the hospital recognize the level of satisfaction of the healthcare providers, as well as what they think of the system. In order to improve the satisfaction of the healthcare professionals, in particular physicians, it is proposed to improve the interface especially the creation of a single view, wherein it is possible analyse all data about a patient in the same window.

It is important in the future to scheduled other evaluations, such as usability testing, as well as to scheduled some workshops and trainings. The aim is to improve the usability of the system, providing better working conditions to the users, as well as improving their satisfaction.

Acknowledgement. This work is financed with the support of the Portuguese Foundation for Science and Technology (FCT), with the grant SFRH/BD/70549/2010 and within project PEst-OE/EEI/UI0752/2011.

References

1. Remagnino, P., Foresti, G.L.: Ambient intelligence: A new multidisciplinary paradigm. IEEE Transactions on Systems, Man and Cybernetics, Part A: Systems and Humans 35(1), 1–6 (2005)
2. Portela, F., Gago, P., Santos, M.F., Silva, Á.M., Rua, F., Machado, J., Abelha, A., Neves, J.: Knowledge discovery for pervasive and real-time intelligent decision support in intensive care medicine. In: KMIS, pp. 241–249 (2011)
3. Portela, F., Santos, M.F., Vilas-Boas, M.: A pervasive approach to a real-time intelligent decision support system in intensive medicine. In: Fred, A., Dietz, J.L.G., Liu, K., Filipe, J. (eds.) IC3K 2010. CCIS, vol. 272, pp. 368–381. Springer, Heidelberg (2013)
4. Rodrigues, R., Gonçalves, P., Miranda, M., Portela, F., Santos, M., Neves, J., Abelha, A., Machado, J.: Monitoring intelligent system for the intensive care unit using rfid and multi-agent systems. In: IEEE International Conference on Industrial Engineering and Engineering Management, IEEM 2012 (2012)
5. Peixoto, H., Santos, M., Abelha, A., Machado, J.: Intelligence in interoperability with aida. In: Chen, L., Felfernig, A., Liu, J., Raś, Z.W. (eds.) ISMIS 2012. LNCS, vol. 7661, pp. 264–273. Springer, Heidelberg (2012)
6. Miranda, M., Duarte, J., Abelha, A., Machado, J., Neves, J., Neves, J.: Interoperability in healthcare. In: ESM 2010 (2010)
7. Hooda, J.S., Dogdu, E., Sunderraman, R.: Health level-7 compliant clinical patient records system. In: Proceedings of the 2004 ACM Symposium on Applied Computing, pp. 259–263. ACM (2004)
8. Isern, D., Sánchez, D., Moreno, A.: Agents applied in health care: A review. International Journal of Medical Informatics 79(3), 145–166 (2010)
9. Miranda, M., Salazar, M., Portela, F., Santos, M., Abelha, A., Neves, J., Machado, J.: Multi-agent systems for hl7 interoperability services. Procedia Technology 5, 725–733 (2012)
10. Dolin, R.H., Alschuler, L., Beebe, C., Biron, P.V., Boyer, S.L., Essin, D., Kimber, E., Lincoln, T., Mattison, J.E.: The hl7 clinical document architecture. Journal of the American Medical Informatics Association 8(6), 552–569 (2001)
11. Schoeffel, R.: The concept of product usability. ISO Bulletin 34(3), 6–7 (2003)
12. Pereira, R., Duarte, J., Salazar, M., Santos, M., Abelha, A., Machado, J.: Usability of an electronic health record. IEEM, 5 (2012)
13. Nielsen, J.: Heuristic evaluation. John Wiley & Sons, New York (1994)

Wide-Input Intelligent Environments
for Industrial Facilities

Gabriel Urzaiz[1], José Luis Escalante[1], David Villa[2], and Juan Carlos López[2]

[1] Universidad Anahuac Mayab, Merida, Yucatan, Mexico
{gabriel.urzaiz,jose.escalante}@anahuac.mx
[2] Universidad de Castilla-La Mancha, Ciudad Real, Spain
{david.villa,juancarlos.lopez}@uclm.es

Abstract. Several factors affect the productivity and efficiency of an industrial facility. We made a revision of some of these factors, and we noticed that not all of them happen close to the workplace. There are also some of them that take place outside the industrial facilities having an impact in productivity and efficiency, and therefore they should also be taken into consideration. In this paper we propose a Wide-Input Intelligent Environment (WIIE) concept which includes local and remote factors. We also propose a conceptual model based on a simple black box concept in order to correlate input factors and output variables, in which the input factors are classified according to three dimensions (environmental vs. person-related, constant vs. variable, local vs. remote) and where the output variables are the productivity and the efficiency. We finally propose an implementation model based on a heterogeneous intelligent sensor-actuator network, which enables for the possibility of using local and remote factors as an input having an impact on the intelligent environment, and for the implementation of advanced distributed functionality.

Keywords: ergonomics, human-factors, workplace, heterogeneous, sensors.

1   Introduction

There are a lot of factors that affect the productivity and efficiency of an industrial facility. In most cases, these factors are neither monitored nor controlled, and they are just kept within subjectively adequate levels.

These factors typically refer either to aspects of environmental (temperature, humidity, lighting, noise level, etc.) or to issues involving the person (blood pressure, heart rate, body temperature, fatigue, etc.). In very few cases some of these factors are monitored and controlled, but always considering only the elements close to the workplace, ignoring those factors occurring outside.

Our proposal is based on the hypothesis that environmental and person-related factors can be controlled to improve the conditions of the person himself and the process, and the greater the number of relevant factors to be considered and the higher the rank of these factors, the better the knowledge of the problem and consequently

G. Urzaiz et al. (Eds.): UCAmI 2013, LNCS 8276, pp. 62–69, 2013.
© Springer International Publishing Switzerland 2013

the greater the possibility of improving the conditions of the person and the productivity and efficiency of the process.

The aim of this paper is to design a model to monitor and control the factors involved in phenomena or processes, including not only those who are close to the workplace, but also relevant information from other nodes, including remote, possibly in a heterogeneous network.

2   Revision

Several factors affect the productivity and efficiency of an industrial facility. Some of these factors take place close to the workplace, some others happen outside the industrial facility, and not all of them are evident.

The presence of musculoskeletal disorders [1] is an example of a local factor that should be taken into consideration. There are cases such as an Ontario car parts manufacturer which opened its doors to researchers who helped implement a participatory ergonomics program to improve the musculoskeletal health of workers. Depressive symptoms [2] are pervasive among workers disabled by musculoskeletal disorders. For those whose symptoms persist, sustainable work-returns are less likely, and treatment by a mental health professional may be needed to improve recovery. Previous studies in the agricultural sector showed that the high level of manual handling risk with the task that required carrying heavy loads with awkward postures [3] which are the probable causative factors of musculoskeletal disorders among the rice farmers. A study revealed [4] that musculoskeletal disorders have become a severe problem in small and medium scale enterprises. Awkward posture in the workplaces should be avoided and these industries should be encouraged to follow ergonomic practices and installation of proper machines which will undoubtedly decrease the risk of musculoskeletal problems and therefore workload can be decreased and efficiency can be increased.

Another example of a local factor is the existence of new workers [5] or young people with dyslexia [5], who may be at greater risk of work injury due to their learning inexperience or disability. This early finding underscores the importance of accommodating different learning styles in health and safety training. The higher risk of work injury among new workers has persisted over the past ten years. Workplaces need to do more to ensure new workers get the training and supervision they need to stay safe on the job.

Workplace characteristics are another important factor. Ergonomics plays a key role by ensuring that the dimensions, clearances, space, layout, efforts, visibility and other factors, incorporated in the equipment design, are matched to human capabilities and limitations [7]. Operations and safety were developed separately into mature areas of management practice, but they are not mutually exclusive. The firms that integrate safety [8] and operations are building a successful business model for both realms.

The occupational overuse [9] problems also known as Repetitive Strain Injuries ("RSI") begins in the early of the 1980's and ends with the present-day problems of pain, fear and stress.

The value of people must not be underestimated, and workers should be considered the key to the profit. Work environment should be good for all workers. There is a premise that says "good ergonomics is good economics" [10].

In many countries of the world, retirement is mandatory at the age at which persons who hold certain jobs or offices are required by employment law to leave their employment, or retire (60 to 65 years), this is justified by the argument that certain occupations are either too dangerous or require high levels of physical skills and mental work. Every worker has to leave the workforce at that age. However, starting from the last two decades of the last century, it is observed that retirees live more years in retirement than ever before, all type of employment should be ergonomically designed to fit the aged worker characteristics, such as physical, mental and affective characteristics [11].

Work insecurity and unemployment [12] can have a negative effect on the physical and mental health of workers. Workers who have kept their jobs during the recession may have had to face more unpaid overtime, wage freezes or cutbacks, roll-backs of benefits and general job insecurity.

A look at the skull-and-crossbones on a container and most people know they are in the presence of poison. This speaks to the power of visual symbols [13] to effectively and quickly convey hazard information to workers. It is advisable to broaden the use of such visual symbols called pictograms within the health and safety context.

Most of the factors mentioned so far take place close to the workplace, but there are also some other factors that happen outside the industrial facility, such as the economic and social changes, economic crisis, globalization [14], the technological development [15], changes in the ecosystem (political demands based on ethical and humane values) [16], among others.

It is necessary to use a model which can include both, the local and the remote factors, because both of them have an impact on the output variables (i.e. productivity and efficiency) of the industrial facility.

3   The Concept of Wide-Input Intelligent Environment (WIIE)

An Intelligent Environment (IE) is a space in which information technology is seamlessly used to enhance ordinary activity. The idea is to make computers invisible to the user [17]. An IE is a physical environment in which information and communication technologies and sensor systems disappear as they become embedded into physical objects, infrastructures, and the surroundings in which we live, travel, and work.

Types of IE range from private to public and from fixed to mobile; some are ephemeral while others are permanent; some change type during their life span [18].

We define a new WIIE concept, understood as an IE in which not only local variables are considered, but other elements from remote nodes, probably connected through a heterogeneous wide area network, are also taken into consideration.

The idea of adding the possibility of having remote elements to be used as part of the input (Fig. 1) enables for the possibility of determining the corresponding action that is to be applied at the environment.

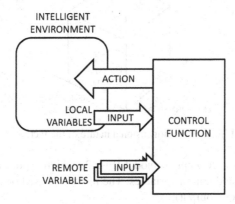

Fig. 1. Local and remote variables as part of the input

Consider as an example the environmental temperature control system. It is clear that the environmental temperature has a direct impact on the productivity and the efficiency of the industrial facility. If the environmental temperature is too high, the air conditioning equipment is activated and therefore productivity is enhanced because the workers are confortable, but efficiency is reduced because it raises the energy consumption.

The common way of controlling the environmental temperature of a workplace is by turning on or turning off the air conditioning equipment at the specific workplace, which takes its thermostat as the control signal.

In our solution it is possible to include as inputs not only the environmental temperature at the workplace, but also temperature of other work areas close to the workplace, the average temperature at the whole industrial facility, and even the environmental temperature at the outside or any other atmospheric variable that is considered relevant, such as the moisture, thermal sensation, etc. It is also possible to consider the total energy consumption of the industrial facility, the instantaneous cost per kilowatt-hour depending on the time and the accumulated consumption, or almost any other variable that may be considered relevant.

4   Conceptual Model

We first classified the input factors according to three dimensions (Fig 2). It can be noticed that some of them are related to the person, i.e, they are within the worker, physically, emotionally or psychologically, and others are specific to the environment, i.e. they are outside the worker and do not belong to him or her. Some are constant or could be considered as such due to its slow rate of change, and others are variable. And finally, some factors are local because they happen within the industrial facility and others are remote because they happen outside the industrial facility.

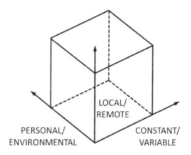

Fig. 2. Three-dimensional nature of the factors

We then developed a conceptual model (Fig. 3) which represents the relationship between input factors and output variables. The model is based on a simple concept of black box (input, process, output).

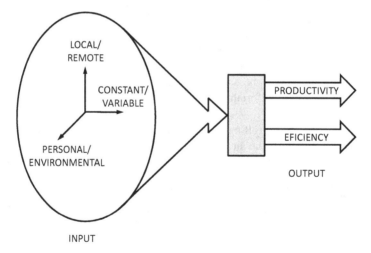

Fig. 3. Conceptual model

We considered two output variables, which are the productivity, which is defined as the ratio between output and resources, and the efficiency, which is defined as the ratio between output and capacity.

5   Implementation Model

The local/remote dimension has impact on the implementation of the platform. The implementation model is based on a heterogeneous intelligent sensor-actuator-network (SAN) which considers local and remote inputs. Due to this fact it is possible to relocate the control function far from the environment, or even to implement a distributed control function (Fig. 4), by implementing functionality not only in the terminal nodes, but also in network nodes.

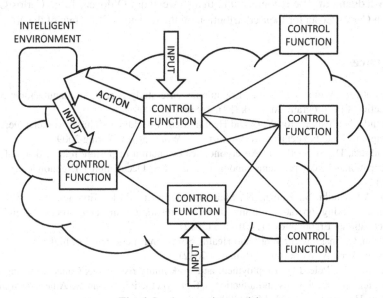

Fig. 4. Implementation model

The model enables for the possibility to provide advanced distributed functionalities based on Process-in-Network (PIN) [19], such as pre-processing, data simplification or data enrichment.

6   Conclusions and Work in Progress

We have proposed a new concept of Wide-Input Intelligent Environment (WIIE) which involves not only local variables but also remote elements that may be relevant as inputs to the phenomenon being analyzed. The idea of including remote elements also allows the possibility of implementing distributed functionality, which brings significant benefits to the model.

We have identified the main factors that have an impact in the productivity and the efficiency of an industrial facility, and they have been classified according to three dimensions: environmental/person-related, variable/constant, and local/remote. We have developed a simple conceptual model in order to correlate these input factors to productivity and efficiency, which are the two considered output variables.

We also proposed an implementation model based on an intelligent heterogeneous sensor-actuator network, which enables for the possibility of advanced distributed functionality.

Work in progress is focused on the experimental tests to identify the most relevant input factors to be implemented, and the experimental construction of the platform (consisting of both software and physical elements such as sensors, actuators and communication). Future work includes the implementation in a real environment.

Acknowledgement. We recognize and thank Alejandra Ordoñez, Jorge Carlos Chapur and Juan Carlos Costa for their contribution on the revision of the state of the art.

References

1. Institute for Work and Health. Ergonomics case study: Car parts manufacturer realizes benefits of PE program. At Work (57), 4 (Summer 2009)
2. Carnide, N.: Institute for Work and Health. Mental health and injured workers: Depressive symptoms linked to delayed work-returns. At Work (56), 5 (Spring 2009)
3. Banibrata, D., Somnath, G.: An ergonomics evaluation of posture related discomfort and occupational health problems among rice farmers. Occupational Ergonomics 10, 25–38 (2011)
4. Rai, A., Gandhi, S., Kumar, N., Sharma, D.K., Garg, M.K.: Ergonomic intervention in Aonla pricking operation during preserve preparation in food processing industries. Occupational Ergonomics 41, 401–405 (2012)
5. Breslin, C.: Institute for Work and Health. Study finds persistence of higher injury risk for new workers. At Work (69), 3 (Summer 2012)
6. Breslin, F.C., Pole, J.D.: Employment and work injury risk among Canadian young people with learning disabilities and attention deficit/hyperactivity disorder. American Journal of Public Health 99(8), 1423–1430 (2009)
7. O'Sullivan, J.: Ergonomics in the Design Process. Ergonomics Australia 21(2), 13–20 (2007) ISSN 1033-875
8. Pagell, M.: Institute for Work and Health. Research finds safety and operations can enhance each other. At Work (71), 3 (Winter 2013)
9. Brown, D.: Ergonomics in a subjective world. Ergonomics Australia 16(3), 20–32 (2012) ISSN 1033-875
10. Blewett, V.: Book review of Increasing productivity and profit through health & safety: The financial returns from a safe working environment. Ergonomics 18(4), 26 (2004) ISSN 1033-1875
11. Mokdad, M.: Ergonomics of bridge employment. Occupational Ergonomics 41, 307–312 (2012)
12. Institute for Work and Health. Economic crisis taking toll on worker health, IWH research suggests. At Work (58), 1 (Fall 2009)
13. Institute for Work and Health. Picture This: Using visual symbols to identify MSD hazards. At Work (60), 5 (Spring 2010)
14. Warner, M.: Management in China: Systems reform, human resources and emergent globalization. Human Systems Management 30(1), 1–9 (2011), doi:10.3233/HSM-2011-0734

15. Nankervis, A., Chatterjee, S.: The resurgence of China and India: collaboration or competition? Human Systems Management 30(1-2), 97–113 (2011)
16. Prieto, S., García, E.: Beneficios de aplicar políticas de responsabilidad social empresarial. Salud de los Trabajadores 20(1) (June 2012)
17. Steventon, A., Wright, S. (eds.): Intelligent Spaces: The Application of Pervasive ICT. Springer (2006)
18. Intelligent Environments Conference (2007), http://www.uni-ulm.de/ie07/ (accessed on May 13, 2013)
19. Urzaiz, G., Villa, D., Villanueva, F., Lopez, J.C.: Process-in-Network: a comprehensive network processing approach. Sensors (6), 8112–8134 (2012), doi:10.3390/s120608112

Citizen-Centric Linked Data Apps for Smart Cities

Diego López-de-Ipiña[1], Sacha Vanhecke[2], Oscar Peña[1], Tom De Nies[2], and Erik Mannens[2]

[1] Deusto Institute of Technology, DeustoTech, University of Deusto, 48007 Bilbao, Spain
[2] Ghent University – iMinds – Multimedia Lab, Gent, Belgium
{dipina,oscar.pena}@deusto.es,
{sacha.vanhecke,tom.denies,erik.mannens}@ugent.be

Abstract. Open Government Data combined with dynamic data collected from either citywide sensor networks or apps running in citizens' smartphones offer ample potential for innovative urban services (apps) that realize Smarter Cities. This paper describes IES CITIES, a platform designed to facilitate the development of urban apps that exploit public data offered by councils and enriched by citizens. This solution addresses the needs of three main stakeholders in a city: a) citizens consuming useful data services in different domains but also contributing with complementary data to the city, b) companies leveraging the simple JSON-based RESTful API provided by IES CITIES to create novel urban apps, and c) the City Council, using the platform to publicize its urban datasets and track services assembled around them.

Keywords: Smart City, Linked Data, Apps, provenance, trust, JSON.

1   Introduction

The world is undergoing the largest wave of urban growth in history. Experts predict the global urban population will double by 2050 meaning 70% of the total world population will be living in a major town or city. Consequently, there is an increasing need to assemble Smart Cities that effectively and efficiently manage the resources required by their increasing populations. A city may be considered smart when it improves the citizens' quality of life and the efficiency and quality of the services provided by governing entities and businesses.

The IES Cities platform is defined to promote user-centric mobile micro-services that exploit open data and generate user-supplied data. It contributes with an open citizen-centric Linked Data apps-enabling technological solution. Importantly, it focuses on enabling citizens to create, improve, extend and enrich the open data associated to a city in which micro-services, i.e. urban apps, are based. The main stakeholders of the resulting urban apps ecosystem are the citizens, SMEs and public administration within a city.

This platform takes advantage of the progress achieved lately in two key technological areas: a) *open government and urban sensor generated datasets*, b) *smartphones equipped with different sensors*, e.g. GPS, which can execute urban apps, i.e. offering services for citizens in different domains (e.g. transport, security and so on).

G. Urzaiz et al. (Eds.): UCAmI 2013, LNCS 8276, pp. 70–77, 2013.

Following the "Apps for Smart Cities Manifesto"[1] approach, IES CITIES aims to enable an ecosystem of urban apps that help citizens in their daily activities and actions within the city. In order to accomplish this, it addresses three main challenges: a) *extract and adapt heterogeneous structured and non-structured data* from council repositories, sensor networks, web sites and social networks, b) *validate, promote and integrate user-provided data* with open government data and c) *facilitate the development of urban apps by end developers*, thus fostering urban-related innovation.

2 Related Work

Citizen execution of urban mobile apps may generate new data that enriches the datasets associated to a given city. However, the quality of the data generated has to be assessed and qualified, thus promoting valuable and trustable information and decrementing and eventually discarding lower quality data. The W3C has created the PROV Data Model [1] for provenance interchange on the web. PROV is a specification to express provenance records, which contain descriptions of the entities and activities involved in producing and delivering or otherwise influencing a given object. Provenance can be used for many purposes, such as understanding how data was collected so it can be meaningfully used, determining ownership and rights over an object, making judgements about information to determine whether to trust it, verifying that the process and steps used to obtain a result complies with given requirements, and reproducing how something was generated [2].

Human Computation [3] enables to leverage human intelligence to carry out tasks that otherwise would be difficult to accomplish by a machine. Different techniques are used to incentivise user participation, e.g., gaming with a purpose (GWAP) [4] to encourage people to help in human-computation through entertaining incentives. Mobile games with a purpose have already been used to annotate and enrich urban data, e.g. UrbanMatch [5] validates links between points of interest and their photos whilst Urbanopoly [6] adds and validates Venue-Feature-Value (VFV) facts. This work fosters the generation of provenance-based trusted citizen contributed Linked Data. Users' contributions are mediated by the IES CITIES-enabled apps that leverage the back-end provenance support of our platform, comprising a generic infrastructure for developers to easily create urban apps that consume and provide confidence ranked Linked Data about a given city.

Lately, some JSON query[2] languages and schemas[3] have emerged that intend to enable end-users to more easily specify and exploit the JSON data model. In our view, urban apps will be assembled from structured and non-structured data in the form of RDF, CSV or even applying web scrapping to HTML pages. Information in such models can be mapped into JSON, a *lingua franca* for web and mobile developers that do not necessarily have to be exposed to the complexities of semantically

---

modelled data. This work employs the TheDataTank (TDT)[4], a distributed open-source web framework that serves as a dataset adaptor to transform online data of different formats into a user-friendly Restful API.

3   The IES CITIES Platform

The preliminary IES CITIES solution is composed of the following elements: a) a *mobile application*, namely the *IES CITIES player*, that allows users to search for and browse over available urban apps, based on their location and filters, and then execute these services and b) a *server* that acts as a mediator among urban apps front-ends played in citizens' smartphones and their business logic implementing back-ends accessing, exploiting and enriching publicly available datasets. Notably, IES CITIES allows users to contribute with and validate others' contributed data, through a mechanism for tracking information provenance and its associated trust and confidence.

The *modus operandi* of the platform is as follows. Firstly, the municipality registers with the IES Cities server its datasets descriptions, by means of a web form. It indicates where the dataset can be located and accessed (URI), what is the original format of the data (CSV, RDF, XML and so on), a description of the dataset expressed in JSON-Schema and, optionally, a mapping script between the original data source format and JSON, and *vice versa*. Secondly, a developer finds which datasets are available by browsing or searching in the IES Cities' dataset repository, and decides which ones best fit his application. Through a RESTful JSON-based API, she issues queries over the datasets abstracted as JSON data structures and retrieves results also expressed in JSON. Thirdly, once the application development has been completed, the developer registers it with the platform through a web form, providing among other details where the application is (URI), its type (Google Play, Local app repository, Web) and a description of its functionality, including snapshots. Finally, end-users, i.e. citizens, with the help of the IES CITIES player app, browse or search for available registered urban apps according to their location and interests.

3.1   Linked Data Design

Involving end-users in the creation of Linked Open Data implies that these data should be published according to some RDF specifications, adding some particular characteristics to the data that associate it to the IES Cities platform, and enforcing its reusability inside or outside the context of the IES Cities platform. Several widely used vocabularies were considered, such as Dublin Core (DC), which defines general metadata attributes such as title, creator, date and subject, and FOAF, that defines terms for describing persons, their activities and their relations to other people and objects. Reusing terms maximizes the probability that data can be consumed by applications that may be tuned to such well-known vocabularies, without requiring further pre-processing of the data or modification of the application [7].

---

[4] http://thedatatank.com/

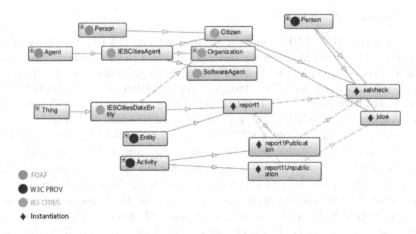

Fig. 1. IES Cities RDF schema

The IES Cities ontology[5] (see Fig. 1) defines two general classes. Firstly, the base for any data generated through the platform is the class `IESCitiesDataEntity`, which should at least include a DC term identifier property to easily query the data and if possible a description. Secondly, in order to incorporate the users of the platform in the model, a general `IESCitiesAgent` class is defined, that extends FOAF's Agent, and several subclasses such as `Citizen`, inheriting from FOAF's Person class, `Organization` and `SoftwareAgent`.

Enabling user contribution to open datasets requires incorporating metadata that enables tracking down the creator of a particular data entity, known as provenance data. A complete provenance ontology that fits the needs of the IES Cities project by separating the data from actual creation, modification and invalidation tasks is the PROV Ontology [8]. Starting Point classes, such as Entity, Activity and Agent, provide the basis for the rest of the PROV Ontology. Expanded terms provide additional terms that can be used to relate classes. These two categories are used in the IES Cities vocabulary to associate users as the publishers or invalidators of particular data.

Related to provenance are the credibility of data and the trustworthiness of their authors. IES Cities currently incorporates a simple mechanism to measure data credibility. Credibility is modelled in a 0 to 1 scale. A credibility score of 1 is assigned to each `IESCitiesDataEntity` at initialization, i.e. the system initially gives 100% credibility to the contents created. The resulting credibility level (CL) is recalculated every time a user votes up or down the published data, by following the simple formula: `CL = numPositiveVotes/numTotalVotes`. A more sophisticated credibility score calculation should take into account the user's reputation, based on earlier contributions. Additionally, contents could be rated according to a scale (e.g. 1 to 5) rather than applying the simple binary (correct vs. incorrect) approach now used.

---

[5] http://studwww.ugent.be/~satvheck/IES/schemas/iescities.owl

3.2   Implementation Details

Fig. 2 shows the IES CITIES platform architecture. The IES CITIES player mobile application is provided to access the services registered in the platform. Information about the services and users is persisted in a PostgreSQL database whilst open datasets are registered and accessible through two publication engines, namely CKAN[6] for structured RDF datasets and TheDataTank[7] for unstructured data. A Virtuoso RDF store is used to maintain linked datasets and store user-provided RDF data.

Open data is fetched through a JSON-formatted query sent to the server's RESTful "/data/" interface, together with the name of the requested datasets. This query consists of key/value pairs to specify required fields and optionally some parameters. The server-side's DataManager component resolves the location of the requested dataset from the publication engines and transforms the JSON query into the query language specific to the nature of the data's resolved endpoint. Currently, a query mapper for both SPARQL, the query language for RDF, and SPECTQL, the query language used by TheDataTank, is available. After executing the query, the resulting data is returned, in JSON format. The structure of the JSON submitted queries is:

```
{
"type":"data",
"requested":{ "predicate1":"object1", "predi-
cate2":"object2" },
"optional" :{ "predicate3":"object3" },
"given"     :{ "predicate2":{ "type":"string",
                 "value":"object2_value" }}
}
```

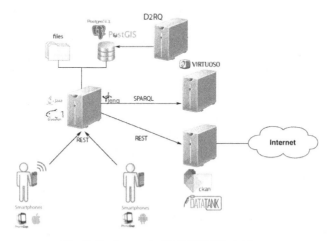

Fig. 2. Deployment of IES CITIES platform

---

[6] http://ckan.org
[7] http://thedatatank.com

A similar mechanism is also used for the generation and validation of data, using the SPARQL/Update extension and adding provenance meta-data compliant to the PROV-O vocabulary. This makes it, however, only available for linked datasets.

The IES Cities Player was developed using PhoneGap[8]. Fig. 3 shows a listing of services available on the user's location and ordered by average rating shown by the player app. Apart from location based look-up, users can also browse services using a set of keywords. When the user selects a service, a description is displayed, along with a list of reviews by other users and the average rating (Fig. 3). By clicking the Start button, the player launches the actual urban app.

4   Validation

The 311 Bilbao (Fig. 4) app has been implemented and deployed to validate the IES Cities platform. It uses Linked Open Data to get an overview of reports of faults in public infrastructure. It demonstrates how a developer can create a complex mobile app relying on semantic data, without technical knowledge of the SPARQL query language or underlying OWL ontologies. A query using the JSON query format proposed has to be assembled and issued to the "/data/" RESTful interface.

During initialization, the service queries for reported faults, and displays the result on a map (Fig. 4a). Using the filter functionality on the second tab (Fig. 4b), a user can choose to see reports of only a certain type. By clicking on the marker of a particular report, the ID and the underlying nature of the reported fault (Fig. 4a) is displayed. When the user decides to inspect the report an information page (Fig. 4c) is shown. On this page, users can see the full description and a photo of the report. Notably, they are also able to vote the credibility of the report up or down. Finally, they can create their own reports (Fig. 4d), specifying the faults nature, its location, a description and optionally add an image.

Fig. 3. Searching and browsing servicers

---

[8] http://phonegap.com/

From the data owner's point of view, enrichment of their datasets by third parties, such as users of the 311 Bilbao app, revealed two problems. The first one is the fact that data does not need to be approved before being published. Despite the fact that users are offered functionality to first review earlier submitted reports in the location where they are placed, some people may still add redundant reports. A future version of this application should enable users to further enhance and comment an already available report. In addition, proximity and content similar reports should be automatically grouped. Additionally, there is a need for a way to consider the reputation of the different authors, e.g. citizens and council staff. The owner of the dataset could use this to prioritize the processing of data from particular sources.

Fig. 4. 311 Bilbao IES CITIES service

5   Conclusion and Further Work

The IES CITIES platform can be used by developers to facilitate the use of open data from arbitrary formats, relying on CKAN and the adaptor functionality of TheData-Tank; all of it through a simple JSON query language. Moreover, the exemplary mobile app developed demonstrates how citizens' involvement in the management of a city can be increased by allowing them to actively participate in the creation of new data and the validation of open data provided by other users. These services also show the IES Cities platform's added value for public bodies, who can easily publish their open data in different non-proprietary formats, while making them accessible as common machine-readable format (JSON) through uniform REST interfaces.

Further work should address the following issues. More complex, derived provenance information should be incorporated, allowing tracing back the full revision chain of data modifications. Recent research has shown that the reconstruction of provenance, when it is (partially) missing, is feasible [9] and can be incorporated to complement our tracking approach. The current mechanism for defining credibility should also be extended. Instead of only setting a default score at creation time of the data, some level of 'trust' should be calculated as well, in an algorithmic manner, based on the data's actual source and its changes [10], making it possible to prioritize the processing of data of more trusted parties, such as official public bodies, over data provided by citizens. The reputation of certain sources is to be calculated over time, and used to set an initial value for a source's credibility. However, in addition to reputation, provenance is an essential component towards trust assessment as well [11]. Applying automatic reasoning over the provenance of the data, seems a feasible method to implement these principles, as it only requires the addition of lightweight annotations to the provenance that is currently tracked [12]. These annotations allow for an on-the-fly selection of data, based on the preference and trustworthiness of its source trace.

References

1. W3C.: PROV Model Primer. Working Group. Note (2013),
   http://www.w3.org/TR/2013/NOTE-prov-primer-20130430/
2. Groth, P., Gil, Y.: Editorial - Using Provenance in the Semantic Web. Web Semantics: Science, Services and Agents on the World Wide Web 9(2) (2011)
3. Bozzon, B., Galli, L., Fraternali, P., Karam, R.: Modeling CrowdSourcing scenarios in Socially-Enabled Human Computation Applications. To Appear in Journal on Dada Semantics (2013)
4. von-Ahn, L.: Games with a Purpose. IEEE Computer 39(6), 92–94 (2006)
5. Celino, I., Contessa, S., Corubolo, M., Dell'Aglio, D., Della Valle, E., Fumeo, S., Krüger, T.: Linking Smart Cities Datasets with Human Computation – the case of UrbanMatch. In: Cudré-Mauroux, P., et al. (eds.) ISWC 2012, Part II. LNCS, vol. 7650, pp. 34–49. Springer, Heidelberg (2012)
6. Celino, I., Cerizza, D., Contessa, S., Corubolo, M., Dell'Aglio, D., Della Valle, E., Fumeo, S.: Urbanopoly – a Social and Location-based Game with a Purpose to Crowdsource your Urban Data. In: Proceedings of the the 4th IEEE International Conference on Social Computing, Workshop on Social Media for Human Computation, pp. 910–913 (2012), doi:10.1109/SocialCom-PASSAT.2012.138
7. Heath, T., Bizer, C.: Linked Data: Evolving the Web into a Global Data Space, 1st edn. Synthesis Lectures on the Semantic Web. Morgan & Claypool Publishers (2011)
8. Lebo, T., Sahoo, S., McGuinness, D. (eds.): Prov-o: The prov ontology (2013),
   http://www.w3.org/TR/2013/REC-prov-o-20130430/
   (last accessed May 10, 2013)
9. Magliacane, S.: Reconstructing provenance. In: Cudré-Mauroux, et al, et al (eds.) ISWC 2012, Part II. LNCS, vol. 7650, pp. 399–406. Springer, Heidelberg (2012)
10. Halpin, H.: Provenance: The missing component of the semantic web for privacy and trust. In: Trust and Privacy on the Social and Semantic Web (SPOT 2009), Workshop of ESWC (2009)
11. Ceolin, D., Groth, P.T., van Hage, W.R., Nottamkandath, A., Fokkink, W.: Trust Evaluation through User Reputation and Provenance Analysis. In: URSW, pp. 15–26 (2012)
12. De Nies, T., Coppens, S., Mannens, E., Van de Walle, R.: Modeling uncertain provenance and provenance of uncertainty in W3C PROV. In: Proceedings of the 22nd International Conference on World Wide Web Companion, pp. 167–168 (2013)

Pervasive User Interface Elements as Synthetic Networked Files

Francisco J. Ballesteros, Gorka Guardiola, and Enrique Soriano-Salvador

Laboratorio de Sistemas – Universidad Rey Juan Carlos, Madrid, Spain
{nemo,paurea,esoriano}@lsub.org
http://lsub.org

Abstract. Current computing environments include multiple I/O devices in a highly heterogeneous, distributed, dynamic, multi-user environment. Most UIMS and toolkits fail to address such environments. The O/live UIMS that we built, and have been using for several years, decouples applications from their interfaces by using distributed synthetic file system interfaces to export user interface elements. O/live supports transparent distribution, replication, and migration of user interface elements among highly heterogeneous devices. It is highly programmable without any application support. This paper briefly describes the ideas underlying O/live.

1 Introduction

Standard UIMSs (User Interface Management System) do not address modern computing environments, such as smart spaces and ubiquitous computing scenarios. In order to do so, a UIMS must integrate distributed I/O devices to support User Interfaces (UIs in what follows) on behalf of users and applications. In addition, it must be able to combine highly heterogeneous devices to implement UIs. Moreover, it must allow both the user and applications to combine and re-arrange elements from distributed UIs, at will. It must also provide a programmatic interface for distributed, heterogeneous UIs and preserve user sessions across machine reboots, connection hang ups, and location changes.

As far as we know, no existing UIMS currently satisfies all of these requirements. We built O/live, a UIMS and a window system, for Octopus [1]. It is the evolution of an earlier prototype [2] aimed at providing support for UIs for ubiquitous computing applications.

In O/live, UI elements (UIEs in what follows, also known as widgets) are represented as an abstract set of synthetic (virtual) networked files, describing their state. There are three actors in our scheme: the synthetic file server (the UIMS), the clients (viewers), and the applications. Applications operate on the synthetic files (i.e. the UIEs) to update their interfaces. A file server provides these "files" and dynamically processes operations over them. The file server coordinates their replication and the concurrent access for both applications and viewers, and provides notifying services. UI subtrees may be freely replicated and re-arranged without disturbing the application. All I/O and editing activity is

G. Urzaiz et al. (Eds.): UCAmI 2013, LNCS 8276, pp. 78–85, 2013.

confined to viewers. Viewers choose UI trees or subtrees to display by remotely accessing file subtrees. Therefore, viewers are able to operate on remote UIEs.

The list of benefits deriving from the use of synthetic files is too large to be detailed and thoroughly discussed in this paper. For a more complete discussion of this topic, please refer to [3,2,1]. All programming languages provide support for using files. Therefore, they provide support for UI programming on O/live, because the interface is just a file system. Using distributed files as the interface for building UIs greatly helps portability. A good example of this is Jolive [4], an O/live viewer implemented for Java Swing and Android.

Viewers are free to represent data in any way that fits the particular devices they use. It is trivial for the application to support highly heterogeneous I/O devices: It has to do nothing on that respect. The application is only in charge of updating the state of its UIEs. Representation and most interaction tasks are transparent for the application.

It is easy to compose different elements within UI container. Files can be easily copied, moved, modified, and inspected. The flexibility of this technique permits us to implement a language easily to operate on distributed elements, similar to the Sam language [5], with the advantage of managing elements from different UIs that may be in different machines. Because UIs and UIEs seem to be files, any shell scripting environment and file-manipulation tool can be used to deal with them. Simple scripts and file utilities are now able to operate on UIs and UIEs.

As far as the user is concerned, the layout and state for all sessions in use seem to persist, because they are represented by the particular layout of a file tree kept on the UIMS, which may be left running separated from the clients (the viewers) and, perhaps, apart from the applications using it. Note that by separated we mean they may be distributed among different machines.

The work presented here is in production and we have been using it daily for some years now. You can refer to http://lsub.org/ls/octopus.html for source code, documentation, and some demonstrations.

2   UI Elements

In O/live, any UI consists of a tree of widgets known as panels. There are two kinds of panels: *groups* (called *rows* and *columns*, after two popular types of groups) and *atoms*. Rows and columns group inner panels and handle their layout. A row/column arranges for inner panels to be disposed in a row/column. All groups are similar and describe how to handle the layout, as a hint to represent the widgets on graphic devices. Atoms include text, tables, buttons, (text) tag-lines, images, gauges, sliders, panning-images, and vector graphics. The particular set of panels is just a detail of our implementation, but not a key point in our approach, which would still work as long as the panels implemented are kept abstract enough.

Each panel is represented by a directory. Panels can be created and deleted programmatically by making and removing such directories. They usually contain two files: `ctl` and `data` (attributes for widgets and their data). Many widgets include another file in their directories, named `edits` (a log of changes). Grouping panels (e.g., rows) contain a subdirectory for each widget they contain.

To avoid confusion, we must emphasize once more that none of these files are actual files on disk. The same happens with directories. They are synthesized on demand by a file server program, which just happens to be the UIMS. That is, they behave as files but are just an interface to the UIMS. Applications perform operations, mainly read and write operations, over the virtual files and directories to access and control the widgets. These virtual files can be used locally or across the network, just like any other remote file system.

The `data` file contains an abstract and portable representation of the panel. It contains plain text for text elements, compressed bitmaps for images, textual representation of draw operations for vector graphics, textual representation of a number between 0 and 100 for gauges, and so on. Data for a widget may be updated by writing its data file, and retrieved by reading from it.

Different types of widgets may use different data formats for their data files (e.g., plain UTF text, textual vector graphics commands, etc.). Moreover, a given type of widget may be designed either as a container or as an atom. This is a choice that the widget developer must make.

The `ctl` (control) file contains a textual representation of the panel attributes. For example, a control file may contain "`sel 5 100`" to state that the text selected in a text widget stands between the 5th and the 100th symbol (unicode character). Another example is "`font T`", which is a hint for viewers to show text using a constant width ("teletype") font. To permit selective updates of individual attributes, the textual representation for an attribute may be used as a control request by writing it to the control file.

The `edits` file, which is present on many panels, is a textual description of changes made to a panel. This is particularly relevant to text panels and relatives (tags, labels, etc.). It is used to maintain a central representation of the history of changes made to a panel. For example, it can be used to undo operations that were made on a previous session, after reopening it (perhaps using a different terminal if the user has moved from one machine to another). The exact details of the set of panels and the format for their data and attributes may be found on the Octopus user's manual.

The widget representation as a file system is up to the developer of the widget. Thus, when adding a new type of widget, the developer can define its language, that is, the data contained in the file(s) that represent the widget.

Regarding concurrency control, file servers involved in O/live (described in the next section) perform a file operation at a time. This means that client programs may consider file operations as atomic. Also, it means that two different (perhaps conflicting) requests are not concurrent. One of them will be performed before the other, and the last one prevails. As an example, it is customary for applications to create entire UIs first, and then write a request to a `ctl` file to make the UI visible at a given screen (or device). Because such a write is atomic, the entire UI can be set for viewing in one or more viewers at once, without races.

When updating a data or control file, the implementation takes care of multiplexing requests from different clients (i.e., from different file descriptors). For example, when updating a large image requiring multiple writes, the widget state will not change before closing the file after writing it. Therefore, the update is also atomic as far as clients are concerned. Should two programs update concurrently the same image, one of them will win the race, but the image will be consistent.

3 Architecture

Unlike most other UI systems, the system is built out of two main programs.

- **O/mero** is the UIMS and provides a single, central, file system interface for all widgets of interest. It is the heart of cooperative and distributed editing and provides support for persistence of widgets across terminal reboots and network partitions. O/mero is designed to be hosted in the cloud. This means that this central point of control can be replicated to provide fault tolerance and availability as needed. This program is not to be confused with Omero, an ancestor of O/live.
- **O/live** is a viewer for O/mero (and gives its name to the entire system). It is responsible for all user interaction and it is the only program that knows how to draw and how to process device input (e.g., mouse and keyboard).

There are two other components in the architecture: O/ports and O/x. O/ports is an event delivery service used by the rest of components. Most of the time, O/live is used in conjunction with O/x. O/x is a file browser, an editor, and a shell to the underlying system. As far as O/live is concerned, it is an application program. It is also in charge of a distributed editing command language, and many applications rely on its services.

O/mero's root directory contains a directory named appl used by applications to create their UIs and operate them. The application is free to adjust its UI and, once ready, replicate it on any screen. By convention, the application replicates its UI in the same screen in which it has been run. Note that this is similar to asking an UI toolkit to *show* it, and does not require the application to be aware of replication facilities. The user may change things later in this respect and move and/or relocate any panel (that has a tag).

O/live is started by giving it the path to a screen (or session) that must be shown. Should the user want, a new screen may be instantiated by creating a new directory in the top-level directory of O/mero. Previously existing panels may be also replicated on it.

The important point here is that applications operate on files, unaware of how many replicas there are, and ignorant for the most part of how are panels going to be depicted on the different screens[1]. On the other hand, O/live (our

---

[1] Refer to demo number 2 at the demonstration web page.

viewer) is the only one who cares about how to render panels. The same holds for input devices but, before getting into details of input processing, we must discuss event handling.

The decoupling of O/live (viewer) from O/mero enables a N:M relationship between them, unlike in systems such as Omero [2]. For example, one O/mero can serve the widgets to several, multimodal viewers (i.e., to different O/lives). Also, a viewer can combine different O/meros to create a mash-up of more than one application; to do so, it only has to use files from different O/meros.

4   Cooperative and Distributed Editing

There may be multiple O/live instances attached to the same O/mero. In fact, that is the case when multiple machines are being used to deploy user interfaces. Usually, there is one O/live per display available (we are referring to the graphical implementation of O/live). Depending on the preferences of the user, different O/lives may be displaying different "screens" (different file subtrees in `/mnt/ui`, siblings of the `appl` directory), or they might be displaying the same one.

All edits are performed inside O/live. For example, an editable text panel implements typical editing facilities within O/live, and notifies O/mero only of text insertions, removals, dirty or clean status change (i.e., unsaved changes), etc. All mouse and keyboard interaction is processed locally, and abstract events are sent from O/live to O/mero, possibly leading to events for the application. The same happens for any kind of interaction with O/live. A consequence of this scheme is that the network link between O/live and O/mero may have high latency (e.g., WAN and 3G networks).

All notifications from O/live to O/mero are done through the `data` or `ctl` files of the panels. O/mero processes the request(s) and then notifies involved parties (i.e., applications and other O/lives using the same tree).

O/mero notifies the different instances of O/live of changes to panels by sending notifications whenever a file changes. When O/live receives such notifications, it updates the panels affected. For example, as text is inserted and removed on a text panel, O/live would send `ins` and `del` events by writing control requests to the panel on its `ctl` file. Then, O/mero would update the panel, and notify other O/lives of the insertion/removal or text. The O/lives would then update their contents accordingly.

In our current implementation we discard a concurrent edit when it happens. The approach taken by O/mero and O/live is not to provide failure transparency (i.e., not to resolve conflicts internally when they happen). O/live is well suited for the two cases it has been designed for: (i) a group of well connected users sharing a common smart space and (ii) a single user using multiple interfaces from local or/and remote locations. In the second case, because there is a single agent using the system, there is no possibility of conflict. Even in that case, there may be several active viewers at the same time at different remote locations.

5   Building Applications

It is quite easy to build regular applications using O/live. Applications only need to create and delete directories, read and write from files and in general interact through the file system with their UI, which they perceive as a single copy.

For example, an application to control the lights of the room 134 which is part of the scenario described in the introduction, would create a button to turn on and off the lights. In order to do this, it must first create the appropriate directory representing the button with a name like:

`/mnt/ui/appl/button:light.2342`

Note that the last number is just a random number to prevent clashes. Then a string like ''appl 34 464'' has to be written to the file:

`/mnt/ui/appl/button:light_room134.2342/ctl`

This string identifies this particular panel and that it belongs to this application instance. Writing the string ''copyto screen1/col:1'' would make the button appear on this screen.

Then, an event channel would be created to receive the events that will be generated for the button. Finally, the application would be in a loop reading from this file. Whenever the read unblocks, the application would turn the lights off and on.

The permissions of the files created by the user interface control what the users can do with it. For example, imagine the ctl file for the button described before has read permission for the public, and write permission just for the owner. This means that anyone can check whether the lights are on but just the owner of the file (which may be the owner of the room) might turn them on and off.

Of course, for more complex applications, a small library can wrap the file system operations to make dealing with the widgets more convenient. This library can look like a normal widget library (for example, GTK+) to the application programmer.

6   Related Work

The literature for UIs and UIMS is very extensive. To the best of our knowledge, this is the only UIMS that allows distributed and highly heterogeneous I/O devices to be freely combined by users to operate on distributed, replicated, widgets in a transparent way for the application. That is the main difference with respect to other related work.

Most related work, including the few systems mentioned here, is either not able to support such a high heterogeneity or not able to do it transparently or does not give users (and programs) the high degree of freedom to, independently, operate on replicated (portions of) distributed widgets. Those that are close to achieving this, require the introduction of new protocols, middleware, languages and/or specific and complex toolkits.

Omero [2] is a direct ancestor of the UIMS presented here. There are several differences between them (architecture, distributed editing, discovery service, I/O, drawing, and so on).

VNC [6] and similar desktop sharing systems take a completely different approach than O/live. They provide viewers for remote virtual framebuffers. In contrast, in O/live, the network dialog involves abstract data, and not pixmaps or mouse and keyboard events, as a consequence the user interface can be reified with all the benefits already described.

One.world [7] migrates application data codified as tuples serialized using Java classes. Again, this means that any device which needs to interact with the infrastructure needs to run Java. One.world also depends on broadcast on a local network. It is unclear how issues like access control, or using a wider scale of integration on the internet would be solved

Closer to our approach is Shared Substance [8]. Shared Substance is completely data oriented, has a tree structure and the distributed interfaces are organized like a file system, except it is not a file system. Instead, it is an ad hoc composition distributed data model accessed through a custom made middleware which has most of the operations and properties of a file system.

There are many systems that use markup languages to describe the interfaces. For example, SUPPLE [9], TERESA [10] and MARIA [11] exploit markup languages to customize interfaces for heterogeneous devices. Another example is CONSENSUS [12], which uses RIML, a language based on XHTML and XForms. Unlike these systems, we suggest using synthetic files as an abstract representation for widgets. This greatly simplifies supporting highly heterogeneous interfaces.

Systems like UBI and Migratable UIs [13,14] enable migration of UIs. However, they do not provide an external interface to use external tools leveraging migration facilities and they require more complexity at the toolkit level. Instead, we simplify and abstract widgets to make migration and replication easier.

UI façades [15] was built on Metisse [16] and permits users to select and rearrange components from interfaces transparently to the application. The problem with their approach is that independent views cannot be handled independently (for example, a scroll in one would scroll others) and that the abstraction level is not enough to enable use of highly heterogeneous devices.

VPRI's work [17] leads to powerful scripting tools to handle widgets. A huge difference is that O/live enables using the system shell and any previously existing scripting or programming language.

7   Conclusions

To conclude, the key contributions of this work are the idea of using synthetic files to decouple user interaction from the interface state, the idea of using synthetic files to decouple the application from its interface state and a revisit of how an architecture for UIMS is built based on the previous two ideas.

References

1. Ballesteros, F.J., Soriano, E., Guardiola, G.: Octopus: An upperware based system for building personal pervasive environments. Journal of Systems and Software 85(7), 1637–1649 (2012)
2. Ballesteros, F.J., Guardiola, G., Algara, K.L., Soriano, E.: Omero: Ubiquitous user interfaces in the plan b operating system. In: IEEE PerCom (2006)
3. Ballesteros, F.J., Guardiola, G., Soriano-Salvador, E.: Personal pervasive environments: Practice and experience. Sensors 12(6), 7109–7125 (2012)
4. Sadogidis, A., Lalis, E.: Add some olives to your coffee: A java-based gui for the octopus system. In: Proceedings for the 7th International Workshop on Plan, vol. 9 (2012)
5. Pike, R.: Acme: A user interface for programmers. In: Proceedings for the Winter USENIX Conference, pp. 223–234 (1994)
6. Richardson, T., Stafford-Fraser, Q., Wood, K.R., Hoppe, A.: Virtual network computing. IEEE Internet Computing 2(1), 33–38 (1998)
7. Grimm, R.: One.world: Experiences with a pervasive computing architecture. IEEE Pervasive Computing, 22–30 (2004)
8. Gjerlufsen, T., Klokmose, C., Eagan, J., Pillias, C., Beaudouin-Lafon, M.: Shared substance: developing flexible multi-surface applications. In: Proceedings of the 2011 Annual Conference on Human Factors in Computing Systems, pp. 3383–3392. ACM (2011)
9. Gajos, K., Weld, D.S.: Supple: automatically generating user interfaces. In: Proceedings of the 9th International Conference on Intelligent User Interfaces, IUI 2004, pp. 93–100. ACM, New York (2004)
10. Bandelloni, R., Paternò, F.: Flexible interface migration. In: Proceedings of the 9th International Conference on Intelligent User Interfaces, p. 155. ACM (2004)
11. Manca, M., Paternó, F.: Extending maria to support distributed user interfaces. In: Gallud, J.A., Tesoriero, R., Penichet, V.M. (eds.) Distributed User Interfaces. Human-Computer Interaction Series, pp. 33–40. Springer, London (2011)
12. The consensus project
13. Nylander, S., Bylund, M., Waern, A.: Ubiquitous service access through adapted user interfaces on multiple devices. Personal Ubiquitous Computing 9(3), 123–133 (2005)
14. Luyten, K., Vandervelpen, C., Coninx, K.: Migratable user interface descriptions in component-based development. In: Forbrig, P., Limbourg, Q., Urban, B., Vanderdonckt, J. (eds.) DSV-IS 2002. LNCS, vol. 2545, pp. 44–58. Springer, Heidelberg (2002)
15. Stuerzlinger, W., Chapuis, O., Phillips, D., Roussel, N.: User interface facades: towards fully adaptable user interfaces. In: Proceedings of the 19th Annual ACM Symposium on User Interface Software and Technology (2006)
16. Chapuis, O., Roussel, N.: Metisse is not a 3d desktop? In: Proceedings of the 18th Annual ACM Symposium on User Interface Software and Technology, pp. 13–22. ACM (2005)
17. Warth, A., Yamamiya, T., Oshima, Y., Wallace, S.: Toward a more scalable end-user scripting language. VPRI Technical Report TR-2008-001 (2008)

Design Lessons from Deploying NFC Mobile Payments

Rui José[1], Helena Rodrigues[1], Ana Melro[1], André Coelho[1], and Marta C. Ferreira[2]

[1] Centro Algoritmi, Universidade do Minho, Portugal
[2] Faculdade de Engenharia, Universidade do Porto, Portugal
{rui,helena,amelro,acoelho}@dsi.uminho.pt, mferreira@fe.up.pt

Abstract. The adoption of mobile payment systems is known to face multiple concerns regarding security, usability and value proposition. In this work, we start from the assumption that initial acceptance will always be weak because of the lack of an established usage frame. Instead, we focus on understanding how we can leverage upon the real contact with the technology to create a solid path for gradual acceptance through the development of new practices and the increasing perception of value. In this study, we report on our findings with a real-world prototype of a NFC-based payment system. We identify a set of design lessons that may help to improve the initial phases of NFC-based payment deployments and provide a path for the adoption that focuses on positive initial user experiences and early adoption scenarios.

Keywords: mobile payments, NFC, user experience.

1 Introduction

Mobile payments have been an emerging technology for some time, but their widespread adoption involves a very broad and diverse range of acceptance factors that go far beyond the mere properties of any particular payment technology. Previous work has largely explored these acceptance factors [1][2][3], highlighting some of the key concerns people have when faced with the prospect of using mobile payment technologies. When considering mobile payments, one should first acknowledge their disruptive effect on many of the practices and respective safeguards people normally resort to when making payments with currently existing methods. For example, from a technology perspective credit cards are known to have multiple risks, but their use is based on a trust model that has evolved over the years to deal with the perception of risk by the users and the management of risk by issuers. These practices have evolved and matured over the years and are now something that people trust and understand. With mobile payments, we must accept that they will necessarily be challenged, leaving a policy and practice vacuum that constitutes a natural obstacle for the adoption of this new payment technologies. In this work, we start from the assumption that initial acceptance will always be weak because of the lack of knowledge about the technology, lack of practices around the technology-based payments and lack of well-known reference scenarios that provide confidence and trust. Our focus is on how to achieve a positive initial user experience and how to leverage upon the real contact with the

G. Urzaiz et al. (Eds.): UCAmI 2013, LNCS 8276, pp. 86–93, 2013.

technology to create a solid path for gradual acceptance through the development of new practices and the perception of value.

For the specific purpose of this study, we define a mobile payment as a payment transaction performed through the use of a mobile device using NFC technology. The use of NFC constitutes an additional challenge, because very few people have experience with NFC in general, which by itself may also constitute an adoption barrier. The contribution of this work is the identification of a set of design lessons and the characterisation of usage experiences associated with real world payment situations with NFC-enabled mobile phones. Based on results from a public deployment of NFC-based payments, we identify a number of challenges and guidelines that may help to shape future versions of NFC-based payments systems. In particular, these design guidelines should help to improve the initial phases of NFC-based payment deployments and provide a path for adoption that focuses on positive initial user experiences and scenarios that can be identified as more feasible for early adoption.

2   Related Work

Existing work on mobile payment systems has largely focused in uncovering the value-chains and qualities that can foster adoption of mobile payment systems. Kindberg et al investigated users' trust and security concerns in mobile payments using a "electronic wallet"[1]. Ease of use, convenience or social issues were reported as being equally important as trust and security issues. Kristoffersen et al. investigated users' attitudes towards m-payments in Norway [2]. The authors conclude that users do not seem to particularly value the mobile payment functionality except if it allows for an immediate use of the product. Mallat et al. conducted a study of mobile ticketing service adoption in public transportation [3]. The analysis of the survey suggests that contextual and mobile service-specific features, such as budget constraints, existing alternatives and time pressure, are important determinants of adoption.

Previous work has also addressed NFC-based payments. A. Zmijewska studies the adoption factors of ease of use, cost, usefulness, trust and mobility to analyze the suitability of available wireless technologies to create mobile payment systems that the user is likely to accept [4]. NFC is described as the easiest, useful and the technology with best-perceived trust. J. Ondrus and Y. Pigneur present an assessment of NFC for future mobile payment systems and conclude that NFC is expected to become an enabler for mobile services, more specifically for mobile payments [5]. M. Massoth and T. Bingel compare the performance of different traditional mobile payment service concepts, namely Interactive Voice Response (IVR), Short Message Service (SMS), Wireless Application Protocol (WAP) and One Time Password Generator (OTP), with a NFC-based mobile payment solution, mainly focusing on user authentication [6]. NFC-based application presented the best performance results mainly due to NFC requiring less manual intervention than other technologies. A. Juntunen et. al have conducted a study on the use of NFC technology for Mobile Ticketing Services [7]. They have concluded that mobile ticketing services offer a clear value proposition to travelers and could contribute to the growth of the NFC ecosystem.

3   The Mobipag Pilot

3.1   Technical Approach

The MobiPag pilot aimed at demonstrating in a controlled real environment the main technologies and services in our mobile payment solution and also to support from various perspectives the evaluation of the technology and the respective user experience. The MobiPag pilot was deployed at the University of Minho Campus, in Guimarães, for a period of one month, and it was a compromise between the simplification needed to run a technology that is still being prototyped and the need to create an evaluation environment that was realistic enough to provide a valuable assessment of the respective user experience.

In this deployment, the devices of users and merchants' were all Android Samsung Galaxy SIII smart phones with NFC. We have used a Universal Integrated Circuit Card (UICC) compliant with the recently available SIMAlliance Open Mobile API as the execution and storage environment for all the security-confine tasks and data related with a payment provider. This implementation and *de facto* standard allows the connection between the applications running in the device processor and the applets running inside the UICC. It contains a secure element running secure applets, which constitute the trust anchors of the payment protocol.

A particular property of Mobipag is the possibility to support many applications on top of the Mobipag API. For this deployment, we created two mobile payment applications: User MobiPag UM and Merchant MobiPag UM. These applications offer the interface and, from the user point of view, also the logic and services to execute the various payment situations supported in this pilot. The merchant MobiPag UM application is actually composed by a Point-of-sale (POS) component and an Automated Payment Terminal (APT) component. The POS interacts with the user and with merchant to agree on the payment amount due from the user to the merchant. The APT is the component responsible to communicate with the payment provider through the MobiPag backend platform.

A backend platform acts as a broker interlinking every service and device, provides facilities to manage all aspects of the associated business model and assures compliance with regulation requirements. It contains several payment adaptors that connect with each financial institution account service. For the purpose of this pilot, a major bank in Portugal acted as the financial institution. Both the merchant POS and APT can contact with the backend platform to make a payment and redeem loyalty or service tokens (the vouchers, tickets, discounts, etc.) provided by the associated external service providers.

3.2   Experimental Methodology

To support the evaluation of the system, we devised six mobile payment scenarios corresponding to common day-to-day transactions, but designed also to include distinct transaction properties, including simple payments, tickets and discount coupons. All prices, products and services were real, but the users did not pay with their own money. Instead, a specific MobiPag account was used and credited with an appropriated initial amount. The threshold for requesting a PIN from users was set to 1 euro, creating situations with and without PIN request. All the scenarios were initiated by both the user and the merchant selecting the mobile payment mode in their terminals. We will now describe the interactions on each of the six payment scenarios (Figure 1).

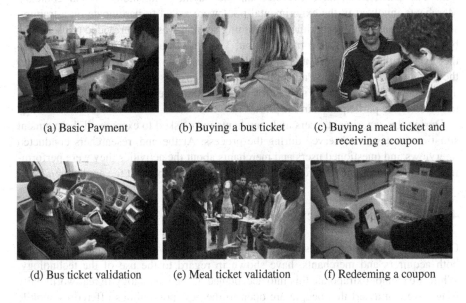

(a) Basic Payment   (b) Buying a bus ticket   (c) Buying a meal ticket and receiving a coupon

(d) Bus ticket validation   (e) Meal ticket validation   (f) Redeeming a coupon

Fig. 1. The six payment situations in the Mobipag pilot

At the bar (Fig.1a), the merchant registers the requested goods in the merchant's application. The user approaches his mobile phone to the merchant's payment terminal. He receives the payment amount in the mobile phone, confirms and enters the security PIN (if applicable). He approaches his mobile phone again to the payment terminal and receives a payment confirmation message. The transaction is then completed. At the bus ticket counter (Fig.1b), users may buy bus tickets. The transactions are the same, but this time an electronic ticket is received in the second tap and stored in the mobile phone for subsequent validation in the bus. At the meal ticket counter, (Fig.1c) the merchant registers the number of tickets in his terminal. All the transactions in previous situations are repeated. The user receives the ticket meal in his mobile phone. In this particular situation, the user also receives a discount coupon. At the bus (Fig.1d), users validate bus tickets stored in the mobile phone. The merchant enters the number of tickets in his terminal. The user selects the corresponding ticket in his mobile phone and approaches the mobile device with the driver's terminal. When the transaction is completed, the user receives a confirmation message. At the meal ticket validation counter (Fig.1e) users pay their meals with a meal ticket previously acquired and stored in their mobile phone. The merchant enters in his terminal the number of required meal tickets. The user selects the corresponding meal tickets in his mobile phone and approaches the mobile device with the driver's terminal. The transaction is then processed as above. At the bar (Fig.1f), the user selects in his application stored discount coupons before paying. The new total amount is then calculated and transaction proceeds as above.

As part of our deployment, we run three evaluation sessions on distinct days and with distinct users. In total, 16 users and 4 merchants have participated in the evaluation. The participants have executed all the payment situations in real contexts. Merchants involved in the experimental pilot were asked to participate on a training session previous to the experiment. A training session was also provided to users, just before the beginning of their participation. The initial training explained the project, the goals of the experiment, and allowed both groups to make an initial approach to the mobile device and MobiPag applications. Both groups (merchants and users) were also asked to answer a small survey for understanding the motivations that have contributed for the participation in the pilot.

During the experiment, users and merchants were asked to execute all the payment situations and were observed during the process. At the end, researchers conducted interviews and questioned users and merchants about the activities they were performing, the difficulties encountered in their execution and also about the application.

4   Analysis and Discussion

Overall, the first general observation is the very positive attitude that participants, both acquirers and merchants, have shown in regard to the use of the technology. While we cannot extrapolate this into acceptance of the technology in real world daily usage, we can assert that people are open to the new possibilities offered by mobile payments and are willing to experiment how they can use them in realistic payment situations. This positive attitude was particularly evident in regard to security perception. While security is clearly the number one concern in any acceptance survey on mobile payments, in a real deployment this concern is strongly mitigated by system feedback and the sense that the system works. Participants expressed the opinion that it must be a secure system, and that the information given by the app provides confidence and security. They indicated that asking for a PIN code in certain transactions, the message "Operation successfully concluded", the confirmation beeps, the NFC connection vibration or even the need to physically approach one mobile phone to another, were all elements that contributed to their perception of trust.

Embodiment of the Payment System
A key property of NFC-based payments is the need to approach the mobile device from the reading device, which in our prototype was always another mobile phone. As a consequence, there was not formally a POS optimized for intensive usage, something that seemed to be part of the expectations and frame of reference of the merchants in our study:

The payment receiving system, if it was a reading system, like on supermarkets, it would be more advantageous and faster. [Ex_Mrch1]

While we anticipate that future instantiations of the technology can have a whole different level of integration with Points of Sale, one of the strong points of this payment system based on mobile phones is also the ability to very quickly establish a payment system using only mobile phones. While not a relevant scenario for major stores, it may constitute a relevant value proposition for many small businesses that due to reduced number of sales or the inherently mobile nature of the their businesses do not justify a full POS system. In our prototype, we considered two approaches, both of which closer to more ad-hoc payment situations: the first was a simple and direct use of two mobile phones that were touched without any particular support for the interaction (Fig. 2a); the second was a simple stand for the merchants' mobile phone (Fig. 2b and Fig. 2c)

Fig. 2. (a) Contact without support (b) Custom support (c) Contact with a custom support

In the first design, both parts of the transaction had to hold their mobile phones and approach them. The main observation is that it clearly forced participants to break the boundaries of social distance and interact at a level of proximity that was more on the range of personal or even intimate distance. The need to approach hands, aligned them to achieve communication and wait in that position for the communication to occur further contributed to this feeling. While the extent to which this is a problem may vary considerably between people, it is still an issue that will always be relevant when considering this form of payment for more than occasional transactions.

In the second design, a very simple physical support was used to hold the merchants' mobile phone and make it stand in a vertical position. This would then allow the acquirers' mobile phone to touch back-to-back with the merchants' mobile phone, while they can both check the information on their display. Our main observation was a clear tradeoff in the stand design between having the merchant's mobile phone facing up to facilitate interaction by the merchant or having it facing down, to make it easier for the acquirer to perform the NFC communication by touching its back. The vertical position offered by our physical stand was an obvious compromise, but it still was not very practical for merchants to interact with the mobile phone while standing at a lower position. For this reason, merchants quickly developed the practice of holding the stand in their hand while inserting the details of a transaction and then placing it next to the acquirer so that he could perform the NFC transaction. The fact that the stand was mobile gave this flexibility to the merchant, but was not so positive for acquirers. When approaching the stand to make the NFC transaction, many people have shown some fear of pushing it away. This has negatively impacted on the performance of NFC operations, as it made the correct alignment a bit harder. With time, many acquirers developed the practice of holding the stand while the person was approaching the mobile phone.

Being in Control

Fundamental to any payment process is that users and merchants can always feel that they are in full control of what is happening. When using NFC, the semantics and implications of the taps, in which the mobile devices are touched, is the core part of this control process.

Even though we had a very high success rate in the transactions made by participants, there were also some error situations. These failed transactions were due to a broad range of issues, the most common being some failure in the contact between mobile phones or network failure on the merchants' device. While we could expect this error rate to become even smaller, what was most striking from our evaluation situations was how people felt lost when it happened. With other payment technologies, both acquirers and merchants have a more developed model of how the system works and what can be tried to circumvent the problem. Faced with a new technology about which they lacked the knowledge that results from previous experience, participants were clearly lost in error situations and unable to initiate any problem solving procedures, other than re-initiating the whole payment process from the beginning and hope it could then work.

One of the strongest points in our solution was the flexibility provided by integrating payments with complimentary services such as tickets and discount coupons. However, we have clearly observed that this flexibility comes with a cost in complexity of the procedures and cognitive overload for users in payment situations. What could be a simple procedure may become very complex from a cognitive perspective when multiple types of coupons, discounts, promotions and fidelity schemes become part of the payment transaction. While the overall procedures were considered simple by participants, coupon redemption and to a lesser extent the use of tickets, were clearly the activities in which participants have experienced more difficulties. While some of the problems could be connected with specific usability problems that could easily be overcome, it was also clear that there was also a problem with the overall mental model associated with these complimentary services.

Payments tasks, coupons, the fact that we could not see the coupons and use them directly. [Lab_Acq3]

There are multiple sequences of procedures that could be followed to achieve essentially the same goals and people do not have established practices for understanding how the system is supposed to work. The fact that certain operations, such as using tickets, required only one tap instead of two was also confusing:

There are situations that it only asks for one tap, and others that asks for two and that is a bit confusing. [Ex_Acq9]

5   Conclusions

The results from this mobile payments pilot demonstrate the range of elements that may have a strong influence in the user experience, and consequently in the value proposition, of mobile payments. Considering acceptance factors regardless of these elements may be useful to establish the broader value proposition of mobile payments technology, but its falls short in the identification of the real world elements that may influence the actual perception of value creation. In this research, we have conducted a set of realistic payment situations to assess this type of elements.

A design guideline for this type of deployments is to clearly address the form factor as a key element in the prototype. This design element can often be neglected on the grounds that the payment system can be instantiated under many different form factors. While being true, the fact remains that the specific form factor being used in a deployment will constitute one of the most influential elements of the user experience with NFC and will have a major impact on the perception of the payment system.

The initial enthusiasm that people can have in regard to the technology means that managing expectations is crucial. First impressions should be strongly focused on quickly creating a sense of confidence, familiarity and added value with the technology that provides the foundations for sustained and subsequent exploration of more advanced features. Design for emerging practices and not let people down can mean focusing at the beginning on simple procedures that, albeit limited in regard to the range of technological possibilities, are much safer and less likely to let people down.

Acknowledgments. This work was co-funded by "Agência de Inovação" and the national QREN program through the COMPETE program, under the project MOBIPAG - National Initiative for Mobile Payments (project 13847).

References

1. Kindberg, T., Sellen, A., Geelhoed, E.: Security and trust in mobile interactions: a study of users' perceptions and reasoning. In: Mynatt, E.D., Siio, I. (eds.) UbiComp 2004. LNCS, vol. 3205, pp. 196–213. Springer, Heidelberg (2004)
2. Kristoffersen, S.: Users ' perception of mobile payment Steinar Kristoffersen * Anders Synstad and Kristian Sørli, vol. X, pp. 122–143
3. Mallat, N., Rossi, M., Tuunainen, V.K., Öörni, A.: An empirical investigation of mobile ticketing service adoption in public transportation. Personal and Ubiquitous Computing 12, 57–65 (2006)
4. Zmijewska, A.: Evaluating wireless technologies in mobile payments - a customer centric approach. In: International Conference on Mobile Business, ICMB 2005, pp. 354–362. IEEE (2005)
5. Ondrus, J., Pigneur, Y.: An Assessment of NFC for Future Mobile Payment Systems. In: International Conference on the Management of Mobile Business, ICMB 2007, p. 43 (2007)
6. Massoth, M., Bingel, T.: Performance of Different Mobile Payment Service Concepts Compared with a NFC-Based Solution. In: 2009 Fourth International Conference on Internet and Web Applications and Services, pp. 205–210 (2009)
7. Juntunen, A., Luukkainen, S., Tuunainen, V.K.: Deploying NFC Technology for Mobile Ticketing Services – Identification of Critical Business Model Issues. In: 2010 Ninth International Conference on Mobile Business and 2010 Ninth Global Mobility Roundtable ICMBGMR, pp. 82–90 (2010)

User, Context and Device Modeling
for Adaptive User Interface Systems

Eduardo Castillejo, Aitor Almeida, and Diego López-de-Ipiña

Deusto Institute of Technology, DeustoTech, University of Deusto, Avda.
Universidades 24, 48007, Bilbao, Spain
eduardo.castillejo@deusto.es
http://www.morelab.deusto.es

Abstract. Personalization and self-customizable environments tend to increase user satisfaction. There are many approaches to face the problem of designing adaptive user interface systems. However, most of the reviewed solutions are very domain dependent. We identify users, context and devices as the most significant entities in adaptive user interface domains. This paper digs into several drawback related to these environments, remarking the incongruity and aggregation of context, and the entities interaction within adaptive user interfaces domains.

Keywords: adaptive user interfaces, context-aware systems, user-adaptability.

1 Introduction

Adaptive user interfaces arise from the need of covering a wide range of users and environment conditions. Besides, there are groups of users who have special needs, e.g., the disabled and the elderly. These people suffer from very concrete limitations and market applications and devices usually are unable to guarantee a comfortable interaction. This situation makes that these groups suffer from inattention. Besides, although nowadays the share of people aged 65 represent a 17% of the current European population, by the year 2060 this figure is projected to rise to 30%[8]. As a consequence, and as the European Commission states, *"the EU would move from having four people of working-age to each person aged over 65 years to about two people of working-age"*. Evidently the current situation shows that it is still a small group, but with a high expected increasing ratio. Nevertheless, this implies that we are still in time of accommodating, adapting and overtaking for future economic and demographic consequences.

In the adaptive systems domain, user interface adaptation has largely evolved. Developers have attempted to customize their applications as far as possible, taking into account user preferences. These adaptations have grown in complexity, covering a wider range of users, as well as taking into account the current context situation. Therefore, context and user modeling have become a real challenge in this domain. This is because of the context variability and the set of different

G. Urzaiz et al. (Eds.): UCAmI 2013, LNCS 8276, pp. 94–101, 2013.
© Springer International Publishing Switzerland 2013

capabilities that users can have. Nonetheless, systems personalization and environment components adaptation has been demonstrated to benefit both users and service providers [19]. However, to achieve a satisfactory adaptation it is necessary to have several inputs, for example, a user characteristics model.

The remainder of this paper is structured as follows: first, in Section 2 we review several significant aspects of users, context and device modeling. Next, in Section 3 we present a study of how the presented entities can affect others. Finally, in Section 4, we discuss several conclusions.

2   Users, Context and Devices

Reviewing the literature solutions in the domain of adaptive user interfaces we found several and significant drawbacks (analyzed in the following sections). We have identified three main entities in this domain: *users, context* and *devices*. This section analyzes several aspects of these entities that are significant within an adaptive user interface domain. Besides, we discuss about different considerations that an adaptive user interface design process should take into account.

From Gerhard Fischer [11] to Heckmann et al. [14] there have been many different solutions for *modeling users*, all of them based in different approaches [3][5][9] and [12]. Nevertheless, these models suffer the same setback: they all are very *domain dependent*. To tackle this problem several solutions have been presented over the past 20 years [19]. For instance, *generic user modeling systems* (i.e., user modeling shell systems) are intended to be: (1) general (including domain independence); (2) expressive and (3) strong reasoners (more concrete reviews of these systems can be found in [10][18] and [20]).

From the *context* point of view, Anind K. Dey defined *context-aware systems* as those systems which, using context data, provide significant information and/or services to the user where the relevancy of the given information depends on the user task [7]. Anthony Jameson studied in 2001 how context-aware computing represent a challenging frontier for researchers [17]. In this work information about the environment, the user current state, longer term user properties and the user behavior are compared to take the correct adaptation decision. Several related researchs base their processes on context changes as triggers. However, they lack a common model of context in their platforms [4][21]. Nonetheless, the first attribute that defines context is its dynamism. This makes modeling context specially troublesome [6][24].

Henricksen et al. [15] and Schmidt et al. [23] defended the existence of a static and a dynamic context. Following the same idea we think that there are several *dynamic device capabilities* that cannot be modeled because of their dynamic nature. This kind of features should be taken into account to perform an adaptation process (see Figure 3).

3   Interaction between Entities

This section digs into the *users, context* and *devices* ability to mutually affect each others in an adaptive user interface domain.

In the software applications developing domain user capabilities are understood as a set of static characteristics that do not change in the interaction process. Current solutions provide several tools for users to customize their applications. However, this "adaptation ability" does not cover more than user specific needs. It does not take context into account, just several parameters that users can manipulate to adjust the applications to their taste. In a user interface adaptation domain we share the same premise. We believe that user capabilities are static (e.g., eyes refraction results of medical tests). Nevertheless, if we also consider context this premise changes. Context has the ability to change other entities capabilities. It can influence them, for example, with noise, lightning or weather. In other words, context has the ability to modify several entities capabilities, improving or impeding them. For example, if we use our device outdoors, making a phone call with a lot of natural sunlight, we may experience several setbacks in the interaction process. Our visual (sensory) capability, as users, is still static. We can see. But the current context is altering our capability of seeing the display properly.

As can be seen in Fig. 1, context combined with user capabilities is able to generate a new and different set of capabilities. To know about these new capabilities it will be necessary to study each context parameter and the corresponding affected user capabilities. To this end, we have remarked several context physical aspects that may be directly affect user capabilities: (1) natural *lightning* levels affect user visual capabilities (brightness, for example, can reflect glossy surfaces); (2) ambient *noise* can affect audio related tasks; (3) current *temperature* may affect the interaction with the device (e.g., cold temperatures in a touch interaction scenario can cause imprecise results) and, (4) as the faster we move, the more imprecise we become, we consider the user *movement* as the last aspect (current devices have several accelerometers and sensors that are capable of capturing acceleration and speed, even the number of steps we take). The Figure 2 details several context characteristics and the corresponding affected user capabilities.

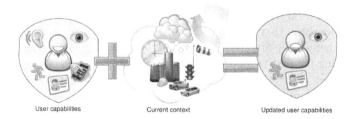

User capabilities   Current context   Updated user capabilities

Fig. 1. User capabilities updated by context

These affected user capabilities point of view is still superficial. For example, to face the interaction process with a blind user, the corresponding platform should adapt the interaction channel to avoid visual information. Therefore, an alternative interaction channel would be based on audio commands and voice recognition. However, what if the user is in a crowed street? This new context condition involves noise, traffic and crowds of people. In this case, should the system still use an audio based interaction channel? This new situation is what we define as a *aggregated context*. Aggregated context is identified as a context that is built from combining two or more context situations. This means that a certain context condition can be affected by unexpected parameters. This way, current context becomes even more dynamic.

Context aspects	User capability	Details

Light	Sensory functions
	• Sight and related
		Visual functions
		• Acuity functions
		   ○ Binocular acuity in short distance
		   ○ Monocular acuity in short distance
		• Useful field of view
		   ○ Vision quality (light sensitivity, color vision, contrast sensitivity, visual image quality)

Noise	Sensory functions • Auditive and vestibular	Hearing functions • Hearing sounds functions • Auditive discrimination • Speech discrimination
Temperature & Weather	Neuromusculoskeletal and movement-related functions	Functions of the joints and bones • Mobility of joint functions (mobility of single joint, several joints and generalized) Muskle functions • Muscle power functions ○ Power of muscles of one limb Movement functions (control of voluntary movement functions, control of simple voluntary movements, coordination of voluntary movements)

Fig. 2. Context influence over user capabilities

There are several situations where the adaptation process is not obvious [1][2][4][13][21]. For example: (1) A user suffers from a visual impairment. This disability obstructs the user from seeing application contents properly. Then the adaptation will intercede to facilitate another interaction channel for the user, e.g., voice recognition and control. But, what if the user is in a library? Or in a hospital? What if the user is doing a exam? (2) A user who sees perfectly well interacts with the application and its default user interface. What if the user starts to drive? (3) Another user is at home, and he/she does not suffer from any severe disability. At 01:00 PM he/she starts to cook. Imagine that the application requests user attention for several tasks. Should we allow the application to distract the user while he/she is cooking? These examples show several situations where users are involved in certain tasks that contradict the current context and user capabilities. We define these situations as *incongruent context adaptations*. An adaptation incongruity is defined by several environment parameters that induce the platform to perform a certain adaptation for the current conditions. However, the result of this adaptation, although it can be linearly aligned with the context characteristics, can be incongruent.

In the previous sections we have discussed about the entities which take part in an adaptation environment domain. We have remarked that these entities (user, context and device) interact with each user. But, in this section, we have presented several complex problems: the aggregated context and incongruent adaptations. These problems are not easily solved. We need something more to characterize the current situation that involves these three entities. Therefore, we introduce the concept of *activity*. Activities help us to understand the current user context and device situation. In other words, it enriches the environment information. Manipulating with hands or being at a certain location (like a library, where people are in silence) are aspects that we have to take into account when we face a context modeling problem. For example, driving or cooking restrict user capabilities momentarily. This way, we can state that these activities impede the user. Here we present several groups of activities that should be modeled and taken into account: (1) activities that limit the use of the hands; (2) activities that limit the use of the voice; (3) activities that limit the user sight capability; (4) activities that limit the user attention and, finally, (5) combinations of these activities. Persad et al. also considered that activities need to be taken into account [22]. They described Human Factors and Ergonomic theory as four components: the user, the product, the context and the activities over time that constitute the interaction. Hong et al. classified context conflicts into several categories [16]: (1) Sensing conflict: Not matching results from several physical data sources. (2) Service resource conflict: The lack of resources in a service offering process may provoke several conflicts. (3) User preference conflict: Users with different profiles or preferences are different but context situation is the same may result in context conflict. These problems are usually faced by using fuzzy algorithms, time stamps and information fusion [16].

Similarly, there are several context aspects that affect devices. Mainly, we have identified those related to infrastructure. Available infrastructure services can directly impede the interaction between the user and the device affecting several device capabilities: (1) Network bandwidth: A low bandwidth level will affect multimedia downloads and requests. (2) Location accuracy: Indoors locations can not be seen with usual GPS systems. New sensor based infrastructure is usually needed to get the user position. (3) Other services: weather and time services, for example, may be affected by similar conditions.

In 2012 Evers et al. [9] introduced the concept of *stress* within these environments. We know that context changes affect users and devices capabilities. Hence an adaptation process will try to reduce the current situation drawbacks to ensure an acceptable interaction. However, this process needs to be very thorough. Uncontrolled adaptations, unreasonable recommendations, and excessive auto-configurations can raise user stress levels.

3.1   Proposed Model

The example depicted in Section 3 shows a situation in which user capabilities are modified by context characteristics (see Figure 2). This brings a real problem to deal with, and there is no simple solution. Approach would be to choose those context situations related to user capabilities that obstructs user interaction in a minor way. For example, if the user is blind, there is no way of making him/her see. This way, although the context can be inappropriate for a voice interaction channel, it is the best adaption option to try to "reach" the user. This may result into an uncomfortable interaction but, at least, there would be a chance to interact. To face this problem a reasoning process would be needed. This process should allow the platform to decide about which would be the best suitable adaptation to be made. Besides, it should permit it to classify the conditions that mainly limit the interaction principally. Hong et al. discuss about the limitations of managing only physical context [16]. This context is limited to the data captured by sensors, involving location data, temperature, time, pressure, lightning levels, etc. As authors state that this information is important, they also defend that, in order to provide personalized services cognitive domains are strongly needed. Authors called this *cognitive context*.

Here we present a model for designing dynamic user interfaces (see Fig. 3). User model is based in R. Casas previous model [5]. This way it is no longer necessary to have any medical knowledge about users' capabilities (e.g., sight and hearing, motor, memory, etc.). The context model is extended in two ways. On the one hand, there is the sensors information and the combination of their measures. On the other hand, a high-level information category built from the combination of context and external pieces of information. The device model is extended by taking into account several dynamic characteristics that are required for every adaptation process.

Entity	Concept	Description
User	Experience	User's experience with technology and several interaction measures (e.g., display, audio...)
Context	Environment metadata	Richer knowledge about context piece of information by combining several sensors data
	Virtual environment	A high-level information category as a result of combining several pieces of information. For example, if a sensor shows that there is a light turned on at office, we can deduce that there is people working
Device	Dynamic capabilities	Battery level, network connectivity, current brightness, sound level, acceleration and orientation.

Fig. 3. Extended model for adaptive user interface systems

Besides, this model allows the combination of several entities aspects. Combining context and user capabilities we can update the user model taking into account the influence that context can have in different user capabilities. What is more, context can be combined with other context situations to generate a new and aggregated context environment.

4   Conclusions

We defend that modeling users, context and devices is challenging due to several aspects: dynamism of context, ignorance about user capabilities, new and unknown devices capabilities... Besides, we remark that current solutions tend to be very domain dependent, although several efforts have been made in this area. This dependency makes difficult to reuse/export these approaches in/to different domains. Actually, mixing users, context and devices in the same domain is troublesome. Beyond the usual static capabilities we have identified how each entity has the ability of mutually affecting each others. This means that each entity capabilities can be altered. This way, we cannot keep talking about static capabilities. So we introduce the concept of *dynamic capabilities*. We have also classified the existing literature solutions for user and context modeling into more formalized groups. In addition, we have added several dynamic characteristics to the device model. Besides this, we have introduced the concept of *aggregated context* and we have defined a set of activities that should be taken into account to avoid *incongruity adaptations*. Nevertheless, our mutually affecting capabilities theory lacks of real data obtained from real users and environment situations.

Acknowledgments. This work has been supported by project grants "UCADAMI: User and Context-aware Dynamically Adaptable Mobile Interfaces" (S-PE12FD006) and "DYNUI: Capability and Context-aware Dynamic Adaptation of User Interfaces for Ambient Assisted Living" (PC2012-73A), sponsored by the Basque Government's Industry and Education Departments, respectively.

References

1. Almeida, A., López-de Ipiña, D., Aguilera, U., Larizgoitia, I., Laiseca, X., Orduña, P., Barbier, A.: An approach to dynamic knowledge extension and semantic reasoning in highly-mutable environments. In: 3rd Symposium of Ubiquitous Computing and Ambient Intelligence 2008, pp. 265–273. Springer (2008)
2. Almeida, A., López-de Ipiña, D.: Assessing ambiguity of context data in intelligent environments: Towards a more reliable context managing system. Sensors 12(4), 4934–4951 (2012), http://www.mdpi.com/1424-8220/12/4/4934
3. Babisch, W.: The noise/stress concept, risk assessment and research needs. Noise and Health 4(16), 1 (2002)
4. Calvary, G., Coutaz, J., Thevenin, D., Limbourg, Q., Souchon, N., Bouillon, L., Florins, M., Vanderdonckt, J.: et al.: Plasticity of user interfaces: A revisited reference framework. In: In Task Models and Diagrams for User Interface Design (2002)
5. Casas, R., Blasco Marín, R., Robinet, A., Delgado, A., Yarza, A., Mcginn, J., Picking, R., Grout, V.: User modelling in ambient intelligence for elderly and disabled people. In: Computers Helping People with Special Needs, pp. 114–122 (2008)
6. Chen, G., Kotz, D.: A survey of context-aware mobile computing research. Tech. rep., Technical Report TR2000-381, Dept. of Computer Science, Dartmouth College (2000)
7. Dey, A.K.: Understanding and using context. Personal and Ubiquitous Computing 5(1), 4–7 (2001)

8. European Commission: Ageing report: Europe needs to prepare for growing older (2012),
   http://ec.europa.eu/economy_finance/articles/
   structural_reforms/2012-05-15_ageing_report_en.htm
9. Evers, C., Kniewel, R., Geihs, K., Schmidt, L.: Achieving user participation for adaptive applications. In: Bravo, J., López-de-Ipiña, D., Moya, F. (eds.) UCAmI 2012. LNCS, vol. 7656, pp. 200–207. Springer, Heidelberg (2012)
10. Fink, J., Kobsa, A.: A review and analysis of commercial user modeling servers for personalization on the world wide web. User Modeling and User-Adapted Interaction 10(2-3), 209–249 (2000)
11. Fischer, G.: User modeling in human–computer interaction. User Modeling and User-Adapted Interaction 11(1), 65–86 (2001)
12. Gregor, P., Newell, A.F., Zajicek, M.: Designing for dynamic diversity: interfaces for older people. In: Proceedings of the Fifth International ACM Conference on Assistive Technologies, pp. 151–156 (2002)
13. Gu, T., Wang, X.H., Pung, H.K., Zhang, D.Q.: An ontology-based context model in intelligent environments. In: Proceedings of Communication Networks and Distributed Systems Modeling and Simulation Conference, vol. 2004, pp. 270–275 (2004)
14. Heckmann, D., Schwarzkopf, E., Mori, J., Dengler, D., Kröner, A.: The user model and context ontology GUMO revisited for future web 2.0 extensions. In: Contexts and Ontologies: Representation and Reasoning, pp. 37–46 (2007)
15. Henricksen, K., Indulska, J., Rakotonirainy, A.: Modeling context information in pervasive computing systems. In: Mattern, F., Naghshineh, M. (eds.) PERVASIVE 2002. LNCS, vol. 2414, pp. 167–180. Springer, Heidelberg (2002)
16. Hong, J.Y., Suh, E.H., Kim, S.J.: Context-aware systems: A literature review and classification. Expert Systems with Applications 36(4), 8509–8522 (2009)
17. Jameson, A.: Modelling both the context and the user. Personal and Ubiquitous Computing 5(1), 29–33 (2001)
18. Jameson, A.: Systems that adapt to their users. Decision Making 2, 23 (2011)
19. Kobsa, A.: Generic user modeling systems. User Modeling and User-Adapted Interaction 11(1-2), 49–63 (2001)
20. Kobsa, P.D.A.: User modeling and user-adapted interaction. User Modeling and User-Adapted Interaction 15(1), 185–190 (2005)
21. Nilsson, E.G., Floch, J., Hallsteinsen, S., Stav, E.: Model-based user interface adaptation. Computers & Graphics 30(5), 692–701 (2006)
22. Persad, U., Langdon, P., Clarkson, J.: Characterising user capabilities to support inclusive design evaluation. Universal Access in the Information Society 6(2), 119–135 (2007)
23. Schmidt, A., Beigl, M., Gellersen, H.W.: There is more to context than location. Computers & Graphics 23(6), 893–901 (1999)
24. Strang, T., Linnhoff-Popien, C.: A context modeling survey. In: Workshop Proceedings (2004)

A Case of Use of Augmented Reality for Supporting Communication in Presentations

Telmo Zarraonandia, Ignacio Aedo, Paloma Díaz, and Alvaro Montero

Computer Science Department, Universidad Carlos III de Madrid,
Leganés (Madrid), Spain
{tzarraon,pdp,ammontes}@inf.uc3m.es, aedo@ia.uc3m.es

Abstract. The Augmented Reality (AR) technology provides unique affordances for education that are only yet started to be explored. In this work the benefits and potential uses of AR technology for supporting communication in presentations are explored. An Augmented Presentation Feedback System (APFs) is presented, which allows a speaker equipped with a pair of Augmented Reality goggles to visualize visual cues depicted over the listeners' heads. These can be used as a way to provide the speaker with feedback on his/her explanations. The results of a case study conducted showed that the system not only assists the speaker in adapting the content and pace of the explanation to the listener, but also helps to better manage their interventions and improve the flow of the presentation.

Keywords: Augmented Reality, Classroom Response System.

1   Introduction

The potential for the use of Augmented Reality (AR) in education has not gone unnoticed in the research community, and such technology has been successfully used to enhance the interaction of learners with the learning content both within the context of a classroom [1] as well as outside [2]. However, its application in this particular area is still in its infancy and little attention has been given to its possibilities for supporting the instructor's tasks. Following this idea in [3] we presented ALFs, an Augmented Lecture Feedback System for supporting the communication between students and teacher during lectures. This communication flow is sometimes hampered by students' fear of showing themselves up in front of their classmates. The system overcomes the problem by allowing students to display graphical representations of their current state close to them, that a teacher equipped with a pair of AR goggles could visualize. Students are then provided with a communication channel that would allow them to communicate with the lecturer in a private and immediate way, without fellow students even noticing and without interrupting the lecture. An experience conducted in the context of a lecture of a university course reported encouraging results [3]. It suggested that the system not only could effectively support communication from the perspective of the students, but it also helps the teacher to adapt the

G. Urzaiz et al. (Eds.): UCAmI 2013, LNCS 8276, pp. 102–110, 2013.
© Springer International Publishing Switzerland 2013

explanations and pace of the lecture to the current knowledge and status of the audience, in a way which had been difficult to achieve previously.

As a continuation of that work, in this paper we present a multiple case study carried out with the aim of exploring the benefits and drawbacks that a similar system might report when used to support communication in a wider range of presentations such as work presentations, student projects or training sessions. The dynamics between the participants of these presentations are usually different from the ones in a lecture, and even if the listeners might be less reluctant to directly address the presenter to communicate difficulties, the system could still report benefits. For example, it can be used to overcome current limitations of traditional Classroom Response Systems [4], allowing the presenter to identify instantly the sender of a response. In addition, it could also allow the listeners to communicate to the speaker information such as level of interest on the current explanation, present mood or suggestions on the way the exposition is being conducted, for example. This type of information is not normally directly elicited during a traditional presentation, and it could help to improve it. To gain a deeper understanding of the specific needs of users of the system and to gather feedback on how its practical application might be improved, an exploratory descriptive investigation has been conducted. Participants of different presentations made use of the different features of a new version of the system named APFs (Augmented Presentation Feedback system), designed to allow greater flexibility in the way the feedback is requested by the speaker and provided by the listeners. The results of the study are presented at the end of the paper, after describing the system, the study objectives and the research methodology followed.

2   The Augmented Presentation Feedback System (APFs)

Figure 1 depicts an illustration of a presentation supported by the APF system. As shown in the picture the listeners use their mobile devices to provide the speaker with feedback on his/her presentation, that he/she visualizes through a pair of AR goggles as symbols depicted over listener's heads. The presenter makes use of a tabletop application to activate and deactivate the different features of the system.

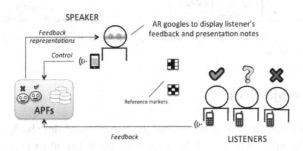

Fig. 1. Representation of an augmented presentation

The process will be as follows. Prior to start the presentation the speaker introduces in the system the position of each listener in the room taking as a reference two AR markers, and using the graphical application depicted in the left hand side of Figure 2. Next, he/she specifies the information he/she wants to elicit from the listeners by introducing in the system a set of "feedback requests". The definition of a request includes a request name, the question to be presented to the listeners, the set of available answers to respond to it and the set of symbols chosen to depict each of the answers in the speaker's AR device. Once the system is configured and the presentation starts, the listeners can use their mobile phones to log onto the system and select responses to the different feedback requests that the speaker makes available (right hand side of Figure 2). The APF system processes this information together with the video captured by the speaker's AR device, and augments speaker's vision accordingly with representations of the listeners' feedback responses, so that he/she has the impression that symbols appear over the corresponding listener's head. In addition, the module also generates a pie chart depicting the distributions of listeners' responses, which could be of help in presentations with many listeners, and a text line with the name of the feedback request whose responses are displayed at that time.

As presentations tend to be more flexible than lectures, the mechanism to activate the feedback request has been changed with respect to the previous version of the system. In that version the activation of the requests followed a pre-established order, not being necessary the intervention of the presenter. On the contrary in APFs the presenter is provided with a tabletop application to allow switching and scrolling between different feedback requests to activate and deactivate them at any given moment.

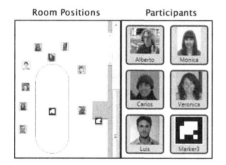 

Fig. 2. Screenshot of the Classroom Positioning system (left) and Screenshot of listener's mobile application (right)

3   Study Objectives

The objective of this study was to explore the benefits and drawbacks that a system like APF might report when used to support communication in presentations. It is necessary to clarify that the research team was aware that the current technology imposes clear and obvious limits to the practical use of the system, as current AR Head Mounted Displays models are still too unwieldy to be used in a real presentation.

However, it is very likely that as the technology evolves these problems will be easier to overcome. Therefore the focus of the study was not the ergonomic or technical requirements of the system, but the gathering of insights into the users' needs and preferences.

4   Methodology

Our methodological approach for the study was based on the design and analysis of an instrumental case study. A case study is defined as an empirical inquiry that investigates a contemporary phenomenon within its real-life context [5], and it is an evaluation method that complies with Design Science Research [6]. In the area of Human-Computer Interaction, exploratory case studies are frequently used to shed light on a specific situation and collect data to help understand problems and the requirements of new solutions [7].

4.1   Case Description

The case study conducted consisted of a series of presentations supported by the APF system and carried out in the Carlos III University of Madrid. A total of 18 lecturers and students collaborated in the study: 5 of them as speakers and 17 as listeners. The presentations were carried out in the conference room of the Computer Science Department, with listeners seated around a table, the furthest being approximately 4 metres from the speaker, and organized in two sessions. In the first one a postgraduate student presented his thesis work to 9 listeners for about 45'. In the second, 4 students presented several different projects of 10' to 15' minutes each consecutively to 8 listeners. The fact that the presentations varied in both length and number of listeners gave us the opportunity to gather feedback from a wider range of presentations. The model of AR device used by the speaker was Vuzix Star 1200 AR eyewear. Figure 3 depicts some pictures taken during the presentations showing the sight from the position of the listeners as well as the image of the room the lecturer obtained through the AR device. As shown in these pictures, the pie chart of the responses was depicted in the top right hand side of the AR display's screen, whereas the name of the feedback request displayed notes appeared at the bottom.

The units of analysis were the speakers' and listeners' responses to the system. In the case of the former, the primary data source were semi-structured interviews conducted at the end of the session, and in the latter, questionnaires including open-ended questions. These are frequently used and preferred methods in HCI research when trying to understand preferences and attitudes of users to a system [7].

4.2   Presentations Configuration

The number of feedback requests introduced by the speakers ranged from 2 to 5 per presentation. Most of the time the speakers used the requests to ask listeners to communicate if they understood some specific concepts or parts of the presentation, such as "how the thesis contributed to existing knowledge". In addition all the presentations included an extra feedback request asking listeners to state their level of understanding on the current explanation. The responses to this request were the ones displayed in the AR display by default. The symbols available to represent the responses included ticks, question marks and crosses in different colours. Green ticks, red crosses and question marks were always assigned to represent positive, negative responses, and uncertainties, respectively, while the other colours were used to indicate the degree of urgency the student gave to his/her questions and uncertainties. With regards to the timing of activation of the feedback requests, only the presenter of the first presentation chose to activate by himself two feedback requests related to two very specific questions he wished to pose. The rest of the presenters made available all feedback requests from the start of the presentation. This means that listeners could respond to them in any order.

Fig. 3. Pictures taken during the presentations of a speaker (left hand side) and the view obtained by the listener (right hand side)

5   Results

Following grounded theory principles [8] the transcripts of the interviews and the responses to the questionnaires were coded into four major categories: communication, presentation, visualization and application control issues. In addition, these categories were subdivided in positive and negative statements and suggestions. The result of the codification process is depicted in Table 1, where the numbers correspond to the number of participants who repeated that comment, and the symbols +, - and S to the three sub-categories just mentioned. Next, more details on the responses obtained from the participants are provided.

5.1   Responses from the Speakers

Interviews began by asking the speaker to give a general overview of the experience and continued by inquiring about the most positive aspects and the ones less satisfactory. Predictably, all of them pointed out the difficulty of carrying out the presentation with an uncomfortable device on their head that restricted their movements. Leaving aside ergonomic factors, they all agreed that the most positive outcome of the system is the opportunity it gives to receive real time and continuous feedback from the listeners. As one of them stated: "It was great to know if they were following my explanation or not all the time". When asked about what they used the feedback for, and if it changed the traditional way they carry out a presentation in any way, one speaker stated that it forced him to take the audience into account more, and avoided "switching on to automatic mode and continuing with the presentation on and on, just going through several slides". Another one explained that the system worked like some sort of "traffic light" in the sense that "when all the symbols were green I moved to the next explanation confident that previous one had been understood". On the contrary, when red crosses and question marks appear on the viewer, most speakers tend to stop and address listeners difficulties. With regards to the visualization, only the speaker from the first presentation found it difficult to discern from which listener the feedback had come, but this problem was only experienced with those participants seated very close to each other. In general the control of the system seemed to satisfy the speakers, although there is still room for improvement, for example by integrating it in the glasses.

5.2   Responses from the Listeners

At the end of the sessions listeners were invited to complete a questionnaire that included four open-ended questions about their overall experience, the system´s major advantages and drawbacks, and suggestions to improve it. As depicted in table 1, listeners valued the option of being able to provide constant feedback to the speaker, and better and more frequent interaction with the speaker. In addition, they also pointed out that the management of the participation also improved, as it was not necessary to interrupt the presentation to communicate with the speaker. On the negative side, some listeners reported that sometimes they were not sure if the speaker received or saw the feedback they had sent. For two listeners in the first session, having several feedback requests available to respond was a little confusing, and two others mentioned that some people might not like the idea of the speaker knowing the answers all the time.

6   Discussion

The opinions gathered from the experience here presented were mainly positive. Both speakers and listeners appreciated the possibility of being able to receive and send continuous feedback throughout the presentation, uninterruptedly. This positive outcome was also reported in the previous experience carried out in the context of a lecture. It is interesting to note that in that case the lecturer used the feedback to adapt the explanation on the fly, whereas in the present experience it was mostly used as an indicator of when to interrupt the presentation and interact with the listeners. A possible explanation to this might lie in the fact that in this experience the feedback responses were assigned by default to positive values, i.e. "I understand", and listeners changed to negative ones, i.e. "I don't understand", whereas in the previous experience in the context of a lecture it worked the other way around. In any case, the five presentations were undoubtedly enhanced in terms of interactivity. Participants' comments suggest that the system provides a less disruptive way of communicating with the speaker than interrupting the presentation by raising your hand. Finally, the

Table 1. Summary of interviews and questionnaire responses

		SPEAKERS	LISTENERS
Communication	+	(5) Receive continuous feedback. (1) Confidence in audience comprehension	(7) Continuous and real time communication. (1) Privacy.
	-		(4) Lack of acknowledgement of responses. (2) Not comfortable having to communicate.
	S		(1) Open responses. (1) Use the system to communicate mood (1) View other listeners answers
Presentation	+	(2) Adapt presentation on the fly (2) Stop when listeners not follow. (1) More interactive presentation.	(4) More interactive. (3) Not necessary to interrupt.
	-		
Visualization	+	(3) Easy to discriminate responses	
	-	(1) Difficult when symbols too close. (1) Distraction.	
	S	(1) Display only negative feedback.	
Control	+	(3) Easy to use.	
	-		(2) Not sure which feedback to respond. (1) Distraction. (1) Keep a fixed position in the room.
	S	(2) Include control in the glasses.	(2) Link feedback requests to presentation.

APF system not only signals to the speaker the most appropriate moment to interrupt the presentation, but can also boost his/her confidence in the knowledge that an explanation has been fully understood.

In addition, the experience conducted also highlighted some requirements that need to be addressed by future implementations. With regards to the speakers, it seem clear that in crowded rooms or when people are too close, the identification of the listener who provides the feedback becomes difficult to ascertain. In addition, despite most speakers considering it easy to use, the observation of the experience showed that the use of the tabletop to change the type of feedback response displayed was generally scarce. This suggests that this control should either be automatic or made redundant. With regards to the listeners, it is clearly necessary to implement mechanisms to acknowledge reception of the feedback sent by the speaker. In addition, if there is any order or timing in which feedback responses need to be provided this should be clearly stated to the listeners, especially in long presentations. Finally, speakers seemed to assume that a less than positive feedback response implied that the listener wanted to be addressed to explain his/her questions, which might not always be true. It seems necessary to discriminate between the communication of a response and the willingness of the listener to participate, and even between different grades of willingness to participate.

Finally, it is also necessary to consider some limitations of the study. This way, the novelty of the system could have influenced listeners, making them more amenable to participating in the presentation and sending responses. It also has to be acknowledged that all the participants of the experience had a technical background, and it is possible that the responses from people with non-technical profiles could be less enthusiastic. However, this also emphasises the criticality of some of the requirements pointed out, such as the automatization of the speakers' control of the application.

7   Conclusions and Future Work Lines

The experience carried out suggests that a future APF system that overcomes the ergonomic limitations of current HDMs could successfully support presentations, improving the communication of the speaker with his/her audience. Receiving continue, private and immediate feedback from the audience seems to increase the speaker's awareness of the reception of the message by the listeners. As reported in the experiences described in this paper, not only can this assist the speaker in adapting the content and pace of the explanation to the listener, but also help to better manage their interventions and improve the flow of the communication with his/her. By modifying the way feedback is requested and represented, it is possible to put the stress on one function or another.

The case study conducted also highlighted some requirements that an APF implementation should carefully consider. For example, a successful implementation should carefully examine how to reduce the number of symbols depicted at a time, and simplify the control of the application by the speaker. There are many different ways in which this can be achieved. One of them could be to display only negative feedback and depicted graphically summarized the other ones. By associating the negative responses to different feedback requests to different symbols the speaker might find easier to discriminate them, without requiring switching between different visualization modes. In addition, colours and sizes can be used to denote intention to participate. Current lines of work include the implementation of new versions of APFs that explore these design solutions.

Acknowlegment. This work is supported by the projects TIPEx (TIN2010-19859-C03-01) and urThey (TIN2009-09687), both funded by the Spanish Ministry of Science and Innovation.

References

1. Chen, G.D., Chao, P.Y.: Augmenting Traditional Books with Context-Aware Learning Supports from Online Learning Communities. Educational Technology & Society 11, 27–40 (2008)

2. Priestnall, G., Brown, E., Sharpless, M., Polmear, G.: A Student-Led Comparison of Techniques for Augmenting the Field Experience (2009)
3. Zarraonandia, T., Aedo, I., Díaz, P., Montero, A.: An Augmented Lecture Feedback System to Support Learner and Teacher Communication. Journal of British Educational Technology 44(4) (July 2013)
4. Caldwell, J.E.: Clickers in the Large Classroom: Current Research and Best-Practice Tips. CBE-Life Sciences Education 6 (2007)
5. Yin, R.K.: Case Study Research: Design and Methods, vol. 5. Sage Publications, Incorporated (2008)
6. Hevner, A.R., March, S.T., Park, J., Ram, S.: Design Science in Information Systems Research. MIS Quarterly 28, 75–105 (2004)
7. Lazer, J., Fenq, J.H., Hochheiser, H.: Research Methods in Human-Computer Interaction. Wiley (2010)
8. Glaser, B.G., Strauss, A.L.: The Discovery of Grounded Theory: Strategies for Qualitative Research. Aldine de Gruyter (1967)

Improving the Process for Developing Augmented Objects: An HCI Perspective

Gustavo López Herrera, Mariana López, and Luis A. Guerrero

Centro de Investigaciones en Tecnologías de la Información y Comunicación,
Escuela de Ciencias de la Computación e Informática, Universidad de Costa Rica
gustavo.lopez_h@ucr.ac.cr,
{mariana.lopez,luis.guerrero}@ecci.ucr.ac.cr

Abstract. The process of designing and creating fine Augmented Objects is not an easy task. In this paper we state that Augmented Objects are just interfaces for specific software systems. In this way, the process of design, construction and testing of Augmented Objects should be part of a Software Engineering methodology, likewise Human Computer Interaction deals with software interfaces. A previously proposed methodology for creating Augmented Objects was evaluated. Three new augmented objects were created. Advantages and disadvantages for using this methodology for creating no-traditional interfaces are reported.

Keywords: Ambient Intelligence, Augmented Objects, Ubiquitous Computing, HCI.

1   Introduction

Since 1993 concepts like Ubiquitous Computing, Ambient Intelligence (AmI), and Augmented Objects have changed the way we see computational influence in the environment [1]. An augmented object is defined as a common object, which has been provided with additional functionalities through integrated computing or software systems [8]. With the heyday of the Internet of Things, the AmI and similar applications of computer science, the use of augmented objects to obtain information from and act over the environment has become very important. However, the design and development of fine augmented objects is not an easy task.

From our point of view, an augmented object is just a non-traditional interface for a computer system. Using augmented objects allows us to interact with a system (through the object), which sometimes is embedded in the same object, but in other cases is running as a specific server and the object only shows information from the system or sends information to it. According to this, we state that the process for designing and developing augmented objects should be part of a Software Engineering methodology, and should be submitted to HCI (Human-Computer Interaction) methods, in a similar way to regular interfaces.

Following this argumentation, it is necessary to define a process for collecting the requirements of the objects to be augmented, and for guiding the design, development

G. Urzaiz et al. (Eds.): UCAmI 2013, LNCS 8276, pp. 111–118, 2013.
© Springer International Publishing Switzerland 2013

and testing stages for the creation of objects that accomplish the requirements. Traditional software and hardware development process fail because they assume traditional interfaces will be developed. Traditional processes do not incorporate the analysis of common real objects in the solution context or the design of new features for these daily objects. Finally, the testing of the augmented objects is a very important activity that, of course, is not considered in traditional software and hardware development processes.

In this sense, Guerrero, Ochoa and Horta [1] have proposed a process perspective for the development of augmented objects known AODeP. In this research project we evaluated this proposal. We design and develop three different augmented objects applying the AODeP methodology; however we also apply HCI methods where we find necessary.

This article presents an improved methodology for analysis, design and evaluation of augmented object as no-traditional interfaces. The next section presents the original AODeP methodology. Section 3 focus on related work. Section 4 presents the way in which the methodology was evaluated in order to generate the proposed improvements presented in section 5. Finally section 6 presents the conclusions of our research.

2   Original Process Description

The use of augmented objects is one way to apply ubiquitous computing by adding computational functionalities to an object [1]. In a previous work, Guerrero et al. [1] proposed a process for developing augmented objects, called AODeP (Augmented Objects Development Process). A diagram explaining this process is shown in Figure 1. This section describes this process and its main characteristics.

AODeP is composed by 6 stages: Problem definition, AO usage context, Requirements definition, Selection of the object to be augmented, Development of the AO, and Testing with users.

The problem definition stage identifies restrictions and searches for opportunities that can be exploited in the development of an augmented object. The main idea of this stage is to obtain the initial set of functional requirements from a business perspective, in a similar way to the Requirement Engineering process.

Once the problem is well defined with a set of requirements the next step is the context definition of where the object will be used. Note that traditional Software Engineering process does not always worry about the context of use of the final application. However, because the interfaces of these systems will be specific objects, the context of use for these new objects acquires significant importance. In this way, the main idea of this stage is to obtain the set of functional and non-functional requirements of the system and the objects. The AODeP suggest different possibilities for achieving this step. All these possibilities regarding the context of use are well described and discussed in Guerrero et al. [1] and Alarcón et al. [3, 4].

The third stage of the process is the formal establishment of the requirements by gathering the information of the previous steps. The main idea of this stage is to create consensus between developers and users. Final users of the augmented objects (non traditional software interfaces of the system) should consider "natural" the new characteristics added to the objects. This point is very important because we want to minimize the mental effort required while the final users are using the objects, and we want to match the user's mental model of what that objects does and what information should be associated to that object.

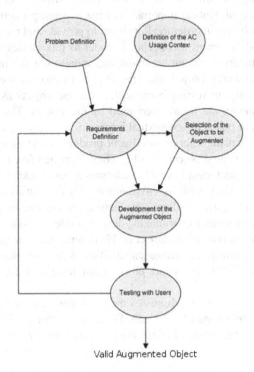

Fig. 1. Development process proposed in AODeP methodology

Once the requirements are properly established the process indicates that the next step is the selection of the object to be augmented. AODeP recommends using a syntactic and semantic analysis of the different options using twelve different dimensions: usage, feedback, history, intention, consequence, action, dependence, opportunity, access, roles, reach and view. Finally the last two steps are the construction of the augmented object and testing it with users.

3   Related Work

Many of the studies in the area of ubiquitous computing and augmented objects are strictly related with the use and communication of the objects but not with the development process itself. In most of those studies the topics of smart objects, the Internet of Things, and Pervasive Computing are being addressed, but most of them are presenting frameworks or solutions to specific problems founded in the development of the objects. Our research differs because it focuses on the development as a process with a real problem as the starting point.

For instance, Vega et al. [5] presented a method to standardize the communication of things through the Internet in order to allow the creation of smart spaces. This work states that the use of augmented objects is essential for incorporating computing in the environment and then feeding the Internet of Things with the information it needs. Works like Vega's et al. hints at importance of implementing a communication protocol on augmented objects in order to allow them to provide and receive information.

Hervas et al. [6] presented a conceptual model to link contextual information by augmenting the objects in the environment and monitoring the interaction with the users. Again this research project uses the objects as providers of the information. This case is especially interesting because they use the objects as holders of awareness marks that contain the information used by the system. The possibility for the augmented objects of providing contextual information is very significant.

Wong et al. [7] explain what an intelligent product is and their definition applies directly to what augmented objects can be. They described five primary characteristics an intelligent product must have: (1) Possesses a unique identity; (2) Is capable of communicating effectively with its environment; (3) Can retain or store data about itself; (4) Deploys a language to display its features, production, requirements etc. and (5) Is capable of participating in or making decisions relevant to its own destiny.

Using these characteristics Sanchez et al. [2] described a new model of five items: identity, sensing capabilities, actuation capabilities, decision-making and networking. The authors propose that any smart object must have at least a subset of these characteristics.

Most of the revised literature discusses the particular characteristics an augmented object should have in a particular domain. However we did not find works related to the design and implementation of augmented objects from a Software Engineering or HCI perspective.

4   Evaluation of a Previous Proposed Methodology

In order to evaluate and then trace possible improvements in the development process proposed by Guerrero et al. [1] we design and develop three different augmented objects following the previous proposed process. In this section we describe our experience utilizing this process for developing these three prototypes.

The first problem we addressed was a notification system for important emails (VIP emails). In this case, we wanted to enhance the visibility of certain emails as they arrive in the inbox, if the sender is important to the user. In order to deal with this requirement, we created a software app that utilizes a Gmail API and creates a filter according to the sender of the messages. In this way, the final user can create a list of "important senders" and the app filters the received messages. This functional requirement was easily solved for Gmail users. However, the most interesting problem was how to notify the arrival of VIP emails? In order to solve this problem we studied several objects in the context of use of the final user (a house or an office). We identified several candidates to become augmented objects. Finally, we decided to use a post-it note metaphor. In this way, when the user receives an important email the system would put a post-it note on the computer monitor. While developing this first augmented object we discovered that the proposed process didn't have an iterative cycle. Actual AODeP is like the waterfall diagram in Software Engineering because it is proposed in a linear process. However, a better approach would be an iterative and incremental series of cycles. Based on this observation, for this first problem space we followed an iterative design and implementation cycle based on user feedback gathered form diary studies.

We also discovered that AODeP involves many perspectives when gathering the requirements. In our case the development group was composed by 3 freshmen of Computer Science, 2 senior students, one graduate student and 3 computer science researchers. In this case, the AODeP fit very well in the work group.

The second prototype was a wearable system for babies that could monitor the baby's position 24/7 and would keep the parents informed about the baby through a mobile application. Several sensors can be added to these augmented clothes and data can be sent to parents or relatives through a monitoring application for instance: temperature, position (accelerometers), microphones, movements, luminosity, etc. While developing this second object we found that the testing part of the proposed process is not clearly defined. We propose that first it is necessary to test with users to validate the object, and afterwards to perform developer testing or functional testing in order to assert that the objects fulfils the functional and not functional requirements.

Finally in the third prototype we developed an augmented door that is able to give a message and to record the response of the user. This prototype follows the metaphor of the answering machines: if nobody answers, the machine plays a previously recorded message and records what the caller said. We decide to add a vibration sensor, a speaker, a camera and a microphone to an office door. When the system is activated and the vibration sensor detects that someone is knocking the door, a message like "nobody is in the office, please leave a message" is given through the speaker and the camera records the message and send it to a mobile app. However, some doubts appeared regarding the best candidate for augmentation when we were trying to design this object. We did not achieve a consensus for the best candidate object in this context. So, we found that before establishing the requirements it would be a good idea to develop a concept validation, and then we discovered that AODeP doesn't incorporate this possibility. A proof of concept, using the HCI technique called Wizard of Oz, was defined in order to evaluate the object before we set out to create the object.

5   Proposed Improvements to the Methodology

In this section we present a list of possible improvements for AODeP by incorporating the things we found while developing the three augmented objects already presented in section 4. Taking into account the taxonomy described by Sanchez et al. [2] which gives five characteristics of smart products (identity, sensing and actuation capabilities, decision making and networking), we decided that it would be a good idea to incorporate two of this characteristics in our augmented objects. These features were also incorporated in the design and development process.

The identity is a problem that has been addressed for many years. Fortunately, the implementation of IPV6 could be the answer to most of the identification problems. If an augmented object is going to have sensing capabilities (like in one of our examples) it should provide an API in order to offer the information gathered to other smart objects that may require it. Similar to the sensing capabilities, the actuation capabilities are given and restricted by the hardware used to develop the augmented object.

The networking capability is interesting and can be approached using some network standards. One particularly interesting approach is proposed by Vega et al. [5]. They present an open and scalable architecture that is service oriented. Finally, the decision-making capability varies depending on the objects that are being developed.

The first step of AODeP is the problem definition. That step could be evaluated observing users in context to reveal problems or other methods of inquiry in order to determine if the problem is correctly specified or if there is something missing. After testing the definition of the problem and the usage context the next validation point could be with a storyboard of the solution that is going to be provided and then with the feedback given by the consulted users the concept can be refined.

One characteristic of the AODeP that might be worth changing is the selection of the object to be augmented. The original process states, "Once concluded the analysis process, the developers could have more than one candidate object to be augmented. In such case, the decision about which object to augment becomes a decision that must be made in consensus between the developers and the users" [1]. We propose that if several objects are viable candidates the development team should validate with final users which one fits her needs best. For example, the team could create a prototype for those objects and once the prototypes are built and evaluated the final user can decide. In addition, if prototypes are hard to build, storyboards can be used to validate concepts before building the augmented objects.

The original AODeP indicates that the final users must be part of the problem solution. We have found that in stages 3 and 4 (requirement definition and selection of the object) it is a good idea to incorporate the use of storyboards to determine if the proposal is correct and if the objects are good enough to be considered as candidates.

Finally, AODeP suggests that the testing process must be done incrementally and present different states for testing the augmented objects. The first testing proof is project inception where the objective is to validate alternatives of solution. Once the implementation starts the AODeP proposes that all prototypes must be evaluated with users. We suggest that the evaluation of the objects must be executed since the beginning of the process. As well, we introduce new ways to test prototypes, such as diary studies to test our concept in the real context of use and Wizard of Oz prototypes to test confidence levels and object characteristics. Figure 2 presents a new diagram that incorporates the improvements proposed to AODeP methodology.

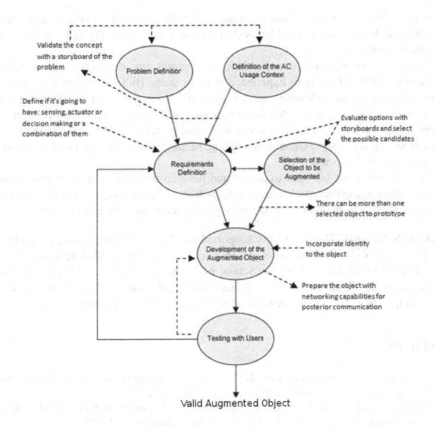

Fig. 2. Diagram of the development process with the proposed improvements

6   Conclusions and Further Work

A "fine" augmented object is an object as natural that we do not need to think in their new functionality. That is, the mental effort for using the object is the minimum, and the final users consider it similar to any other daily object. In this way, the process for creation fine augmented objects was the main objective of our project.

In this paper project we report the evaluation of a previously proposed methodology for developing augmented objects. We design and develop three different objects using this methodology and we find some strength and weakness while using this methodology. A new proposal of an improved methodology was presented. The new version is an iterative and incremental methodology because new features can be obtained in the testing phase and these new requirements must be evaluated and incorporated in the design phase of a new version of the augmented objects.

One of the main questions we asked ourselves during this exercise was: how can we evaluate the usability of an augmented object? The answer is not obvious. In fact we designed the methodology so that the evaluation of the objects is executed as part of the process. We proposed two ways to evaluate the future augmented objects:

Wizard of Oz and Scripting. Both techniques are well known in the HCI area, and we verified that both of them could be used in the process of designing and constructing augmented objects.

During the last year we incorporated into our group new assistants (undergraduate students), which did not have experience in these areas. HCI and augmented objects were very strange and unknown concepts for them. However, when we explained our proposed methodology and stated that augmented objects are just no-traditional interfaces to software systems, the concept was quickly grasped. We accomplished the goal of seeing the design, creation and testing of augmented objects as part of a Software Engineering process.

As a further work we need to design and develop more augmented objects using the improved methodology. We need also to work in enhancing the usability of the augmented objects, in order to define more precise techniques for testing them.

Acknowledgments. This work was supported by CITIC (*Centro de Investigaciones en Tecnologías de la Información y Comunicación*) at Universidad de Costa Rica, grand No. 834-B2-228 and by the School of Computer Science and Informatics at Universidad de Costa Rica. In the project also participated: Christopher Sanchez, Daniela Quesada, Lucia Gonzalez, Brandon Alvarez and Daniel Bonilla.

References

1. Guerrero, L.A., Ochoa, S.F., Horta, H.: Developing Augmented Objects: A Process Perspective. Journal of Universal Computer Science, 1612–1632 (2010)
2. Sánchez, T., Chinthana, D., Patkai, B., McFarlane, D.: Taxonomy, technology and applications of smart objects. Journal of Information Systems Frontiers, 281–300 (2011)
3. Alarcón, R., Guerrero, L.A., Ochoa, S.F., Pino, J.: Analysis and Design of Mobile Collaborative Applications using Contextual Elements. Computing and Informatics, 469–496 (2006)
4. Guerrero, L.A., Ochoa, S.F., Pino, J.A., Collazos, C.: Selecting Devices to Support Mobile Collaboration. Group Decision and Negotiation, 243–271 (2006)
5. Vega, M., Casado, D., Valero, M.: Smart Spaces and Smart Objects interoperability Architecture (S^3OiA). In: Conference on Innovative Mobile and Internet Services in Ubiquitous Computing, pp. 725–730 (2012)
6. Hervás, R., Bravo, J., Fontecha, J.: Awareness marks: adaptive services through user interactions with augmented objects. In: Personal and Ubiquitous Computing, pp. 409–418 (2011)
7. Wong, C.Y., McFarlane, D., Zaharudin, A.H., Agarwal, V.: The intelligent product driven supply chain. In: Proceedings of the IEEE International Conference on Systems, Man and Cybernetics (2002)
8. Ishii, H., Ullmer, B.: Tangible bits: towards seamless interfaces between people, bits and atoms. In: Proceedings of the ACM SIGCHI Conference on Human Factors in Computing Systems, pp. 234–241 (1997)

Tangible Interfaces and Virtual Worlds: A New Environment for Inclusive Education

Juan Mateu[1], María José Lasala[2], and Xavier Alamán[1]

[1] Universidad Autónoma de Madrid (UAM), Madrid, Spain
juan.mateu@estudiante.uam.es, xavier.alaman@uam.es
[2] IES Ernest Lluch, Cunit, Tarragona Spain
mlasala3@xtec.cat

Abstract. In this paper we present an educational application that integrates virtual worlds with tangible interfaces, in what is called "mixed reality", using Kinect and OpenSim as the base technologies. The paper also discusses an experience on applying such technology for the inclusion at a concrete high school in Cunit (Spain). In the initial experiments, the use of mixed reality has shown a great potential for these education requirements.

Keywords: virtual worlds, tangible user interfaces, natural user interface, inclusive education, e-learning, mixed reality.

1   Introduction

In our society, social differences such as language, culture, religion, gender, and socioeconomic status are certainly present at schools. Inclusive education tries to engage all students at the school, offering them equal opportunities regardless of their differences (gifted students, immigrants or students with disabilities) and avoiding segregation or isolation.

This paper focuses on inclusive education for immigrant children that do not know the language and culture of the country where they have recently arrived. Teachers develop a variety of activities that allow students to learn the language and culture, as well as to develop other skills. Many of these activities can be improved making use of computer technologies.

This paper proposes the blend of virtual worlds -which provide a simulated 3D environment- and tangible and natural interfaces -where we use a Microsoft Kinect device to recognize gestures and shapes-.

Kinect devices have been already used successfully for educational purposes. There are communities such as KinectEducation [1] that promote the use of Kinect in the classrooms. An interesting project that allows programming with Scratch using Microsoft Kinect is Kinect2Scratch [2]. Kinect can be used for inclusive education, i.e. for helping children with autism allowing them to interact with videogames and to practice movements that they have difficulties performing.

G. Urzaiz et al. (Eds.): UCAmI 2013, LNCS 8276, pp. 119–126, 2013.

In this paper we propose the use of a Kinect device to enrich a virtual world environment with two types of activities: Natural User Interface (NUI) activities that use gestures to interact with the virtual world and Tangible User Interfaces (TUI) activities that use wooden blocks to interact with the virtual world. The combination of NUI and TUI interactions on a virtual world provides many advantages that will allow the students a more meaningful learning.

2   Virtual Worlds and Inclusive Education

A three-dimensional virtual world is a networked desktop virtual reality in which users move and interact in simulated 3D spaces (Dickey [3]). Virtual worlds allow to work under different educational approaches such as constructivist learning, collaborative learning, situated learning, active learning and role playing.

Many of these learning paradigms cannot be used easily in a traditional classroom. The use of virtual worlds may improve this situation. For example, virtual worlds may allow the students to travel to ancient Egypt to learn about the culture, visit the pyramids, interact with residents, etc.

Virtual worlds have tools that allow voice and text chat, which can be used to learn or improve language skills. According to Babu [4], avatar mediated interactions can facilitate verbal and non-verbal social communication skills.

Virtual worlds can provide the opportunity to try out alternative social interactions reflecting upon feelings and thoughts (Sheehy & Ferguson [5]). Therefore, virtual worlds can be used for inclusive education.

"Accessibility in Virtual Worlds" is an example of a virtual world project aimed to blind students. The position is communicated by sound, allowing blind students to navigate the virtual world and to interact with other students (Sheehy [6]).

Another example of using virtual worlds for inclusion is Brigadoon. Brigadoon is a private island in Second Life aimed to Autism or Asperger Syndrome people, where students can improve their social skills without face to face interactions. Students can build objects in a virtual world, sitting and chatting with other people in a virtual garden, sailing boats, and in general performing activities that provide them new experiences.

Finally, Espurnik Project [7] it is a project that, among other things, tries to facilitate the adaptation and integration of immigrant students to high-school. In this project, there are a lot of activities using virtual worlds where students can learn language abilities, cultural aspects and achieve other skills.

3   Virtual Worlds and Tangible Interfaces in Education

The term "tangible user interface" (TUI) is proposed by Ishii & Ullmer [8] as an extension of the conceptual framework "graspable user interface" proposed by Fitzmaurice [9] in order to link the physical and digital worlds. Tangible interfaces provide a number of advantages:

- Development of motor and cognitive skills through physical activity.
- Development and improvement of collaborative and social skills.
- Learning made more intuitive by the "hands-on" approach.
- Increased interest and motivation of students.

Table 1 lists some of the educational projects which make use of tangible interfaces. As we can see in the table, the tangible elements are generally used for teaching abstract concepts such as programming or mathematics, and are more effective at earlier ages. Although our proposal is aimed at inclusive education, our tangible interfaces can be extrapolated to other areas such as chemistry, geometry, etc. On the other hand, most of the projects shown in Table 1 are very specific for a particular area and can be hardly extrapolated to other areas.

Furthermore, our system uses a cheap and simple infrastructure (it just needs a Kinect device and a few pieces of wood) while most of the other projects in Table 1 require a more complex infrastructure.

Many of these projects reflect the actions of tangible interfaces in fixed applications, such as in AlgoBlock (Suzuki [16]) where the student has to guide a submarine on the computer screen. In our case, the use of a virtual world as the user interface allows the design of quite different learning spaces where you can interact anytime and from anywhere simply by using a viewer. Kinect provides an intuitive and natural interaction through body movements, voice and gestures allowing physical activities. Therefore, our project takes the benefits of both TUI and NUI paradigms using the same infrastructure.

4   Description and Implementation of the System

The system described in this paper is based on a virtual world which is managed using a Kinect device, by means of gestures (NUI interactions) and tangible interfaces (TUI interactions).

OpenSimulator [19] is used as the virtual world platform. Various educational spaces are defined within the virtual world, where students can perform different activities allowing them to practice language skills (see Figure 1). Students can interact with other students and teachers in real time through their avatars (their representations in the virtual world), making extensive use of language in a specific context (situated learning).For example, the students can practice speaking while being at a store, a bank, etc.

Two kinds of interaction were used for these educational spaces: gestures and tangible artifacts. To enable this, a middleware was developed for the communication between the Kinect device and the virtual world.

In order to develop the middleware we used the Visual Studio 2012 as programming environment and several third party libraries: Kinect library SDK 1.7. [20], LibOpenMetaverse [21], and OpenCV libraries [22].

Kinect provides a good support for skeleton tracking and gesture recognition but it is not so good at object detection or recognition. A complementary library for blob recognition called OpenCV was used to overcome this. OpenCV (Open Source

Table 1. Tangible interfaces in education

Author	Project Description	Types of Tangible	Main Goals	Ages or level
Africano [10]	Explore different cultures through the adventures of a fictional character	Postcards, multitouch table, camera, **Ely the explorer** (a computer character on the screen)	Promote collaborative learning, teaching geography and foreign cultures	6-12
Horn [11]	Learn computer programming with tangible programming languages	**Quetzal** (language for controlling LEGO Mindstorm robots), **Tern** (language for controlling virtual robots on a computer screen)	Teaching computer programming using a physical interface	K-12
Raffle [12]	Reconfigurable robotic set of tools with kinetic memory	**Topobo**	Develop sensory capabilities, control their own learning process, learn through personal exploration, enhance creativity	5-13
Scharf [13]	Haptic programmable bricks	**Tangicons**	Learn first steps of programming	7
Gallardo [14]	Tangible programming language	**Turtan** (based on Logo)	Teaching programming for non-programmers	Children
Suzuki [15]	Tangible videogame (guiding a submarine on the computer screen)	**AlgoBlock**	Teaching programming skills, collaborative learning	Children
Stringer [16]	TUI-supported rethorical applications	**WebKit**	Teaching rethorical skills	Children
Zuckerman [17]	SystemBlocks: simulations, dynamic models . FlowBlock: mathematical concepts (couting ,probability...)	**Flow Blocks, System Blocks**	Teaching abstract concepts	4-11
Stanton [18]	Collaborative storytelling technologies	**Magic carpet**	Collaborative learning	5-7

Fig. 1. Activities in a virtual world

Computer Vision) is a powerful library under BSD license used to develop computer vision applications in areas such as augmented reality, robotics, surveillance, object detection, etc. Here the OpenCV library is used for recognition of simple shapes, such as squares, circles and triangles. LibOpenMetaverse is the .NET based client/server library used for accessing and creating 3D virtual worlds. LibOpenMetaverse is used to link the virtual world with the Kinect device. A bot was created to communicate with the virtual world by sending messages. When a certain block (i.e. cube) is shown, the Kinect device detects the shape (using OpenCV libraries), which in turn is created in the virtual world using LibOpenMetaverse (see figure 2).

The Figure 3 shows the prototype. In the real world there are tangible interfaces (wooden blocks) that are recognized by Kinect, the result being reflected in the virtual world, offering a "mixed reality" experience.

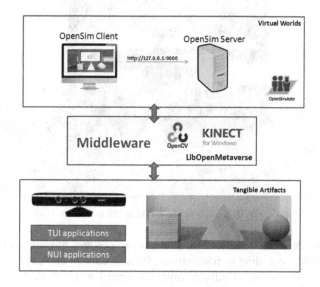

Fig. 2. Architecture of the system

5   Case Study: Applying the System for Inclusive Education at High-School

The system has been tested at a public high school with a high ratio of immigrant children. The IES Ernest Lluch is located at Cunit (north-east of Spain) where the working language is Catalan. New students from other countries (Ukraine, England, China, Morocco…) need to learn Catalan language to follow correctly the rest of classes, as well as to integrate adequately into the local society

In order to integrate these children, the Catalonian Educational System has created the "Welcome Course", where students receive special training several hours per day to learn Catalan language, cultural aspects and other basic skills. The welcome course normally covers ages from 12 to 16, each student being assigned an Intensive Individualized Plan with the adequate curricular adaptations.

Some educational activities were prepared to see the degree of acceptance of the proposed technologies among immigrant students. The work was done in the context of a telematic network called Xtec [23] which has a section of activities and materials for students who participate in "Welcome courses".

Within the developed virtual world, students can explore a virtual island where there are various educational activities to learn new concepts about Catalan and they also can practice speaking through interaction with other students or teachers using the text chat and voice chat.

Fig. 3. Virtual world and tangible interfaces

As an example of NUI interaction, students use gestures to change clock digits in the virtual world, according to instructions given in Catalan language. When the student finishes, she receives feedback from the virtual world indicating whether the activity was correctly done.

As an example of TUI interaction, tangible wooden blocks may represent concepts. For example, the cube represents a noun, the triangle represents a verb and the sphere represents the adjective (see Figures 3 and 4). Different words are shown in the virtual world and the student has to select the correct wooden block for each one.

Another similar activity with the same representation of the blocks (cube as a noun, triangle as a verb, and sphere as an adjective) consists of a set of incomplete sentences where students must guess what kind of word should go in the missing hole. All activities are performed inside the virtual world, and there is feedback indicating whether it has been successful or not.

Our goal is to provide in the future more tangible elements to the system, and to capture also the positions of each block, creating composite shapes. Finally we want to create a toolkit that will allow the teacher to customize the activities.

Fig. 4. Student interacting with the tangible interface

6   Conclusions and Future Work

We have developed a system that combines virtual worlds and tangible interfaces using OpenSim and Kinect technologies, providing a "mixed reality" experience. A prototype has been developed for inclusive education, and a first experience was carried out in a specific high school in Cunit (Tarragona). The case study presented in this paper will be further worked into a full fledged experiment, where we expect to be able to analyze in deep the efficiency and accuracy of the approach.

The work described in this paper was partially funded by the Spanish National Plan of I+D+i (TIN2010-17344).

References

1. Kinect Education, http://www.kinecteducation.com/ (accessed on September 15, 2013)
2. Kinect2Scratch, http://scratch.saorog.com/ (accessed on September 15, 2013)

3. Dickey, M.D.: Three-dimensional virtual worlds and distance learning: Two case studies of Active Worlds as a medium for distance education. British Journal of Educational Technology 36(3), 439–451 (2005)

4. Babu, S., Suma, E., Hodges, L.: Can immersive virtual humans teach social conversational protocols? In: IEEE Virtual Reality Conference, NC, March 10-14 (2007)

5. Sheehy, K., Ferguson, R.: Educational inclusion, new technologies. In: Scott, T.B., Livingston, J.L. (eds.) Leading Edge Educational Technology. Nova Science, NY (2008)

6. Sheehy, K.: Virtual Environments: Issues and Opportunities for Researching Inclusive Educational Practices. In: Peachey, A., Gillen, J., Livingstone, D., Smith-Robbins, S. (eds.) Researching Learning in Virtual Worlds. Human Computer Interaction Series (2010)

7. Peterson, M.: Towards a research agenda for the use of three-dimensional virtual worlds in language learning. CALICO Journal 29(1), 67–80 (2011)

8. Espurna, http://www.espurna.cat (accessed on September 15, 2013)

9. Ishii, H., Ullmer, B.: Tangible Bits: Towards Seamless Interfaces between People, Bits, and Atoms. In: Proceedings of CHI 1997, pp. 234–241 (1997)

10. Fitzmaurice, G.W., Ishii, H., Buxton, W.: Laying the Foundations for Graspable User Interfaces. In: Published in the Proceedings of CHI, May 7-11. ACM Press (2001)

11. Africano, D., Berg, S., Lindbergh, K., Lundholm, P., Nilbrink, F., Persson, A.: Designing tangible interfaces for children's collaboration. Paper Presented at the CHI 2004 Extended Abstracts on Human Factors in Computing Systems, pp. 853–868 (2004)

12. Horn, M.S., Jacob, R.J.K.: Designing Tangible Programming Languages for Classroom Use. In: Proceedings of TEI 2007. First International Conference on Tangible and Embedded Interaction (2007)

13. Raffle, H., Parkes, A., Ishii, H.: Topobo: A constructive Assembly System with Kinetic Memory. In: Proceedings of CHI 2004, pp. 869–877. ACM Press (2004)

14. Scharf, F., Winkler, T., Herczeg, M.: Tangicons: algorithmic reasoning in a collaborative game for children in kindergarten and first class. Paper presented at the Proceedings of 7th International Conference on Interaction Design and Children, pp. 242–249 (2008)

15. Gallardo, D., Julià, C.F., Jordà, S.: Turtan: A tangible Programming Language for Creative Exploration. In: Proceedings of TABLETOP 2008, pp. 95–98. IEEE, Los Alamitos (2008)

16. Suzuki, H., Kato, H.: AlgoBlock: a tangible programming language, a tool for collaborative learning. In: Proceeedings of the 4th European Logo Conference (Eurologo 1993), Athens, Greece, pp. 297–303 (1993)

17. Stringer, M., Toye, E., Rode, J., Blackwell, A.F.: Teaching Rethorical Skills with Tangible User Interface. In: Proceedings of IDC 2004, pp. 11–18. ACM Press, New York (2004)

18. Zuckerman, O., Arida, S., Mitchel, R.: Extending Tangible Interfaces for Education: Digital Montessori-inspired Manipulatives. In: Proc. of CHI 2005, pp. 859–868 (2005)

19. Stanton, D., Bayon, V., Neale, H., Ghali, A., Benford, S., Cobb, S., Ingram, R., Wilson, J., Pridmore, T., O'Malley, C.: Classroom collaboration in the design of tangible interfaces for storytelling. In: CHI 2001 Seattle, pp. 482–489. ACM Press, Seattle (2001)

20. OpenSimulator, http://www.opensimulator.org (accessed on September 15, 2013)

21. Kinect for Windows,
http://www.microsoft.com/en-us/kinectforwindows/
(accessed on September 15, 2013)

22. LibOpenMetaverse, http://www.openmetaverse.org (accessed on September 15, 2013)

23. OpenCV, http://opencv.org (accessed on September 15, 2013)

24. Xtec, http://www.xtec.cat/web/projectes/alumnatnou (accessed on September 15, 2013)

Movement-Based and Tangible Interactions to Offer Body Awareness to Children with Autism

Rodrigo Zalapa and Monica Tentori

Computer Science Department, CICESE
{czalapa,mtentori}@cicese.mx

Abstract. Children with autism have sensory processing disorders impairing their ability of having awareness of their body and movementsso theyfrequently exhibit "atypical" body-interactions they useas "compensatory movements". In this paper, we explore how tangible computing could offer to children with autism the body awareness they need during sensory therapies. We describe the design and development of Sensory Paint, a system that enables children with autism to control a multisensory environment using body-based and tangible interactions. Sensory Paint displays the shadow of the user to provide "biofeedback," monitors users' "atypical movements" to adjust the instrumental music playing in the background, and tracks users' interactions with balls to change colors. Sensory Paint uses the kinect sensor and computer vision techniques for recognizing user interactions. The results of a performance evaluation of the use of SensoryPaint with 10 users shows SensoryPaint is accurate, easy to use, fun, and engaging.

Keywords: Tangible computing, movement-based interactions, autism, object recognition, Kinect.

1   Introduction

Many children with autism have sensory processing disorders (e.g.,[1], [2]); they are hypersensitive or under-sensitive to light([1]), sounds ([2]), and touch ([1]; [3]) –for example, some children with autism hardly bear the sound of a dishwasher or do not tolerate some clothing textures. As a consequence children with autism experience poor behavior [4] and motor skills, displaying "atypical" body-interactions that frequently act as "compensatory movements" helping them to have some sense of agency when interacting with the world ([3]). Therapies for sensory processing disorders involve the use of multisensory environments (MSE) saturated with multimedia information and specialized equipment that reactively offer children with autism their needed sensory stimulation.

A psychologist personalizes a "sensory diet" taking into account each child sensory needs specifying the time and quantity each child needs to "interact" with a particular element of the environment (e.g., a child must play 10 minutes with a fiber-optic rope for visual stimulation). However, children with autism are mainly reactive to stimulus during sensory therapies often disengaged from the therapy, and when

G. Urzaiz et al. (Eds.): UCAmI 2013, LNCS 8276, pp. 127–134, 2013.

they run out of new ways to "interacting" with such environment, they abandon the therapy unable to reach their sensory goals.

Current new models on tangible computing with their ability to control ubiquitous environments with body-movements could empower current MSEs with the "effective interactivity" children with autism need to be more proactive and engaged during sensory therapies. Second, such "interactive MSE" could help children with autism to understand how their actions and experienced sensations have a counterpart in the real world –giving them sense of agency about their body and movements.

We hypothesize that an "interactive MSE" that takes into account users' body movements as an implicit input to adapt such environment could provide the much-needed engagement children with autism need during sensory therapies, and give them feedback about their body and movements. In this paper, we describe the design (section 3), development (section 4), and evaluation (section 5) of SensoryPaint, an interactive MSE that integrates the physical and the digital world to enable children with autism to control visual and audio stimulus through movement-based and tangible interactions, and gives them feedback about their body and movements.

2   Related Work

Research in ubiquitous computing suggests tangible and movement-based interactions are appropriate to support sensory impairments.

Tangible computing has proposed some devices and applications to support sensory disorders, some of them in support of children with autism (e.g., Mediate [5]). Some projects have researched how to use haptic technology to stimulate the "tactile experience" of individuals (e.g., TouchMe and squeeze me [6], Therapeutic Holdig ([7]) helping them to be more tolerant to touch and textures. Other projects have crafted specialized devices to support musical therapies (e.g., Reactable ([8], [9]), Tap and play ([10])) and provide visual stimuli (e.g., ReactTable [8], T3 [11]) to help individuals deal with sensory disorders related to sounds and light. Although these projects have argue that integrating the physical and the digital world supports sensory impairments little has been said about how these "tangible interactions" could give individuals sense of agency about their body and movements.

In this direction, research exploring new models for body-based interactions to give individuals feedback about their movements has mainly explored how to support the motor skills of individuals or how to promote exercising (e.g. exergaming station [12]). These projects have prove being effective in offering "body awareness"(e.g. Mediate [5]) to individuals; however, little has been said about how this body of work could take advantage of the use of physical objects and tangible interactions to engage children with such environments.

Building upon this body of work,in this paper we explore how to take the advantage of the "affordances" of objects (i.e., tangible interactions) to keep children with autism "on task" and engaged during therapies, and how tangible interactions could be integrated with an interaction model that provides "body awareness" to provide effective "interactivity" in a MSE.

3   SensoryPaint: An Interactive Multisensory Environment

We conducted a qualitative study to inform the design of SensoryPaint and uncover the type of interactions children with autism experienceduring sensory therapies. The study followed a contextual inquiry process, including interviews with physiologists (n=2) and therapists (n=4), and 3 hrs. of passive observation of children with autism attending to sensory therapies. Data was analyzed following the techniques to derive grounded theory and rapid contextual design.

3.1   The Interaction Experience of Sensory Therapies

We found out sensory therapies involve a combination of the use of the elements of an MSE to expose children with autism to different visual and audio stimulus, the use of balls and toys to teach children with autism to tolerate a variety of textures and fabrics, and the use of a mirror to give children with autism "biofeedback" –a process of gaining body awareness using your sensory channels (i.e. sight, taste).

Our results indicate children with autism like to play with balls, as these objects have the appropriate affordances to let children be engaged during sensory therapies, and could be transformed to specific colors and textures children need as stimulus. So children move balls around, throw them against walls, or use them to adjust the MSE by tapping on projected objects (e.g., using a ball to hit a star projected in the wall).

To provide "biofeedback" physiologistsplace children in front of a mirror and ask them to move their body(e.g., move your hands from side to side) oridentify their body parts (e.g., "where is your nose?"), so they can gain a sense of awareness of their body and movements. As the MSE is filled with stimulus children frequently ignore the mirror missing the opportunities of improving "biofeedback". So there is a tradeoff between the pervasive stimulation children need and it is provided by the MSE, and the subtle but perceptible "biofeedback" children with autism need and gain when using the mirror. To balance this tradeoff we used movement-based and tangible interactions to design an interactive MSE that takes the advantage of the affordances of balls and mimics the mirror therapy.

3.2   Designing SensoryPaint

Following an interactive user-centered design methodology we iteratively envision several low-fidelity prototypes mimicking the interaction experience of children with autism during sensory therapies. The low-fidelity prototypes were discussed during several participatory design sessions that help us to select the more appropriate proto-type balancing interactivity and "biofeedback".

We envisioned an interactive MSE like a "virtual interactive cave" that enables children to paint in walls using different kinds of brushes and their body to control the instrumental music playing within the cave and the intensity of the color used to paint in the wall (Figure 2). Brushes are balls wearing "skins" of different textures (e.g., rice).To interact with the interactive MSE the child could: (a) move the ball to draw the trajectory (Figure 1 left); (b) throw or kick the ball to create "painting effects" in the form of "splashes" drawn at the contact point (Figure 1 middle);and (c) adjust the music when the child move different parts of his body to adjust the instrumental music being played (Figure 1 right).Here we present a scenario of the use of the system.

Fig. 1. An interactive MSE. A child with autism using balls to draw shapes in the wall (left) and throw balls towards the wall (middle). A child with autism adjusting the instrumental music being played within the cave

Victor is a 5 year-old children with autism who is under sensitive to plastic and fabric textures. Victor enters the interactive MSE and his shadow is projected in the walls to provide him "biofeedback". The teacher Bella gives Victor a box filled of balls with different plastic and fabric textures. Victor starts crying when seeing the textures. Then, the system prompts Victor showing an animation of a child throwing the ball towards the wall. Victor mimics the animation and throws the ball. The ball trajectory is painted in the wall, and a "splash" is drawn at the contact point where the ball fell. When Victor sees the painting, he grabs another ball and moves it from side to side. While Victor moves the ball, a line is being painted in the wall. Then Victor smashes the ball in the wall and it splashes. Victor laughs. Victor changes the ball to use another texture to paint. Victor successfully finishes the therapy.

To further engage the children with autism, the system optionally provides goal-oriented tasks enabling children with autism to draw geometric shapesSensoryPaint randomly displays (e.g., circle, rectangle), oruse the ball to hit a target moving randomly every 5 sec.

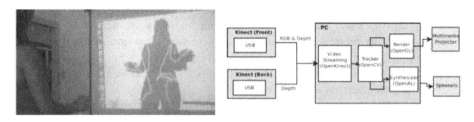

Fig. 2. The SensoryPaint System. A user receiving "biofeedback", and using a yellow and a blue ball to draw (left) The architecture of SensoryPaint (right).

4   Implementing SensoryPaint

We implemented SensoryPaint using the kinect sensor (Figure 2 left). We used
OpenCV to recognize objects, their colors and forms, OpenGL for the 3D rendering,
and openAL to adjust an audio multichannel. The architecture of SensoryPaint is
composed by three main subsystems (Figure 2 right).

4.1   Tracker

This subsystemis responsible for tracking the ball's position, inferring when the ball
hits a surface, and detecting when the child disengages from the therapy.

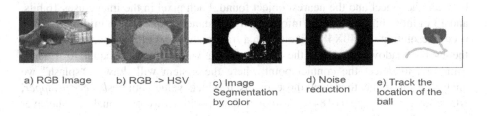

a) RGB Image   b) RGB -> HSV   c) Image Segmentation by color   d) Noise reduction   e) Track the location of the ball

Fig. 3. Image transformations to track its position ball. The original RGB image (a) the RGB
image in its HSV form (b) the image segmented (c) the image after noise is reduced (d) the
"centroid" of the ball located (e).

Tracking the Ball. We use the color and the form of the ball to detect its position
(Figure 3).First, we transformed the image extracted from the kinect's camera from
the RBG model into an HSV model. Then, we segmented the transformed HSV image
(Figure 3a) using thresholding technique [13]. We extracted the pixels that match
a"source color"according to a threshold X=[lower, upper] we pre-defined (e.g., blue
in the case of Figure 3).Then, we obtain a binary imagewith 0xff where the color
matches the "source color" (e.g., the pixels are blue, Figure 3)-, and 0 for the rest of
the colors in the scene (Figure 3c).Then, we reduced the noise (Figure 3d)isolating the
pixels that do not match the form of the original object.

We used the morphological operations of erode to eliminate the little spots that do
not match the form of the binary image (1), andthenwe dilatedthe binary image
connecting the isolated points (2).

$$erode(x,y) = min\ src(x+x',y+y') \tag{1}$$

$$dilate(x,y) = max\ src(x+x',y+y')^1 \tag{2}$$

---

[1] Where x' and y' belong to the Kernel –a small solid square or disk with the anchor point at
the center, in this case we use a rectangular kernel.

Once we reduced the noise from the binary image, we calculated the centroid of the ball and store its position to determine where to paint the line (Figure 3e).For this, we calculated the position (x,y) of the object's centroid using the image moment [13] (3). Then, we define the ball's centroid c(x,y) with an area of $m_{0,0}$(3).

$$m_{p,q} = {}_{i=1}\Sigma^n \ I(x,y)x^p y^q, x_c = m_{1,0}/m_{0,0} \ ; \ y_c = m_{0,1}/m_{0,0} \qquad (3)$$

To draw a line we monitor the variation of the ball's position considering an α value to guarantee the user is significantly moving the ball (4).

$$\|C - C_{past}\| > \alpha \qquad (4)$$

Tracking Depth. We used the kinect's depth camera to infer when a ball hits a wall, and to display the shadow of the user. The depth camera sends a stream of distances between the kinect and the nearest object found. Each pixel in the image uses 16 bits, and 13 of those bits contain the information of distances expressed in millimeters. We used a resolution of 640X480 pixels with a frame rate of 30 FPS. Then, we reproduce the user's shadow extracting the pixels with a value of 1678 (equal to 1.68m). Similarly, to detect the contact point where the system will draw a "splash" we analyze each frame to detect those pixels p which value satisfies $lower < p < upper$, where lower=180, upper=184. . To reduce false positives we only analyze whenever the <<tracker>> detects a variation –meaning the ball is moving.

4.2 Rendererand Synthesizer

When the <<tracker>> subsystem detects one of the abovementioned triggers (*i.e.*, ball movement, "atypical" movement, and a ball contact) given a time t, it communicates this information to the <<rendering>> subsystem which retrieves the appropriate visualization or to the <<synthesizer>> which adjust the sound accordingly. These<<subsystems>>are organized in layers.

5   Usability and Performance Evaluation

We evaluated the usability and performance of SensoryPaint through a controlled experiment with 10 computer science students (age: 23-32, 7 male), and one non-verbal child with autism (age: 9, male). We choose this population to gain feedback about the design of the system, and get a sense of the potential impact of the system with a pilot case. SensoryPaint was installed using two kinect cameras: one in front of the user at 40 cm from the floor, to capture RGB images; and the other one placed in the back at 2.24 m, to capture depth images. We placed the multimedia projector at a height of 2.75 m and at 3.5 m from the screen.

Evaluation sessions were videotaped an lasted around 20 minutes with each participant. During the evaluation participants: (1) use a ball to draw a circle, a triangle, and a square, and (2) throw a ball towards the wall to hit a target moving left, right, up, and down. We used three different ball sizes (i.e., small, medium, and large), and with different colors, to test the performance of our algorithm against form and color.

Participants also had the opportunity to use the system freely.Participants were interviewed about the experiences on using the system.

Overall, participants found SensoryPaint *"easy to use and attractive"*.All participants described the interaction model of Sensory as "intuitive" and explained that they very rapidly learned how to use the system, with almost no instructions from researchers.

"I found [SensorPaint] very intuitive, I just need to throw or bounce the ball and [SensoryPaint] reacts"(p2).

Participants found the system attractive and engaging (8/10), they found new ways for interacting with the system, and were very creative when painting in the wall.

We measured the precision and accuracy of the system to detect when a child hits the wall and the ability of the system to correctly display a "splash" effect with different ball sizes and colors. We asked participants to throw the ball 20 times for each ball size and color.

Table 1. Confusion matrix of the percentage of instances the algorithm correctly detects children hitting the target displayed in the wall with three different ball sizes

	Small ball		Medium ball		Large ball	
	Hit	No hit	Hit	No hit	Hit	No hit
Hit	43.75 %	5 %	81.5%	12.25%	94.5%	58.75%
No hit	56.25%	95%	18.5%	87.5%	5.25%	56.25%

We did not find major differences when using different ball colors, but our results indicate our algorithm is sensitive to ball sizes (Table 1). When users used the small ball the number of false positives were very few (5%); however, the accuracy for detecting when the ball hits the wall is low. With the bigger ball the systems successfully identified when the ball hits the wall (94%), but, the system missed one of every two hits –i.e., there were more false positives. In contrast, the medium ball performed accurate –with more than 80% of hits registered. Overall, the SensoryPaint has good performance in the worst scenario –i.e., the small ball.Our results indicate participants' height influenced the performance of SensoryPaint. SensoryPaint performed 30% better with participants with height between 1.58-1.70m (n=5) than with participants with height between 1.71-1.80m, using the medium ball. The shadow of the user and the kinect's elevation angle also affected SensoryPaint performance. This indicates that the systems should desirable personalized to each participant's height to increase recognition accuracy, mostly in kinect elevation angle.

We measured how many times participants were aware of their "projected shadow" to investigate how much "body awareness" SensoryPaint provides to users. Our results indicate users are highly aware of their "projected shadow" when freely using the system (80%), but when playing with the goal-oriented activities users were highly distracted from gaining "body awareness" (5%). This shows the importance of balancing interactivity and "biofeedback". Most participants (9/10) explained that using SensoryPaint increased their "body awareness".

"While drawing I am more aware of my movements, because I notice how the balls are moving and the painting coming out of the ball " (p3)

6   Conclusions

The primary contribution of this work was to articulate and explore the design space of using tangible computing to provide body awareness to children with autism. Our results indicate integrating the tangible and body-based interactions are good constructs for controlling MSEs, and building such system is accurate enough to deploy it in naturalistic conditions and with a considerable amount of users and objects. We are conducting a deployment evaluation of the system with children with autism to explore the impact of an "interactive MSE", an specifically the impact of Sensory Paint, during the sensory therapies of children with autism.

References

[1] Leekam, S., Nieto, C., Libby, S., Wing, L., Gould, J.: Describing the Sensory Abnormalities of Children and Adults with Autism. J. Autism Dev. Disord. 37(5), 894–910 (2007)

[2] Tomchek, S.D., Dunn, W.: Sensory processing in children with and without autism: a comparative study using the short sensory profile. Am. J. Occup. Ther. Off. Publ. Am. Occup. Ther. Assoc. 61(2), 190–200 (2007)

[3] Ornitz, E.M.: The modulation of sensory input and motor output in autistic children. J. Autism Dev. Disord. 4(3), 197–215 (1974)

[4] Beaudry Bellefeuille, I.: Un trastorno en el procesamiento sensorial es frecuentemente la causa de problemas de aprendizaje, conducta y coordinación motriz en niños. SCCALP / ERGON 46(197) (July 2006)

[5] Parés, N., Carreras, A., Durany, J., Ferrer, J., Freixa, P., Gómez, D., Kruglanski, O., Parés, R., Ribas, J.I., Soler, M., Sanjurjo, À.: Promotion of creative activity in children with severe autism through visuals in an interactive multisensory environment. In: IDC, New York, NY, USA, pp. 110–116 (2005)

[6] Vaucelle, C., Bonanni, L., Ishii, H.: Design of haptic interfaces for therapy. In: Proceedings of CHI, New York, NY, USA, pp. 467–470 (2009)

[7] Berrios, C.D., Jacobowitz, W.H.: Therapeutic holding: outcomes of a pilot study. J. Psychosoc. Nurs. Ment. Health Serv. 36(8), 14–18 (1998)

[8] Jordà, S.: The reactable: tangible and tabletop music performance. In: CHI, New York, NY, USA, pp. 2989–2994 (2010)

[9] Jordà, S., Geiger, G., Alonso, M., Kaltenbrunner, M.: The reacTable: exploring the synergy between live music performance and tabletop tangible interfaces. In: TEI, New York, NY, USA, pp. 139–146 (2007)

[10] Piper, A.M., Weibel, N., Hollan, J.: TAP & PLAY: an end-user toolkit for authoring interactive pen and paper language activities. In: CHI, New York, NY, USA, pp. 149–158 (2012)

[11] Catalina, I., Monica, T.: Things that think for the cognitive skills training of students with autism. In: CHI EA 2012, Austin, TX, USA (2012)

[12] Hernandez, H.A., Graham, T.C.N., Fehlings, D., Switzer, L., Ye, Z., Bellay, Q., Hamza, M.A., Savery, C., Stach, T.: Design of an exergaming station for children with cerebral palsy. In: CHI, New York, NY, USA, pp. 2619–2628 (2012)

[13] Bradski, G., Kaehler, A.: Learning OpenCV: Computer Vision with the OpenCV Library. O'Reilly Media (2008)

Development Challenges in Web Apps for Public Displays

Constantin Taivan[1], José Miguel Andrade[1], Rui José[1], Bruno Silva[1],
Hélder Pinto[1], and António Nestor Ribeiro[2]

[1] Centro Algoritmi, Universidade do Minho, Portugal
{constantin,jma,rui,bruno.silva,helder}@dsi.uminho.pt
[2] Department of Informatics, University of Minho & HASLab/INESC TEC, Braga Portugal
anr@di.uminho.pt

Abstract. Digital public displays can have a key role in urban ubiquitous computing infrastructures, but they have not yet managed to fill this role. A key step in that direction would be the emergence of an application model for open display networks that would enable anyone to create applications for display infrastructures. In this work, we study the development of web-based applications for public displays. We report on our experience of application development for real world public deployment and also on an experiment with external web developers to assess their ability to create such applications using our own development tools. The results show that the web-based app model can effectively be used in the context of public displays and that web developers are able to leverage upon their expertise to create this type of applications.

Keywords: public displays, ubiquitous computing, applications.

1 Introduction

Pervasive computing technology is increasingly present in urban spaces aiming to provide new types of support for our everyday tasks [1]. Public displays, in particular, have the properties to become an important infrastructural element for Intelligent Urban Environments. Digital public displays have always been part of the ubiquitous computing vision. They were called the "boards" in the original Weiser's work [2], where they were essentially seen as interactive, yard-size displays that would complement pads and tabs to enhance spaces by enabling a broad range of casual information exchanges. However, public displays have not yet managed to fill this role. Existing display systems are designed around a content management model in which content is first orchestrated at a central location and then distributed to the displays. They are essentially seen as mere end-points for content distribution or devices that are isolated from the people and the data around them.

The recent trend towards open networks of public displays [3] challenges many of those assumptions and creates the opportunity for any third parties to create and publish content in the form of applications, promoting openness as a source of value for all the parties involved. Together with mobile phones, wireless access points and associated sensors, public displays can become an appropriate execution environment

G. Urzaiz et al. (Eds.): UCAmI 2013, LNCS 8276, pp. 135–142, 2013.
© Springer International Publishing Switzerland 2013

for new and innovative applications. The global nature of pervasive display applications and their strong portability requirements match very well with the core values of web technologies, such as openness, wide-spread availability and high portability [5]. Web technologies not only have the advantage of being easily available across multiple platforms and operating systems, they can also make applications much easier to deploy in large scale and they benefit from a large developers base.

In this paper, we present our experience with a web-based model for display apps. We have created and publicly deployed multiple applications and we have conducted an experiment with external web developers to assess their ability to create such applications using our own development tools. The results show that the web-based app model can effectively be used in the context of public displays and that web developers are able to leverage upon their expertise to create this type of applications.

2   Related Work

There are some obvious similarities between the concept of display apps and other popular app models such as the mobile applications market, e.g., Apple Store or Google' Play [6]. Clinch et al. [16] present a set of design considerations for app stores for public display applications. Conceiving such application stores faces specific challenges when compared with the mobile application market, such as dealing with multiple stakeholders, new business models and scheduling requirements. While in mobile devices market there are well established platforms for running the applications (Android, iOS), in public displays there is no uniform application model for crafting display applications.

Multiple public display infrastructures have experimented with web applications as a way to share content from various sources and prompt user interaction. A remarkable example is UBI hotspots – the real world displays deployment from city of Oulu, Finland [4][7]. Oulu's multi-application public displays based its design on the Web paradigm and enable content contribution from multiple third parties through the publication of services. A service that is associated with a public display and resides anywhere on the Internet may present content using a simple URL. A UBI hotspot can employ interactive services by interacting with users' mobile phones or by distributing its interface to nearby mobile devices. e-Campus public display infrastructure from Lancaster University [8] is another relevant example for using web applications as means to personalize user experience in front of large displays [9]. Based on a mobile Android application users can locate the nearby displays and configure what content to see as part of the associated display web applications. Instant Places from University of Minho [10] is yet another display infrastructure based on web technologies that aggregates place-based screen media and explores new concepts for user-generated content. Many diverse display applications have been proposed for many different domains, e.g. maps, bus schedules, galleries to interactive content generation [11][12]. The research on display prototypes was mostly conducted as part of single display and single application installations (e.g. [13][14]) and lately as key enabler for large scale of open display networks [3]. The commercial sector is mainly concentrating on broadcasting static content though there is a growing market on personalized and interactive content enabled by third party applications [15].

While the research community is already working on applications for public displays, this study is the first to specifically consider the extension of web development practices and expertise to support that type of development.

3   Web Applications for Public Displays

For the purpose of this work, a display app is a web application whose primary goal is to render content on a public display. A display application encapsulates both the content and the means to render that content on the screens. They are based on web technologies and standards, e.g., HTML, JavaScript and CSS. They are deployed on public servers from where they can be used in any public display. Display apps run in any standard web browser or other types of specially tailored web stacks and their model is optimized for the distinctive execution context and user experience of public displays.

This approach is similar to the well-known iPhone, Android or SmartTV web app models that specify how an app should be designed and implemented for a specific platform. In our case, the key property is a rich client model in which the core of the application is running on the display node. Each application will have its own JavaScript code to handle on the display side issues such as obtaining and managing the content items that the application will need, cache and pre-fetch policies, visual adaptation and network disconnections. To support interaction, applications may include a mobile contact point that allows mobile applications to expose their interactive features to users.

While we are not claiming this to be the only possible model for web apps, this is a model that has evolved over the years with our ongoing research in this topic, and we have now developed and deployed multiple display apps based on these principles [10], like the ones represented in Fig. 1. The Posters app shows posters shared by local community. The Football pins app presents content that reflects the football preferences of the users around the display.

(a) Posters   (b) Footbal Pins apps

Fig. 1. Instant Places web applications

3.1   Development Process and Tools

To facilitate development of display web apps we created a developers web site with key information on how to develop these apps and also with the following set of development tools: Application Generator, Instant Places library and Media Simulator.

The Application Generator provides developers with the possibility to generate a ready-made application structure. This considerably reduces the initial development effort and it promotes the use of patterns and components that are known to work better with this type of application. This was achieved by the generation of a Hello World display app, which constituted the skeleton for the creation of other apps.

The Instant Places library provides an abstraction layer for the Instant Places service that enables applications to integrate dynamic data into their content, more specifically place-based information about their surrounding settings, i.e. sensing and interaction information associated with displays (see [10] for a detailed description).

The Media Simulator allows display apps to be tested in their target execution environment, i.e., display nodes' web browsers. Instead of deploying applications to the real display infrastructure, developers have the ability to use this tool to check in advance if a display app is ready to be shown on a public display. Based on a set of guiding reference tests, e.g., resizing the window of the application, unplug the network cable, a developer could observe the behavior of the app.

In addition to these tools, we also provided developers with a few additional guidelines on how to handle key issues such as network disconnection and visual adaptation. Building a fault-tolerant app is essential to public display environments, because we do not have an end-user that is ready to solve the problem. We included a set of code blocks for the cases when no data was fetched or it took too much time to show up, e.g., splash screens routines for masking application startup delays or show something to its audience while external data is being fetched. For example, the Hello World application generated by the Application Generator already included a splash screen hiding the error of no connectivity. To handle the diverse resolutions and orientations that public displays can have, there is a need to employ at least some basic techniques for making the application content look good and – especially – readable. Our initial Hello World app already included a technique based on CSS media queries. Is allows developers to add expressions to media type to check for certain conditions and apply different style sheets. For example, one can have one style sheet for large displays and a different style sheet specifically for mobile devices. The technique is really helpful because it allows adjusting to different resolutions and devices without changing the content. The condition that is often verified to trigger the changes is the viewport width. When the viewport is too narrow, applications can adjust the font and some box sizes.

4   Experience with Third-Party Developers

In order to consolidate our view on creating display web apps, we conducted a short term development experiment in which we investigated the learnability and usefulness of our development tools by other programmers. The assessment of our development tools was achieved by adopting the same evaluation method as [17] and [18], that is, *informal and controlled laboratory evaluation*. We invited five participants to create a given display web app by using our guidelines and tools and interviewed them about their experiences. All of them had basic web development skills, e.g., JavaScript, HTML and CSS, and had never built a display web app.

A week before the experiment, we sent participants the URL of the development web site so that they could learn the basics of the process. At the beginning of the experiment we gave them a brief tutorial of about 10 minutes in which we introduced the concept of display apps and explained the APIs. They were then asked to build a new display app, i.e., a poster grid app, based on the Hello World example. To do this, we formulated three development tasks that led developers to create the given app. The first task was to put the Hello World app running and test its execution. For this, they needed to install the App Generator and output the necessary application example and Media Simulator for being able to test it. The second task was to use the Instant Places library for getting place related data, such as the *place name*, *place image* and *posters*. Finally, participants were asked to show the posters in a grid by using some CSS rules. In this step, developers needed to use splash screens and configure them to last for at least 3 seconds; support fault tolerance functionality (lack of data, lack of connectivity); prepare the app to be displayed correctly in an iPad or in another device of similar dimensions and test the application using a desktop web browser and Media Simulator tool. Throughout the experiment, participants were encouraged to raise questions and they had four hours to complete all the tasks. At the end, each of them was interviewed about their experiences with our display apps development tools. The interviews were audio recorded and the code produced by developers was kept for subsequent analysis.

4.1   Results and Discussions

The overall view of this experiment was positive, even for the less skilled developers. All the participants have achieved the key development goals without wasting too much time in writing the code. They also preferred to use our toolkit rather than starting to build the application from scratch.

Participants had some initial effort to grasp the specific concepts associated with displays apps, but after that they were quickly able to master the process. Developers could easily follow the documentation provided by our development web site. Even though this was optional, all participants used the Hello World app generated by the App Generator tool as a template to start implementing the new display app. The participants didn't even think very much about the structure of the application, so we may conclude the Application Generator was effective. When we asked developers how it would be to develop without this tool all of them responded that would it be difficult or even very difficult.

Developers had enthusiasm for this experiment despite their weaker experience with some the required web technologies. This is demonstrated by the fact that all of them succeeded in applying their web development skills to develop a display app. However, some of them experienced some difficulties in understanding and using all specific development and testing scenarios, e.g., implementing the splash screens or providing the required code blocks for a fault tolerant display app. Only one of them could entirely test the app execution behavior.

Due to the fact that our display app was not too complex, it just required a set of API requests, the code source is quite identic among the participants and the final applications share the same structure and very similar lines of code. Having a previously scaffold app structure proved to be comfortable to the participants and reduced the amount of code they had to write. Developers ended up not writing much code and not changing the application structure at all. Instead their effort was mostly applied into answering questions like "What do I need to change from this app?" instead of "What do I need to build my app?". One student noted that the integration of our code blocks was straightforward, while making various customizations of the provided code fragments was not so easy.

Using the Instant Places API library was something that proved to be very handy. Although there were some initial problems in understanding the meaning of our API and the related code blocks, after getting the place name, they easily succeeded to get further data, such as posters.

Developers had difficulties when testing their apps because they weren't familiar with any tools to accomplish this task, e.g. Fiddler. Most tests were made using a common web browser while the Media Simulator tool was just periodically used to rule out eventual errors related to the different web engine of display players. Only one student did not test at all the new application execution, neither in desktop web browser nor in Media Simulator tool. The others tested the application but encountered various difficulties.

Participants were really motivated by the innovative field of usage of display web apps and recognized their big potential when deployed in real world settings. They associated display apps with mechanisms to publish content, such as replacing the traditional paper based posters with digital forms of content. In their final comments, they all referred particular features for display web apps, e.g., a display app should provide content that is dynamic, personalized and place-based. In Table 1 we provide a short description about the development challenges that we addressed in this work.

Table 1. Summary of the develoment challenges

Development Challenges	Techniques employed	Developers' opinions
Content management policies	Rich client model includes logic to cache and pre-fetch content.	Instant Places API library helps with high-level application concepts.
Fault tolerance support	Code blocks that can be configured for specific purposes, e.g., splash screens	Code blocks are easy to integrate but not to customize ; Fault-tolerance testing scenarios were complex
Rich visual adaptation	CSS media queries	No special issues were mentioned. Most participants did not test this feature.

5   Conclusions

In this paper we have presented our early experiences in developing display web applications. In order to guide development and speed up the process of creating display application we implemented a collection of tools, which were evaluated based on an experiment with developers. The experiment showed that there is a short learning curve even for first-time developers and building a display web app is quite an appealing challenge for web skilled persons. The participants were able to put in practice their web programing experience though this was not straight-forward. The specific field of public displays put forward a set of specificities that requires clear development specifications and guidelines. These have a strong effect in leveraging on the expertise of web developers to create display apps and subsequently attracting an increasing number of people with appropriate web development skills. Based on these insights we are looking forward to collect long-term development feedback from more web experienced developers and to extend the specification of our model for display web applications.

Acknowledgment. The authors acknowledge the financial support of the Future and Emerging Technologies (FET) programme within the 7th Framework Programme for Research of the European Commission, under FET-Open grant number: 244011 and "Fundação para a Ciência e a Tecnologia", under the research grant SFRH/BD/75868/2011.

References

1. Greenfield, A.: Everyware: The Dawning Age of Ubiquitous Computing, p. 272. New Riders Publishing (2006)
2. Weiser, M.: The Computer for the 21st Century. Scientific Am., 94–104 (1991)
3. Davies, N., Langheinrich, M., José, R., Schmidt, A.: Open Display Networks: A Communications Medium for the 21st Century. IEEE Computer, 58–64 (May 2012)
4. Ojala, T., Kostakos, V., Kukka, H., Heikkinen, T., Linden, T., Jurmu, M., Hosio, S., Kruger, F., Zanni, D.: Multipurpose Interactive Public Displays in the Wild: Three Years Later. Computer 45(5), 42–49 (2012)
5. Pawan, V.: Web Applications Design Patterns, p. 448. Morgan Kaufmann (2009)
6. Holzer, A., Ondrus, J.: Mobile application market: A developer's perspective. Telematics and Informatics 28(1), 22–31 (2011)
7. Lindén, T., Heikkinen, T., Kostakos, V., Ferreira, D., Ojala, T.: Towards multi-application public interactive displays. In: Proceedings of the 2012 International Symposium on Pervasive Displays, PerDis 2012, pp. 1–5 (2012)
8. Friday, A., Davies, N., Efstratiou, C.: Reflections on Long-Term Experiments with Public Displays. Computer 45(5), 34–41 (2012)
9. Kubitza, T., Clinch, S., Davies, N., Langheinrich, M.: Using mobile devices to personalize pervasive displays. ACM SIGMOBILE Mobile Computing and Communications Review 16(4), 26–27 (2012)

10. José, R., Pinto, H., Silva, B., Melro, A., Rodrigues, H.: Beyond interaction: tools and practices for situated publication in display networks. In: Proceedings of the 2012 International Symposium on Pervasive Displays, PerDis 2012, pp. 1–6 (2012)
11. Memarovic, N., Elhart, I., Langheinrich, M.: FunSquare. In: Proceedings of the 10th International Conference on Mobile and Ubiquitous Multimedia, MUM 2011, pp. 175–184 (2011)
12. Alt, F., Kubitza, T., Bial, D., Zaidan, F., Ortel, M., Zurmaar, B., Lewen, T., Shirazi, A.S., Schmidt, A.: Digifieds: insights into deploying digital public notice areas in the wild. In: Proceedings of the 10th International Conference on Mobile and Ubiquitous Multimedia, MUM 2011, pp. 165–174 (2011)
13. Huang, E.M., Mynatt, E.D.: Semi-public displays for small, co-located groups. In: Proceedings of the Conference on Human Factors in Computing Systems, CHI 2003, vol. 5(5), p. 49 (2003)
14. Izadi, S., Brignull, H., Rodden, T., Rogers, Y., Underwood, M.: Dynamo: a public interactive surface supporting the cooperative sharing and exchange of media. In: Proceedings of the 16th Annual ACM Symposium on User Interface Software and Technology, UIST 2003, pp. 159–168 (2003)
15. Locamoda, Fifteen Seconds or More. Engaging Audiences With Place-Based Social Media, In: White Paper (2010)
16. Clinch, S., Davies, N., Kubitza, T., Schmidt, A.: Designing application stores for public display networks. In: Proceedings of the 2012 International Symposium on Pervasive Displays, PerDis 2012, pp. 1–6 (2012)
17. Klemmer, S.R., Li, J., Lin, J., Landay, J.A.: "Papier-Mâché: Toolkit Support for Tangible Input," in. In: Proceedings of the 2004 Conference on Human Factors in Computing Systems, CHI 2004, pp. 399–406 (2004)
18. Heer, J., Card, S.K., Landay, J.A.: prefuse: a toolkit for interactive information visualization. In: Proceedings of the SIGCHI Conference on Human Factors in Computing System, CHI 2005, p. 421 (2005)

Towards a Technology for Caregivers' Emotional Expression and Self-reflection

Carolina Fuentes[1], Valeria Herskovic[1], Jurgen Heysen[1], and Monica Tentori[2]

[1] Computer Science Department, Pontificia Universidad Católica de Chile, Santiago, Chile
cjfuentes@uc.cl, vherskov@ing.puc.cl, jdheysen@uc.cl
[2] Department of Computer Science, CICESE, Ensenada, México
mtentori@cicese.mx

Abstract. The care of individuals with cancer is a difficult and draining task. The care responsibility is in many cases, taken over by a family member, usually the mother in the case of pediatric cancer. We studied the needs of these mothers, related to their particular situation: they live in a community of caregivers, while their families are in distant cities and they must deal with the stress of being healthcare providers and emotional support to their children. This paper presents a qualitative study to understand emotional wellbeing in caregivers, and the development and evaluation of *Ohana*, a tangible user interface to allow caregivers to easily express their emotions to their families and physicians, and reflect on their emotional-wellbeing and needs. The Ohana System was reported to be easy to use, and easy to learn, and we believe it could be integrated into the lives of the interviewed mothers and their children. This work will be continued by improving the interface, adding communication functionality, and further evaluation.

Keywords: tangible user interface, caregivers, emotions.

1   Introduction

Cancer is a major worldwide health challenge. The care of individuals with cancer is a difficult, draining task, and this responsibility is often taken over by a family member, e.g. a spouse or parent. This creates burdens on the caregivers, e.g. in the areas of time, finances, mental health, and emotions [1]. A study found over half of all caregivers evidence clinically significant levels of depression [2]. Monitoring caregivers' emotions could help detect and treat early symptoms of depression. Moreover, allowing caregivers to express and review their emotions may induce self-reflection and self-knowledge [3]. However, emotional well-being monitoring presents challenges including accurate detection of emotions and user adoption [4].

Occasionally, and perhaps more frequently in a developing country, cancer patients do not have access to high quality medical care in a location close to their home, and they must relocate to a larger city. In the case of pediatric cancer, caregivers are frequently mothers [5] and may live in a house with other caregivers.

We studied the needs of these mothers, related to their particular situation: they live in a community of caregivers, with part of their families far away in distant cities or countries, and they must deal with the pressures of being healthcare providers and

G. Urzaiz et al. (Eds.): UCAmI 2013, LNCS 8276, pp. 143–150, 2013.

emotional support to their children. Using the results of our qualitative study, we then developed a tangible user interface (TUI) called the *Ohana¹ Bear*, caregivers use to easily express and communicate their emotions to their families or physicians, and promote emotional-wellbeing self-reflection.

This paper is structured as follows. First, it describes related work in the field of understanding caregivers and providing technology to them. Then, it presents our study of caregivers, followed by a TUI we designed to allow caregivers to express their emotions. Then, we present evaluation results and our conclusions.

2   Related Work

When a person becomes chronically ill, a family member usually takes the role of main caregiver, providing informal care to the patient. Usually, caregivers are the patient's spouse or partner [6], or adult children or friends [7]. Care requirements include physical care, housekeeping, transportation, and financial support [8]. Being a primary caregiver is a complex task: over 60% of caregivers present high rates of depression, anxiety disorders or emotional distress [9]. Some of their main problems are related to relationships and family life, social isolation, depression, anxiety and loneliness [10],[11],[12]. A caregiver with negative emotional states cannot adequately perform his/her task [7], so caregivers require attention, communication and emotional support to prevent physical and mental health problems.

In the context of caregiving, commonly a network support of family is created to support the main caregiver [13]. Therefore, it is also important to understand how families communicate. Another important factor is geographic distribution [14].

Technology to support family caregivers may be classified as: technology to stay healthy, safe and secure, to stay in touch and to stay strong [15]. Some applications, such as CareNet display [16], which is a prototype with a user-centered design, investigate the coordination between the different members of a network of caregivers to elderly patients. The prototype is a photo frame, showing a picture of an older adult and information about his/her condition, nutrition, falls, mood and a calendar. Estrellita System [17] is a mobile web application developed to help caregivers of premature babies. Astra [18] is designed to provide and evaluate awareness, connecting households and family members supported with mobile systems. Their results are interesting, because they provide a concept called *connectedness*, which implies "positive emotional appraisal, characterized by a feeling of being in touch within ongoing social relations". Sparcs [19] presents a prototype for sharing photos and calendar information between large families to stay connected. Aurora [20] is a prototype in a mobile device to promote emotional awareness, sharing emotion and social behavior support. Its main objective is to share emotions, drawing on the work of affective computing indicating that systems must act as a medium to convey emotions. From this sample of technologies, we may see that it is important to provide connectedness and communication between families, and that capturing and sharing emotions is central to healthcare.

---

¹ "Ohana" is a broad Hawaiian concept encompassing families, friends, and staying together.

3   A Qualitative Study of Mother Caregivers

3.1   Methodology

To understand caregivers' needs, we conducted six semi-structured interviews with mothers who act as main caregivers for their children receiving treatment for cancer, and live at a residence for caregivers in Chile. The participants were recruited and interviewed at the house, which allowed them to be more relaxed and open.

The main interviewer was one of the authors of the article, a young female Ph.D. student who has a child. It is important to note this because of the bias the interviewees might have had towards a female who is also a mother - interestingly, all of the potential interviewees refused to contact male interviewers and only would talk to them after being introduced by the female student.

The interviews began with a brief demographic and computer-skills questionnaire, followed by semi-structured questions about their routines and their emotional states. The interviewees ranged in age from 20 to 46 (avg: 37.2), and from 1 to 8 children (avg: 3). They were all from other cities (one from another country), separated from their families by 120-1900 kms (straight line measurement, avg: 822).

3.2   Analysis

We codified the interviews by selecting recurring topics and summarizing the thoughts of the interviewees (E1 to E6) for each one. This section presents three themes that were recurrently discussed by the mothers.

Communication with Their Families. The mothers all are living far from their families while their children are treated for their illness. They communicate through phone, text, Facebook and videoconferencing. The mothers appreciate the connectedness technology can provide: "*My family is supportive; technology helps inform them about my child's illness. I am disconnected from my home, the bills.*" (E1). However, several of them complained about the fact that their families do not really understand what they are going through. One of them shared the following story about another caregiver: "*One mother arrived at the house, and her husband wanted her to return to her city as soon as possible. Her child was still in treatment, but everyone was calling her, her in-laws, everyone was giving her instructions about what she should do: 'You must do this and you must do that'. She was crying and feeling down after every phone call. So the residence mothers told her, 'Your child is first, tell your husband to take a hike.'*" (E2). This also highlights the sense of community among the mothers. Another mother expressed that: "*Your family is always there, but they don't understand, they don't live it, because I am living it with my child by myself. They can call me everyday, but they won't ever feel the pain I feel.*" (E3). Although the families are informed of how treatment is going, and how the child is feeling, there is little shared about the toll the situation is taking on the caregiver.

Sharing Emotional States. We selected 8 negative emotions from Russell's circumplex model [21], e.g. sad, lonely, depressed, irritable, overwhelmed, annoyed, hopeless, and asked the mothers how often they feel each of these emotions, and whether they feel any other emotions. The interviewees reported frequently feeling sad (5 out of 6) and overwhelmed (4 out of 6), and they also reported feeling lonely, scared, and hopeless. Some interviewees expressed that they don't want to share their feelings: *"I try not to share my emotions, I would rather keep them to myself"* (E6)), while one identified that this was harmful: *"When I was depressed I locked myself in my room, turned the lights off, closed the windows. I kept what I felt inside, until I started to show physical symptoms"* (E4). Some of them do share their feelings: *"I get distracted by chatting with other caregivers who are going through the same as me"* (E2), *"I search for someone online, like my sister, to talk about how I feel"* (E6)) or do other activities to unwind: *"I relax, go shopping, or go to the gym"* (E3).

Self Reflection. The interviewees had different outlooks on the need for analyzing or reflecting on their own emotions: two of them expressed that they are not interested in expressing their emotions nor sharing them: *"I just live day to day"* (E5), while two others attend psychological therapy, which allows for some self reflection and sharing, albeit with the limited audience of the therapist. All of them reported having a very close relationship to their child's physician, and our preliminary interviews of the doctors involved in cancer and palliative care confirmed that they try to monitor the caregivers' emotional states as well as their patients' health and treatment.

4   The Ohana Bear: A System to Express and Reflect on Emotions

We developed the Ohana Bear to allow caregivers to record their emotions, with the goal of registering how they feel and potentially sharing them with their families. The system was developed using a Gadgeteer FEZSpider Kit, using .NET Framework 4.0, .NET Micro Framework 4.2, GHI Electronics SDK and Visual Studio 2010. This kit was incorporated into a decorative, soothing element to decorate the mother and child's space: a medium-sized teddy bear (Figure 1a, 1b). Information is stored in a SD card, and could be sent through IOStreams through Wifi, Bluetooth, or Ethernet modules, which were not available at the moment of implementation. The next sections describe the interaction capabilities of the system, and how they implement the emotional and communicative needs detailed in the previous section.

4.1   Emotions, Reflection and Communication Design

The literature usually reports on caregivers' negative feelings, however, we also wanted to include positive and neutral feelings to help caregivers share and reflect on the changes in their emotions. Therefore, we chose to represent the negative emotions the mothers reported feeling more often (angry, sad, overwhelmed), as well as an emotion-neutral feeling (serene) and two positive emotions (happy, excited).

Second, we wanted to give the mothers a space to reflect on their recent emotions: e.g. for a mother to see whether she has been feeling down lately and take action about it (as they reported in their interviews, go shopping, or talk to someone). For this reason, we wanted to incorporate a visualization of the mother's recent emotions, classified by emotion type, to see whether this would induce behavioral change.

(a) Emotions are selected by pressing on one   (b) Happy emotion, closeup.
of the bear's hands.

Fig. 1. Ohana Bear

Third, the device should allow sharing these emotions with far-away family, in the same visualization format and in a more detailed view in which the family can see how the caregiver has been feeling. This can be done in the form of a once-a-day and once-a-week email report to a registered loved one. In the current system implementation, the data is stored in an SD card and can be shared in a manual way.

4.2   Interaction Design

The bear incorporates the screen in its stomach area. Each of the bear's hands has a button that allows users to interact with it. The screen also allows touch to record an emotion. Figure 2 summarizes how a user may interact with the bear: (1) The screen displays an image (size 320x240) representing an emotion. (2) If the bear's left hand is pressed, the displayed emotion changes. (3) The screen displays six different emotions, which change with each button press. (4) If the screen is tapped, the emotion is saved and (5) a message confirming this pops up. This records the data, along with contextual data in the SD card. (6) Whenever the bear's right hand is pressed, the screen displays (7) a simple graph summarizing the saved emotions (grouped by whether they are positive, negative or neutral).

4.3   Evaluation

We conducted a first usability evaluation of the Ohana bear to understand whether the device is easy to use and could potentially become a part of the caregivers' routines and lives. For this reason, we decided to evaluate the system with regular users, who could give us insights on how to improve the system, before involving the mothers.

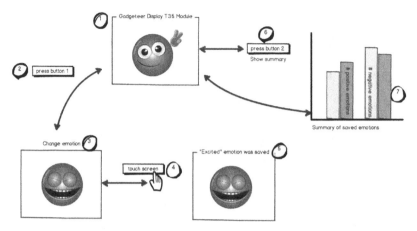

Fig. 2. Ohana Interaction Diagram

Procedure. We recruited participants at a university campus near a walkway used by students, faculty and staff from several academic programs. The evaluation was done with 11 participants, ages 18-34, 8 female and 3 male. Participants were all volunteers and were not compensated. Before the evaluation, the participants were briefly introduced to the research project and shown the prototype system. They were allowed to freely interact with the Ohana bear, and were asked to fill an anonymous, brief questionnaire afterwards. They were also asked for additional comments.

Results. We collected questionnaire results and user comments about the Ohana bear. We adapted the questionnaire from the TUI evaluation questionnaire used in [22], asking 10 questions about learnability, tangibility, interaction and collaboration. We used a 5-point Likert scale (1=completely disagree, 5=completely agree).

Table 1 shows the questions and their average results. The Ohana bear got high scores in learnability and interaction, and lower scores in Collaboration and Tangibility. The users commented on the ease of use, on the lack of more emotions that they wanted to express, and on the associations created by the device being a bear: *"The object, by being a teddy bear, is inviting me to be playful,..., and I forget its real purpose"*.

Discussion. The results from the user study were encouraging: the device was found easy to use, and all its functions were easy to interact with. The fact that it was a teddy bear and therefore invited playfulness and relaxation, making a user forget that she was "working" to express her emotions, also seems like a positive indicator that Ohana could be a nonintrusive addition to relaxation routines in the mothers' lives.

However, the scores for collaboration and tangibility were lower. This may be explained by the fact that the participants of the study were mostly students and not parents, and none of them corresponded to parents of cancer patients. Therefore, they did not know and could not imagine the complex, stressful context of the target users. For this reason, the user study mainly evaluated usability rather than usefulness. The other low score for tangibility was that the bear clearly manages digital data, and this is especially evident in a university campus where students are highly connected and technology-savvy. Future Ohana system designs should work to make emotions a more subtle part of the interface, rather than displaying them centrally on the screen.

Table 1. Results for learnability, interaction, collaboration and tangibility questions

Question type	Question	Avg score	Avg per type
Learnability	It was immediately clear to me how to use the system	4.45	4.39
	It was easy to learn how the system is used	4.91	
	I always knew how to perform a desired action	3.81	
Interaction	It was easy to select a picture/emotion	4	4.58
	It was easy to record an emotion	4.81	
	It was easy to view the graph	4.91	
Collaboration	I would use this to share with someone how I feel	2.9	2.9
Tangibility	I was able to manipulate the object naturally	4	3.21
	I was not aware that I was working with a computer program and digital data	1.91	
	I would be able to integrate this device into my environment	3.64	

5   Conclusions

We presented the Ohana bear: a TUI designed for mothers of pediatric cancer patients to express and self-reflect on their emotions. The bear was designed to become a part of the mothers' rooms while away from home, as a decorative, soothing element. It was also designed to incorporate two aspects concerning emotions that are central to caregivers' routines: allowing them to express how they feel and allowing them to review their own emotions. A third aspect (permitting their far-away families to know about their emotional states) will be incorporated in future versions. Results from a small-scale user study were encouraging: users reported easily learning and interacting with the device, and a natural manipulation of it. However, it is necessary to evaluate the device further, with mothers of pediatric cancer patients and their families, to gauge not only usability but usefulness and adoption. This may be done by giving the device to mothers for prolonged periods of time, to register e.g. a week's worth of emotions and then evaluate device use and satisfaction. We also believe that the results of the experiment gave us insights to redesign the bear, by making the screen a less central part of the device to allow users to interact with the object more naturally, "forgetting" that it is actually a computer device.

Acknowledgements. This work was partially supported by the LACCIR Project Grant R1212LAC001.

References

[1] Rabow, M.W., Hauser, J.M., Adams, J.: Supporting family caregivers at the end of life. JAMA 291(4), 483–491 (2004)

[2] Haley, W.E., LaMonde, L.A., Han, B., Narramore, S., Schonwetter, R.: Family caregiving in hospice: effects on psychological and health functioning among spousal caregivers of hospice patients with lung cancer or dementia. Hospice Journal (2001)

[3] Li, I., Dey, A., Forlizzi, J.: A stage-based model of personal informatics systems. In: Proceedings of the 28th International Conference on Human Factors in Computing Systems, pp. 557–566 (2010)

[4] Dickerson, R.F., Gorlin, E.I., Stankovic, J.A.: Empath: a continuous remote emotional health monitoring system for depressive illness. In: Proceedings of the 2nd Conference on Wireless Health, p. 5 (2011)

[5] Marsland, A.L., Long, K.A., Howe, C., Thompson, A.L., Tersak, J., Ewing, L.J.: A Pilot Trial of a Stress Management Intervention for Primary Caregivers of Children Newly Diagnosed With Cancer: Preliminary Evidence That Perceived Social Support Moderates the Psychosocial Benefit of Intervention. Journal of Pediatric Psychology (2013)

[6] Grunfeld, E., Coyle, D., Whelan, T., Clinch, J., Reyno, L., Earle, C.C., Willan, A., Viola, R., Coristine, M., Janz, T., et al.: Family caregiver burden: results of a longitudinal study of breast cancer patients and their principal caregivers. Canadian Medical Association Journal 170(12), 1795–1801 (2004)

[7] Northouse, L., Williams, A., Given, B., McCorkle, R.: Psychosocial care for family caregivers of patients with cancer. J. of Clinical Oncology 30(11), 1227–1234 (2012)

[8] Given, B.A., Given, C.W., Sherwood, P.R.: Family and caregiver needs over the course of the cancer trajectory. J. of Supportive Oncology 10(2), 57–64 (2012)

[9] Haley, W.E.: Family caregivers of elderly patients with cancer: understanding and minimizing the burden of care. J. Support Oncol 1(4) (suppl. 2), 25–29 (2003)

[10] Chen, Y., Ngo, V., Park, S.Y.: Caring for caregivers: designing for integrality. In: Proceedings of the 2013 Conference on CSCW, pp. 91–102 (2013)

[11] George, L.K., Gwyther, L.P.: Caregiver Well-Being: A Multidimensional Examination of Family Caregivers of Demented Adults. The Gerontologist 26(3), 253–259 (1986)

[12] Flaskerud, J.H., Carter, P.A., Lee, P.: Distressing Emotions in Female Caregivers of People With AIDS, Age-Related Dementias, and Advanced-Stage Cancers. Perspectives in Psychiatric Care 36(4), 121–130 (2000)

[13] Hudson, P.L., Aranda, S., Kristjanson, L.J.: Meeting the supportive needs of family caregivers in palliative care: challenges for health professionals. Journal of Palliative Medicine 7(1), 19–25 (2004)

[14] Pang, C., Neustaedter, C., Riecke, B.E., Oduor, E., Hillman, S.: Technology Preferences and Routines for Sharing Health Information during the Treatment of a Chronic Illness (2013)

[15] UnitedHealthcare, "e Connected Family Caregiver: Bringing Caregiving into the 21st Century"

[16] Consolvo, S., Roessler, P., Shelton, B.E., LaMarca, A., Schilit, B., Bly, S.: Technology for care networks of elders. IEEE Pervasive Computing 3(2), 22–29 (2004)

[17] Hirano, S.H., Tang, K.P., Cheng, K.G., Hayes, G.R.: The estrellita system: A health informatics tool to support caregivers of preterm infants. In: Pervasive Health, pp. 195–196 (2012)

[18] Romero, N., Markopoulos, P., Baren, J., Ruyter, B., Ijsselsteijn, W., Farshchian, B.: Connecting the family with awareness systems. Personal and Ubiquitous Computing 11(4), 299–312 (2007)

[19] Brush, A.J., Inkpen, K.M., Tee, K.: SPARCS: exploring sharing suggestions to enhance family connectedness. In: CSCW 2008, pp. 629–638 (2008)

[20] Gay, G., Pollak, J., Adams, P., Leonard, J.P., et al.: Pilot study of aurora, a social, mobile-phone-based emotion sharing and recording system. Journal of Diabetes Science and Technology 5(2), 325–332 (2011)

[21] Russell, J.A.: A circumplex model of affect. Journal of Personality and Social Psychology 39(6), 1161–1178 (1980)

[22] Waldner, M., Hauber, J., Zauner, J., Haller, M., Billinghurst, M.: Tangible tiles: design and evaluation of a tangible user interface in a collaborative tabletop setup. In: Proc. of the 18th Australia Conference on CHI, pp. 151–158 (2006)

A Sleep Monitoring Application for u-lifecare Using Accelerometer Sensor of Smartphone

Muhammad Fahim[1], Le Ba Vui[1], Iram Fatima[1], Sungyoung Lee[1], and Yongik Yoon[2]

[1] Ubiquitous Computing Laboratory, Department of Computer Engineering,
Kyung Hee University, Korea
{fahim,lebavui,iram.fatima,sylee}@oslab.khu.ac.kr
[2] Department of Multimedia Science, Sookmyung Womens University, South Korea
yiyoon@sookmyung.ac.kr

Abstract. Ubiquitous lifecare (u-lifecare) is regarded as a seamless technology that can provide services to the patients as well as facilitate the healthy people to maintain an active lifestyle. In this paper, we develop a sleep monitoring application to assists the healthy people for managing their sleep. It provides an unobtrusive and proactive way for the self-management. We utilize the embedded accelerometer sensor of the smartphone as a client node to collect the sleeping data logs. Our proposed model is server-driven approach and process the data over the server machine. We classify the body movements and compute the useful sleep analytics. It facilitates the users to keep the record of daily sleep and assists to change their unhealthy sleeping habits that are identified by our computed sleep analytics such as bed time, wake up, fell asleep, body movements, frequent body movements at different stages of the night, sleep efficiency and time spent in the bed. Furthermore, we also provide our pilot study results to demonstrate the applicability with the real-world service scenarios.

Keywords: Sleep Monitoring, Accelerometer Sensor, Smartphone, u-lifecare.

1   Introduction

Ubiquitous lifecare (u-lifecare) is a proactive approach to adopt healthy lifestyle in our daily routines. For instance, daily exercise, diet, sleep and social relationships are the wellbeing indicators. A progressive health effects can be observed if they are well managed. Among these sleep in one of the most important health attribute as almost one-third of the human lifetime is spent by sleeping [1]. Insufficient sleep or poor quality has direct impact on person mood, decision capabilities, mental and physical health conditions. Furthermore, serious complexities in sleep may cause the chronic disease such as cardiovascular problems, depression and stress.

The ways to monitor the sleep are polysomnography [2], actigraphy [3] and maintaining sleep diary [4]. Polysomnography is a reliable method due to heterogeneous invasive sensors to monitor the quality of sleep and adopted in the hospital environments. However, it is an intrusive and uncomfortable way to monitor

G. Urzaiz et al. (Eds.): UCAmI 2013, LNCS 8276, pp. 151–158, 2013.
© Springer International Publishing Switzerland 2013

the sleep. Actigraphy is another way to monitor the sleep but less intrusive as compared to polysomnography. Still subjects need to wear the accelerometer embedded watch/bracelets during the sleep. Sleep diary is an easy and simple way to monitor the sleep but it is difficult to remember every night situation and needs sometime to manage it regularly. The adoption of any sleep monitoring solution depends on the sleep complications, severity level and symptoms.

Current generation smartphones are an alternative solution to wearable sensors due to their many diverse and powerful embedded sensors. The smartphone includes accelerometer, magnetometer, gyroscope, proximity, ambient light, GPS and cameras. Furthermore, it is one of the best choices for u-lifecare applications due to its unobtrusive characteristics, high storage capacity and computation, low energy consumption and programmable capabilities. In order to practice healthy sleeping pattern in daily routines, we proposed a sleep monitoring application based on the accelerometer sensor of smartphone. It can help the ordinary people to monitor the sleep in a proactive way that may avoid the sleep complications. For self-management, our application provide the visualization of the body movement patterns and useful analytics to assess the efficiency of sleep. We detect the body movement patterns through Support Vector Machine (SVM) and compute the important sleep analytics that may help to adopt active lifestyle.

Although, sleep monitoring is complex study in case of sleep disorders and other complications related to sleep. The scope of our study is to consider the healthy people in a u-lifecare context and ultimately integrate sleep monitoring application with our under developed u-lifecare research project [5]. We will provide the recommendations over sleep analysis such as music therapy, physical activities and control the physical objects to improve the quality of life and make the u-lifecare vision true.

We structure our paper as follow: Section 2 provides information about some of the existing approaches for sleep monitoring. Section 3 presents our proposed smartphone-based approach. In Section 4, we illustrate the experimental results followed by discussion. And finally the conclusion and future work are drawn in Section 5.

2   Related Work

Several research studies have been presented and a large number of sleep monitoring applications are available in the market. Adriana et al. [6] detected the body movements in bed using unobtrusive load cell sensors. They identified the movement when forces sensed by the load cells under the bed legs. Basically, they calculate the energy in each load cell signal over short segments to capture the variations caused by the body movements. The evaluated their system over the dataset collected in the laboratory. This solution is not possible to adopt in daily routines because extra hardware (i.e., load cell sensor) is required to build the system.

In the market, developers also developed other handy solutions to monitor the sleep like Wakemate [7]. It is a sleep monitoring system, which consists of wearable accelerometer band and communicate with the smartphone over the Bluetooth. Smartphone act as a server to receive the accelerometer signals and process them to monitor the sleep. It is able to record the body movements and provide intelligent alarm services to wake up the subject within the 20 minutes window prior to the desired alarm time. One of the first smartphone-based applications is sleep cycle [8] to monitor the sleep and predict the optimal wake up points. They utilized the embedded accelerometer of smartphone for sleep monitoring and process the signals using a proprietary algorithm.

Similarly, some other applications [9] [10] [11] with same functionalities are also available on the app store but details are still not available how they process the sensory data. A technical detail to process smartphone accelerometer data is still vacant to make this vision a reality. In this study, we provide the technical details to process the accelerometer data as well as pilot study implementation results.

3   The Proposed Approach

The proposed approach consists of a smartphone application as a client node to record the accelerometer data and server machine to process the logs for computing the body movements with sleep analytics. The architecture of proposed approach is shown in Fig. 1 and details of sub-components are as follow:

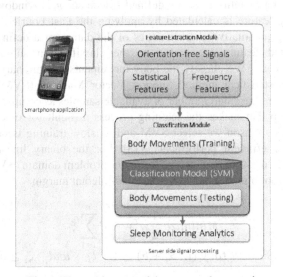

Fig. 1. The architecture of the proposed approach

3.1   Smartphone Application

An Android based smartphone application is developed to log the sensory data. It activate the accelerometer sensor and record the three dimensional data inside storage of the smartphone. In our study, we analyzed and recorded the data at 50 Hz, which is a suitable sampling rate for detecting the body movements over a window of fifteen seconds. The application is server-driven and allows the phone to transfer the data over the Wi-Fi/4G for further processing. Consequently, it resolves the limited data logging issues and allows easy access to sleep data by users themselves as well as, if necessary, physicians or researcher community.

3.2   Server Side Signal Processing

It is composed of *(a) Feature Extraction:* It is highly domain specific method to transfer the raw signals into meaningful region. Firstly, we solve the orientation issue of accelerometer data suggested by Mizell [12] and then extract the following time and frequency domain features.

$$\mu = \frac{1}{n} \sum_{i=1}^{n} x_i^2 \tag{1}$$

$$E = \frac{1}{n} \sum_{i=1}^{n} |FFT_i|^2 \tag{2}$$

In eq. 1, the mean (μ) is a statistical time domain feature to measure the central tendency of varying quantity over the defined fifteen seconds window. Similarly, in eq. 2, the energy feature is calculated by applying the Fast Fourier Transformation (FFT) to find the quantitative characteristics of the data over a defined time period. After it, extracted feature are passed to the classification sub-component. *(b) Classification Module:* We classify the body movements or stationary states through theoretically rich statistical method Support Vector Machine (SVM). In our case, body movements are the small number of available samples as compared to stationary states during sleep that makes the learning process difficult for other classification algorithms. For this reason we select SVM and its slow training issues are resolved through SMO for efficient performance [13]. For the binary linear classification problem (i.e., body movement or stationary in our problem domain) SVM requires the following optimization model including the error-tolerant margin.

$$Minimize \ \frac{1}{2} w^T w + C \sum_{i=1}^{n} \xi_i \tag{1}$$

$$Subject \ to: y_i(w^T x_i + b) \geq 1 - \xi_i, \quad and \quad \xi_i \geq 0 \tag{2}$$

Where "w" is a weight vector and "b" is bias. "C" is the error penalty and "ξ_i" are slack variables, measuring the degree of misclassification of the sample "x_i". The maximum margin is obtained by minimizing the first term of objective function, while the minimum total error of all training examples is assured by minimizing the second term. The above optimization model can be simplified by using the Lagrangrian multiplier techniques and kernel functions:

$$Maximize \ (w.r.t \ \alpha) \sum_{i=1}^{n} \alpha_i - \frac{1}{2} \sum_{i=0}^{n} \sum_{j=1}^{n} \alpha_i \, y_i \alpha_j y_j K(x_i, x_j) \qquad (3)$$

$$Subject \ to: \sum_{i=1}^{n} \alpha_i y_i = 0, \quad 0 \le \alpha_i \le C \qquad (4).$$

Where "K" is the kernel function that satisfies $K(x_i, x_j) = \Phi^T(x_i)\Phi(x_j)$. We used generic polynomial kernels function and is defined by:

$$K(x_i, x_j) = x_i^T x_j \qquad (5)$$

After training, we store the trained model over the server for further classification of unseen sleep data. *(c) Sleep Monitoring Analytics:* After recognizing the body movements, we also keep the record of bed time, wake up time and calculate the fell asleep, frequent body movements patterns, sleep efficiency and time spent in the bed. These are the important parameters to understand the individual sleep and irregularities can be found by computed analytics.

4   Experiments and Discussion

For our pilot study, seven healthy adults (five male and two female) between 25 to 33 years old participated in this study for two weeks. The participants are also requested to complete their sleep diary as a reference. Data is collected using two different scenarios, bed with spring mattresses and plain mattress on the floor, to assess the generalization of proposed approach. We perform the experiments in which subject start the application and keep the mobile phone near the pillow during sleep. Accelerometer sensor of the smartphone is activated and logs the raw signals during the whole night. In the morning, the application is stopped by the subject. Before sending data to the server, first time it requires the user credentials and server authentication to transfer the logged data.

In order to get the training data for classification, four subjects are request to performed five trails of body movement in a natural and comfortable way. The data is collected and transferred to the server through our developed application. We extract the features from accelerometer data and trained the classification module over the server for further analysis of sleep. Time scale for inferencing is set to a one minute epoch that is sufficient to distinguish the stationary state or body movement. For discussion, we are presenting one subject sleep monitoring trail results of working days over one week span in Fig. 2.

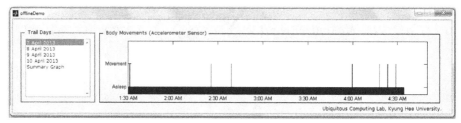

(a)   Detected body movements of the subject during the night of 7th April

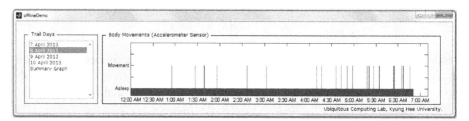

(b)   Detected body movements of the subject during the night of 8th April

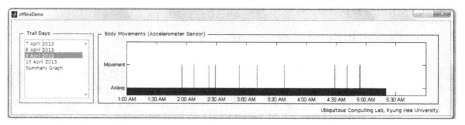

(c)   Detected body movements of the subject during the night of 9th April

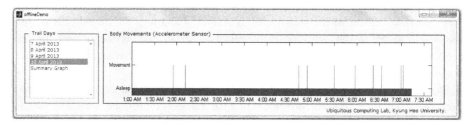

(d)   Detected body movements of the subject during the night of 10th April

Fig. 2. Movement and asleep pattern during the four night trial

Fig. 2, shows the trail days with the body movements and asleep states graph for each day. In order to get useful information, we compute the following sleep analytics (as shown in Table 1) that may help the subject to adopt a healthy lifestyle in a proactive way.

Table 1. Sleep analytics of working day over one week of span

Sleep Analytics	04/07/2013	04/08/2013	04/09/2013	04/10/2013
Bed time	1:30 a.m.	12:00 a.m.	1:00 a.m.	1:00 a.m.
Wake up	4:50 a.m.	6:50 a.m.	5:20 a.m.	7:20 a.m.
Fell asleep	5 min	< 5 min	< 5 min	<5 min
Body movements	6 times	21 times	10 times	10 times
Frequent movements	Morning	Morning	All Night	Morning
Sleep efficiency	80%	84%	88%	92%
In bed time	3hr 20 min	6hr 50 min	4hr 20 min	6hr 20 min

In Table 1, we can infer the irregularity pattern for going to sleep by observation of bed time analytics. It has an important impact on the mood and freshness level on the person daily life routines. For instance, according to the subject sleep diary, after the day 10th April sleep, feels more fresh and active as compared to the last night sleep. It is due to sufficient sleep, on time going to bed and average body movements during the whole night. In our study, we analyze that too much body movements also cause the low quality of sleep and has direct impact on the person's mood. Sometime people feel some problem to fell asleep once they are in the bed. Fell asleep statistic may help to know the duration of it and may correlate with the coffee intake or any other activity before going to bed. The number of body movement and the frequent body movements at the part of the night (i.e., start, midnight, and morning) can tell us about the movement pattern and helpful to find disturbance if it is observed too much. In Figure 4(b), subjects frequent body movements are observed after 4:30 a.m. According to subject report, the room temperature is too cold last night. This kind of analysis may facilitate the automation of other dependent technologies like adjust the room temperature when such kind of situation happens. Furthermore, we also calculate the sleep efficiency according to Michael [14] by the following equation.

$$Sleep\ Efficieny = \frac{(Total\ Sleep\ Time - Awakened\ Time)}{Total\ Sleep\ Time} \qquad (5)$$

We also computing the summary graphs and analytics to provide a quick review over the monitored sleep. Fig. 3 shows the weekly summary graph and analytics of four night sleep.

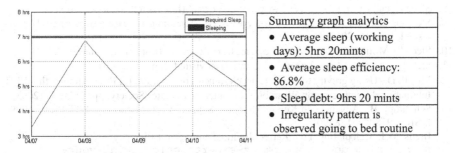

Fig. 3. Summary graph and analytics of four night sleep

5   Conclusion and Future Work

In this study, we designed and developed the sleep monitoring application in a client-server environment. Where smartphone act as a client node to collect the acceleration data during sleep and server process the raw signals. Our method classify the body movements and asleep states by SVM algorithm. We compute the sleep analytics like bed time, wake up, fell asleep, body movements, frequent body movements at different stages of the night, sleep efficiency and time spent in the bed. Our application facilitates the healthy individuals to monitor their sleep and provide a proactive platform for self-management. Currently, our application evolve server side processing and limited to the sleep analytics only. We have plan to implement the proposed model inside the smartphone, commercialize it and provide recommendations for self-management of sleep.

Acknowledgments. This research was funded by the MSIP (Ministry of Science, ICT & Future Planning), Korea in the ICT R&D Program 2013.

References

1. Jeong, C., Joo, S.-C., Jeong, Y.S.: Sleeping situation monitoring system in ubiquitous environments. Journal of Personal and Ubiquitous Computing, 1–8 (2012)
2. Khai, L.Q., Khoa, T.Q.D., Toi, V.V.: A tool for analysis and classification of sleep stages. In: International Conference on Advanced Technologies for Communications, pp. 307–310 (2011)
3. Gironda, R.J., Lloyd, J., Clark, M.E., Walker, R.L.: Preliminary Evaluation of the Reliability and Criterion Validity of the Actiwatch-Score. Journal of Rehabilitation Research & Development, 223–230 (2007)
4. Sleep Diary, http://sleep.buffalo.edu/sleepdiary.pdf (last visited: June 10, 2013)
5. Le, H.X., Lee, S., Truc, P., Vinh, L.T., Khattak, A.M., Han, M., Hung, V.D., Hassan, M.M., Kim, M., Koo, H.K., Lee, K.Y., Huh, E.N.: Secured WSN-integrated cloud computing for u-life care. In: 7th IEEE Consumer Communications and Networking Conference, pp. 1–2 (2010)
6. Adriana, M.A., Pavel, M., Tamara, L.H., Clifford, M.S.: Detection of Movement in Bed Using Unobtrusive Load Cell Sensors. IEEE Transactions on Information Technology in Biomedicine 14(2), 481–490 (2010)
7. Wakemate, http://wakemate.com/ (last visited: June 10, 2013)
8. Sleep Cycle, http://www.sleepcycle.com/ (last visited: June 10, 2013)
9. Sleep as android, https://sites.google.com/site/sleepasandroid/ (last visited: June 10, 2013)
10. Sleep by MotionX, http://sleep.motionx.com/ (last visited: June 10, 2013)
11. Sleepbot, http://mysleepbot.com/ (last visited: June 10, 2013)
12. Mizell, D.: Using gravity to estimate accelerometer orientation. In: Proceeding of the IEEE International Symposium on Wearable Computers, Computer Society, pp. 252–253 (2003)
13. Scholkopf, B.: Advances in Kernel Methods: Support Vector Learning. MIT Press (1999) ISSBN: 9780585128290
14. Breus, M.J.: Calculating Your Perfect Bedtime and Sleep Efficiency, http://blog.doctoroz.com/oz-experts/calculating-your-perfect-bedtime-and-sleep-efficiency (last visited: June 10, 2013)

HARF: A Hierarchical Activity Recognition Framework Using Smartphone Sensors

Manhyung Han[1], Jae Hun Bang[1], Chris Nugent[2], Sally McClean[3], and Sungyoung Lee[1]

[1] Department of Computer Engineering, Kyung Hee University (Global Campus), Korea
{smiley,jhb,sylee}@oslab.khu.ac.kr
[2] School of Computing and Mathematics, University of Ulster, Jordanstown, U.K.
cd.nugent@ulster.ac.uk
[3] School of Computing and Information Engineering, University of Ulster, Coleraine, U.K.
si.mcclean@ulster.ac.uk

Abstract. Activity recognition for the purposes of recognizing a user's intentions using multimodal sensors is becoming a widely researched topic largely based on the prevalence of the smartphone. Previous studies have reported the difficulty in recognizing life-logs by only using a smartphone due to the challenges with activity modeling and real-time recognition. In addition, recognizing life-logs is difficult due to the absence of an established framework which enables utilizing different sources of sensor data. In this paper, we propose a smartphone based Hierarchical Activity Recognition Framework which extends the Naïve Bayes approach for the processing of activity modeling and real-time activity recognition. The proposed algorithm demonstrates higher accuracy than the Naïve Bayes approach and also enables the recognition of a user's activities within a mobile environment. The proposed algorithm has the ability to classify fifteen activities with an average classification accuracy of 92.96%.

Keywords: Activity Recognition, Smartphone, Multimodal Sensors, Naïve Bayes, Life-log.

1 Introduction

Activity Recognition (AR) solutions are capable of identifying physical actions, postures or movements using various sensors which have the ability to capture the intention and the condition of the current situation of the subject. Existing AR research has utilized wearable sensors which have been attached on the human's body or 2D/3D cameras for the purposes of capturing video based images [1,2]. A range of studies have also considered the use of mobile phones for the purposes of AR [3,4,5]. In these studies, the data is collected using a mobile phone and the AR is normally performed offline. Thus, the AR algorithms are not implemented in real-time on the phone and the classification is not performed in real-time. In [6], an AR system running purely on a smartphone is presented. The system can be trained on the mobile phone itself

G. Urzaiz et al. (Eds.): UCAmI 2013, LNCS 8276, pp. 159–166, 2013.

and also as the ability to perform the classification in real-time on the phone. The recognition is based on features calculated using a geometric template matching approach and a support vector machine (SVM) is used as the classifier.

There are multiple sensor devices embedded on a smartphone and the smartphone is able to process collected data independently. For recognizing physical movements of the user, accelerometer and gyroscope sensors are utilized. Also for gathering context data such as location, situation or environmental information, data from GPS, proximity sensor and MIC are used. A smartphone also has enough storage space, processing capability and communication modules. So we selected a smartphone as a sensing and processing platform for recognizing human's activities.

General AR is divided into two phase. Firstly a training phase is required to build the activity models and secondly a recognition phase where based on activity models the data collected is proposed. Probability-based AR algorithms for example hidden markov models (HMM), SVM or k-nearest neighbor (kNN) are difficult to apply to smartphone applications given that they requires sample data for modeling in addition to their computational complexity [11].

In this paper, a lightweight activity modeling and recognition framework defined as the Hierarchical Activity Recognition Framework (HARF) which enables the modeling and recognition the user activities on a smartphone is proposed. The proposed HARF has the ability to recognize 15 activities and uses the accelerometer, Gyroscope, Proximity sensor and GPS modules all from the smartphone.

2   Related Works

AR using multimodal sensors on a smartphone has been widely investigated due to the ability of the smartphone to collect various sensor data on a single mobile device. Previous studies have considered recognizing the activities of walking and running using accelerometer data [7,8] and moving activities by transportation using GPS data [9,10]. Nevertheless, the majority of approaches have mainly considered a single sensor and exploited multiple sensor data. To a certain extent this limits the type of activities which can be recognized in addition to the recognition accuracy. In [11], the researches utilizing multimodal sensors in a Smartphone are similar to this paper. They have, however, used HMM and GMM algorithms which require significant computing resources. In [2], the authors proved that utilizing multiple sensor data helps to improve accuracy levels through a combination of accelerometer and audio data.

There are several existing studies for activity modeling and recognition algorithms. In [12], the authors used multiple sensors or heterogeneous sensors for recognizing user's activities by attaching to the body. The approach required a physical connection between the sensors, however, such an approach is not suitable for long-term AR. For accelerometer data classification, several approaches to feature extraction and classification have been investigated [13]. Nevertheless, existing approaches are difficult to apply to mobile devices which have relatively less resources than computers or servers for the initial stages of training.

3   Adaptive Naïve Bayes Algorithm

In this paper the Naïve Bayes algorithm is used as a basic algorithm for recognizing a human's activities. If the activity information of users is matched to the model which has the highest possibilities among pre-constructed activities models, it is chosen by the algorithm. Generally the Naïve Bayes classifier achieves faster modeling time and less computation overheads than other machine learning algorithms. The Naïve Bayes classifier can be generate an activity model quickly, however, it has several limitations such as relatively low processing speed and it is difficult to deploy into a mobile environment which is resource constrained. In addition, one of the inherent characteristics of the Naïve Bayes classifier is that every attribute has the same priority which results in a lower accuracy of posterior probability. In the current work, an Adaptive Naïve Bayes approach is proposed in an effort to address the aforementioned issues.

Naïve Bayes is a statistical classification method which can estimate the possibility of a given sample. The Naïve Bayes probabilistic model assumes that sample data F_1 to F_n have possibilities to relating to an independent class C. The probability of C after the sample data $F_1 \dots F_n$ are collected is $p(C|F_1, \dots, F_n)$ and which is referred to as the posteriori probability. In order to calculate $p(C|F_1, \dots, F_n)$, $p(F_1, \dots, F_n)$ and $p(C)$ are required. These can be estimated from training data and are referred to as the boundary probability. By using Bayes's theorem a posteriori probability is defined as presented in equation (1):

$$p(C|F_1, \dots, F_n) = \frac{p(C)p(F_1, \dots, F_n|C)}{p(F_1, \dots, F_n)} \tag{1}$$

Only considering a maximization of $p(C)p(C|F_1, \dots, F_n)$ because $p(F_1, \dots, F_n)$ has values to every class. If the boundary probability of the class is now known, only $p(F_1, \dots, F_n|C)$ may be considered. $p(F_1, \dots, F_n|C)$ is calculated by the independent assumption of Naïve Bayes. As a result, $F_1, \dots, F_n$ can be classified as the class which has the largest posteriori probability. If a sample data F_i is a classification attribute and contains one value out of several limited values, a calculation of $p(F_i|C)$ may be made according to traditional probability. However the characteristic of the training data for AR is continuous data. In this case, the distribution of probability is utilized for calculating conditional probability. And the Gaussian distribution is utilized for representing a distribution of F_i.

$$P(F_i = v|C) = \frac{1}{\sqrt{2\pi\sigma_C^2}} e^{-\frac{(v-\mu_C)^2}{2\sigma_C^2}} \tag{2}$$

In equation (2), the mean value of F_i in class C is μ_c and distribution is σ_c^2, In the current work, the proposed approach utilizes multiple sensor data gleaned from a smartphone. Taking this into consideration a lightweight modeling and recognition algorithm is therefore required due to the limited resources. In addition, given the performance issues associated with the Naïve Bayes approach a lightweight classification algorithm A-NB, which enables activity modeling and recognition in a

Smartphone, is proposed. When a system builds an activity model using Naïve Bayes, the complexity of the calculation is dependent on the number of sample data i. If features for AR are increased, it requires significant processing capabilities while calculating the mean value μ_C and the distribution σ_C^2 of data F_i. For overcoming memory overflow which may occur during real-time activity training, A-NB calculates the mean and distribution values of data F_i periodically. The repetitive approach considering memory usage and efficiency is described below:

$$\mu_N = \frac{\mu_{(N-1)} \times (N-1) + F_N}{N}, \; v_N = \frac{v_{(N-1)} \times (N-1) + F_N^2}{N}, \sigma_N^2 = v_N - \mu_N^2 \tag{3}$$

In equation (3), N is the number of collected data for time t, μ_N is the mean of data N, v_N is the mean of the square of data N and σ_N^2 is the distribution. If the number of calculated mean and distribution is j, the proposed A-NB approach calculates the total mean value by combining μ_1 to μ_j, the total distribution value by mean value of σ_1^2 to σ_j^2. In order to calculate the $p'(F_i|C)$ value, equation (2) is transformed to equation (4)

$$P'(F_i = v|C) = \frac{1}{\sqrt{2\pi\mu_v}} e^{-\frac{(v-\mu_m)^2}{2\mu_v}} \tag{4}$$

μ_m is the mean value of $\mu_1 \dots \mu_j$, μ_v is also the mean value of the distribution $\sigma_1^2 \dots \sigma_j^2$. Hence the mean and distribution are calculated by data sample F_i, and by using these values the posteriori probability $P'(F_i = v|C)$ are able to can subsequently be calculated.

4   Proposed Hierarchical Activity Recognition Framework

Although the AR using multimodal sensors can increase recognizable activities and enable the recognition various situations, it lowers the accuracy of the overall recognition result given that the classifier is required to consider more factors from input data. In order to overcome this issue, HARF which recognizes activities in hierarchical approach has been proposed. The approach includes the ability to not only recognize a simple act, however, also to consider the spatial location of the user and their activity within a given context. The approach also considers that there may be different meanings associated with the user's location. The activities are categorized into 3 types as presented in Table 1.

Figure 1 depicts the proposed HARF architecture for real-time AR processing based on the A-NB algorithm. If the A-NB is applied to AR, classification is performed firstly using location information and the heuristic approach is applied as described in Table 1. Once recognition is performing, a system recognizes the location first for differentiating indoor (Home and Office) and outdoor. If the user is at unregistered location, the system tries to recognize the current activity among outdoor activities (Walking, Sitting, Standing, Jogging and Riding a car) with heuristic-based approach. However if the user is at registered location, the system firstly look up the location-based activity list. If the user is at the home or office, the system tries to recognize the activity using the proposed approach with multimodal sensor data.

Table 1. Activity categorization for hierarchical activity recognition

Type	Area	Activity	Sensors
Location & multimodal sensor based activity recognition	Home	Walking Sitting Standing	Accelerometer, Gyroscope, Proximity and GPS
	Office	Walking Sitting Standing	
	Outdoor	Walking Sitting Standing Jogging	
Location based activity recognition	Outdoor	Waiting for bus at bus stop Having a meal at cafeteria Exercising at gym Visiting a park	GPS
Heuristic based activity recognition	Outdoor	Riding a car	Accelerometer, Gyroscope, Proximity, GPS and Heuristic

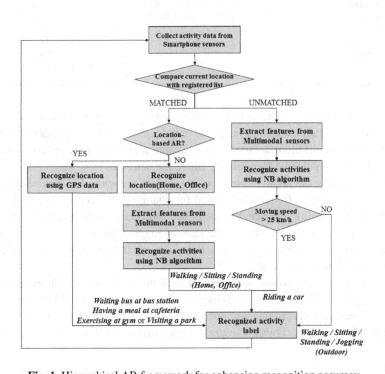

Fig. 1. Hierarchical AR framework for enhancing recognition accuracy

5   Performance Evaluation

For the verification of the A-NB algorithms and the HARF framework, a real-time AR system has been implemented in the form of a Smartphone application using the Android OS. Table 2 presents the results of the AR using the developed Smartphone application. The experiments were conducted on 15 activities including 4 location based activities (Waiting for bus at bus stop, Having a meal at cafeteria, Exercising at gym, Visiting a park). However, the results of recognizing 4 location based activities are not presented. There was only 1 misrecognized case out of 200 testing samples. Nevertheless, if the GPS on the Smartphone is guaranteed to work well, location based activities are well recognized in the proposed system. Therefore, the experimental results in Table 2 present the accuracy of 11 activities without location-based activities.

Table 2. Activity recognition accuracy table of 11 activities for validating proposed HARF

Location		Home			Office			Outdoor				
		Standing	Walking	Sitting	Standing	Walking	Sitting	Standing	Walking	Sitting	Jogging	Car
	Standing	**90.32**	-	9.68	-	-	-	-	-	-	-	-
Home	Walking	10.43	**83.47**	6.1	-	-	-	-	-	-	-	-
	Sitting	2.56	-	**98.44**	-	-	-	-	-	-	-	-
	Standing	-	-	-	**95.2**	-	4.8	-	-	-	-	-
Office	Walking	-	-	-	4.84	**94.35**	0.81	-	-	-	-	-
	Sitting	-	-	-	1.2	0.61	**98.19**	-	-	-	-	-
	Standing	-	-	-	-	-	-	**94.34**	-	5.66	-	-
	Walking	-	-	-	-	-	-	12.77	**80.85**	6.38	-	-
Outdoor	Sitting	-	-	-	-	-	-	2.5	-	**97.5**	-	-
	Jogging	-	-	-	-	-	-	2.17	10.86	1.47	**85.5**	-
	Car	-	-	-	-	-	-	16.25	6.25	1.25	-	**76.25**

The recognition result of 15 activities shows an accuracy of 92.96% and the result of 11 activities, without activities based on only location, is 90.4%. There are several cases which show different accuracy on the same activities. This indicates that the activity can be recognized differently on where the activities took place. For example, walking activities in the home or outdoors are seldom recognized as a standing activity given that the user is frequently stopped for changing a direction. The recognition accuracy of both sitting and standing activities are relatively higher than others because of their static characteristic. In the case of jogging and car, there are some misrecognition results because a jogging activity is similar to walking and a car is frequently stopped or driven slowly.

A performance comparison of the HARF and the Naïve Bayes algorithm is presented in Figure 2. The result of the Naive Bayes and the proposed HARF are 81.17% and 89.88% respectively. In the case of recognizing Car Driving, HARF showed 76% and but the Naïve Bayes showed a lower accuracy of around 50%.

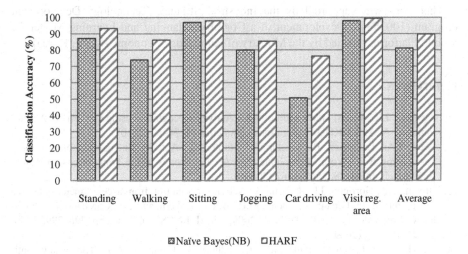

Fig. 2. Accuracy comparison between Naïve Bayes and HARF for 15 activities

6   Conclusion and Future Work

In this paper, we proposed a personalized activity modeling and real-time activity recognition framework for understanding a human's intention or requirements based on multimodal sensors in a Smartphone. A Hierarchical Activity Recognition Framework for modeling and recognizing user activities on resource restricted smartphone was proposed. For compensating a memory overflow error which may occur within the constrained resources of the smartphone when considering data from multimodal sensors, we proposed a hierarchical activity modeling and recognition approach. The testing results show that the proposed system can recognize 15 activities with an accuracy of 92.96%. This is 10.73% higher than using a conventional Naïve Bayes approach.

The proposed HARF exhibited relatively high accuracy when recognizing simple or fixed patterns of activities (jogging, standing). In the case of activities such as riding a car or walking, which may have various patterns, it showed lower accuracy. In order to compensate for these problems, other studies using not only smartphone, however, external sensor devices or utilizing environmental sound are required. A compound approach utilizing multimodal sensor data and external sensor data is expected to enhance the accuracy of activity modeling and recognition.

Acknowledgements. This research was supported by the MSIP (Ministry of Science, ICT & Future Planning), Korea, under the ITRC (Information Technology Research Center) support program supervised by the NIPA (National IT Industry Promotion Agency) (NIPA-2013-(H0301-13-2001)).

This work was supported by the Industrial Strategic Technology Development Program (10035348, Development of a Cognitive Planning and Learning Model for Mobile Platforms) funded by the Ministry of Knowledge Economy (MKE, Korea).

References

1. Kwapisz, J.R., Weiss, G.M., Moore, S.A.: Activity Recognition using Cell Phone Accelerometers. ACM SIGKDD Explorations Newsletter 12, 74–82 (2010)
2. Ward, J.A., Lukowicz, P., Troster, G., Starner, T.: Activity Recognition of Assembly Tasks using Body-Worn Microphones and Accelerometers. IEEE Transactions on Pattern Anal. Mach. Intell. 28, 1553–1567 (2006)
3. Brezmes, T., Gorricho, J.L., Cotrina, J.: Activity recognition from accelerometer data on a mobile phone. In: Omatu, S., Rocha, M.P., Bravo, J., Fernández, F., Corchado, E., Bustillo, A., Corchado, J.M. (eds.) IWANN 2009, Part II. LNCS, vol. 5518, pp. 796–799. Springer, Heidelberg (2009)
4. Lu, H., Yang, J., Liu, Z., Lane, N.D., Choudhury, T., Campbell, A.T.: The Jigsaw continuous sensing engine for mobile phone applications. In: Proceedings of the 8th ACM Conference on Embedded Networked Sensor Systems, SenSys 2010, pp. 71–84 (2010)
5. Peebles, D., Lu, H., Lane, N.D., Choudhury, T., Campbell, A.T.: Community-guided learning: Exploiting mobile sensor users to model human behavior. In: Proceedings of the Twenty-Fourth AAAI Conference on Artificial Intelligence, AAAI 2010, Atlanta, Georgia, USA, July 11-15 (2010)
6. Frank, J., Mannor, S., Precup, D.: Activity recognition with mobile phones. In: Gunopulos, D., Hofmann, T., Malerba, D., Vazirgiannis, M. (eds.) ECML PKDD 2011, Part III. LNCS, vol. 6913, pp. 630–633. Springer, Heidelberg (2011)
7. Khan, A.M., Lee, Y.K., Lee, S.Y., Kim, T.S.: A Triaxial Accelerometer-Based Physical-Activity Recognition Via Augmented-Signal Features and a Hierarchical Recognizer. IEEE Transactions on Information Technology in Biomedicine 14(5), 1166–1172 (2010)
8. Ravi, N., Dandekar, N., Mysore, P., Littman, M.L.: Activity Recognition from Accelerometer Data. In: Proceedings of the Seventeenth Conference on Innovative Applications of Artificial Intelligence, pp. 1541–1549 (2005)
9. Liao, L., Fox, D., Kautz, H.: Extracting Places and Activities from GPS Traces using Hierarchical Conditional Random Fields. Int. J. Rob. Res. 26, 119–134 (2007)
10. Vinh, L.T., Lee, S.Y., Park, Y.T., d'Auriol, B.: A Novel Feature Selection Method Based on Normalized Mutual Information. Appl. Intell. 37, 100–120 (2012)
11. Han, M., Vinh, L.T., Lee, Y.-K., Lee, S.: Comprehensive Context Recognizer Based on Multimodal Sensors in a Smartphone. Journal of Sensors 12(9), 12588–12605 (2012)
12. Minnen, D., Starner, T., Ward, J., Lukowicz, P., Troester, G.: Recognizing and discovering human actions from on-body sensor data. In: Proc. IEEE Int. Conf. Multimedia Expo, pp. 1545–1548 (2005)
13. Shen, K.Q., Ong, C.J., Li, X.P., Wilder-Smith, E.P.V.: Novel Multi-Class Feature Selection Methods using Sensitivity Analysis of Posterior Probabilities. In: Proc. of the IEEE International Conference on Systems, Man and Cybernetics, pp. 1116–1121 (2008)

An Affective Inference Model
Based on Facial Expression Analysis

Paula Andrea Lago and Claudia Lucía Jiménez-Guarín

Department of Systems Engineering and Computation,
Universidad de Los Andes, Bogotá, Colombia
{pa.lago52,cjimenez}@uniandes.edu.co

Abstract. Ubiquitous computing aims to reduce the complexity of interacting with computing devices. Analyzing psychological user states helps in this task. In this work we propose a computational model for analyzing psychological user states that takes into account three emotions that have not been explored deeply: interest, boredom and confusion. The model was constructed based on a video analysis of 35 engineering students during two class activities, all of whom reported the emotions they were feeling as they performed the activity. From the video, facial expressions features were extracted and matched with the emotion reported. This allowed us to construct patterns of facial expression and emotion inference rules. Our model is based on distances and indicators of change with respect to a user baseline, which allows the model to adapt to different users, moods and personal manners. Recognizing these emotions can be used as an implicit feedback in different systems.

Keywords: analysis of psychological user states, affective computing, facial expression, implicit feedback, computational model of emotion, interest, boredom, confusion.

1 Introduction

Ubiquitous computing aims to help people be more productive or live more easily by reducing the complexity of interacting with computing devices. However, current computing devices and applications leave to the user the burden of exactly telling the computer what she is trying to achieve or what she really wants. This is often not easy and can leave the user with an unaccomplished or unsuccessful task and feeling frustrated.

Just as when people interact with other people, when they use their computers they are feeling different emotions. If the user finds some piece of information that helps them with the task at hand, she feels interested; if she gets information that is not currently relevant for her, she will feel bored; and so on. If computers could understand these emotions, they could interact better with their users.

Humans communicate emotions through their facial expressions, and computers can take advantage of this fact to better interact with users. For example, if the user feels confused at an error message the computer could suggest possible actions or

G. Urzaiz et al. (Eds.): UCAmI 2013, LNCS 8276, pp. 167–174, 2013.
© Springer International Publishing Switzerland 2013

give a step to step guide to correct the error. In the same way, if the user is interested in a piece of information, the application could recommend other related articles. In sum, understanding emotions can give computers the ability to tailor their actions and results based on the emotional state of their users.

Most of the current emotional models focus on the six basic emotions proposed by Ekman [1] or the measurement of valence based on physiological signals (Section 2). In this work we present a computational model of emotion based on facial expression analysis which will be used for inferring confusion, boredom and interest. We selected the set of emotions and parameters for the model based on the emotional self-reporting of 35 engineering students at Universidad de Los Andes, 2011 while taking an exam or performing a guided activity and the corresponding video of their facial expressions (Section 3). Our model is based on changes of the facial expression of the user with respect to a baseline (Section 4). This allows the model to adapt to different moods and personal manners. We discuss our model and some considerations for facial expression analysis in section 5.

This model will be used as an implicit feedback for MagPie [2], a pervasive environment for information retrieval in academic contexts. The implicit feedback from the emotional response enables MagPie to build pervasive features and adapt to the user.

2 Current Affective Models Based on Facial Expression Recognition

Affective computing comprises the study and creation of technologies that "relate to, arise from, or deliberately influence emotion or other affective phenomena" [3] [4]. This consists of the following steps: definition of the emotions to be studied or recognized, definition of the expression of the emotion to be used, identification of features from this expression and interpretation of the features in order to recognize the emotion. Each of the steps will be described in the following paragraphs.

The work in affective computing usually focuses on recognizing the six basic emotions proposed by Ekman (sadness, happiness, anger, surprise, disgust and fear) [1]. However, this set is not used in MagPie. This is because when interacting with computing devices for academic activities these emotions do not arise as frequently as in interactions between humans. Instead, we use a set of emotions relevant to both the work with computational devices and the interaction with content in academic contexts. We chose the set of emotions (interest, boredom, confusion, neutral) after observation of people in our community interacting with their computers (section 3).

The expression of emotion includes physiological changes such as changes in breath and heart rhythm, sweating, changes in brain signals and others [5]. Measuring these physiological signals generally require the use of sensors attached to the user that cannot be considered pervasive since they are highly obtrusive. Other forms of emotional expression include facial expression, posture, gestures, speech and behavior [5]. We are working with facial expressions for they can be recognized using a web camera which is a highly available device for numerous users.

Facial expressions have been studied in depth by Ekman [6] [7]. He states that there are three forms of facial expression: macroexpressions [6], microexpressions [6] and subtle expressions [8]. We are working with micro and macro expressions, which have durations of 1/50 seconds to 4 seconds. This imposes a requirement of timing in the samples of facial expressions and a challenge in the performance of the application. Fasel and Luettin [9] and Beristain and Graña [10] provide extensive surveys of the different techniques for facial expression recognition and emotion recognition based on its analysis. One of the most used techniques is to encode the facial expression using the Facial Action Coding Systems (FACS) [7].

We are basing our model in the models of Chang [11] and Cerezo [12], adding the indicators of change for each distance. Their models are based on the extraction of feature points over the face and corresponding distances among them.

3   Data Gathering and Analysis

Facial expression databases for emotion recognition such as Cohn-Kanade [13], MUG [14], the CMU [15], PIE [15] and MMI [16], have facial expression samples for the six basic emotions or a subset of them. Since we want to work with different emotions, acquiring samples of facial expressions for these emotions was one crucial task. Moreover, we want to work with video instead of single pictures in order to detect changes in the expression.

For taking real examples of different facial expressions in an academic context, we recorded an exam of 22 first-semester engineering students (14 male, 8 women) and a guided activity of 13 senior students (11 male, 2 female). The activities were prepared trying to elicit some emotions such as interest, confusion, boredom, curiosity, frustration, etc. Along with the exam and activity, students were handed a questionnaire to report emotions felt at each moment of the test. In this questionnaire, they also had to report at what time they felt the emotion so we could match it to their facial expressions in the video. The results are summarized in Table 1, in which we show the total number of reports for each emotion.

Table 1. Number of reports for each emotion obtained

Emotion	Number of reports
Interest	60
Concentration	64
Fulfillment	35
Confusion	31
Frustration	9
Boredom	9
Distraction	15
Tiredness	6
None/Other	2

From these emotions we chose the set of emotions that could be easily matched to facial expressions in the video. Some of the emotions were often reported together, so we grouped them in one single emotion. The final set of emotions is then: interest, boredom, confusion, and a neutral state. Figure 1 shows some examples of the data.

Fig. 1. Example of a sequence of confusion (top) and interest (bottom) captured during an exam and a guided activity

From the data gathered we make the following remarks:

1. Some people have "constant" gestures that do not indicate an emotion but a mood or a personal manner or another affective state. For example, some people frowned all the time while performing the test. Our model must be able to identify these gestures and adapt accordingly.
2. Facial expressions have durations from fractions of seconds to almost 5 seconds, as was stated by Ekman. This means the model should not process all data but only the segments that could indicate an emotion.
3. Some emotions are expressed with posture more than with facial expression. Combining posture and facial expression can thus improve accuracy. However, the scope of this paper is only concerned with facial expression.

4   Proposed Model

We base our model on the models of Chang and Cerezo, both of which use distances as the features that describe a facial expression. In addition, our model considers a baseline of the user expression and changes with respect to it, so it can adapt to different moods and personal manners.

The process for recognition consists of four steps: (i) extract facial features points, (ii) calculate distances between these points, (iii) compute change indicators, (iv) define expression characteristics and (v) estimate probabilities for each emotion based on a vector of change indicators.

To extract facial features points we use the library LuxandFace SDK [17] which extracts 64 feature points. Among these points we calculate the distances and the change indicators, shown in figure 2. The change measure is taken with respect to a baseline of the user expression, which is the average of a window over time for each distance measure.

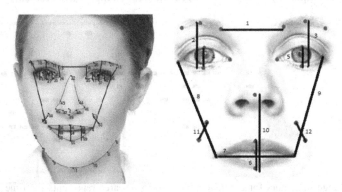

Fig. 2. Feature points extracted by Luxand Face SDK (numbered) and distances calculated for inference model (lines on black). On the right, change measures calculated from the distances.

Each change measure is calculated as follows: If most of the current measures (m) are greater than the baseline (b) plus a threshold (μ), then we set the indicator to one, corresponding to a positive change. If most of the current measures (m) are less than the baseline (b) minus a threshold (μ), the indicator is set to minus one, indicating a negative change. If neither condition is met, the indicator is set to zero, indicating there was no significant change. This is shown in (1).

$$I = \begin{cases} 1 \; if \; m > b + \mu \\ -1 \; if m < b - \mu \\ 0 \; otherwise \end{cases} \tag{1}$$

Figure 3 illustrates this concept for the distance between the eyebrows during confusion. As can be seen, at time 16, 17 and 18 this distance has a negative change since the points lie below the threshold area.

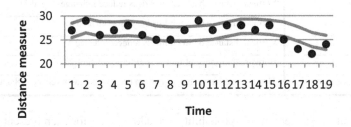

Fig. 3. Distance measures for the distance between eyebrows during confusion. The area between both lines represents the threshold area. Points outside of this area indicate change.

As an example of the change indicators calculated, figure 4 shows the indicators of change for the sequence of confusion shown in figure 1. By the time the user reports confusion and shows it with a facial expression, more indicators of change are present at the same time than when the emotion is not being expressed. Each row represents a facial distance (as numbered in figure 2) and the squares in each row show when a positive (gray squares) or negative (black squares) change was detected.

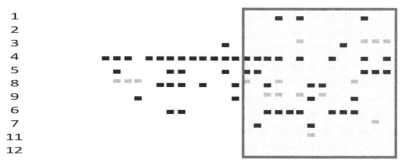

Fig. 4. Change indicators for confusion. The shadowed area represents the time at which the expression is present.

Change indicators allow us to decide if a facial action has been made. We show the actions used in this work and the changes associated to it in Table 3.

Table 2. Expression characteristics and change measures associated

Expression Characteristic	Changes associated
Smile	The distance between eyes and lip corners is reduced (changes 8 and 9) and the distance of the wrinkles on the side of the mouth increases (changes 11 and 12)
Open eyes	Vertical distance between eyelids increases (change 4 and 5)
Frown eyebrows	Horizontal distance between eyebrows is reduced (change 1)
Raise eyebrows	Vertical distance between eyebrows and eyelid increases (changes 2 and 3)
Lower eyebrows	Vertical distance between eyebrows and eyelid is reduced(changes 2 and 3)
Close eyes	Vertical distance between eyelids is reduced(changes 4 and 5)
Open mouth	Vertical distance between lips increases (change 6)
Close mouth	Vertical distance between lips is reduced(change 6)
Pucker lips	Horizontal distance of mouth is reduced (change 7)
Lower lip corners	The distance between eyes and lip corners increases (changes 8 and 9)

To calculate each emotion's probability, we add a factor for each present characteristic. These factors were carefully hand-tuned based on the data collected and are shown in Table 4. Based on the data, there are indicators of change that are more significant in some emotions, thus the factors are tuned accordingly.

Table 3. Heuristics to compute the probability of each of the emotions of the model

Emotion	Heuristics
Interest Happiness	Smile (0.5), Open eyes (0.1), Look at the device (0.2), No frowns (0.05), Eyebrows rise (0.1), Open mouth (0.05)
Confusion Frustration	Frown (0.5), Lower eyebrows (0.05), Pucker lips (0.2), Open mouth (0.1), Close eyes (0.05), No smile (0.1)
Boredom	No smile (0.2), Close eyes (0.2), Open mouth (0.3), Lower lip corners (0.3)

5   Discussion

In this section we review the proposed model and the main challenges and quality attributes that should be taken into account when implementing an affective computing application.

- First of all, facial expressions are very short in duration which makes sampling and processing intense.
- It is important to remember that some people have gestures that they often make but do not express an emotion. This is why we work with changes in facial expression and not with a static view.
- Taking into account the previous point, it would be desirable to learn from each user to personalize inferences and make them more correct.
- Lastly, emotion expression is not only present for one point in time but for a window of time, so it can be seen as a process and the analysis should be done over a period of time and not just in a single point.

6   Conclusions and Future Work

In this work, we have proposed a computational model of emotion for analyzing user's psychological states. The model is used for inferring interest, boredom and confusion; emotions that are relevant to human computer interaction. The model consists of patterns of facial expression and emotion inference rules. This model enables pervasive features to MagPie such us gathering implicit feedback for the construction of user profiles.

Planned future work includes adding a personal model which can take into account variables that affect emotion expression such as gender, personality and culture. Also, adding posture detection to improve accuracy of inference.

References

1. Ekman, P.: Basic Emotions. de Handbook of Cognition and Emotion, pp. 45–60. John Wiley & Sons, Ltd. (2005)
2. Lago, P., Jimenez, C.: MAGPIE:Pervasive Environment with Emotional Awareness for Managing Information in the Context of Collaborative Communities. In: Conference Proceedings Ucami 2011 – 5th International Symposium on Ubiquitous Computing And Ambient Intelligence, Riviera Maya, Mexico (2011) ISBN 978-84-694-9677-0

3. Höök, K.: Affective Computing. In: Soegaard, M., Dam, R.F. (eds.) The Encyclopedia of Human-Computer Interaction, 2nd edn. The Interaction Design Foundation (2013)
4. Picard, R.W.: Affective Computing: From Laughter to IEEE. IEEE Transactions on Affective Computing 1(1), 11–17 (2010)
5. Bradley, M.M., Lang, P.J.: Measuring emotion: behavior, feeling, and physiology. In: Lane, R.D., Nadel, L. (eds.) Cognitive Neuroscience of Emotion, pp. 242–276. Oxford University Press (2000)
6. Ekman, P.: Emotions Revealed. Times Books, New York (2003)
7. Ekman, P.: Facial Action Coding System: A Technique for the Measurement of Facial Movement. Consulting Psychologists Press (1978)
8. Warren, G., Schertler, E., Bull, P.: Detecting Deception from Emotional and Unemotional Cues. Journal of Nonverbal Behavior
9. Fasel, B., Luettin, J.: Automatic facial expression analysis: a survey. Pattern Recognition 36(1), 259–275 (2003)
10. Beristain, A., Graña, M.: Emotion Recognition Based on The Analysis of Facial Expresions: A Survey. New Mathematics and Natural Computation (NMNC) 5(2), 513–534 (2009)
11. Chang, C.-Y., Tsai, J.-S., Wang, C.-J., Chung, P.-C.: Emotion recognition with consideration of facial expression and physiological signals (2009)
12. Cerezo, E., Hupont, I., Baldassarri, S., Ballano, S.: Emotional facial sensing and multimodal fusion in a continuous 2D affective space. Journal of Ambient Intelligence and Humanized Computing, 1–16
13. Lucey, P., Cohn, J.F., Kanade, T., Saragih, J., Ambadar, Z., Matthews, I.: The Extended Cohn-Kande Dataset (CK+): A complete facial expression dataset for action unit and emotion-specified expression. In: Third IEEE Workshop on CVPR for Human Communicative Behavior Analysis (2010)
14. Aifanti, N., Papachristou, C., Delopoulos, A.: The MUG Facial Expression Database. In: 11th Int. Workshop on Image Analysis for Multimedia Interactive Services (WIAMIS), Proc. 11th Int. Workshop on Image Analysis for Multimedia Interactive Services (WIAMIS), Desenzano, Italy (2010)
15. Sim, T., Baker, S., Bsat, M.: The CMU Pose, Illumination, and Expression Database. IEEE Transactions on Pattern Analysis and Machine Intelligence 25(12), 1615–1618 (2003)
16. Valstar, M.F., Pantic, M.: Induced Disgust, Happiness and Surprise: an Addition to the MMI Facial Expression Database. In: Workshop on Emotional Corpora (2010)
17. Face SDK. Luxand, http://www.luxand.com/facesdk/

Probabilistic Situation Modeling from Ambient Sensors in a Health Condition Monitoring System

Gustavo López and Ramón Brena

ITESM, Campus Monterrey
Av. Eugenio Garza Sada 2501 Sur, Monterrey, N.L., México
gustavo.alh@gmail.com, ramon.brena@itesm.mx

Abstract. The abundance of sensors in daily life infrastructures and mobile devices can allow to determine what the users are doing, which is the situation of the environment they are in, and therefore what needs they can have and take action accordingly. Artificial Intelligence techniques are applied in order to give the users the functionality that best suits their needs. This is what is called "context-aware computing". The term "Ambient Intelligence" refers to this technology and emphasizes the incorporation of local intelligence to computing components. Ambient Intelligence is a huge field that goes from the acquisition of data from the environment, to fusioning the gathered information and data, to extracting situation characteristics, and to finally selecting and providing adequate information and services based on the extracted context. There are many applications of this technology. In this research paper, we present a Temporal Probabilistic Graphical Model based on Context Extraction Modules for Situation Modeling applications. This model is implemented and analyzed in the context of a Health Condition Monitoring System for recognizing and keeping track of changes in the Activities of Daily Living, an elderly care indicator used to detect emerging medical conditions.

1 Introduction

Nowadays, we live in a world where information and knowledge have a great effect in our daily activities. Different types of sensors and actuators are being embedded in daily life infrastructures and mobile devices are ubiquitous. These computing devices will have to be coordinated by intelligent systems that integrate the resources available to provide an "intelligent environment". [6] This confluence of topics has led to the introduction of the area of "Ambient Intelligence" (AmI): *"a digital environment that proactively, but sensibly, supports people in their daily lives."* [1]

An important part of an Ambient Intelligence System is the context or situation awareness. It allows the system to take intelligent decisions based on the situation of the environment. A situation is a particular set of circumstances

G. Urzaiz et al. (Eds.): UCAmI 2013, LNCS 8276, pp. 175–182, 2013.

(conditions and states) of the surrounding environment defined by context variables. The notion of "Situation Modeling" refers to the representation and use of situations in a system, therefore providing the situation awareness capability.

One field that can take a good advantage of the implementation of Ambient Intelligence [9,6,5] applications is the Health Care and, specifically, the Health Condition Monitoring. In elderly care, activities of daily living (ADLs) are used to assess the cognitive and physical capabilities of an elderly person [4]. An activity recognition system allows to automatically monitor their decline over time and detect anomalies.

2   Proposed Solution Model

The *main problem* in the subject of *Situation Modeling in Ambient Intelligence* that we address in this paper is the recognizing of ADLs in an application of a Health Condition Monitoring System. In this section, the Solution Model is presented.

2.1   Model Description

In this work we propose a Temporal Probabilistic Graphical Model [2,8] based on Context Extraction Modules. Thus, it has the advantage of handling uncertainty and time, and implements concepts from the Ambient Intelligence and Situation Modeling framework. The characteristics of the model are:

- The probability of time-dependent Random Variables (RV) is defined by probability functions of time. These functions automatically handle values in intervals and points of time.
- The probability of non time-dependent RVs is defined by conventional probability tables.
- Since in Ambient Intelligence, time is given by the system. The value of a RV is already defined according to the time.
- Sensors provide the real-time values of the observed nodes.
- Relationships between two RVs are handled by their connecting edges in the network. Causation can only extend forward in time.
- A monitored variable can save a history of past values.
- If the current value of a variable depends on its past value, it can be checked in the history (avoiding dependency cycles over the same variable in the network).
- Dependency on past values can be handled for both self-dependence and dependence in other variables past values.
- The values of the nodes in the network come from developed modules that extract specific contextual information from the diverse inputs of the system.

2.2   Model Parameters

As a system, our model has input parameters and output parameters. The inputs provide the raw data about different variables of the environment. The outputs provide a way to act on the environment or take action according to its state. A list of those parameters is provided next.

Internally, the system is based on five modules that take care of the exaction and account of each of the context dimensions: Identity (Who), Activity (What), Objects (How), Time (When) and Location (Where). Each module extracts its context dimension from the inputs of the system.

A schematic of the proposed model is shown in Figure 1. The system is represented as a black box with the five context aware modules and their interactions. These context modules are explained next. The inputs and outputs are represented outside.

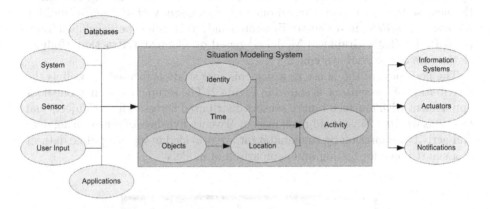

Fig. 1. Situation Modeling System Schematic

2.3   Context Awareness Modules

For the design and implementation of the system, the AmI awareness concepts are applied. The five types of Context-Awareness [5] implemented in modules for Situation Modeling in the system are:

1. *Identity-awareness (IAw)*: this is the user module which stores and makes use of information regarding the profile, preferences and past actions (historic information) of the person using the system and its use of it.
2. *Location-awareness (LAw)*: this module extracts the location of the user from the inputs of the system. In some applications it can be extracted directly from the availability of location dedicated sensors like RFID or location triangulation, in others it is provided indirectly from the mapping of sensing objects to locations.

3. *Time-awareness (TAw)*: the time is taken directly from the system and provides valuable information. Depending on the application, time is discretized into time periods or used by means of functions of time and intrapolation.
4. *Objects-awareness (OAw)*: this module associates the sensors data with the use of objects. This provides valuable information most of the objects that a person uses are application or task specific.
5. *Activity-awareness (AAw)*: the activity carried out by the user is inferred from the information extracted from the other context modules. The different dimensions allow for a precise determination of activities.

3 Case Study: Health Condition Monitoring

In this section the functionality and implementation of the model in a real life application is analyzed. The implementation shown here and the experiments of the next section have been carried out in the case study of a *Health Condition Monitoring System*, in a "Smart Environment", [6,5] using the developed Temporal Probabilistic Graphical Model [7] based on Context Extraction Modules as the core of the AmI system.

The floor plan of the house in which this case study is focused, as well as the distribution of the sensors, is shown in Figure 2. The setup consists in a one floor appartment with fourteen binary sensors distributed across different objects and locations where a 26 year old male lives in. Twenty five days of sensor firing data and activity annotation by the inhabitant are provided in [3] as a public dataset of a smart home for testing and comparison of models.

Fig. 2. Floor Plan and Sensor Distribution of the House

3.1 Objects Module

For this particular application, this module maps each ambient sensor with a corresponding object. Thus the fourteen sensors in the house are mapped to their corresponding objects: *CupsCupboard, Dishwasher, Freezer, Fridge, Frontdoor, GroceriesCupboard, HallBathroomDoor, HallBedroomDoor, HallToiletDoor, Microwave, PansCupboard, PlatesCupboard, ToiletFlush* and *Washingmachine*. Each of these objects is used according to the activity or task. In the system, each time one of the sensors fires, the corresponding flag of the associated object activates indicating its current use or deactivates if the sensor changes state again.

3.2 Time Module

This module takes the time global variable of the environment into account. Modeled scenarios and processes change over time. Also the distribution of the probabilities of events vary according to the time. In the Health Condition Monitoring Application, the Activities of Daily Living are carried out on some specific time more than another. A distribution of the probabilities as a function of time of the nine activities considered from the annotated dataset is shown in Figure 3. It can be seen that the probability of each activity changes over time. By considering the time variable and either discretization or probability functions of time, this module accounts for those changes instead of giving each activity a static prior probability.

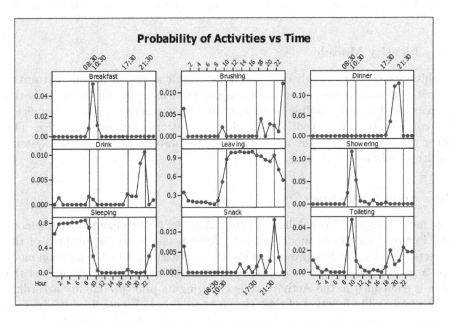

Fig. 3. Probability of Activities vs Time in the Experiment Data

3.3   Location Module

In this application, there are no devices or location dedicated sensors which provide direct access to the location of the user. There are sensors located in doors of specific locations of the house, but these have the issue that door sensors are ambiguous, i.e. the person could have left the door opened, never entered the room or left it.

The solution of this module for working with the current infrastructure, is a *Location based on objects used* approach. Each object from the objects module is mapped to a specific location of the house where it belongs or is used. The user is in the location given by the last object used. Since the objects are distributed across the house, each time the user goes from one place to another, a different sensor is firing (either activating or deactivating) providing the location.

Table 1 is taken from the mapping performed by this module and shows the correlation between the nine ADLs and five locations. As can be seen, location extraction provides useful information for activity identification.

Table 1. Distribution of Locations for each Activity (Values are percentages)

	Brush	Drink	Snack	Sleep	Leave	Breakfast	Dinner	Shower	Toilet
Bathroom	15.38	0.00	0.00	0.16	0.01	0.00	0.00	0.00	30.89
Bedroom	3.85	0.00	0.00	99.39	0.01	0.00	0.00	0.00	0.52
Kitchen	0.00	100.00	100.00	0.00	0.01	100.00	99.38	0.90	1.05
Outside	7.69	0.00	0.00	0.00	99.95	0.00	0.00	1.35	2.09
Toilet	73.08	0.00	0.00	0.45	0.03	0.00	0.62	97.75	65.45

3.4   Identity Module

In this scenario there is only one user. This module stores his historic pattern of activities in a database for analysis and posterior use. One direct use is in the activity identification module as an input for previous activity. This accounts for the consideration of sequential activities and patterns between activities. The other use of the data is the main reason of the implementation of the system: Health Condition Monitoring.

3.5   Activity Module

The main Temporal Probabilistic Graphical Model is implemented in this module. Figure 4 shows the model with its input nodes being the outputs of the objects module, a node representing the location extracted by the location module, a node providing the sequential pattern distribution of activities, and the time is embedded in the Activity node changing its prior probability according to the probability function of time shown previously in Figure 3.

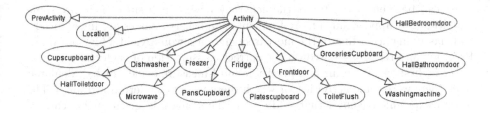

Fig. 4. Temporal Probabilistic Graphical Model for Activity Recognition

4   Experimentation and Results

Here the performance of the system is evaluated. There can be several performance measures on this topic but since the task at hand is the identification of activities given the inputs, the ones of interest are: the Accuracy, the Precision, the Recall and the F-Measure scores. [3]

The experiments are set up in this way: The provided datasets are in two parts, one is the sensor data tables with timestamps and the other is the manually annotated activities with time stamps. Inconsistencies are removed and only the nine activities shown earlier are considered. The two sets of information are merged and a dataset of sensor firing status along with activity of each minute is prepared. Using a Cross Validation *Leave One Day Out* approach, each instance of one day of sensor data is fed to the system and the remaining days are used for training. The system takes the input and infers the contexts and activity. The scores come from the confusion matrix of the inferred and actual activities. Each experiment consists of separately testing different combinations of the context extraction modules under this same experimental setup.

The results of the experiments for each of the modules are shown in Table 2. The main four classification performance measures are in the table. The letters O, T, L and P correspond to the Objects, Time, Location and Past Activity respectively. The Experiment column shows the number of the experiment.

Table 2. Results of the Experiments for different Context Modules combinations

Experiment	Accuracy	Precision	Recall	F-Measure	O	T	L	P
1	0.8365928	NA	0.3153969	NA	X			
2	0.9035513	NA	0.4160937	NA	X	X		
3	0.9935742	0.6456631	0.6048490	0.6245900	X		X	
4	0.9680884	0.7432225	0.8492201	0.7926936	X			X
5	0.9975166	0.8189433	0.8362290	0.8274959	X	X	X	
6	0.9827715	0.7444976	0.8346259	0.7869897	X	X		X
7	0.9986341	0.8883097	0.9217288	0.9047107	X		X	X
8	0.9989446	0.9182971	0.9467268	0.9322953	X	X	X	X

As can be seen in the table, the accuracy begins high since there are some activities that appear much more frequent than others (classes are imbalanced), and classifying according to the most frequent class would yield a high accuracy. Precision and recall are based on the correct classification of each class.

In the first two experiments, precision and f-measure could not be calculated since there were some activities for which there were not inferred instances. The second experiment shows that adding the Time module gives an increase in the accuracy and recall scores. Also the location and previous activity modules give a significant performance improvement to the system. Experiments five to seven show the combinations of the modules, while experiment eight shows the complete model with all context extraction modules.

Thus, it can be seen from the results of the experiments that each one of the context variables expands the model and improves its performance when considered. A synergistic effect is observed between variables. Also, the complete model shows very high accuracy and f-measure scores for this application. Following the Ambient Intelligence paradigm proposed in the solution model can help in identifying and monitoring situations and activity changes for elderly care.

5   Conclusions and Future Work

The solution model proposed here demonstrated to improve the scores of activity recognition. The case study was limited to one individual and fourteen sensors, but the model aims to be scalable by adding additional sensors to its inputs and user profiles to handle additional individuals.

Future work includes analyzing other scenarios and scalability of the model, optimizing the context extraction modules to make the system more robust, and comparing the model with other models for Situation Modeling.

References

1. Erman, L.D., Lark, J.S., Hayes-Roth, F.: ABE: An Environment for Engineering Intelligent Systems. IEEE Trans. Software Eng. 14(12), 1758–1770 (1988)
2. Hopgood, A.A.: Intelligent Systems for Engineers and Scientists. CRC Press (2001)
3. van Kasteren, T.L.M., Englebienne, G., Kröse, B.J.A.: Transferring Knowledge of Activity Recognition Across Sensor Networks. In: Floréen, P., Krüger, A., Spasojevic, M. (eds.) Pervasive 2010. LNCS, vol. 6030, pp. 283–300. Springer, Heidelberg (2010)
4. Katz, S., Downs, T.D., Cash, H.R., Grotz, R.C.: Progress in development of the index of ADL. The Gerontologist 10(1), 20–30 (1970)
5. Mikulecký, P., Lisková, T., Cech, P., Bures, V. (eds.): Ambient Intelligence Perspectives: Selected Papers from the first International Ambient Intelligence Forum 2008, Ambient Intelligence and Smart Environments, vol. 1. IOS Press (2008)
6. Nakashima, H., Aghajan, H., Augusto, J.C. (eds.): Handbook of Ambient Intelligence and Smart Environments. Springer, New York (2010)
7. Neapolitan, R.E.: Learning Bayesian Networks. Prentice Hall (2003)
8. Russell, S.J., Norvig, P.: Artificial Intelligence: A Modern Approach, 2nd edn. Prentice Hall (2002)
9. Weber, W., Rabaey, J.M., Aarts, E. (eds.): Ambient Intelligence. Springer (2005)

Heterogeneous Device Networking
for an AmI Environment

José Jaime Ariza, Cristina Urdiales García, and Francisco Sandoval Hernández

ISIS Group, ETSI Telecommunications, University of Malaga, 29071 Malaga, Spain
jariza@uma.es, {cristina,sandoval}@dte.uma.es

Abstract. Assisted living environments involve a wide range of different devices. Most of them are commercially available, but typically associated to standard domotics buses not compatible with each other. Besides, in many cases it is desirable to integrate new devices to a system that might not support the installed bus protocol. Interconnection between devices is far from simple, specially because domotic buses are often proprietary. The most popular solution to this problem is to export information to Ethernet as a system meeting point, but it is not always simple and accessibility in proprietary buses is limited. This paper proposes a method to integrate a variety of platforms through a shared memory interface, including a proprietary bus, commercial devices and ad hoc systems. Its main novelty is that compatibility between different standards is achieved without additional expensive hardware.

Keywords: Domotics, KNX, Ambient Intelligence, protocols, integration.

1 Introduction

An Ambient Intelligence (AmI) environment is one that can raise context awareness through the use of sensors embedded in everyday objects. Whereas in traditional domotics systems do not need major intelligence, e.g. smoke and gas sensors or HVAC (Heating, Ventilation, and Air Conditioning) systems, AmI systems require further smartness, but also connectivity, so decisions can be made regarding all available information. Hence, AmI devices are networked and control can be performed in a distributed, hybrid way.

Many AmI systems are typically built on top of a domotics system, where several sensors are embedded in usual domestic elements like lights, smoke alarms, switches, presence detectors, etc. There are many commercial domotics protocols, both open, like X10 or BatiBUS and proprietary like Lonworks or KNX. Every bus has its typical niche depending on factors like how many devices it can support, its reliability or its cost. In many AmI applications it can be interesting to mix different buses for several reasons: i) some non critical devices are significantly cheaper in less reliable buses like X10; ii) critical devices like smoke or gas alarms might not be available in less reliable buses; iii) it might be necessary to combine different medium accesses. Besides, it is often interesting to include

G. Urzaiz et al. (Eds.): UCAmI 2013, LNCS 8276, pp. 183–190, 2013.

in our systems other elements that do not have a domotics bus interface, like biometric sensors, robots, computers, etc. However, most protocols are meant to operate as a standalone installation, where each device is preprogrammed via commercial hardware to work in a deterministic way. This problem can be solved via a gateway that taps in the bus and make it available to external systems. While there are hardware gateways to provide partial access to the bus, they are usually meant for tele control and limited to activating/deactivating a device or group[1]. Other gateways may provide translation up to layer 2 or higher[2] to allow communication via USB, IP (KNXnet/IP) or even web services; in some cases KNXnet/IP to webservice conversion relies on external middleware software. The main drawback of IP communication is a significant protocol overhead; as all connection oriented protocols, TCP needs more process than non connection oriented ones. This is specially relevant in domotics networks, where messages are small and scarce. This could be partially solved by using UDP instead of TCP, but the overall overhead remains high. If communication relies on a web service, the overhead is even larger: there is XML over HTTP over TCP over IP[1], and XML and HTTP are quite heavy. Most of these web services use REST instead of SOAP to reduce the load [2], but it is still large. Alternatively, the middleware can run on a local computer using a light communication protocol, whereas web services run in remote ones [3], but, as most systems in a smart house are remote, web service usage would be high.

Web services have another drawback: since domotics buses operate on interruptions, the middleware needs to be able to both send and receive push notifications. This implies a duplicity in implementation, as both ends need a webserver and a webclient to work both ways. Finally, we need a translation system to abstract the inner addressing in the bus so that the user can send orders or receive status in a transparent way. This translation, when implemented, tens to be poor and doesn't extract all the information that every KNX message has [4].

This paper focuses on integrating a set of proprietary bus devices and other external devices in a common framework to implement an AmI system, while avoiding the problems commented above. In our case, we will focus on the KNX-EIB standard because it is widely available and supports almost every sensor and actuator in the market. Next section focuses on describing the protocol.

2   Proposed Distributed Architecture

In order to bring all possible devices together, we are going to use the DLA (Distributed and Layered Architecture)[3], originally proposed in [5] to control autonomous robots. Robotics (open) architectures are interesting for AmI applications because they support mechanisms to cope with physical agents and sensors in potentially unpredictable environments that fit well the AmI paradigm.

---

[1] http://www.cdinnovation.com/page1.html

[2] http://www.knxshop.co.uk/catalog/Catalog.aspx?NavID=000-009-1041

[3] Available at (GPL): http://webpersonal.uma.es/de/eperez/

DLA relies on a shared memory schema at local level, avoiding most protocol overhead. Remotely, although DLA is also based on sockets, it is much lighter than webservices and does not need to duplicate servers for push notification because its management server handles interruptions.

The main advantages of DLA are that it supports intuitive adaptation to different physical agents and simple expansion of their capacities via addition of new modules. This feature is specially interesting because it allows addition of different sensors and actuators in the same way that we could add a new robot with its own set of sensors. DLA combines the responses of different deliberative and reactive algorithms through the interaction of freely distributed processes in an asynchronous way. This is particularly interesting to implement the AmI paradigm of Ubiquitous Computing, where different devices may present different computing capacities and processors may also be distributed in the network.This architecture provides transparency to the user through a high simplicity and portability. Besides, it has a very low computational load. There are alternatives to DLA, specially in the robotics field. ROS (Robotic Operating System) is probably, the most popular one, but there are others like OpenRDK, OROCOS or MARIE. However, most of them are very oriented to robotic applications and neglect integration of domotic devices. Besides, they usually provide a full software framework to operate. While this means that they support a wide variety of hardware and software, the require more computational resources than DLA, that can run perfectly on devices like, for example, a Raspberry Pi. Besides, most frameworks tend to favor a specific OS. ROS, for example, runs on Ubuntu Linux and it is reported to have limited support on Mac OSX, but it is not easy to configure on Mac. DLA supports Unix, Linux and Windows alone or combinedly and devices simply need an API library to connect to the system. It also supports applications in C, Java and Matlab and can easily be extended to any programming language supporting sockets. Finally, regarding scalabitity, we can improve the system processing capability by adding new processing units on demand and extend functionality but progressively adding new equipment and behaviors to the system. We have already used DLA in different robotic platforms to achieve autonomous behaviors [6][5]. In this work we are going to add two new capabilities to a DLA based system: i) interaction with standalone hardware; and ii) interaction with a KNX bus.

2.1   Accessing the KNX Bus

KNX is based in the EIB protocol stack but extended with several capabilities from BatiBUS and EHS. KNX is the de facto European standard and, although it is expensive when compared to open bus standards, it is within acceptable margins for domestic use. Its main advantages are:

- Interoperability: (KNX-compatible) devices from different manufacturers can be mixed; allowing high flexibility level installations.
- Quality: To use the KNX brand, manufacturers have to fulfill ISO 9001 and EN50090-2-2 (European standard for home and builds electric systems).

– Specific functionalities implementation: manufacturers that share the same interests can proposed the inclusion of new functionalities into the standard.
– Agnostic platform: KNX can be developed into any kind of hardware or software platform, even from already existing commercial products.
– Devices variety: KNX is supported by most manufacturers and offers a wide catalogue of device, including critical alarms.

The bus can be accessed in a standardized way through the BCU (Bus Coupling Units), which can be programmed, configured and commanded via the KNX bus. There are commercial software packages that show information on the installation state and alarms, usually via a graphic interface, but most don't support M2M (Machine to machine), so they are not very interactive.

Alternatively, there are some APIs that allow enhanced access to the bus like Falcon[4], Windows-only official API, or Calimero[5], Java-based API but unable to connect through KNX/USB adapter. In our case, we are going to use a set of free, Linux-based tools with the capacity of accessing through KNX/IP or KNX/USB and programming and commanding the BCU: BCUSDK [7]. BCUSDK provides a daemon for bus access, EIBD, that provides interaction with KNX via UNIX sockets or even TCP/IP (with reduced capabilities). Interfacing with the daemon is much easier than understanding the full protocol itself.

2.2   Integration of KNX into DLA

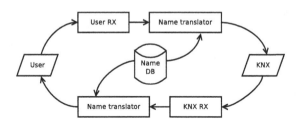

Fig. 1. Gateway functional schema

In order to interact with a KNX installation, we need to send commands to the devices and receive their status Fig. 1. We have two interfaces: i) communication with KNX, via EIBD using a UNIX socket; and ii) communication with DLA (shared memory system). Our system must perform a name translation from KNX group and device address. Our gateway runs two independent threads:

– sender, takes commands from DLA, translates the names into KNX group address and and sends the requests to EIBD. This thread is blocked until the user sends a command to KNX.

---

[4] http://www.knx.org/knx-tools/falcon/description/
[5] http://sourceforge.net/p/calimero/wiki/Home/

```
if send to KNX then
    groupaddr = GetFromTable(T1, 'group addr WHERE
    name=data[destname]');
else
    name = GetFromTable(T2, 'name WHERE source addr=data[source] AND
    group addr=data[group]');
    if name == " then
        name = GetFromTable(T3, 'name WHERE source addr=data[source]');
    end
end
```

Algorithm 1. Name lookup process where data is the information to be send
or the information received respectively

– receiver, monitorizes communications in KNX. Every time there is a tele-
  graph flowing in the KNX bus, it is read by EIBD and send to the gateway.
  The telegram sender address is translated into a name and notified to DLA.
  This thread is blocked until EIBD sends any notification.

All telegrams sent to KNX are also read by the receiver thread, to log the user
commands, in case we want to implement some kind of data verification. The
gateway understands three commands: i) WRITE sets the value of a parameter
of a KNX element, and is used to control the domotic elements; ANSWER is
generated when any KNX device send a telegram; and iii) READ ask a device to
resend its status to the bus. It's used for forcing updates. The name translation
(Alg. 1) is supported by three lookup tables (Table 1) and performed in 2 steps:

1. If the user wants to send a command to the KNX bus, it uses an address
   group, so we need a lookup table to translate names into it (T1).
2. If a device sends a telegram, we have a source address (device address) and
   a destination address (group address). There are two possibilities depending
   on how relevant the destination address is:
   (a) Relevant: the same binary input can send orders to several actuators.
       We can figure out from the destination address which input has been
       activated depending on our design. The system has a lookup table (T2)
       that combines both addresses to perform name translation.
   (b) Irrelevant: several inputs from the same binary adapter send orders to
       the same actuator. We can't know which input has been activated, since
       the information is duplicated. Hence, we use a third lookup table (T3)
       to relate source address with names.

All lookup tables are stored in a MySQL database. When the gateway receives
a telegram from the KNX bus, all tables are queried and results are logged and
used to track the devices status. When the user sends a command to KNX, only
T1 is queried to translate the name in the command into a group address. The
gateway also tracks the status of every element in the bus.

Table 1. Database schemas for lookup tables T1, T2 and T3

T1		T2		T3	
Column	Type	Column	Type	Column	Type
id	int(11)	id	int(11)	id	int(11)
group addr	varchar(15)	source addr	varchar(15)	source addr	varchar(15)
name	varchar(100)	group addr	varchar(15)	name	varchar(100)
		name	varchar(100)		

Since all the data needed for the name translation is stored in MySQL tables, devices can be added or removed in run-time by simply adding or removing the requiered row in the lookup tables.

3   A Test Scenario

We have tested the proposed integrated system in different scenarios. The following one consists of responding to a fire, and it follows the 112 emergency system recommendations[6]. We present this one because it involves all the commented interconnected systems, namely:

- A commercial home robot (Pioneer AT), with audioconference capabilities.
- A KNX basic installation with several sensors, actuators and alarms.
- A multiparametric physiological monitor (Equivital from Hidalgo).
- Wearable RFID reader for object and location detection.

Our KNX installation includes access to lights and blinds, plus information on the different rooms status via motion sensors. It can also cut off power input via a shut trip releaser. The key element for this scenario is a smoke detector that is not available in all domotic standards, but fairly common in KNX. In our specific case, it was purchased from Jung.

Whenever the smoke detector is triggered, KNX exports the information to the DLA system, that dispatches three parallel tasks: i) notify caregiver, ii) KNX actions; and iii) biometric monitoring:

- According to recommended safety protocols, commands are directed to the KNX bus to enhance visibility by turning on all the lights and also to close all the blinds to prevent air flows and, consequently, fire propagation.
- If the user is wearing the biometric sensor, it start to monitorize the user health parameters to check if he has already started suffering from smoke intoxication.
- The authorized caregiver is notified of the problem.

The caregiver may choose to contact the user and check if everything is all right. At their command, the system can send the robot to the room where the

---

[6] http://www.112.es/consejos/incendio-de-un-edificio.html

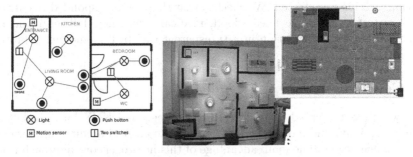

Fig. 2. KNX installation, simulation panel and user interface

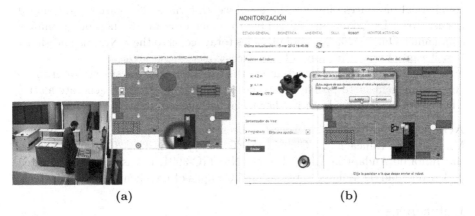

(a)   (b)

Fig. 3. a) RFID tag detection a) robot targeting and producing audio warnings

KNX system detected the user last. The robot detects where it is and where the user is within the room by means of a set of passive RFID tags set around the house and worn by the user Fig.3a. The robot carries around the reader itself. Both the reader and the robot are connected to the DLA architecture. When both robot and user are close, an audio conference is enabled to check the status of the emergency and provide instructions to leave the house Fig. 3b. It is up to the caregiver to call the firemen and health services, because the system can not do it automatically due to current legislation. The user of the system can do it as well, but in case of emergency early evacuation is advised. The user's progress through the house is followed by the KNX motion sensors and the RFID tags reader. When the system detects that the user has left the house, the KNX system cuts off the electricity input Fig.2, according to safety protocols.

If the user cannot reach the main door, the caregiver can lead him via robot audioconference to the nearest window, which is automatically opened via a KNX command, and warn firemen about the situation. The location of the user within the house is constantly updated as long as the system is on-line.

The system was throughly tested in a controlled environment where all physical sensors were deployed. All name translation possibilities exposed in the previous section were tested. We checked that the system responded as expected in every test scenario we tried (flood, medical emergency, fall, etc) and that all devices shared information in a transparent way to the emergency protocol programmer.

4   Conclusions

This work has presented an architecture to integrate a KNX bus, a robot and different assistive and monitorization devices into an AmI architecture for emergency management. The main advantage of this heterogeneous approach is that the developer can choose the most appropriate device for each task, rather than focusing on a single standard or resigning to whatever (limited) information commercial interfaces offer via the usual web interface. The gateway developed is based on EIBD daemon and is able to understand all the non-programming commands. Our translation tool provides total access to the KNX bus and shows how it can interact with any other devices.

Future work will focus on extending the capabilities of the system from emergency management to profile construction, so that we can also generate alarms when the user deviates from his/her usual activities of daily living (ADL).

Acknowledgements. This work has been partially supported by the Spanish Ministerio de Educacion y Ciencia (MEC), Project n. TEC2011-06734 and by the Junta de Andalucia, SIAD Project No. TIC-3991. It has been also granted by Universidad de Málaga, International Campus of Excellence Andalucía Tech.

References

1. Kastner, W., Szucsich, S.: Accessing knx networks via bacnet/ws. In: 2011 IEEE International Symposium on Industrial Electronics (ISIE), pp. 1315–1320 (2011)
2. Bovet, G., Hennebert, J.: A web-of-things gateway for knx networks. In: Proceedings of 2013 European Conference on Smart Objects, Systems and Technologies (SmartSysTech), pp. 1–8 (2013)
3. Cruz-Sanchez, H., Chehaider, H.L., Song, M., Mpigate, Y.Q.: A solution to use heterogeneous networks for assisted living applications. In: 2012 9th International Conference on Ubiquitous Intelligence Computing and 9th International Conference on Autonomic Trusted Computing (UIC/ATC), pp. 104–111 (2012)
4. Nazabal, J.A., Nazabal, J., Matias, I., Fernandez-Valdivielso, C., Falcone, F., Branchi, P., Mukhopadhyay, S.: Home automation based sensor system for monitoring elderly people safety. In: 2012 Sixth International Conference on Sensing Technology (ICST), pp. 142–145 (2012)
5. Pérez Rodríguez, E.J.: Distributed intelligent navigation architecture for robots. AI Commun. 21(2-3), 215–218 (2008)
6. Poncela, A., Urdiales, C., Perez, E.J., Sandoval, F.: A new efficiency-weighted strategy for continuous human/robot cooperation in navigation. IEEE Transactions on Systems, Man and Cybernetics, Part A: Systems and Humans 39(3), 486–500 (2009)
7. Kögler, M.: Free development environment for bus coupling units of the european installation bus. Master's thesis, Institut für Rechnergestützte Automation, Technische Universität Wien (2011)

Low Cost and Easy to Deploy Real Time Location System Based in Radio Frequency Identification

Ignacio Angulo[1,*], Enrique Onieva[1], Asier Perallos[1], Itziar Salaberria[1],
Leire Azpilicueta[2], Francisco Falcone[2], José Javier Astráin[3], and Jesús Villadangos[3]

[1] Deusto Institute of Technology (DeustoTech), University of Deusto, 48007 Bilbao, Spain
{ignacio.angulo,enrique.onieva,perallos,
itziar.salaberria}@deusto.es
[2] Electrical and Electronic Engineering Department,
Universidad Pública de Navarra, 31006 Pamplona, Spain
{leyre.azpilicueta,francisco.falcone}@unavarra.es
[3] Mathematics and Computer Engineering Department,
Universidad Pública de Navarra, 31006 Pamplona, Spain
{josej.astrain,jesusv}@unavarra.es

Abstract. Real Time Location Systems (RTLS) provide great benefits to society in safety and can lead to sensitive information to optimize resource planning in public facilities and major events. The current cost of people locator systems and deployment difficulty hinders installation in multiple scenarios despite the potential benefits posed therein. In this paper we present a low cost and easy deployment RTLS based on RFID technology and active tags. The proposed system can be optimal for scenarios where location accuracy is not a key factor, being enough to know an approximation of the position and mainly the presence or absence of a person in the area monitored.

Keywords: Real Time Location Systems, RTLS, RFID, Active Tag, Smart Antenna, Assets and individuals tracking.

1 Introduction

The cost and difficulty of installing the current real-time location systems (RTLS) hinders its deployment in environments where ROI cannot be measured from an economic standpoint. However to locate people in a bounded area or even verify their presence provides very clear benefits to society from the point of view of safety and leisure.

In that sense, providing a RTLS easily deployable on any installation and low cost in both infrastructure and tracking devices can be extremely advantageous in many scenarios. To ensure the presence of a person with a tendency to cognitive problems in orientation or memory, such as Alzheimer's disease or senile dementia in elderly within a controlled area for their care and detect when they leave the same or enter into a hazardous area, improves the quality of life not only of the monitored person but also staff in care assistant [1]. In parallel, the implementation of a system of this

G. Urzaiz et al. (Eds.): UCAmI 2013, LNCS 8276, pp. 191–198, 2013.

nature in big areas designated for children's entertainment, combined with new apps compatible with smartphones can be used to notify caregivers when a child leaves the monitored area or even to facilitate location when it's time to go home. In addition, the proliferation of social networks raises new possibilities of social interaction with geo-located individuals. Facilitate the location of friends and acquaintances in multitudinous events or estimate the flow of people in a particular installation can open a wide range of marketing possibilities and help optimize the management and planning of resources.

The aim of the work presented in this paper is to develop a real time location system based on radio frequency identification (RFID) and low cost active tags that allows easy deployment in indoor and outdoor areas for the provision of telematics services aimed at increasing the safety of people and offer new opportunities for leisure and resource planning.

In the following paragraph is contextualized the scope of the proposed system in comparison with other alternatives, section 3 shows the system architecture and describes the implementation of the main elements that make it up. Later section 4 describes the real scenario where the system is to be tested, where a detailed radioelectric analysis has been performed for the proper deployment of the system. Finally conclusions of the system will be presented and future lines opened by the proposed system.

2   Context of the Work

The main challenge of the proposed system in this paper is to develop a system capable of monitoring real-time people in indoor and outdoor scenarios with significant size, with the minimum possible cost. Currently there are multiple technologies used in indoor real time location systems [2]. Existing commercial location systems provide location accuracy varies from a few inches in systems based on proprietary microwave solutions (UWB) (e.g. Ubisense), accuracies below 1 meter by systems based infrared sensors technologies (e.g. Firefly) or systems that provide a lower accuracy using wireless technologies such as WLAN, Bluetooth, ZigBee or DECT (e.g. Ekahau). These systems employ multiple schemes to estimate the location. Many systems employ techniques and algorithms based on measurements on the Angle of Arrival (AoA), Time of Arrival (TOA) or Time Difference of Arrival (TDOA) that require additional hardware, increasing the cost of deployment [3]. Other systems, mainly those based on RFID technology, are based on the Received Signal Strength Indication (RSSI) to optimize the location estimate [4]. According to the characteristics of the scenario and considering the economic factor as main feature of the system, the chosen technology has been active Radio Frequency Identification [5]. The consolidated statement of this technology and the proliferation of manufacturers facilitates finding reader units and bracelet shaped tags at very low cost. In this sense multiple Asian manufacturers have launched numerous identification solutions in different ranges. From integrated units including directional antenna, the reader and the embedded platform for managing the acquired information, to simple readers that only provide located tags. The proposed system is based on those bottom range devices that considerably help to get a cheaper solution but difficult to estimate the location not providing any analyzable measure as those previously identified (RSS, AOA, TOA, TDOA). Therefore, the proposed system is based primarily on the location of the antennas and the order in which the reader provides the identified tags.

3   System Architecture

The system architecture is shown in Fig. 1. The proposed solution presents a distributed RTLS system based on three distinct levels.

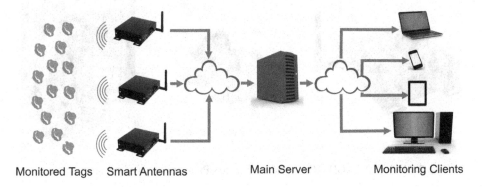

Monitored Tags   Smart Antennas   Main Server   Monitoring Clients

Fig. 1. System Architecture

3.1   Smart Antennas

It is the main component of the system. The implementation of this element is carried out by integrating a 2.4GHz RFID omni-directional active reader with a reading range up to 80 meters (MR3002A from Marktrace®) and a low-cost embedded platform with Internet connectivity (Raspberry Pi). The total cost of this item, including the reader (175€), the embedded platform (30€), an IP66 enclosure (Fig. 2) and all necessary accessories, does not exceed €400. The cost of implementing the system depends directly on the number of smart antennas to ensure proper coverage of tags monitored in the controlled environment. In chapter four discusses in detail the optimum antenna number and positioning of these for the chosen test scenario. A public 13,000 square meters area can be covered with five smart antennas. The low cost of the hardware deployed, together with the low cost of active tags compatible with the system (4 €) and the use of mobile platforms as monitoring clients, facilitates the implementation of the system.

The embedded platform, connected via Ethernet to the RFID reader constantly query RFID tags that are in the coverage range. The embedded platform manages a list of tags that are in the area of coverage. For each tag the platform stores the identifier and a sensing factor. When the reader identifies a tag that had not previously been identified, the antenna sends a SOAP POST request to the server, indicating the entry of the individual associated with that label in the coverage area. Each time a tag is identified, the sensing factor is restored to a pre-set value. When a tag in the list is not received after a query, the sensing factor is decremented. If the sensing factor reaches zero, the label is removed from the list and a SOAP POST request is sent to the server indicating the exit of the monitored person out of the coverage area of the antenna.

The configuration of each antenna to be deployed in the system requires two actions: setting the IP address and the HTTP port of the main server in the embedded platform (1) and inserting the positioning information and the transmission power into the database of the main server (2).

Fig. 2. MR3002A 2.4GHz RFID reader, raspberry Pi an prototype of the smart antenna

3.2   Main Server

The main server is responsible for analyzing the information sent from the smart antennas and monitor proper people in the user interfaces of the clients.

A database stores the physical location of the antennas installed, links the RFID tags with the users of the system and stores each alteration in the people locations referred by each antenna. Microsoft SQL Server 2008 DBMS has been used in this context

All data transfer between smart antennas, monitoring clients and the main server are performed through asynchronous web services in order to facilitate scalability of the system and improve reliability. The implementation of this distributed architecture has been developed using .NET technology and Windows Communication Foundation (WCF).

Although tests of the system have been carried out on a development server, the technologies used in the development facilitate the deployment of the system in a cloud platform during the production stage. The estimated monthly cost of the system hosted on the Windows Azure platform including a Extra small Virtual Machine, 1Gb SQL Azure storage and bandwidth of 30Gb is € 20.76

3.3   Monitoring Clients

According to the nature of the test scenario, which is presented in the next section, it has been developed a native application for iOS compatible devices that enables to locate people who wear tags. The link between people and tags is performed from within the application via QR code printed over the tag. In addition to displaying the estimated location of the monitored person the application receives PUSH notification when the person leaves the controlled area.

4   Test Scenario

The proposed system will be deployed in a playground for children of recent construction. The park located in the town of Getxo in northern Spain, has 13000m2 and provides different recreational areas as three zones of swings, a bar, a soccer field, a basketball court and open area for free play (Fig. 3). The proposed system must allow tutors to monitor the estimated location where are children under their responsibility and report immediately when they leave the park.

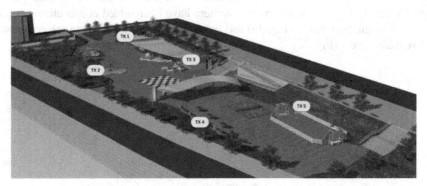

Fig. 3. Scenario under consideration with the representation of the deployment of five readers RFID

The most important requirement for the proper functioning of the system is the correct positioning of the antennas, which requires a complete radio-electrical analysis of the controlled area.

4.1   Radio-Electrical Analysis

The effects of radio wave propagation are highly important in order to analyse the behaviour of the wireless communication system. The assessment on electromagnetic spectrum is of importance to model overall performance of the system under analysis in terms of coverage and capacity analysis. In this work, a deterministic method based on an in-house developed 3D ray launching code [6-8] is used to analyze the performance of the wireless communication system of the considered scenario.

This scenario is depicted in Fig. 3 with the representation of five transmitters which have been analyzed in terms of coverage, capacity and sensitivity.

The use of deterministic modeling leads to a previous radio planning analysis in order to achieve an optimal configuration of sensors to bear a competitive, flexible and scalable solution. Firstly, the whole scenario has been created, taking into account the material parameters of all the elements within it in terms of conductivity and dielectric permittivity. Electromagnetic phenomena such as reflection, refraction and diffraction have been taken into account based on Geometrical Optics (GO) and the Uniform Geometrical Theory of Diffraction (GTD). The commitment between accuracy and computational time is acquired with the number of launching rays and the cuboids size of the considered scenario. Several transmitters can be placed within the scenario and parameters such as frequency of operation, radiation patterns of the antennas, number of multipath reflections, separation angle between rays and cuboids dimension are introduced.

3D ray launching simulation results have been obtained for the whole volume of the simulation scenario (Fig. 3). The positions of the transmitters have been chosen in order to simulate a possible morphology of a real wireless network.

Fig. 3 shows the obtained received power levels for the bidimensional plane at height 1m for different number of transmitter. For each of the represented planes (from Fig. 3a to Fig. 3c), two new transmitters have been added consecutively, starting with a single transmitter (Fig. 3a) and finishing with a wireless network composed by five transmitters (Fig. 3c).

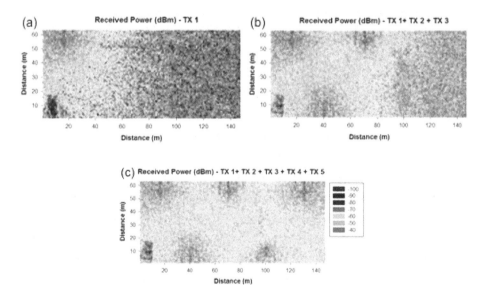

Fig. 4. RSSI 3D-ray simulation results obtained at a bidimensional plane at a height of 1m for different number of transmitters (a) TX 1 (b) TX1,TX2,TX3 (c) TX1,TX2,TX3,TX4,TX5

As it can be seen from the previous figure, received power level is strongly dependent on the position of the potential receiver element and the morphology of the wireless network. Variations can be in order of 10dB within 1 meter when the number of transmitters is low, which has a strong impact on the performance of the sensors, not only in terms of receiver sensitivity limits but also on overall system capacity, which is dependent on signal level as well as on signal to noise ratio.

The multipath propagation is absolutely noticeable in this type of complex environments; hence, to appreciate the variability of estimated received power level more accurately, Fig. 4 represents the power delay profile for a single point at the center of the considered scenario. As it can be seen, there are a large number of echoes in the scenario in a time span of approximately 0.10 to 2.10µs.

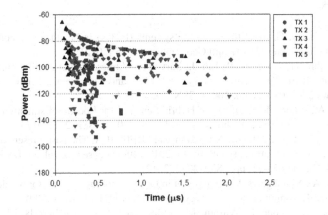

Fig. 5. Power Delay Profile in the central point of the scenario for a height of 2.75m

5   Conclusions and Future Work

The constant advancement in RFID technology and the general fall of prices on readers and tags allows the development of low cost RTLS lacking high location accuracy but able to detect the presence of people who should be monitored in large indoor and outdoor areas. These systems generate new application scenarios improving the safety of public facilities and major events and promoting leisure between users.

In the coming months the presented system will be deployed in Guernica Park, in the town of Getxo in northern Spain.

As future work, we will consider the application of fuzzy finite state machines (FFSMs) and fuzzy rule based classifiers (FRBCs) in order to obtain relevant information from data collected in the environment. Thanks to the near-human rules generated under the field of fuzzy logic, it is expected to be able to filter large amounts of data in the form (time + ID + Location) in order to obtain valuable information in the way: "at about 5pm, most of the parents are in the cafeteria, while their kids are in the play-zone 1". This information is quite valuable in order to program maintenance operations in the environment as well as for to improve its characteristics.

To this purpose, FFSMs allow us to abstract the environment as a finite state machine, where events are responsible in changes of the state. The use of fuzzy logic allows dealing with imprecisions and uncertainties derived from the environment or the sensors. In the other hand, FRBCs provide the classification of such states and transitions in a formal way. Finally, by using computational perceptions techniques and expressions constructors it is expected to "translate" obtained results in a set of human-like sentences, to be sent to the environment's operator or manager.

Acknowledgments. This work has been funded by the Bask Government under Gaitek funding program (Gizain project, IG-2013/01387).

References

1. Boulos, K., Berry, G.: Real-time locating systems (RTLS) in healthcare: a condensed primer. International Journal of Health Geographics 11, 25 (2012)
2. Liu, H., Darabi, H., Banerjee, P., Liu, J.: Survey of Wireless Indoor Positioning Techniques and Systems. IEEE Transactions on Systems, Man, and Cybernetics, Part C: Applications and Reviews 37(6) (November 2007) ISSN: 1094-6977
3. De Gante, A., Siller, M.: A Survey of Hybrid Schemes for Location Estimation in Wireless Sensor Networks. Procedia Technology 7, 377–383 (2013) ISSN 2212-0173
4. Li, Z., Zhou, Z., He, C., Huang, X.: Advances in RFID-ILA: The past, present and future of RFID-based indoor location algorithms. In: 2012 24th Chinese Control and Decision Conference (CCDC), May 23-25, pp. 3830–3835 (2012)
5. Gu, Y., Lo, A., Niemegeers, I.: A survey of indoor positioning systems for wireless personal networks. IEEE Communications Surveys & Tutorials 11(1), 13–32 (2009)
6. Azpilicueta, L., Falcone, F., Astráin, J.J., Villadangos, J., García Zuazola, I.J., Landaluce, H., Angulo, I., Perallos, A.: Measurement and modeling of a UHF-RFID system in a metallic closed vehicle. Microwave and Optical Technology Letters 54(9), 2126–2130 (2012)
7. Nazábal, J.A., Iturri López, P., Azpilicueta, L., Falcone, F., Fernández-Valdivielso, C.: Performance Analysis of IEEE 802.15.4 Compliant Wireless Devices for Heterogeneous Indoor Home Automation Environments. International Journal of Antennas and Propagation (2012)
8. Aguirre, E., Arpón, J., Azpilicueta, L., de Miguel, S., Ramos, V., Falcone, F.: Evaluation of electromagnetic dosimetry of wireless systems in complex indoor scenarios with human body interaction. Progress In Electromagnetics Research B 43, 189–209 (2012)

METADEPCAS: Introducing Semantic RFID Data Management

Ismael Abad, Carlos Cerrada, and José Antonio Cerrada

Departamento de Ingeniería de Software y Sistemas Informáticos,
Escuela Técnica Superior de Ingeniería Informática. UNED, C/ Juan del Rosal. 16,
28040 Madrid, Spain
{iabad,ccerrada,jcerrada}@issi.uned.es

Abstract. Traditional Radio-Frequency IDentification (RFID) applications have been centered on replacing physical codes in supply chain management. The article presents a framework allowing both quick decentralized on-line item discovery and centralized off-line massive business logic analysis, according to needs and requirements of supply chain actors. A semantic-based environment, that we call METADEPCAS where tagged objects become resources exposing to an RFID reader not only a trivial identification code but a semantic annotation, enables tagged objects to describe themselves *directly* without depending on a centralized infrastructure. On the other hand, facing on data management issues, a proposal is formulated for an effective *off-line* multidimensional analysis of huge amounts of RFID data generated and stored along a supply chain.

Keywords: RFID Data Management, DEPCAS, supply chain, semantic data.

1 Introduction

A supply chain is a complex system constituted by organizations and people with their activities involved in transferring a product or service from a supplier to a final customer. The key to make a successful supply chain relies on an extended collaboration, implying the integration among actors involved in the productive and logistic network. An integrated and flexible management of logistics (physical and information flows) has to be set-up both inside and outside factory boundaries. Specialized production and distribution processes suffer from the limited interactions allowed by rigid networks. As a result, nowadays a relevant component of competition in the market occurs among logistical chains. The supply chain can no longer be represented as static or linear, but it needs to be evaluated dynamically, as a complex system made of interactions and connections among actors operating along the chain.

Many empirical investigations have demonstrated there is a positive correlation between enterprise performances and its propensity and attitude to be integrated into larger systems. This is the reason why enterprises are more and more attentive to the opportunity offered by both coordination and cooperation among their internal functions and the other external actors contributing in different ways to the business.

G. Urzaiz et al. (Eds.): UCAmI 2013, LNCS 8276, pp. 199–206, 2013.

Hence, information has been an increasingly strategic asset in the last few years. It covers a determinant position in both logistics and marketing. The physical flow of raw materials, products and their related information is considered as a strategic element for quality standards of products/services, for business analysis and evaluation and finally to allow corrective actions. In particular, current trends in the consumer products market assign a growing significance to retailers in the governance of supply chains. The growing dimension of retail groups – sustained by the reached degree of concentration in that field – increases their power against producers and makes them privileged centers of value accumulation, acting as filters for the information flow for the whole chain. As a result, the main retailers are investing in new technology in order to boost the information exchange and are mandating the adoption of interoperable solutions to commercial partners [1].

Radio-Frequency IDentification (RFID) is an automatic identification (AutoID) technology, interconnecting via radio two main components: (1) transponders (commonly named tags) carrying data, located on the objects to be identified; (2) interrogators (also known as readers) able to receive the transmitted data. Benefits introduced by RFID technology with respect to barcodes include: (i) unlike optical scan, alignment between reader and tag is not needed; (ii) longer read range (up to few meters); (iii) nearly simultaneous detection of multiple RFID tags; (iv) higher tag storage capacity [2]. Because of these features, RFID provides better levels of automation in the supply chain and helps prevent human errors. In latest years, industry is progressively rallying around few world- wide standards for RFID technologies. In this effort a leading role is played by the EPCglobal (Electronic Product Code, EPC) consortium. However, two main issues appears with a more advanced exploitation of RFID capabilities. Firstly, the original identification mechanism only enables a trivial string matching of ID codes, providing exclusively "yes/no" replies. Furthermore, RFID-based technology usually relies on a stable support infrastructure and fixed information servers where massive data analysis is quite difficult without the support of proper data management and aggregation schemes. Serious data management issues are then inevitably inherited and they must be faced on.

In this article an innovative model for supply chain management is presented, aiming to overcome these limitations by adopting the Ubiquitous Computing paradigm. As originally introduced by Mark Weiser [3], this paradigm requires both information and computational capabilities to be deeply integrated into common objects and/or actions and the user will interact with many computational devices simultaneously, exploiting data automatically extracted from "smart objects" permeating the environment during his/her ordinary activities.

Leveraging a distributed architecture, the model provides a unified framework for both quick run-time analysis (with respect to a local fragment of the overall infrastructure) and stand-alone massive business logic elaborations (with respect to a centralized Data Base Management System, DBMS) following needs and requirements of the supply chain actors. An extension of current RFID technology supporting logic-based formalisms for knowledge representation is exploited. Semantic-based object/product annotations are stored into RFID tags, exploiting machine-understandable ontological languages originally created for the Semantic Web effort and based on

Description Logics (DLs), such as Resource Description Framework (RDF) and Web Ontology Language (OWL). Semantically rich and unambiguous information is allowed to follow a product in each step of its life cycle. The model allows to trace and discover the information flow –associated to products thanks to their RFID tags– along the supply chain, and to formalize various supply chain analyses. Different perspectives can be so followed (e.g., product-centric, node-centric, path-oriented, time-oriented). Exploiting semantic-based queries, product and process information can be read, updated and integrated during manufacturing, packaging and supply chain management, thus allowing full traceability up to sales, as well as intelligent and de-localized interrogation of product data.

2   Scenario

A simple reference example should clarify our approach, also highlighting its benefits. Let us suppose monitor the life cycle of an apparel item, a cotton shirt, and to follow every production step surveying and extracting relevant product/process information. Each production stage will see the progressive joining of annotations to enhanced RFID tags attached – for instance – to cotton yarn containers shipped to the factory (first production stage), shirt pallets (logistic step) and single product packages (final sale phase). Because of traceability requirements, a tag will store: (1) quantitative data belonging to the product besides EPC identifier; (2) high-level qualitative information about production or delivery/logistics processes, expressed as semantic annotations with respect to reference ontology of the specific industry domain. Information extracted via RFID can be used for a variety of purposes. First of all – at each stage of the product evolution – accurate verifications can be performed about expected quality requirements of the product/process. Moreover, intelligent deliveries can be routed from warehouse to different production departments according to their specific characteristics.

A product can inherit (relevant parts of) the semantically annotated description of its raw materials, through properties defined in the reference ontology for the relevant domain. Further product attributes can also be stored on the RFID tag, such as size, production date and (for perishable products) expiration date. Finally, location, entering and exiting times are stamped by each supply chain actor conveying the item, such that advanced applications can be enabled. Beyond rather basic features allowed by a traditional data-oriented usage of RFID, a semantic-based approach makes possible further interactions.

A relevant aspect of the approach is that the semantic-enhanced RFID technology allows sharing information, so for example optimizing the supply chain and improving performance both in terms of logistics features and by providing innovative services available for all involved actors. The envisioned framework can support a range of use cases, involving different stakeholders along a product life cycle. Several tangible (economic) and intangible benefits are expected. During product manufacturing and distribution, a wide-area support network interconnecting commercial partners is not strictly needed. This is a significant innovation with respect to common RFID supply chain management solutions.

Semantic-enabled RFID tags contain a structured and detailed description of product features, endowed with unambiguous and machine-understandable semantics. Goods auto-expose their description to any RFID-enabled computing environment is reached. This favors decentralized approaches in order to offer context- aware application solutions, based on less expensive and more manageable mobile ad hoc networks. In addition to improved traceability, a semantic-based approach provides unique value-added capabilities. By combining standard and non-standard inference services devised in [4], several semantic-based matchmaking schemes can be designed to meet goals and requirements of specific applications. Adopting a logic-based approach, query flexibility and expressiveness are much greater than both keyword-based information retrieval and standard resource discovery protocols, which support code-based exact matches only. This enables an effective query refinement process and can increase user trust in the discovery facility. Semantic-enhanced RFID object discovery can be leveraged also for sales and post-sale services, by assisting customers in using their purchased products more effectively.

3   METADEPCAS

3.1   DEPCAS

The high performance enabled through RFID technology evolution applied to automatic identification has caused the needed to research, define and propose new standards and practical architectures. Data EPC Acquisition System (DEPCAS) [5] architecture is a proposal that is included in this area. The main idea when we started to work in DEPCAS conception was the definition and the development of a practical approach to use EPC data acquisition system. The characteristics and behaviors of this system are: open, configurable and customizable in different scenarios (tracking, aggregating, identifying, classificating, etc.). The architecture definition is based on supervisory control and data acquisition systems. The development of these systems, generically known as Supervisory Control and Data Acquisition (SCADA), has defined a well-recognized software architecture. This software structure is used in a wide range of applications and with different scalability options. Like in SCADA systems, the next RFID systems will be characterized by huge input information in real time. This information should be processed, filtered, supervised and consolidated to be able to employ it in these same systems or transferred to others external.

3.2   METADEPCAS RFID Data Representation

Whatever RFID application usually generates a tuple stream in the form of a triple (E, l, t), where:

- E is an *EPC*, i.e., a unique identifier stored in a tag and associated to each tagged object;
- l is the *location* where an RFID reader has scanned an object having the E EPC;
- t is the *time* when the reading took place.

As a single tag may have multiple readings at the same location – thus producing a great amount of raw data – cleaning techniques have to be applied. The most used compression converts raw data in stay records in the form: (E, l, t_{in}, t_{out}) where t_{in} is the time when the object enters the location l, and t_{out} is the time when the object leaves it. Although this basic solution reduces the amount of data to be stored (even if not considerably), previous data representation loses object transitions information. So an alternative representation of RFID data has been proposed involving trace records and has the form:

$$E : \; l_1[\; t_{in}^1; t_{out}^1] \rightarrow \dots \rightarrow l_k[\; t_{in}^k; t_{out}^k] \tag{1}$$

where:

- $l_1, .. \; l_k$ are locations along the path followed by the tag with E EPC;
- t_{in}^i is the entering time at location l_i
- t_{out}^i is the exiting time at location l_i
- the sequence is ordered by t_{in}^i

The drawback of such data representations is that they are path-dependent, and therefore only path queries over objects moving together can benefit from them. To overcome this limitation, the notion of entry records is introduced, which describes product information that can be used in multidimensional analysis. Entry records have the form:

$$E : [A_1, v_1], [A_2, v_2], \dots, [A_n, v_n] \tag{2}$$

where:

- A_i describes an attribute representing the object with E EPC;
- v_i is the value associated to A_i for this object.

Notice that: (i) an entry record can be used to represent collections of RFID data at different level of details (e.g. raw data or stay records) and (ii) aggregates are based on different combinations of attributes A_i.

3.3   Supply Chain Indexing

In supply chain management, a basic need is to analyze object transitions. A product with an RFID tag can cross many locations in a chain. Tracing its movements, transitions can be expressed as a path $l_1, ..., l_n$ in a graph describing the supply chain itself. Different approaches and techniques have been proposed for supply chain indexing in order to effectively compute the path of a tag. Currently they are supported by DBMS physical optimizations. In [6] and [7], EPC data features are exploited to group tags and arrange them through bitmap indexes. Lee and Chung [8] devised an alternative encoding scheme that assigns to each path a pair (Element List Encoding Number (ELEN) - Order Encoding Number (OEN)). By assigning a prime number to each node in the chain, ELEN is obtained by multiplying path nodes (with related values) among them. In this way, the path followed by a tag is computed as factorization of the integer assigned to the path itself. Primarily of assigned numbers guarantees the correctness of the result. Additionally, OEN is a value able to encode the arrangement among nodes in the path.

Both the above solutions present some non-negligible drawback. Approaches [6] and [7] are dependent on DBMS optimizations and on the similarity assumption between EPCs, whereas framework in [8] does not cope with computational complexity of prime factorization of an integer. Since a supply chain can present several levels (typically from four to ten), to the best of our knowledge, no efficient algorithms are available for very large values.

To efficiently manage the object transitions, an elementary method was introduced in a model for the supply chain s as a directed sc-graph G_s whose nodes are locations of s and there is an edge from a node l_1 to a node l_2 if there is some movement of objects from l_1 to l_2 in s. The source nodes of a sc-graph, i.e., the nodes having no incoming edge, usually represent the place where objects are produced, whereas target nodes of a sc-graph, i.e., nodes having no outgoing edge, are usually the final stores where products are sold. Then, a token is associated to each possible path from a source to a target node. Finally, the encoding is performed in each node n of a sc-graph by assigning to n the set of tokens representing each path from a source to a target node traversing n.

3.4   Data Compression

In order to aggregate queries over a large amount of RFID data, it is useful to compress them with respect to different aggregation factors. For instance, considering location, data can be aggregated either at city, region or country levels. Similarly, a product can be grouped by brand, category or price.

Let us consider a set of attributes $S = \{A_1, A_2..., A_n\}$ describing available entry records. By borrowing a typical OLAP approach, attributes are grouped in S according to different factors such as location, time or product. Moreover, each factor allows to build a set $R = \{(x, r, y): x, y \in S\}$, where r is a binary relationship between attributes such as *is-a*, *part-of*, and so on. In this way *taxonomies* can be built starting from the original attribute set.

The set R, augmented with taxonomies defined over proper factors in R, suggests interesting attribute aggregations. An aggregation factor is defined as a propositional logic expression ϕ involving attributes occurring in $A_1, ..., A_n$. It can be easily noticed that ϕ depends on taxonomies defined over them. For instance, if $A_i \wedge A_j$ occurs in ϕ and $(A_i, \text{part-of}, A_j)$ then the conjunction can be replaced by A_j because A_j has a higher aggregation degree than Ai. Hence, a set of rules can be defined to simplify an aggregation factor using taxonomies. For example, with respect to a set of attributes related with location and time, a possible aggregation factors for that domain are $\phi 1$ = (location $\wedge$ time_in $\wedge$ time_out) and $\phi 2$ = (model).

Intuitively, ϕ_1 aggregates records for items entering and leaving the same location at the same time, while ϕ_2 aggregates records for items which are similar among them. Given two entry records; $r_1 = \{E_1; [A'_1, v'_1], \ldots, [A'_n, v'_n]\}$ and $r_2 = \{E_2; [A''_1, v''_1], \ldots, [A''_m, v''_m]\}$ an aggregated record r_A has the form: $\{E_{rA}; [r1, r2]\}$. Two entry records r_1 and r_2 are aggregated with respect to an aggregation factor ϕ if r1 and r2 satisfy ϕ as following definitions.

Definition 1 (ϕ-satisfiability). Given an expression ϕ over a set of attributes A1, ... , An, and two entry records $r_1 = \{E1; [A'_1, v'_1], \ldots, [A'_n, v'_n]\}$ and $r_2 = \{E2; [A''_1, v''_1], \ldots, [A''_m, v''_m]\}$, r_1 and r_2 satisfy ϕ if, by replacing each A_i in ϕ with the atom $(v'_i = v''_i)$ for $1 \le i \le n$, the obtained formula is true.

This notion can be used to introduce the one of aggregation based on a given aggregation factor.

Definition 2 (ϕ-aggregation). Given an aggregated record r_A, r_A is a ϕ-aggregate if for each pair of entry records r_1, and r_2 occurring in r_A:r_1 and r_2 satisfy ϕ.

Hence, an aggregation F can be obtained by a sequence of aggregation factors ϕ_1, $\phi_2, \ldots, \phi_n$. Basically, in a supply chain an aggregated record is an item *stock*. Object movement can be seen as a collection of stocks that split moving from sources to targets. Under this assumption, a useful definition is reported hereafter.

Definition 3 (subsumption). Given two aggregated records, $r_{A1} = \{E_{rA1}; [r_1, r_2, \ldots, r_n]\}$ and $r_{A2} = \{E_{rA2}; [r'_1, r'_2, \ldots, r'_{1m}]\}$, r_{A1} is subsumed by r_{A2} denoted $r_{A1} \blacktriangleleft r_{A2}$, if each r_i occurring in r_{A1} also occurs in r_{A2}.

An object transition can be then seen as a movement from a stock to another one. Hence, an observation is defined as an object transition event and it can be represented by a pair (s_1, s_2), where s_1 is a stock including a set of items coming from the stock s_2. It ensures that $s_1 \blacktriangleleft s_2$.

4   Conclusion

This paper presents two alternative approaches for data management in supply chains based on RFID identification technology. One based on on-line semantic-based object discovery and, other based on off-line analyses involving large amounts of RFID data. Distinguishing features are: (i) definite modifications to the EPCglobal standards allowing to exploit ontology-based data as well as to support nonstandard inference services, while keeping backward compatibility, (ii) advanced compression techniques enabling a significant space saving also maintaining a logical representation of data aggregation.

Such an approach may provide several benefits. Information about a product is structured and complete; it accurately follows the product history within the supply chain, being progressively built or updated during object lifecycle. This improves traceability of production and distribution, facilitates sales and post-sale services thanks to an advanced and selective discovery infrastructure. Indexing techniques, with an efficient data access, have been also proposed in a tool implementing the proposed approach. Some experimental results are presented to show the feasibility of the proposed framework also evidencing its effectiveness. The coherent development of the approach allows a strengthening of the information to be shared between the actors involved in supply chains, reducing the costs of adoption of RFID in business. Furthermore, an increase in transparency and trust is achieved not only between supply chain partners, but also between retailers and customers. This may be a direct competitive advantage for companies that adopt the technology.

Acknowledgements. This work has been supported by (i) the Spanish Government under the CICYT projects DPI-2011-26094 and DPI-2011-24588, (ii) the Comunidad de Madrid under the RoboCity2030-II excellence research network S2009/DPI-1559.

References

1. Smith, A.: Exploring radio frequency identification technology and its impact on business systems. Inf. Manag. Comp. Secur. 13, 16–28 (2005)
2. Ayoub, K., Manoj, S.: A Survey of RFID Tags. International Journal of Recent Trends in Engineering 1(4), 68–71 (2009)
3. Weiser, M.: The computer for the 21st century. SIGMOBILE Mob. Comput. Commun. Rev. 3, 3–11 (1999)
4. Di Noia, T., Di Sciascio, E., Donini, F., Ruta, M., Mongiello, M.: A system for principled matchmaking in an electronic marketplace. Int. J. Electron. Comm. 8, 9–37 (2004)
5. Abad, I., Heradio, G., Cerrada, C., Cerrada, J.A.: A SCADA Oriented Middleware for RFID Technology. Experts Systems With Application 39(12), 11115–11124 (2012)
6. Ban, C., Hong, B.-H., Kim, D.: Time parameterized interval r-tree for tracing tags in RFID systems. In: Andersen, K.V., Debenham, J., Wagner, R. (eds.) DEXA 2005. LNCS, vol. 3588, pp. 503–513. Springer, Heidelberg (2005)
7. Gonzalez, H., Han, J., Li, X., Klabjan, D.: Warehousing and analyzing massive RFID data set. In: Proceedings of the 22nd Int. Conference on Data Engineering, ICDE (2006)
8. Lee, C.H., Chung, C.-W.: Efficient storage scheme and query processing for supply chain management using RFID. In: Proceeding of the ACM SIGMOD Int. Conf. on Management of Data (2008)

E-Flow: A Communication System for User Notification in Dynamic Evacuation Scenarios

Augusto Morales, Ramon Alcarria, Tomás Robles, Edwin Cedeño,
Erno Peter Cosma, Javier Bermejo, and Francisco Perez Arribas

Technical University of Madrid,
Av. Complutense 30, 28040, Madrid, Spain
{amorales,ralcarria,trobles,edwinc}@dit.upm.es,
{erno.peter,javier.bermejo,francisco.perez.arribas}@upm.es

Abstract. Most of the current evacuation plans are based on static signaling, fixed monitoring infrastructure, and limited user notification and feedback mechanisms. These facts lead to lower situation awareness, in the case event of an emergency, such as blocked emergency exits, while delaying the reaction time of individuals. In this context, we introduce the E-Flow communication system, which improves the user awareness by integrating personal, mobile and fixed devices with the existing monitoring infrastructure. Our system broadens the notification and monitoring alternatives, in real time, among, safety staff, end-users and evacuation related devices, such as sensors and actuators.

Keywords: evacuation, communication system, publish/subscribe, MQTT.

1   Introduction and Background

The evacuation analysis of infrastructures is a long-studied problem that has been tackled with route modeling, decision support systems and so on. Some weaknesses of current evacuation plans relate to the way users perceive information using fixed visual, acoustic and light signals regardless of the emergency type, as these signals generally provide the static information and evacuation routes. For example, if emergency exits are unusable during the evacuation, individuals might not be aware of this situation until it is probably too late to react, and this fact affects the overall safety procedures and user awareness. Therefore, it is clear that a number of factors (e.g. humans and environmental) could alter the evacuation scenario, so they shall be considered as factors to take into consideration for a successful evacuation.

Most of the current research in evacuation scenarios has tackled [1][3] decision, route planning, and simulations, but few of them tackle the evacuation from the user awareness perspective. Nowadays, there are technologies that indeed permit wireless sensorized environments to provide information in these situations. Nevertheless, there are also challenges [2] related to the human factor, such as: reducing the reaction time of personnel, reduce the interpretation time, providing easy interaction mechanisms and dynamic signaling. Hence, the aim of dynamic evacuation scenarios is

G. Urzaiz et al. (Eds.): UCAmI 2013, LNCS 8276, pp. 207–214, 2013.

also associated to the availability of flexible user notification mechanisms and the interaction capabilities with the evacuation communication infrastructure in the critical moments.

In this paper we present our communication system for enhancing the user awareness, which has been developed under the E-Flow project [5]. It improves evacuation scenarios by integrating computing capabilities (human or machine-oriented) with end-users in order to improve their chances of survival through better situation awareness. Our system is composed of several communication layers, ranging from nodes in wireless sensor networks to end-user messaging. Therefore, this paper addresses the novelties of our system from a holistic approach and describes the integration of communication enhancements, produced from previous works [7][11]

Most of the solutions that may help to foresee and correctly react to evacuation scenarios are based on simulations [4]. They optimize evacuation plans for specific infrastructures, test them and detect critical points before the building is even planned. Our proposal focuses on the communication capabilities and allows broader situation awareness that lead to better individuals' decisions; so it can work as a complementary input for these solutions. Other approaches regarding implementations of evacuation scenarios take into account the dynamic characteristic by providing adaptation models that enable the fast creation of prototypes based on agent systems [19] or autonomous navigation systems [15]. These systems are often focused on route optimizations that can be based on colony algorithms [16], fuzzy logic [17] and also with algorithms inherited from communication networks. Other approaches also consider the movement of pedestrians as a homogeneous mass that behaves like a fluid flowing along corridors at a specific rate [20]. Our system differs from others, as it offers a comprehensive knowledge of the scenario in real time so it can work on top of other solutions.

The organization of the paper is as follows. In section II we detail the requirements of communication system from the human perspective. Section III states our proposed system. In Section IV we describe our implementation. Section V reviews previous works. Finally, we end with conclusions and future works

2   The Human Context in Evacuation Scenarios

The evacuation of buildings and other spaces is solved by means of static-like evacuation plans. These plans are obtained from the use of regulations and experiences prior to their construction. Evacuation plans can also be implemented over buildings or spaces already built due for example to new regulations or distribution changes. Thus, current evacuation plans associated to buildings barely take into account specific incidents people might face in an emergency [2], and the consequences of particular circumstances (e.g. fire near the emergency exit, changes in meeting points). Also, in many of these plans, both signals and evacuation devices are not suitable for persons with special needs.

Another weakness of current evacuation plans is the fact that the information given, based on labeled signs, acoustic and/or illuminated signals, is displayed in a static way, regardless of the emergency situation. For example, if one of the emergency exits cannot be used during the evacuation, people are unaware of this up to the very last moment, and probably this will probably lead to a late reaction. This non-flexible way to perform the evacuation clearly affects people's safety as it assumes a lack of variance when it is evident that there are plenty of different situations that can alter its progress. Therefore, a *user notification system* can contribute to a broader and flexible view of the whole situation.   Currently, communication among the head of the evacuation and the rest of the assigned staff is mostly carry out by using push-to-talk technologies and radio-frequency devices; however, these proprietary devices generally lack integration capabilities with the rest of the communication platform of the site, and are difficult to enhance with new functionalities. Thus, communication flexibility and pluggability merge as needs. Currently, external and emergency response teams are informed through phone calls or the activation of their emergency switchboard. Nevertheless, once these procedures have been initialized the subsequent information feedback is susceptible to the subjective point of view of the safety staff and human error. Hence, a key challenge consists of *offering richer communication capabilities* to arriving emergency services and allowing them to interact with humans and the existing evacuation infrastructure (e.g. communication systems, route signals, smoke sensors and mechanical actuators).

2.1   Motivation Scenario

This motivation scenario describes an example of an evacuation scenario which is tackled by our system. We start from the fact that it is a scenario with many machine-to-machine (M2M) communication links among sensors/actuators. The scenario comprises of a university with scholar buildings with students, faculty and safety staff. In normal conditions sensors provide humidity, air quality and temperature readings. Sensors are connected through several middleware solutions running over low-capable wireless devices. Hence, all the collected data are forwarded to servers which store and categorized them.   Security staff can access this information through a mobile application on their mobile devices. Faculty and students also have access to collected data from their facilities. There are three different roles: *standard staff* (faculty/students). The *safety staff* includes all the staff which has safety duties and permission to access and modify the evacuation infrastructure. The *emergency response team* is an external team (e.g. firefighters) that has access to the system upon request of the safety staff in emergencies.

Suddenly, a building goes on fire. Sensors and actuators fail because either they burn or their communication capabilities have collapsed. As some sensors and actuators have lost their connectivity, the evacuation system allows a reallocation of evacuation routes and the corresponding evacuation signals that guide all the personnel to a safe exit. In addition, the infrastructure informs safety staff where the fire originated, and which facilities have more evacuation priority depending on the fire level. In this situation, staff is capable of consuming the information produced by sensors from their respective building, as well as manually communicating with people. Hence the infrastructure disseminates all this generated data to interested parties and allows authorized safety staff to interact with sensors and actuators.   At the same time, the emergency response team arrives to a facility, for example a laboratory, which is probably contaminated with poisoning gases. As they need to activate a set of mobile and sophisticated sensors (e.g. a carbon monoxide sensor) the system is ready to plug their data into the content dissemination network without modifying the core communication system.

3   Communication System for User Notification

The core communication system of the E-Flow system is based on a topic-based Publish/Subscribe network, which is implemented using the Message Queue Telemetry Transport protocol (MQTT) [6]. Our system supports a topic-based subscription model which employs lightweight and compatible with M2M protocols. Hence, we include our mobile broker [12] as a functional component in our system which provides pluggable and mobile support for the information dissemination network. In addition, we employ our previously extended topic-based model [17] to enhance the information delivery process whenever subscribers express multiple interests at the same time; so the system can overcome the limitations of single topic-based language while maintaining compatibility with standard MQTT. In order to provide a broader information access, a proxy provides interoperability between MQTT and Web interfaces. Regarding identification, we made use of a topic hierarchy, similar to the WS-topic* specification [13] in order to ensure a common understanding of existing resources through and their identifiers. This hierarchy depends on the level of organization of the information that will be produced and the physical (e.g. floor types, halls), networking (e.g. sensors, networks), or human (e.g. staff roles) resources of the environment (e.g. a school, a hospital). The system integrates sensors and actuators through a *concentrator* which maps these resources to valid identifiers using the topic hierarchy. As resource identification depends on the protocols that are being used, and these protocols could vary from many sensors (e.g. 6LowPan and Zigbee), the concentrator abstracts them while acting as the front-end interface and performing as a MQTT client. It can also modify the behavior of back-end sensors upon receiving a notification from the Publish/Subscribe network. Figure 1, shows the different elements of the communication system.

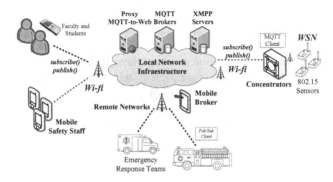

Fig. 1. Communication system for user notification

The system provides updated evacuation information that helps to reduce the reaction time of individuals, minimize the interpretation time, and offer capabilities for interacting with the communication system. The system provides user awareness in two forms: through a native application installed in their mobile devices and using a web-based application. Even if new HTML5/JavaScript technologies have access to mobile devices resources they are still less powerful than native applications. Hence, we use this type of technologies for actions that requires a lower level of integration with the existing resources of the mobile device (e.g. access to sensors). Regarding the user-to-user interaction, the system is designed to allow multimedia communication between several users through the XMPP protocol [10], as well as to consume information from sensors using MQTT. Concerning to safety staff and emergency response teams, the system offers native and web-based applications to detect in real time the status of sensors, and execute actions in actuators. In the native application, if the standard messaging system (through infrastructure of XMPP servers) fails, it automatically switches to modes: local Peer-to-Peer and GSM/UMTS communication (and their SMS and MMS capabilities). Hence, users maintain the same level of information awareness inside the system so they can still pay attention to critical actions.

4   Implementation

Our system comprises of different software or hardware developments, so in this section we clarify them as well as the end-to-end integration.

Sensor integration: All the hardware developments that integrate sensors have been designed from scratch; it includes the printed circuit board and electronic design. The core processor is a low-power OMAPL127 (DSP+ARM) [24] of Texas Instruments. Nodes use the chip PSOC3 [25] of Cypress Semiconductor. The communication between sensors nodes is made following the 802.15.4 standard and a WSN topology based on trees. Central nodes act as data proxies between the WSN and the concentrator. Both are connected using an USB interface and the middleware developed in C++. The concentrator runs Montavista Linux and acts as a MQTT client. The MQTT client was developed in Java using open-source libraries [9]. Its interconnection with the central WSN node is implemented using a Java Native Interface (JNI) and a USB connection. Figure 2 shows the integration of sensors.

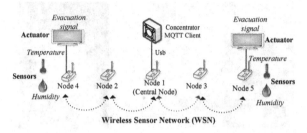

Fig. 2. Integration of sensors and actuators

Communication system: The system provides two functionalities: multimedia messaging using XMPP, and sensor/actuator over MQTT. In our testbed, a virtual machine running Ubuntu 12.04 supports both functionalities. In the first case, we have used the open-source XMPP Openfire 3.8 server [12]. We have set up three groups of standard staff, safety staff and emergency staff with the corresponding persistent chat rooms. Regarding the MQTT broker, we have implemented a modified version of the java-based Moquette broker [9] in order to extend the topic-based support intersected subscriptions [11]. This extension allows staff to have a tailored notification based on their status and location (e.g. status/available&building/a). The MQTT-to-Web proxy has been implemented using Node.js [14] and works with Websockets. It runs on a different virtual machine Ubuntu 12.04 machine than the broker.

User notification and interaction: We developed two applications: a native Android application and a web-based application. In the first case, the application implements three modes: a centralized XMPP, the P2P and cellular network. In the first mode, the application connects to the Openfire, in the P2P mode is built using AllJoyn [22] libraries. In the third case the UMTS/3G messaging is used. This application also integrates a MQTT client [13]. Regarding the graphical user interface we have also set visual and audible signals in order to alert users whenever an emergency occurs. There are also predefined messages that let users quickly publish some emergency warnings such as: "fire", "stair blocked help please".

The second web-based application is focused on evacuation management and decision support; so it is the front-end for fixed safety staff, and emergency staff (upon previous login). It runs together with the MQTT-to-web proxy. The application shows a map of pre-loaded locations and allows collecting information from sensor and modifying actuators' states.

4.1   Deployment

The system has been partially deployed in the Telecommunication School of the Technical University of Madrid. It includes the entries of building and halls. Wireless nodes have been provided with a rechargeable USB battery. In this topology and conditions the average bandwidth between nodes is about 255Kbps and 5ms of delay between WSN nodes. Concentrators and mobile devices are connected using 802.11g, with the local gigabit network that leads to the broker and proxy.

Fig. 3. Physical deployment in: entry of the building; second, boiler room; third, basement

Table 1 shows the information timeliness of our implementation. In this experiment, we use a Nexus S with Android 2.3.7. Case a) shows the delay from the concentrator publishes sensor data until they are received by the web application in a PC. Case b) shows the same case but for a mobile MQTT client and the web application. Case c) show the delay the MQTT-to-Web proxy introduces to the system. We have checked the normality of the three samples with the Shapiro-Wilk normality test [23] and conclude that the three samples came from a Normal distribution (p-value <= 0.05). Differences between fixed and mobile devices are the result of the low optimization level of the libraries and continuous garbage collection processes in the native applications, which increase the delay. Nevertheless, user experience and awareness are still acceptable for these values. This affirmation is based on the work [18] of Jacob et al., which states that delays less than 1.0 second need no special feedback.

Table 1. Information Timeliness (milliseconds)

	End-to-End MQTT-to-Web using Websockets			Pub/Sub Network MQTT only		
	Mean	Median	SD	Mean	Median	SD
a) Fixed devices	30,977	29,770	1,056	4,740	4,515	0,904
b) Mobile devices	246,983	250,989	11,893	65,904	66,938	4,111
c) Proxy Delay	4.402	4.520	0.830	-	-	-

5   Conclusions

This paper presents our solution for enhancing evacuation scenarios through user awareness. We outlined requirements of evacuation-oriented communication system from the human perspective and cover them in our system design. We also presented the advantages of our communication model in terms of user notification, M2M integration, resource identification and pluggability. We presented our implementation and show that our system offers an acceptable response rate in fixed and mobile scenarios. As future works we are planning a massive deployment of the system. It also includes evacuation exercises. Regarding the technical part we will improve the WSN nodes in order to directly support the MQTT-S and extract experimental data about their interaction with mobile brokers. We will implement mechanisms for extending the WSN node life and the performance of the mobile applications.

Acknowledgment. This work is supported by the E-Flow project TSI-020302-2011-5, under the TRACTOR Program of the Ministry of Industry, Energy and Tourism of Spain. We would like to thank the ETSIT.

References

1. Hamza-Lup, G.L., Hua, K.A., Minh Le, P.R.: Dynamic Plan Generation and Real-Time Management Techniques for Traffic Evacuation. IEEE Transactions on Intelligent Transportation Systems 9(4), 615–624 (2008)
2. Lovas, G.G.: On the importance of building evacuation system components. IEEE Transactions on Engineering Management 45(2), 181–191 (1998)

3. Georgoudas, I.G., Sirakoulis, G.C., Andreadis, I.T.: A cellular automaton crowd tracking system for modelling evacuation processes. In: El Yacoubi, S., Chopard, B., Bandini, S. (eds.) ACRI 2006. LNCS, vol. 4173, pp. 699–702. Springer, Heidelberg (2006)
4. Galea, E.R., Brown, R.C., Filippidis, L., Deere, S., Peacock, R.D., Kuligowski, E.D., Averill, J.D.: Pedestrian and Evacuation Dynamics. Springer, Boston (2011)
5. Avanza, Proyecto Tractor. E-Flow Project (2011), `http://gisai.dit.upm.es/index.php/projects`
6. MQTT Protocol Specificacion v3.1, `http://public.dhe.ibm.com/software/dw/webservices/ws-mqtt/mqtt-v3r1.html` (accessed on June 2013)
7. Morales Dominguez, A., Robles, T., Alcarria, R., Cedeño, E.: A Rendezvous Mobile Broker for Pub/Sub Networks. In: Mauri, J.L., Rodrigues, J.J.P.C. (eds.) GreeNets 2012. LNICST, vol. 113, pp. 16–27. Springer, Heidelberg (2013)
8. WS-Topics 1.3 OASIS Standard, `http://docs.oasis-open.org/wsn/wsn-ws_topics-1.3-spec-os.pdf` (accessed on June 2013)
9. Moquette MQTT Java, `http://code.google.com/p/moquette-mqtt/` (accessed on June 2013)
10. Extensible Messaging and Presence Protocol (XMPP): Core. IETF RFC6120
11. Morales Dominguez, A., Alcarria, R., Cedeno, E., Robles, T.: An Extended Topic-Based Pub/Sub Broker for Cooperative Mobile Services. In: 27th International Conference Advanced Information Networking and Applications Workshops (WAINA), pp. 1313–1318 (2013)
12. OpenFire, `http://www.igniterealtime.org/projects/openfire/` (accessed on June 2013)
13. Fusesource MQTT libraries, `https://github.com/fusesource/mqtt-client` (accessed on June 2013)
14. Node.js, `http://nodejs.org/` (accessed on June 2013)
15. Filippoupolitis, A., Gorbil, G., Gelenbe, E.: Autonomous navigation systems for emergency management in buildings. In: GLOBECOM Workshops IEEE, pp. 1056–1061 (2011)
16. Cheng, N.: An Optimization Method for Dynamic Evacuation Route Programming Based on Improved Ant Colony Algorithm. In: International Conference on Intelligent System Design and Engineering Application (ISDEA), pp. 265–267 (2010)
17. Sharma, S., Vadali, H.: Modeling Emergency Scenarios in Virtual Evacuation Environment. In: WRI World Congress on Computer Science and Information Engineering, vol. 4, pp. 759–763 (2009)
18. Jakob, N.: Usability Engineering. Academic Press (1993)
19. Almeida., J.E., Kokkinogenis., Z., Rossetti, R.J.F.: NetLogo implementation of an evacuation scenario. In: 7th Iberian Conference on Information Systems and Technologies, pp. 1–4 (2012)
20. Hamacher, H.W., Tjandra, S.A.: Mathematical Modeling of Evacuation Problems: A State of the Art. In: Schreckenberg, M., Sharma, S.D. (eds.) Pedestrian and Evacuation Dynamics, pp. 227–266. Springer, Berlin (2002)
21. Luh, P.B., Wilkie, C.T., Chang, S.-C., Marsh, K.L., Olderman, N.: Modeling and Optimization of Building Emergency Evacuation Considering Blocking Effects on Crowd Movement. IEEE Transactions on Automation Science and Engineering 9(4), 687–700 (2012)
22. Alljoyn Website, `https://www.alljoyn.org/` (accessed on June 2013)
23. Shapiro, S.S., Wilk, M.B.: An analysis of variance test for normality (complete samples). Biometrika 52, 591–611 (1965)
24. Texas Instrument OMAP-L137, `http://www.ti.com/product/omap-l137` (Accessed on June 2013)
25. Cypress Semiconductor PSOC3, `http://www.cypress.com/?id=2232` (Accessed on June 2013)

Subtle Interaction
for a Non Intrusive Communication

Fernando Olivera, Alfredo Rivas, and Felipe Iturriaga

Unidad Profesional Interdisciplinaria de Ingeniería Campus Zacatecas (UPIIZ),
Instituto Politécnico Nacional (IPN),
Zacatecas, México
foliverad@ipn.mx

Abstract. Human communication is not completely supported by current technology. This is due to the richness and variety of our social interactions. Information and Communication Technologies have grown in recent decades to provide multiple communication services in the most varied devices. But most of them are highly intrusive, forcing us to focus our attention and having in many cases to temporarily leave the activity we were doing. This paper presents a proposal for implementing a non-intrusive communication based on the common context that conversational partners share. To achieve this we make use of the concept of Subtle Interaction, to implement Calm Technology and study how we can exploit the periphery of our attention to accomplish less intrusive ways of communication supported by current technology. Finally we present a proof of concept and a brief user study.

Keywords: subtle interaction, calm computing, peripheral interaction, ambient displays.

1 Introduction

Weiser was a visionary who surprised us with revolutionary ideas as Ubiquitous Computing. We have seen in our world how Ubiquitous Computing has kept expanding slowly. We now have microcontrollers embedded in many different devices, that make use of various computational capabilities in a way invisible to our perception to make our life easier. We have also seen how the computational capabilities of personal computers were distributed among various devices: laptops, PDAs, netbooks, smartphones ... Going from having a computer per person (at best), to count each person with multiple devices with different computational capabilities. And having advanced as well on the integration of these devices to access any information anytime, anywhere. However this progress has not been as Weiser intended and we are still far away from feeling the use of computers "as refreshing as taking a walk in the woods" [1].

But if there is one aspect of Weiser's vision whose development has hardly been conducted outside research laboratories, that is certainly Calm Technology [2]. Calm Technology involves both the center and the periphery of our attention. Designing Calm Technology systems has proved difficult, even to the point

G. Urzaiz et al. (Eds.): UCAmI 2013, LNCS 8276, pp. 215–222, 2013.

that some researchers have proposed to move on from Weiser's vision of Calm Technology to pursue more easily achievable goals [3]. We feel it is difficult to design Calm Technology and more difficult to evaluate it because of its own nature. Calm Technology can only be calm when it is not a novelty. It's like when a child learns to read. At first any text catches his attention and the child tries to read every written word that he sees. But once reading is mastered, and after this initial period of fascination, the child will perceive writing as a ubiquitous technology and as long as the streets are not full of dozens of billboards and other signs, he will perceive all these words in the periphery, moving them to the center of his attention only when it becomes necessary. We think that research in Calm Technology is the one which has to focus on small reachable projects to attain favorable results. Only when we fully understand Calm Technology we could pursue further goals. In this paper we present our little contribution to develop Calm Technology for a limited non intrusive communication system.

1.1   Communication Technologies

Today we live in a world in which any information is within our reach to the point of having an information overload, however unlike other aspects of our life, the only way to access this information is focusing our attention. This is because most of existing communication technologies are highly intrusive, forcing users to drive most of their attention into the communication itself (think of how dangerous it can be to answer the phone while driving). Areas with no phone signal or Internet connection are disappearing, so we have no more excuses to avoid answering our conversational partners almost immediately. We are forgetting that the person making a phone call has the available time to do it, and yet the receiver may be engaged in other activities. Also it is not strange that we feel disappointed when they interrupt us in an important activity or when someone refuses to answer us for unknown reasons. Therefore, there are reasons to be concerned about the communication demands that new devices can impose.

Also these forms of communication are often stressful, not only for the information overload, but also for the way it is displayed. It's easy to have a feeling of stress when you find the information you need with a level of detail beyond what you need, or when you have to interrupt a task to approach your device's screen to search for something. The screens are a common interface, but they require that we focus our attention and are not suitable to display more relaxing information in our periphery. It is not the same to feel how less light enters the room and to hear the first drops of rain on the glass while immersed in a task, to having to search the Internet for the weather in your city. Some of the information that screens provide could be shown in a similar way to how we perceive climate in the windows of our home.

We think there is a need for technology to support less intrusive ways of communication that occur in daily life outside our cell phones. There are many examples of less intrusive communication in everyday life: When we wink, our interlocutor interprets the meaning depending on the context. When we hit the glass wall of someone's office, the meaning also depends on the context, it may mean that we are still waiting for the report or may be a proposition to go for coffee. We can answer to this communications in a similar way without nearly losing focus, for example returning the wink back or waving our hand in a negative answer. This type of communication has being referred to in previous work as Subtle Interaction [4]. A communication in which less is more and in which special attention should be paid to balance capabilities and intrusion. Subtle Interaction is based on the context, therefore the information transmitted is not present for the most part on the message, but in the knowledge that sender and receiver have of each other, based in all the experiences that they have shared. We are looking for the development of appropriate interfaces that make use of the concept of Subtle Interaction, to implement Calm Technology and study how computing devices that take advantage of the periphery to develop new forms of communication. The work presented here explores the development of new forms of remote communication through devices which act on the periphery of human attention, using the context in a similar way as people do in any daily communication.

When we face the problem of exporting this model of communication to Ubiquitous Computing area, the common household objects, being perfectly integrated into the environment, can provide a deployed network of possible communication tools for ubiquitous and subtle interaction. With the only necessity being to provide computing capabilities to those objects, which then are called smart objects or augmented objects. For the design of these new interfaces it is possible to exploit previous research in Augmented Objects, by enhancing common objects [5], and the closely related Internet of Things(IoT) paradigm [6].

We have explored enhancing a lamp to allow establishing communication between small networks of people (such as extended family or close friends) that do not live together, through the use of context information (information that conversational partners have about each other based on previous experiences).

2   Related Work

There has been previous efforts to accomplish similar ways of Calm Technology. Ambient Displays have sought to exploit human capabilities to perceive events in the periphery of their attention. Examples might be a display that offers information about the time it takes to reach each of the bus lines to the nearest bus stop, or a lamp showing a light level similar to the outside, letting us know about the time of the day [7]. Even they have come to market lamps that change color depending on some variable, such as the values of certain shares on the stock market. Nevertheless, Ambient Displays are one-way information channels, through which the user can only receive information but not interact.

Also communication between people that live apart has been explored. One-way communication has been developed for the home, including picture frames connecting elderly people to their extended family members [8] [9] and entangled lamps [10]. But they only connect one home to another through ambient awareness, without exploiting communication based on the context. Other systems like

ASTRA [11] or HomeinTouch [12] attempted to strengthen unmet communication needs, but instead ended up opening a powerful but demanding channel of communication by using screens and text messages, which is not what we have tried to accomplish. Pheriperal Interaction systems [13] [14], nevertheless, have proven that it is possible to open parallel channels of communication without greatly disturbing the main activity. These channels can be exploited to create a less intrusive communication.

Examples of two-way communication systems include InTouch [15], which enables a tangible connection channel, or Lumitouch [16], a system limited to two users that uses two distant picture frame that are entangled, by touching one of them the other lights up. These communication systems can be based on context but they are not easily defined.

3 Designing the Interaction

The aim of this paper is to demonstrate that it is possible to develop Calm Technology, using Subtle interaction, to create less intrusive communication technologies based on context. We think there are other scenarios where Calm Technology could also be applicable, provided that small problems are addressed.

Calm technology should be natural. So in the case of an interface based on this technology, ideally, it should not be necessary to teach the device's operation to users. We think that creating a specific functionality for an interface and trying to explain to the user the meaning of each event or action, may not be the best way for the user to consider it natural. Therefore, we wanted to create an interface that allows different ways of interacting, in which all events and actions are very simple, but have no predefined meanings. We think that in this way, the interface designer may favor some meanings or others based on her experience, but she does not discourage any other meaning.

In the case of this work, we have tried to use Calm Technology to communicate small networks of people (as extended family), so it is mandatory that the interface acts both as output and input, allowing to have bidirectional communication. It also needs an Internet connection for establishing a remote communication. We have argued before about the advantage of using common objects as they are perfectly integrated into the environment. Also light has proved to be associated in many cases with presence [10], letting us know for example, if our neighbor is at home or even if he is already asleep. For these reasons we decided that our prototype should be an augmented lamp. We chose to have RGB color lights, because previous work have made us realize the ease of establishing and remembering color-person associations [4]. This could allow to remain in contact with more than one person by associating different colors to different people.

Although the interaction should be unobtrusive and may be easily ignored, we think that the device should have a more intrusive form of communication, to draw attention if necessary. This could be very useful in case of an emergency. We decided that the device could make a sound if needed.

3.1   Prototype

Our first prototype is a pair of augmented objects. Each one consists of a lamp illuminated by RGB LEDs which has several sensors and a buzzer (see figure 1). On the one hand it has some PIR sensors (Passive infrared sensor) to detect any movement that occurs near the lamp. On the other hand it features several capacitive touch elements including a scroll wheel, button and proximity sensor for explicit user interaction. It also has a switch button that is activated when someone presses slightly on the top of the lamp.

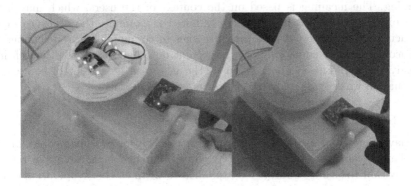

Fig. 1. Augmented Lamp prototype

It has two microcontrollers, one handles the capacitive touch elements and the other controls the LEDs, the buzzer and the switch button. The second one has an ethernet module to establish an Internet connection to send and receive data from a server which was programmed in Java. It can record the various actions that occur in each lamp and send the action to take in response to the corresponding associated lamp. The operation is as follows:

- When someone is moving near the lamp, the PIR sensors detects this motion and the microcontroller send this information to the server. The server passes the information to any attached lamp and their LEDs are turned on with the color associated to the first lamp. If motion is not detected again for a few minutes the lights will slowly turn down. If more than one augmented lamp detects presence, the lamps will slowly change color, going through all the colors that correspond to the lamps which have detected motion.
- When a user's finger approaches the capacitive scroll wheel, the proximity sensor sends a signal to the microcontroller and some LEDS in the capacitive sensor are turned on, meaning that the capacitive sensors are ready for interaction. Now the user can move her finger above the scroll wheel to select which augmented lamps she wants to contact, the lamp color is turned on going through all the colors corresponding to the other lamps, for the user

to select one color (an its associated lamp) with the capacitive button inside the wheel. When a lamp is contacted its LEDs will blink with the color corresponding to the lamp that has made contact. To dismiss this flickering the user at the contacted lamp only needs to press the top of the lamp.

– If the user selects the option to contact a particular lamp 3 times in less than five minutes, the buzzer will produce a melody in case of detecting presence near the lamp that she wanted to contact, or it will wait to detect some motion to produce the sound.

In this way the lamps can provide three types of information: awareness, desire for contact and the urgency to make contact. This messages have no associated meaning. The meaning is based on the context of the users, which may have been previously decided by the users or not. For example, the desire to make contact could indicate that the person wishes to communicate by telephone or videoconference, or could simply try to point out that the football match has already started. The meaning is up to the users, as it is a lot of contextual information we provide daily to our conversational partners.

3.2   User Study

We have conducted a brief user study with the help of two augmented lamps. The lamps were used for two weeks by three different couples living in remote cities within the same country. We explained to them the basic operation of the prototype (e.g. what action makes the other lamp turn on) without revealing the possible meanings of such actions. We also let them choose the color they wanted their lamps to light on. When we asked them about the reasons for their selection, we found out that in the case of two of the couples their motives were not related to their sentimental partner. The other couple chose blue because it is the favorite color of both. Despite this, we think that if there were more lamps, the selection of colors would have been probably associated with the persons on the other side of the communication link in order to remember this association easily, but it is only a hypothesis that still has to be proven.

After the experience, a brief interview was conducted with every couple. We asked them about things like their feelings when the lamp was emitting any of the visual or acoustic signals, and what they think the other was doing or thinking. We are aware that with such a limited amount of participants and time, our results are only preliminary, but the results were similar to those expected. All couples stressed that seeing the light on indicating the recent presence of the other gave them peace of mind. One of the couples said that they sent each other less SMS when they were home, because the lamp made them realize their sentimental partner was fine. Another woman pointed out that the lamp helped her to synchronize calls to her boyfriend when he had just gotten home, instead of calling him when he was driving. Therefore, at least in some cases the new communication device tends to partially replace more intrusive forms of communication or ensure that these intrusions occur at appropriate times. Two of the men expressed some concerns about a feeling of surveillance, especially during the weekend.

The first and in one case the second day, they had not yet established a meaning for the different forms of interaction. We believe that they experienced a brief testing phase. As a few days passed, all the couples agreed that any attempt to make contact would mean that they were available for communication by phone. The rules of communication were not explained, but all the couples arrived to the same conclusions. The sound alarm was only used frequently at first, except for one of the couples who used it more often to call the attention of their partner. Two couples stressed that during those two weeks they felt closer to each other, the other couple view the device as a funny way of communication. The Java server stored the different messages the couples send to each other. Studying the data we realized that the three couples went through a period of initial fascination between 3 and 6 days in which the lamps were often used. After this, their use was slowly declining.

This brief preliminary study raises new questions: How will the system work with more attached lamps? What will happen when people have the device for such a long time that it becomes a natural part of their homes? How do these devices affect the bond between sentimental partners? How do these devices affect other forms of communication in the long place? These and other questions must be studied.

4   Conclusions and Future Work

Human communication is complex and nuanced. Current technologies are not supporting every way in which humans communicate with each other. We have pointed out that communication technologies are highly intrusive and that new devices are imposing their communication demands. It seems that this globalized and always connected world, has changed the way we communicate, however it is just that communication technologies do not capture the variety of our social interaction.

We have proposed the development of new interfaces that make use of the concept of Subtle Interaction to implement Calm Technology. We have suggested a mechanism to support this kind of interaction using the periphery of our attention to display information based on the context between conversational partners. We have also developed a proof of concept consisting of a set of augmented lamps which support communication based on context. We have presented a brief case study which suggests that good results are going to be obtained. Despite the difficulty to evaluate it, it seems that Calm Technology can be achieved using Subtle Interaction. We certainly believe that supporting the types of communication and interaction that we are accustomed to in face to face scenarios, could provide closeness to those living apart from their families.

We need to increase the population of the user study to have more reliable data. We are planning to build more lamps to answer further questions. Also, we are about to conduct a transnational user study, because we believe that this type of interface can be very suitable for families in which one of its members lives in another time zone. In this situation we think that it could be very interesting for them to have some contextual awareness information about their whereabouts, and specially to know when they can engage in a higher level conversation (by phone, videoconference...).

References

1. Weiser, M.: The computer for the 21 century. Scientific American 256(3), 94–104 (1991)
2. Weiser, M., Brown, J.: Designing calm technology. PowerGrid Journal 1(1), 75–85 (1996)
3. Rogers, Y.: Moving on from Weiser's vision of calm computing: Engaging ubicomp experiences. In: Dourish, P., Friday, A. (eds.) UbiComp 2006. LNCS, vol. 4206, pp. 404–421. Springer, Heidelberg (2006)
4. García-Herranz, M., Olivera, F., Haya, P., Alamán, X.: Harnessing the interaction continuum for subtle assisted living. Sensors 12(7), 9829–9846 (2012)
5. Gellersen, H., Beigl, M., Krull, H.: The MediaCup: Awareness technology embedded in an everyday object. In: Gellersen, H.-W. (ed.) HUC 1999. LNCS, vol. 1707, pp. 308–310. Springer, Heidelberg (1999)
6. Ashton, K.: That internet of things thing. RFiD Journal 22, 97–114 (2009)
7. Mankoff, J., Dey, A.K., Hsieh, G., Kientz, J., Lederer, S., Ames, M.: Heuristic evaluation of ambient displays. In: Proceedings of the SIGCHI Conference on Human Factors in Computing Systems, pp. 169–176. ACM (2003)
8. Mynatt, E., Rowan, J., Craighill, S., Jacobs, A.: Digital family portraits: supporting peace of mind for extended family members. In: Proceedings of the SIGCHI Conference on Human Factors in Computing Systems, pp. 333–340. ACM, New York (2001)
9. Consolvo, S., Roessler, P., Shelton, B., LaMarca, A., Schilit, B., Bly, S., Res, I., Seattle, W.: Technology for care networks of elders. IEEE Pervasive Computing 3(2), 22–29 (2004)
10. Tollmar, K., Persson, J.: Understanding remote presence. In: Proceedings of the Second Nordic Conference on Human-Computer Interaction, pp. 41–50. ACM (2002)
11. Romero, N., Markopoulos, P., Baren, J., Ruyter, B., Ijsselsteijn, W., Farshchian, B.: Connecting the family with awareness systems. Personal and Ubiquitous Computing 11(4), 299–312 (2007)
12. Petersen, M.G., Hansen, A.B., Nielsen, K.R., Gude, R.: HOMEinTOUCH designing two-way ambient communication. In: Aarts, E., Crowley, J.L., de Ruyter, B., Gerhäuser, H., Pflaum, A., Schmidt, J., Wichert, R. (eds.) AmI 2008. LNCS, vol. 5355, pp. 44–57. Springer, Heidelberg (2008)
13. Olivera, F., García-Herranz, M., Haya, P., Llinás, P.: Do not disturb: Physical interfaces for parallel peripheral interactions. In: Campos, P., Graham, N., Jorge, J., Nunes, N., Palanque, P., Winckler, M. (eds.) INTERACT 2011, Part II. LNCS, vol. 6947, pp. 479–486. Springer, Heidelberg (2011)
14. Hausen, D.: Peripheral interaction: facilitating interaction with secondary tasks. In: Proceedings of the Sixth International Conference on Tangible, Embedded and Embodied Interaction, pp. 387–388. ACM (2012)
15. Brave, S., Dahley, A.: inTouch: a medium for haptic interpersonal communication. In: Extended Abstracts on Human Factors in Computing Systems: Looking to the Future, CHI 1997, p. 364. ACM (1997)
16. Chang, A., Resner, B., Koerner, B., Ishii, H.: LumiTouch: an emotional communication device. In: Conference on Human Factors in Computing Systems, pp. 313–314. ACM, New York (2001)

Characterizing Mobile Telephony Signals in Indoor Environments for Their Use in Fingerprinting-Based User Location

Alicia Rodriguez-Carrion, Celeste Campo, Carlos Garcia-Rubio,
Estrella Garcia-Lozano, and Alberto Cortés-Martín

Department of Telematic Engineering
University Carlos III of Madrid
28911-Leganés, Madrid, Spain
{arcarrio,celeste,cgr,emglozan,alcortes}@it.uc3m.es

Abstract. Fingerprinting techniques have been applied to locate users in indoor scenarios using WiFi signals. Although mobile telephony network is used for outdoor location, it is widely deployed and their signal more stable, thus being also a candidate to be used for fingerprinting. This paper describes the characterization of GSM/UMTS signals in indoor scenarios to check if their features allow to use them for constructing the radio maps needed for fingerprinting purposes. We have developed an Android application to collect the received signal information, such that makes the measurement process cheaper and easier. Measurements show that changes in location and device orientation can be identified by observing the received signal strength of the connected and neighboring base stations. Besides, detecting this variability is easier by using the GSM network than with UMTS technology. Therefore mobile telephony network seems suitable to perform fingerprinting-based indoor location.

Keywords: fingerprinting, indoor location, mobile device-based location, GSM, UMTS.

1 Introduction

Location represents one of the most used aspects of users' context. In order to provide intelligence to our surroundings, first we need to know exactly what our concrete surrounding is. In the concrete case of indoor location, many techniques have been proposed in the literature, but one of the most investigated nowadays is the so called fingerprinting technique. The foundation of this method lies in two steps: first, in an offline phase, the received signal strengths (RSSs) from the transmission stations of certain wireless technology are collected at different locations in order to construct a radio map of the place; and second, in an online phase, we could locate the user by comparing her current RSSs with the information stored in the radio map, looking for the closest measurement to estimate her position. The wireless technologies used include WiFi, RFID, Ultra WideBand (UWB) systems or the mobile phone network. Section 2 deals with

G. Urzaiz et al. (Eds.): UCAmI 2013, LNCS 8276, pp. 223–230, 2013.

this variety of technologies, both for indoor and outdoor environments. Since the device performing the measurements also influences the collected data, it seems reasonable to use the same device to collect the fingerprints and to perform the online phase. In Sect. 3 we describe a mobile phone based application to perform the offline phase for mobile telephony networks.

Since WiFi signals fluctuate due to many factors (multipath fading, obstacles...), and they are variable through time because of the dynamic character of these networks, we decide to test how the mobile network works instead. This work is not focused on the final positioning performance, but on studying the features of the signal strengths received from different base transceiver stations (BTSs) in indoor environments, analyzing the differences between GSM and UMTS networks. Different measurements were made at several locations using different device orientations to see how these factors impact the RSSs, and if it is feasible to identify such changes by looking at the RSS fluctuations. Sections 4 and 5 focus on the testbed carried out to perform such analysis, using the application previously described, along with the data gathered and the results drawn from it. Finally, Sect. 6 summarizes the main conclusions together with an outline of the future work.

2   Related Work

Many location techniques are available nowadays, varying in diverse parameters such as scale, output, measurements needed or estimation method [1]. Methods based on fingerprinting gained popularity during the last years. Much research have been done on this area, which can be tackled from mainly three points of view: the fingerprint collecting process, the features conditioning the RSSs, and the algorithm used to estimate the position based on the fingerprints.

Most works propose location algorithms [2,3] based on different approaches: probabilistic methods [4,5], Bayesian frameworks [6], entropy-based methods [7,8], principal component and multiple discriminant analysis [9], decision trees [3], ray-tracing models [10], neural networks or clustering methods [11,12]. These algorithms rely on different technologies: WiFi, mostly for indoor environments [2,16,7,17,9,15,12,3,5,8]; mobile phone networks [4,11]; RFID [13,14]; or UWB [6].

Not so many works are devoted to the fingerprint collection process. Some authors use information from third party services like Google or Skyhook [4], and very few give specific details on the system and software used to collect the fingerprints [15], since they are usually collected using ad-hoc frameworks.

Both the algorithms and the fingerprint collection process depend also on complementary information besides the received signal: fingerprints becoming out of date with time [16], the environment conditioning the RSS values [12], or the importance of taking into account the receiver information [3,2,17].

3   Fingerprint Collecting Application for Mobile Devices

Most of the research on fingerprinting has been devoted to the algorithmic part, but the first step, the fingerprint collection, cannot be ignored in order to obtain precise and useful raw data. The devices used for obtaining the fingerprints, called dongles, are expensive equipments. In many cases, the interested parties hire them to afford the cost, limiting the availability to perform measurements. This device measures a wide variety of parameters with high accuracy, but for fingerprinting purposes we may not need such varied and high quality data. Considering that the devices to be located are mobile phones, which radio hardware is not as precise as the measurement equipment, the RSS perceived by the phone hardware may not be similar to the measurement made by the dongle.

These reasons led us to develop a fingerprint collecting application for mobile phones, so that the radio map constructed by the collected fingerprints (offline phase) may be more similar to the signals received by the phones that want to be located (online phase). The main requirements for the application are the following ones: it must be able to collect the network type, identifier and RSS of all detected BTSs, both for GSM and UMTS networks; it should show this information on screen and record it in a file for post processing; it should be aware of the terminal orientation; it has to take into account that mobile devices have limited memory and battery, which requires high efficiency; it must allow on demand measurements as well as a pooling mechanism, where the pooling period can be configured.

With these requirements in mind, we have designed and implemented an application for Android devices, made of five blocks: Telephony Network, which provide all the data about the received signal; Sensor Management, which obtains the device orientation data; File Management, in charge of creating the files and recording the data obtained; Core Service, the main player of the application, in charge of managing the interaction among the rest of the blocks; and User Interface, which takes care of showing the information on screen and providing a human interface to control the application.

During the implementation and testing phases of the application, we have noticed that, whilst LG and HTC devices provide all the available data offered by Android Telephony API, Samsung devices restrict the data about the neighboring BTSs. Therefore, we should take into account the concrete device to use for the radio map construction, since we may not obtain all the desired information with certain devices.

4   Test Scenarios and Measurements

This work is focused on studying how GSM and UMTS signals behave in indoor environments, in order to make sure that mobile network signals are suitable for constructing radio maps. We should remind that, unlike WiFi networks, BTSs coverage area can be very wide and therefore the RSS differences perceived in a small indoor environment may not be sufficient to locate a user.

Therefore, we have performed different testbeds in order to observe the behavior of GSM and UMTS signals from different points of view, using the fingerprint collecting application described in Sect. 3.

We made tests in two different scenarios: outdoor, in order to set a reference when multi path and obstacles are minimum, and indoor, as it is the actual environment where we would like to make the locating task. Several different devices should be tested in order to see the differences among their measurements, but because of space limitations this aspect is left for future works. In this case, with a mobile phone HTC Desire with Android version 2.2.2 and the pooling mode of the application at a sampling rate of 2 samples per second, we performed different tests:

- In the outdoor scenario, we have measured the signal for 15 minutes in each of four orientations: 0°, 90°, 180° and 270°. We have done two sets of measurements: one for GSM signal, and another one for UMTS signal.
- In the indoor scenario two different measurements took place. The first one is analogous to the test done in the outdoor scenario: the signal level is measured with the device running the aforementioned application during 15 minutes for each orientation. Once again, two test sets were performed, for GSM and UMTS cases. The second measurement set was done as follows. We covered a laboratory measuring RSSs along two parallel hallways separated 4 meters between them, performing measurements each 4 meters along each hallway. At each of the eight locations, the device collected data during 5 minutes for each orientation. The measurements were done twice, once for GSM and once for UMTS sginals.

5   Results and Discussion

In this section we describe some results drawn from the dataset obtained in the experiments described in Sect. 4. As mentioned in the introduction, the main goal of the paper is to determine if it is possible to use fingerprinting-based positioning techniques in indoor scenarios using mobile phone network signals. Therefore the final positioning performance (i.e. localization error) is not addressed. The goal is to characterize both GSM and UMTS signals in such indoor scenarios.

First we compare the RSSs in an outdoor scenario with respect to a near indoor one, therefore the serving BTSs in both cases are roughly the same. Figure 1 shows the RSSs of all the GSM BTSs the device has detected during 15 minutes, for the outdoor environment in the left-hand plot, and for the indoor scenario in the right-hand one. The plots only represent the RSS of the main BTSs, i.e. the signals that have a received power above −95dBm during at least 5 minutes. In the outdoor scenario the device detected 9 BTSs and in the indoor scenario 11 BTSs. As we can see, in both cases there is a main signal that reaches around −65dBm, and then the rest of the signals are received with lower levels above −90dBm. In general, the RSSs are stable in both cases, varying in 2dBm due to the discrete values returned by the Android API.

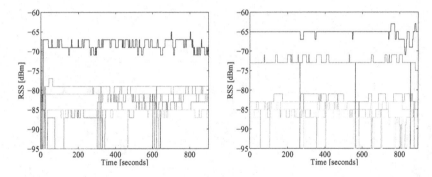

Fig. 1. RSS of all GSM BTSs detected, for outdoor (left) and indoor (right) scenarios

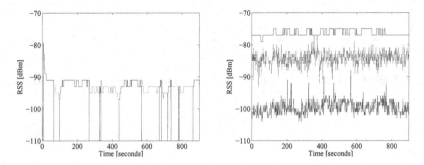

Fig. 2. RSS of all UMTS BTSs detected, for outdoor (left) and indoor (right) scenarios

Therefore we can see that although we are in an indoor environment, the signals are not affected by effects as absorption and obstacles. Moreover, several BTSs signals can be detected, and the total number is not lower when measuring in the indoor scenario. We will see later that the number of BTSs detected is important in order to have more information with which determine the user's position.

The case of UMTS signals is very different, as pictured in Fig. 2. The device only detected significative signal strength from two different BTSs for the outdoor scenario, and three for the indoor one. Moreover, in the case of the indoor environment, the received signals with lower strength have an important ripple not observed in the rest of cases, where all signals are very stable. Therefore, UMTS network does not offer as much information as GSM one and it seems that with so few signals the fingerprinting algorithms would lack of data to perform the positioning task.

Focusing on GSM case and the indoor scenario, Fig. 3 shows the RSSs of the 8 BTSs with strongest level received. The white and grey rectangles mark out the time periods the device was in each orientation. We can observe that the terminal orientation impacts clearly the signal received from all BTSs. We can see that as the orientation changes, so the signals level does, and then they maintain approximately that same level throughout the measurement period.

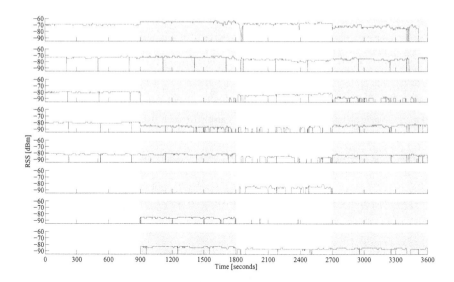

Fig. 3. RSS of all GSM BTSs detected, for a fixed location and four orientations

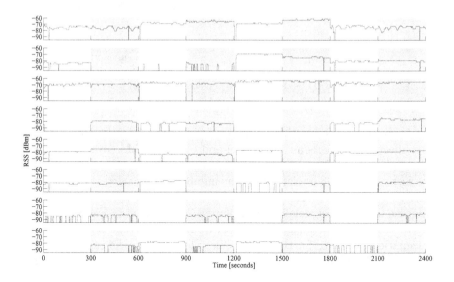

Fig. 4. RSS of all GSM BTSs detected, for a fixed orientation and eight locations

Combining the levels of all the BTSs we could determine the device orientation. Therefore we can leverage this information to create richer radio maps that include orientation data. This way, during the online phase we can obtain the device orientation from its sensor and filter the radio map database to consider only the data corresponding to that orientation, potentially improving the resulting location estimation.

Finally, Fig. 4 shows how different locations are represented in terms of signal strength of the different BTSs. In this case the device orientation is fixed all time, and 5 minute measurements have been made in 8 locations, differentiated by the white and grey rectangles. As happened with device orientation, location changes reflect in the RSS profile, which remain almost constant for each location. Therefore, by looking at the signal level of all the BTSs we could determine the location of the device, thus concluding that GSM signals seem suitable for fingerprinting purposes in indoor scenarios.

6   Conclusions and Future Work

Although fingerprinting positionig has been proposed mostly for WiFi deployments in indoor environments, we have shown that GSM network also has potential to be used for this purpose. In order to check it, we have developed an Android application for collecting data about the RSSs of the detected BTSs, both for GSM and UMTS networks, as well as the device orientation. With this application we have performed tests that showed: (i) GSM received signals in indoor environments preserve the useful information of the signals observed in outdoor scenarios; (ii) the number of detected BTSs signals vary depending on the concrete location, but they usually account for 6-8 significative signals in places with dense BTS deployment; (iii) UMTS technology does not show as much potential as GSM, since only 2-3 signals are received; (iv) by looking at the combination of RSSs of all the detected GSM BTSs we can distinguish the location and device orientation, which could be useful for the radio map database, in order to further filter the data corresponding to the current device orientation during the fingerprinting online phase.

A large number of future lines keep opened. Several improvements for the fingerprint collecting application can be developed, such as detecting automatically when to stop to measure the signal level when its variance lowers to certain threshold. Regarding the fingerprinting process itself, it would be interesting to repeat these characterization with different terminals to see the differences among different devices, and test different algorithms with GSM signal data to determine the performance of the locating process, analyzing also how orientation information may improve positioning process by filtering the radio map according to the current device orientation.

Acknowledgments. The authors would like to thank Dmitry Dudá, Guillermo Fernández and David Roncero for the application development and their help in the measurement process. This work has been partially supported by the Spanish Ministry of Science and Innovation through the CONSEQUENCE (TEC2010-20572-C02-01) and MONOLOC (IPT-2011-1272-430000) projects.

References

1. Bejuri, W., Mohamad, M., Sapri, M.: Ubiquitous Positioning: A Taxonomy for Location Determination on Mobile Navigation System. Signal & Image Processing: An International Journal (SIPIJ) 2(1), 24–34 (2011)
2. Honkavirta, V., Perälä, T., Ali-Löytty, S., Piché, R.: A Comparative Survey of WLAN Location Fingerprinting Methods. In: 6th Workshop on Pos., Nav. and Comm. (WPNC 2009), pp. 243–251 (2009)
3. Sanchez, D., Quinteiro, J.M., Hernandez-Morera, P., Martel-Jordan, E.: Using data mining and fingerprinting extension with device orientation information for WLAN efficient indoor location estimation. In: 2012 IEEE 8th Int. Conf. on Wireless and Mob. Comp., Netw. and Comm (WiMob 2012), pp. 77–83 (2012)
4. Ibrahim, M., Youssef, M.: CellSense: A Probabilistic RSSI-Based GSM Positioning System. In: 2010 IEEE Global Telecomm. Conf (GLOBECOM 2010), pp. 1–5 (2010)
5. Meng, W., Xiao, W., Ni, W., Xie, L.: Secure and robust Wi-Fi fingerprinting indoor localization. In: 2011 Int. Conf. on Indoor Pos. and Indoor Nav. (IPIN 2011), pp. 1–7 (2011)
6. Steiner, C., Wittneben, A.: Low Complexity Location Fingerprinting With Generalized UWB Energy Detection Receivers. IEEE Trans. on Signal Proc. 58(3), 1756–1767 (2010)
7. Zhou, M., Krishnamurthy, P., Xu, Y., Ma, L.: Physical Distance vs. Signal Distance: An Analysis towards Better Location Fingerprinting. In: 2011 IEEE 13th Int. Conf. on High Perform. Comp. and Comm. (HPCC 2011), pp. 977–982 (2011)
8. Alsindi, N., Chaloupka, Z., Aweya, J.: Entropy-based location fingerprinting for WLAN systems. In: 2012 Int. Conf. on Indoor Pos. and Indoor Nav (IPIN 2012), pp. 1–7 (2012)
9. Fang, S., Wang, C.: A Dynamic Hybrid Projection Approach for Improved Wi-Fi Location Fingerprinting. IEEE Trans. on Vehicular Tech. 60(3), 1037–1044 (2011)
10. Khanbashi, N.A., Alsindi, N., Al-Araji, S., Ali, N., Aweya, J.: Performance evaluation of CIR based location fingerprinting. In: 2012 IEEE 23rd Int. Symp. on Personal Indoor and Mobile Radio Comm (PIMRC 2012), pp. 2466–2471 (2012)
11. Arya, A., Godlewski, P., Mellé, P.: A Hierarchical Clustering Technique for Radio Map Compression in Location Fingerprinting Systems. In: 2010 IEEE 71st Vehicular Tech. Conf. (VTC 2010), pp. 1–5 (Spring 2010)
12. Shih, C., Chen, L., Chen, G., Wu, E.H.-K., Jin, M.: Intelligent radio map management for future WLAN indoor location fingerprinting. In: 2012 IEEE Wireless Comm. and Netw. Conf. (WCNC 2012), pp. 2769–2773 (2012)
13. Jiang, X., Liu, Y., Wang, X.: An Enhanced Location Estimation Approach Based on Fingerprinting Technique. In: 2010 Int. Conf. on Comm. and Mob. Comp (CMC 2010), vol. 3, pp. 424–427 (2010)
14. Ni, W., Xiao, W., Toh, Y.K., Tham, C.K.: Fingerprint-MDS based algorithm for indoor wireless localization. In: 2010 IEEE 21st Int. Symp. on Personal Indoor and Mob. Radio Comm. (PIMRC 2010), pp. 1972–1977 (2010)
15. Kim, Y., Chon, Y., Cha, H.: Smartphone-Based Collaborative and Autonomous Radio Fingerprinting. IEEE Trans. on Systems, Man, and Cybernetics, Part C: Applications and Reviews 42(1), 112–122 (2012)
16. Koweerawong, C., Wipusitwarakun, K., Kaemarungsi, K.: Indoor localization improvement via adaptive RSS fingerprinting database. In: 2013 Int. Conf. on Information Netw. (ICOIN 2013), pp. 412–416 (2013)
17. Kjærgaard, M.B.: Indoor location fingerprinting with heterogeneous clients. Perv. Mob. Comp. 7(1), 31–43 (2011)

Easing Communication Means Selection Using Context Information and Semantic Technologies

Koldo Zabaleta, Pablo Curiel, and Ana B. Lago

Deusto Institute of Technology, DeustoTech
MORElab, Envisioning Future Internet
University of Deusto, Avda. Universidades 24, 48007, Bilbao, Spain
{koldo.zabaleta,pcuriel,anabelen.lago}@deusto.es

Abstract. Due to the advances in the ICTs in recent years, the variety of communication means at our disposal has noticeably increased. Some communication means offer simple tools to inform users about the status and availability of their contacts. However, not all of them offer this functionality, and indeed, elements like context, preferences and habits of the contact, which currently are not considered, should be taken into account before trying to stablish communication with a contact. In order to tackle this problem, we propose a platform that takes into account these features to assist users in deciding what communication means to use with each contact in each moment. Considering the real-time constraints of the system, a series of performance tests are also presented.

Keywords: semantics, mobile technology, communications, social networks.

1 Introduction

Due to the advances made in the ICTs in recent times, the variety of communication means at our disposal has noticeably increased. Latest smartphones, rather than providing users with just voice call and short message-based communication, enable them to keep in touch with their contacts using most of the communication means available nowadays. Taking into account the remarkable market share increase of these devices, a great number of mobile users have access to several communication means at their fingertips and thus, whenever they want to talk to their contacts, have to decide which to use among them.

This decision is not straightforward, as many variables must be taken into account. For this purpose, some communication means offer tools which inform users about their contacts' availability. For instance, many instant messaging systems have a user state which allows users to know if a contact is online, busy or absent, offline or its time of last connection. Similarly, some social networks give users the option to establish a custom state where they can give out what they are doing. However, other elements like context, preferences and habits of the contact determine the success or failure of a communication attempt. And currently no communication tools which consider these variables exist. Therefore, in many

G. Urzaiz et al. (Eds.): UCAmI 2013, LNCS 8276, pp. 231–238, 2013.

cases the person initiating the communication has to follow a trial-and-error approach, performing several attempts or trying with different communication means before successfully getting in touch with a contact.

In order to address this problem, in this paper we propose a platform that assists users in deciding what communication means to use with each contact in each moment. This platform enables users to define diverse use preferences about their communication means (which can be either general use preferences, like liking or disliking a particular communication means, or context-based preferences, like not using a specific communication means at certain place or time). Using these preferences, when users want to talk to one of their contacts, the system recommends them the most appropriate communication means to use for this purpose. This recommendation has real-time constraints, as users would hardly find it useful if they had to wait for too long before receiving the suggestion. Thus, to determine if response times comply with this mentioned requirement, a performance analysis of the system is also presented.

The remaining of the paper is structured as follows. The next section discusses related work. Section 3 gives a generic description of the platform. Section 4 describes tests carried out in order to assess the performance of the communication means recommendation mechanism. Finally, in Section 5, conclusions and future work are exposed.

2   Related Work

The Semantic Web is an idea promoted by Tim Berners-Lee [3]. The objective pursued with this idea is to add semantic content to the web. With this addition it is possible to share, reuse and process with different applications the data available on the web.

Ontologies, which are used to model the different domains of a software solution, are one of the main tools of the Semantic Web. To create an ontology a knowledge representation language is needed. Nowadays Web Ontology Language (OWL) [16] is the standardized and recommended language by the W3C.

Thanks to the work carried out in this field in recent years, there are several reference ontologies which can be used to represent a specific domain. An example of this type of ontology is FOAF [6], which is used for modelling information about people and relationships among them. Many projects that need to model users make use of this ontology [1] [7] [13]. SIOC [5] is other relevant ontology, designed for representing concepts related to social networks, and which is used in several projects that model this domain [1] [7] [10].

These ontologies can be perfectly used for modelling the areas for which they were designed. The problem arises when there is a need to model an environment that spans more concepts than a single ontology supports, as it is the case of the working domain of this article. Thus, the reviewed ontologies model certain subdomains, such as users and social networks, but we could not find any ontology for representing all the communication means considered and the preferences to define over them, not at least with the minimum details that are required.

For this reason we designed an ad-hoc ontology which adds and extends terms from existing ontologies and vocabularies such as FOAF, WGS84 [15] and OWL-Time [14].

On the other hand, one of the key features that ontologies provide is reasoning over the knowledge represented using them, enabling applications to perform personalized recommendation of products and services. For instance, Rung-Ching Chen et al. [4] present an application that models characteristics of diabetic patients, and which through reasoning about this information is capable of recommending the user which drug to take. A similar approach is followed in our work, which, after modelling the communication means of the users and their preferences over them, reasons about this information to suggest users which communication means to use at each moment.

On to other matters, Knittel et al. [9], carried out different studies in which they determine the most appropriate type of context information to use in order to identify users' status. And Tang et al. [12] developed a prototype which enables users to share context information with their contacts. Although these proposals deal with context information as a means to ease interpersonal communication, neither of them provide the caller with a recommendation about which communication means to use in order to stablish a communication with a callee.

3   The System Architecture

With this work we try to solve the problem of deciding which communications channel to select when a mobile user wants to communicate with a contact. In this section we describe the platform we propose for recommending users the best communication means to use in each situation. This platform is composed of a mobile application and of a central server. These two components are described in detail below.

3.1   The Server

The server is in charge of storing all the information related to the users of the platform, their communication means and the preferences defined over them. The server has two main components, which are the ontological model used to represent the mentioned information, and a rule engine, which processes this information to generate the recommendation about which communication means to use in each situation.

The Ontology. To model the elements that are part of the solution developed we designed an OWL ontology. This ontology models three main concepts.

First, we have the user modelling. Currently there are several ontologies created for modelling user profiles, among which FOAF is the one that has received more support. For this reason FOAF has been used as the basis for user modelling in the proposed platform.

The second main modelled concept are the communication means, represented as a class hierarchy to favour extension and reuse. This part of the ontology is entirely of our own design and does not use any external element. We have modelled the majority of the communication means available on a smartphone as a class hierarchy.

The third concept modelled in the ontology are the communication preferences defined by the users. These can be of general purpose (e.g., "I like telephone calls") or linked to the user's context (e.g., "At work I do not use instant messaging" or "Weekends I do not check my work email account") and allow users to express which communication means are the best to get in touch with them in each particular moment, and which are less likely to be appropriate or successful.

The Rule Engine. Rules are a useful and simple tool to generate additional information from a model. In our case, a rule engine is used to rate communication means based on user context and their preferences. And based on this rating, a sorted list of communication means is obtained, from the most appropriate to get in touch with a contact to the least appropriate one.

Rules are divided into four different groups. The first group identifies whether a user has network connection in the moment of its execution. The second rule group rates communication means according to the user having or not network connection. The third rule group rates communication means which provide users' status (e.g., instant messaging services) according to that kind of information. And the last group rates communication means based on the preferences associated with them.

3.2   Mobile Application

The mobile application is the client of the platform and acts as interface for the users to access its functionalities. Due to its ubiquitous nature, the access it provides to most of the communication means available nowadays and its ability to provide rich context information, it is the perfect device for this task.

Thus, this application enables users access and configure its profile in the platform, registering the communication means they have access to and the use preferences they want to define over them. It also provides a personalized contact agenda, which requests the server the best communication means to use to talk to each contact when the user wants to do so. Finally, in order to enable this recommendation, the mobile application is responsible for periodically reporting to the central server user-specific context information (location, status of the connection, user status in those communication means that provide that kind of information, etc.).

4   Evaluation

In this section we describe the different types of tests we have carried out in order to evaluate the server performance regarding the communication means recommendation. This functionality is the most computationally demanding among the ones exposed by the server, as involves executing a rule engine and semantic inference tasks. At the same time, this functionality has real-time constraints, as it is requested by the mobile application when the user wants to talk to a contact and users would hardly find it useful if they had to wait for too long before receiving the suggestion. In order to evaluate this response time from the end-users' perspective, we have defined the user experience levels shown in Table 1, which are based in the study by Shaikh et al. [11].

Table 1. User experience depending on server response time

Time (t)	User Experience
$t < 1$ s	Very satisfactory
1 s $< t < 3$ s	Satisfactory
3 s $< t < 5$ s	Acceptable
5 s $< t < 8$ s	Poor
$t > 8$ s	Not Acceptable

Therefore, a series of tests were carried out to assess the performance of this recommender service under diverse situations and with different configuration parameters. In the first test case we made requests to the server from the mobile application via Wi-Fi, 3G and 2G networks. In the second test scenario concurrent calls with a different number of clients were made to the server. The third test scenario consisted in making calls to the server with a different number of users registered in the system. And the fourth and last test case consisted in requesting the communication means recommendation for users who have defined a different number of preferences. Except for the third test scenario, we registered two users in the system. And excluding the last test scenario, each user had four preferences defined.

For these tests, the server was executing on a virtual machine. The host server was an Intel Xeon Quad-Core at 2.83 GHz and with 12 GiB of memory, running an Ubuntu Server 10.04.4 LTS 64 bits edition and with a VirtualBox 3.0.14 installation. The virtual machine had the 4 cores and 2 GiB of memory assigned and was running an Ubuntu Server 12.04 LTS 64 bits edition. The web service was deployed in a Tomcat 6.0 using JDK 1.6. Regarding the client side, two different configurations where used. For the network types test scenario a Samsung Galaxy Nexus with Android 4.2 was used with an ad-hoc version of the mobile application which registered and saved the request times to a CSV file. For the other three test cases Apache Bench [2] was used from a laptop computer through Ethernet connection. This enabled simulating scenarios of up to 64 concurrent clients without network being a bottleneck, and also having a more stable network connection which minimises the added noise to the conclusions of these three tests. JConsole [8] utility provided by the JDK was also used to monitor CPU and memory demand of the server side in the concurrence tests.

In the first test scenario, requests with different network types (Wi-Fi, 3G, 2G and 2G under low coverage) were tested. These tests involved making rounds of 100 requests repeated under diverse situations (different locations and times). In Fig. 1 minimum, maximum and median request times of each network type are shown. As we can observe, response times when requests are made via Wi-Fi and 3G connections are very satisfactory. In good coverage 2G networks response times still remain noticeably restrained. In contrast, when coverage is low in 2G networks ("Bad 2G" in the graph), response times moderately increase. Even so, this times remain in the satisfactory and acceptable user experience ranges.

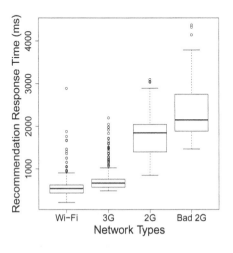
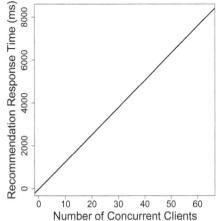

Fig. 1. Request times with different network types

Fig. 2. Request times with concurrent clients

In the second test case, requests to the server with an increasing number of concurrent clients were made, up to 64 concurrent clients. Results obtained (see Fig. 2) show that even when around 35 concurrent clients are querying for recommendations, response time is acceptable. And attending about up to 60 concurrent clients could still be tolerable with a hardware equivalent to the one used in the tests if it is a punctual situation. Regarding CPU usage in this test cases, the lower concurrency scenarios show a linear increase, from around 10% in the single client test up to 30% in the 4 clients one. For higher concurrency cases, CPU demand increased at a slower pace, being the medium demand around 50% in the 64 concurrent clients test. Finally, memory consumption is quite constrained throughout all the test case even in the scenarios with a higher number of concurrent clients. In fact, memory usage remained similar through all the concurrence tests, with a maximum demand of around 250 MiB.

The third test case consisted in studying recommendation task response times with an increasing number of users registered in the platform. This aspect should have low impact in this response time, as the server only executes the rule engine against the data of the requested user. Therefore, response time increases as a function of the number of registered users only due to the query to the triplestore to retrieve this information being slightly slower. Server answering times with different numbers of registered users can be checked in Fig. 3.

In the last test scenario we measured the impact that the user having a different number of preferences defined has in the server response time. Preferences are the main element that rules use for grading communication means, so inference task will take longer for users who have a higher number of them defined. In Fig. 4 response times for users with different number of preferences are shown. As it would be expected, response times increase together with an increase in the number of preferences, though even for 50 preferences registered, which is an extreme case, this task takes around 2 seconds.

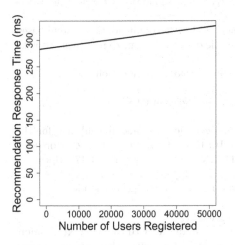

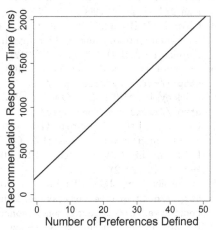

Fig. 3. Request times related to registered users number

Fig. 4. Request times related to defined preferences number

5   Conclusion

In this article we have presented a platform that assists mobile users in the task of deciding which communication means to use to communicate with their contacts. This platform enables users to register their communication means and define different use preferences over them. Combining this preferences with users' context, the system is capable of inferring which communication means they would prefer to be contacted with in each situation.

Due to the real-time constraints of this system, we have also presented a series of tests aimed at assessing system performance executing this recommendation task. These tests have shown that the platform offers satisfactory response times even under poor mobile connections, with several communication preferences defined by each user and with both a considerable number of users registered in the system and concurrently working against it.

Having tested the technical viability of the proposal, as future work we plan to perform a large scale experiment with real users so as to evaluate the efficacy of the server, that is, if the communication means recommended by the platform in each situation are the most appropriate ones to get in touch with other users.

References

1. Abel, F., Henze, N., Herder, E., Houben, G.J., Krause, D., Leonardi, E.: Building blocks for user modeling with data from the social web. In: Proceedings of the International Workshop on Architectures and Building Blocks of Web-Based User-Adaptive Systems (WABBWUAS 2010), vol. 609, CEUR-WS. org (2010)
2. Apache Bench: ab - Apache HTTP server benchmarking tool, `http://httpd.apache.org/docs/2.2/programs/ab.html`
3. Berners-Lee, T., Hendler, J., Lassila, O., et al.: The semantic web. Scientific American 284(5), 28–37 (2001)
4. Chen, R.C., Huang, Y.H., Bau, C.T., Chen, S.M.: A recommendation system based on domain ontology and swrl for anti-diabetic drugs selection. Expert Systems with Applications 39(4), 3995–4006 (2012)
5. Berrueta, D., Brickley, D., et al.: SIOC core ontology specification, `http://rdfs.org/sioc/spec/`
6. Brickley, D., Miller, L.: FOAF vocabulary specification 0.98, `http://xmlns.com/foaf/spec/`
7. Gao, Q., Abel, F., Houben, G.J.: Genius: generic user modeling library for the social semantic web. In: Pan, J.Z., Chen, H., Kim, H.-G., Li, J., Wu, Z., Horrocks, I., Mizoguchi, R., Wu, Z. (eds.) JIST 2011. LNCS, vol. 7185, pp. 160–175. Springer, Heidelberg (2012)
8. JConsole: Using JConsole: Java SE monitoring and management guide, `http://docs.oracle.com/javase/6/docs/technotes/guides/management/jconsole.html`
9. Knittel, J., Sahami Shirazi, A., Henze, N., Schmidt, A.: Utilizing contextual information for mobile communication. In: CHI 2013 Extended Abstracts on Human Factors in Computing Systems, pp. 1371–1376. ACM (2013)
10. Orlandi, F., Passant, A.: Enabling cross-wikis integration by extending the sioc ontology. LSSM+ (Cit. on p.) (2009)
11. Shaikh, J., Fiedler, M., Collange, D.: Quality of experience from user and network perspectives. Annals of Telecommunications-Annales Des télé Communications 65(1-2), 47–57 (2010)
12. Tang, J.C., Yankelovich, N., Begole, J., Van Kleek, M., Li, F., Bhalodia, J.: Connexus to awarenex: extending awareness to mobile users. In: Proceedings of the SIGCHI Conference on Human Factors in Computing Systems, pp. 221–228. ACM (2001)
13. Tao, K., Abel, F., Gao, Q., Houben, G.J.: Tums: twitter-based user modeling service. In: García-Castro, R., Fensel, D., Antoniou, G. (eds.) ESWC 2011. LNCS, vol. 7117, pp. 269–283. Springer, Heidelberg (2012)
14. W3C: OWL-Time: time ontology in owl, `http://www.w3.org/TR/owl-time/`
15. W3C: WGS84 Geo Positioning: an RDF vocabulary, `http://www.w3.org/2003/01/geo/wgs84_pos#`
16. W3C OWL Working Group: OWL 2 Web Ontology Language document overview, 2nd edn., `http://www.w3.org/TR/owl2-overview/`

Emergency Event Detection in Twitter Streams Based on Natural Language Processing

Bernhard Klein[1], Federico Castanedo[1], Iñigo Elejalde[1], Diego López-de-Ipiña[1],
and Alejandro Prada Nespral[2]

[1] Deusto Institute of Technology (DeustoTech), University of Deusto
Avda. Universidades 24, 48007 Bilbao, Spain
{bernhard.klein,fcastanedo,ielejalde,dipina}@deusto.es
[2] Treelogic, Parque Tecnológico de Asturias, Parcela 30
E33428 Llanera - Asturias, Spain
alejandro.prada@treelogic.com

Abstract. Real-time social media usage is widely adapted today because it encourages quick spreading of news within social networks. New opportunities arise to use social media feeds to detect emergencies and extract crucial information about that event to support rescue operations. A major challenge for the extraction of emergency event information from applications like Twitter is the big mass of data, inaccurate or lacking metadata and the noisy nature of the post text itself. We propose to filter the real-time media stream by analysing posts seriousity, extract facts through natural language processing and group posts using a novel event identification scheme. Based on a manually tagged social media feed corpus we show that false or missed alarms are limited to posts with highly ambiguous information with less value for the rescue units.

Keywords: Emergency detection, social media mining, natural language processing, incremental clustering.

1 Introduction

Online social media applications have become an invaluable tool to gather users feelings and comments and spread them in real time to the rest of the world. Popular social media applications generate a big amount of data during important events. For instance, during last U.S elections Twitter was serving a peak of 15000 tweets per second and currently is sending a billion tweets every two and a half days on average[1]. Several companies are using these social data to perform data analysis and drive marketing decisions. The use of social media applications became very popular in the last disaster events such as hurricane Sandy, the earthquake in Haiti or the tsunami in Fukushima. Observations show that social media is meanwhile also used as an alternative communication tool

---

[1] see Twitter Blog, http://alturl.com/v4mpe

G. Urzaiz et al. (Eds.): UCAmI 2013, LNCS 8276, pp. 239–246, 2013.

for disasters victims [1]. In fact, people tend to communicate emergency information faster and more effective within their social network rather than using other communication media like phone or email [2]. However, real-time social media communication tools, such as Twitter, are used to communicate and share different type information which is usually not related to emergency detection and management. Thus the signal to noise ratio in these domains is very low and detecting emergency events is like finding a needle in a haystack. In addition, these type of media sources are highly dynamic and make the early detection of an event really complex since there is no historical data about new events.

One of the main goals of the Social Awareness Based Emergency Situation Solver (SABESS) project is the development of an emergency event detection tool for twitter streams to aid the emergency operation and rescue teams in the decision support process. In order to achieve this goal it is necessary to detect an event from a continuous media stream and to provide a good summarization. In this work, we present an approach to the problem of real-time event detection in Twitter streams.

The rest of the article is as follows. The next section present the related works. Then, in Section 3 the problem statement is presented together with our proposed clustering approach. Section 4 describes the research model and the experiment corpus. Experimental results are provided in Section 5. Finally, Section 6 concludes the article.

2   Related Work

Several researchers have worked on similar analysis tools to improve information for rescue teams by exploiting data from social networks: SensePlace [3], the TEDAS system [4] and the Crime Detection Web3 use an iterative crawler which monitors the global Twitter stream to identify emergencies within a given region. Queries are issued as a set of keywords specifying specific time points (July 2010), locations (Houston) and emergency types (car accidents). Their user interface allows rescue organizations to parametrize emergency filters, visualize emergency information on the map and summarize the content of emergency messages through tag clouds. The Twitcident project [5] goes one step further and enriches structured emergency information with data obtained from Twitter streams. They use natural language processing (NLP) techniques, more specifically part-of-speech (POS) tagging and named entity recognition (NER), to tag tweets and enrich tweet contents for incident detection and profiling. Gnip and DataSift are further examples which interface with different social media, provide complex query syntax for more general events and integrate event based information through NLP techniques. Above that, it is important to aggregate tweets which describe the same emergency event. Marcus et al. [6] and Becker et al. [7] describe ways how to cluster tweets based on the inferred topic similarity measured through the keyword distance obtained from an emergency taxonomy. Alarms are automatically issued if the amount of tweets belonging to an event exceeds a certain threshold value. Pohl et al. [8] extend this clustering concept with the capability of sub-event detection. In case tweet clusters are not strongly coherent, less frequently used keywords in the tweet cluster are used to identify sub clusters which point for instance to different hot spots in the emergency region.

All these clustering approaches use knowledge about a new evolving emergencies e.g. from the 911 hotline to improve the focus of the crawler by specifying more adequate query keywords. This first set of data can then be enhanced through finding similar tweets or better organized by identifying important sub topics. They work, however, is less reliable in identifying new emergencies just from the Twitter stream without a prior knowledge. Within the SABESS project the objective is to identify emergencies completely in a autonomous process.

3   Stream Filter and Event Clustering Approach

For the SABESS project we consider different type of natural and human disasters. These include weather related disasters like hurricanes, flooding and fires but also geological disasters like an earthquake or even health related events like epidemics. Disasters can have varying complexity with respect to scale, spatial distribution and dynamics. Small scale disasters like a fire center around a single hotspot with a coverage range not more than few hundred meters. Large scale events like a hurricane have usually multiple hotspots which can span entire regions and may includes several hundred victims. Of course, large scale events are usually easier to detect as more people would report about them.

From all these messages generated by all the users in the Twitter system we are able to retrieve some messages by using an external API. For this we use a bag of words approach and query the Twitter stream with manually selected keywords frequently appearing in emergency posts like *112, 911, Accident, Affected, Aid, Alarm, Alert, Ambulance, Bodies, Casualties, Collapse, Collateral, Corpses, etc.*. In addition, we limit the potential geographic scope of detected emergencies by specifying observation ranges through the Twitter API. Although the retrieved messages represents approximately a 10% of the complete communication in the system the number of collected tweets may still very large. Given the size of the data, it is important to separate emergency from non-emergency messages in a very fast and effective pre-filtering process. Since a survey [9] shows that the degree of information extracted from tweets strongly correlates with the slang or sentiment degree of a given post, we automatically remove tweets with several letter/punctuation repetitions or other obvious misspellings. Examples for removed tweets are *"Set my life ...ON FIRE!!!!"*, *"burn baby burn, light a fire"*, *"make it pondeeeemmmm whitee boii ya betta runnnnnnnn* and *"Dont be a fire stone bitxhhhhh!!!!"*.

The goal is to group posts that share some data about emergency event. Before this can be done, emergency relevant knowledge has to be extracted from the post. Such event data can be extracted indirectly from the metadata of the tweet or directly from the tweet text. Several studies show that the majority of users do not maintain personal profile data nor do they agree on sharing e.g.

spatio-temporal data attached to the tweet. Even if such a metadata is available it is not necessarily secure to use it for the clustering process, as the authoring location may differ significantly from the event location if the user just forwards an emergency message. For this reason we use natural language processing tools to extract emergency facts direct from the post text written by the user. More specifically we apply the Stanford NER library which can extract tags referring to person, organisation, and location knowledge. NLP tools, however, were originally designed for larger texts and may fail not only due to the short size of tweets but also because of their noisy writing style. For this reason we process post texts with adequate slang/text cleaners, and stop word removers prior to the NLP processing. The event grouping process differentiates between two sub processes. First an emergency is classified according to an emergency taxonomy and second a specific emergency event is identified from further clues in the post text. In an abstract view, words in a tweet message can be roughly distinguished in words specifying a given emergency e.g. hurricane sandy, words correlated with emergencies e.g. injured people and relative meaningless stop words providing the kit between the previous word groups.

More formally we define the emergency classification as follows:

Definition (Emergency Classification). Given an emergency taxonomy t we define a message m belonging to the emergency domain if more than n words exist where $\forall x = \{1 \ldots n\} w_x \in t \land w_x \in m$.

In order to increase the matchmaking probability we apply a tolerant matchmaking approach by comparing the word stem through the startWith() function. In this case abbreviations, plural forms or other word concatenations can still be classified correctly. For the identification of specific emergencies like a fire in Bilbao more complex concatenated expressions have to be considered. Since small-scale emergency events center around a single hotspot (see above paragraph), any location tag found in the tweet text during the preprocessing phase can be used. Because people may refer to locations with varying precision it is important to compare locations along administrative hierarchies e.g. on city or district level. Geocoding services like Google or Geonames provide functions that allow a complete hierarchical specification of a given location. This approach, however, cannot be applied for large scale events where multiple hotspots are usually involved. Here we make use of the fact that humans tend to name bigger emergency events. Disaster names usually follow the emergency category term e.g. hurricane *Sandy*, and can thus be easily extracted from the tweet text. More formally we define an emergency identifier as follows:

Definition (Emergency Identification): An emergency identifier is a concatenated string that is build after following syntax: $\langle emergency\ identification \rangle :=$ $\{\langle emergency\ keyword \rangle + \langle disaster\ name \rangle \lor \langle emergency\ keyword \rangle + \langle location\ hierarchy \rangle\}$ whereas $\langle location\ hierarchy \rangle := \{\langle country \rangle + \langle region \rangle + \langle city \rangle + \langle district \rangle\}$.

4   Research Model and Test Corpus

Clustering algorithms can be evaluated with internal (measuring the similarity) or external assessment approaches (comparing predictions with an 'external' golden standard). As the success of the SABESS project depends finally on the applicability for real-world rescue operations the second approach is the more appropriate.

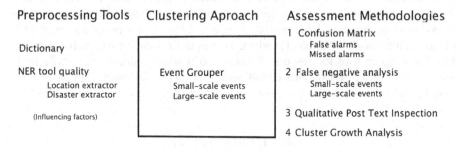

Fig. 1. Research Model

For all experiments we collected a corpus through a Twitter crawler using different emergency keywords. These include events like fires in Tasmania, a cyclone in the Fiji islands, hurricane Sandy and the tsunami in Japan. From this corpus we extracted randomly 1000 tweets for manual tagging. We have developed a tagging tool that enables us to classify posts in emergency and non-emergency messages, and assign each message to an concrete pre-specified emergency event. We further enlarged the tagged corpus up to 10000 tweets with a corpus generator that added new tweets by copying them and randomly replacing a given percentage of the words in the corpus with words from a dictionary. In order to keep the same the emergency classification, words identifying the tweets have been excluded from this process. The analysis of the ground truth (actual emergencies) reveals an almost similar amount of emergency (55%) and non-emergency tweets (45%) in the test corpus.

In the following we describe our research model illustrated in Fig. 1. In a first step we evaluate the overall performance of the event grouper. More specifically, we have been interested in determining the failed detection rate (percentage of incorrect detected emergencies). By representing these results through a confusion matrix, we are able to derive the proportion of missed and false alarms. As rescue operations require a lot of resources and planning both cases need to be considered. As the clustering process generally differentiates between small-scale and large-scale events (see Section 3) it is important to evaluate them separately in more detail. Therefore, the corpus has been separated based on the pre-defined ground truth facts so that one corpus contains only small-scale events and the other large-scale events. For each corpus we perform a false alarm analysis to see the efficiency difference between both approaches. We finalize the evaluation with an inspection of the incorrect classified posts to gain qualitative impression of the failed cases and ideas on how to improve the event grouper in future.

5   Results and Interpretation

In the following we present the results of the experiments and the corpus we presented above. First we take a look on the confusion matrix. Here we are interested in the missed and false alarms, both are problematic for rescue teams as rescue measures need a non significant amount of time and resources. The majority of events have been correctly classified (see 87% emergencies and 76% of non-emergencies in Table 1), which represents a mandatory prerequisite to build a support tool for rescues. However, still some failures exist. 23% false alarms were generated (tweets classified as emergency although they were not) and 12% of al emergencies have not been detected.

Table 1. Confusion Matrix

Predicted / Actual	Positive	Negative
Positive	0.8726236	0.2347826
Negative	0.1273764	0.7652174

Fig. 2 a) shows the true and false positive rate analysis for small and large-scale event clustering techniques. The dotted line represents small scale events (e.g. fire events) whereas the solid line large scale events (e.g. hurricanes). Small scale events show a much higher true positive rate than large scale events. Since large-scale emergencies are identified through a corresponding disaster name, name misspellings (see noisy character of tweets) or incorrect word ordering may lead in some cases to an incorrect event identification. In contrary, the small scale event detection process is less error prone, as missing location references in the text or incorrect identified location tags immediately lead to exclusion of the clustering process by marking them as noise.

Looking at the non detected emergency cases reveals that they have been due to word connections, misinterpreted word order or the mentioning of multiple locations or most often due to unclear message content. An example for unidentified emergency tweets are *"CycloneEvan appeal launched to aid displaced people in Fiji amp Samoa"* or *"Nails hammers tarpaulins blankets arrived from Australia Aid from govt for Western Fiji heading to Lautoka CycloneEvan"*.

In order to still assure adequate rescue team support false clusters should not be displayed to the end-user. In the following we want to show how this can be achieved with reasonable effort. Since incorrect identified large-scale clusters are based on individual spelling errors or less frequent occurring word order problems, we can assume that these clusters will (in comparison to correctly identified emergency event clusters) evolve much slower and usually remain small.

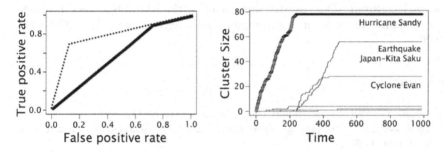

Fig. 2. a) Comparison of small (dotted line) and large-scale (black line) event detection quality and b) evolution of emergency cluster sizes

Figure 2 b) shows exemplary the cluster size increase for the test corpus. The thick line represent the hurricane sandy event (large scale event), and the following curves fires in Australia and Tasmania (small scale events). The curves on the button represent false identified emergency events like *hurricane superstorm, hurricane photos, hurrican san.* or events which have just emerged e.g. *accident west birkshire*. A threshold value for the cluster size of 10 tweets was good enough in our experiment to remove all meaningless emergency events or incorrect identified emergency events. It is however important to not remove these small clusters from the memory unless the last tweet has not been detected for a very long time ago. This age assumption for a cluster makes sense as tweets usually occur close to the event because the tweet time line for the users is limited.

6   Conclusion

We have presented a novel real-time clustering technique for performing event grouping on public tweet messages. Our approach is based on extracting event information from post texts and therefore outperforms approaches utilizing post metadata. Emergencies are classified based on emergency taxonomies and identified through a widely applied disaster name scheme or alternatively through location information extracted based on natural language processing tools. Posts are finally assigned to specific emergency clusters by a matchmaking approach.

The approach has been evaluated with a tagged emergency corpus containing several disaster events collected during the evaluation period. The results show that the event clustering works quite well and only few emergencies are missed or false alarms created. The application of preprocessing tools such as slang cleaning, word separators and stop word removal generates a positive influence on the results of the event clustering- Whereas small-scale events can be reliably detected by extracting location information through NER tools, large-scale events require an additional post processing step because disaster names can not be safely detected due to spelling errors or word order problems. As these type of problems occur much less frequently than correctly detected events we can do a thresholding step to show only relevant emergency clusters in the user interface.

Acknowledgment. This research was funded by the SABESS project, Innpacto Project Funding of the Spanish government, grant agreement no. IPT-2011-1052-390000.

References

1. Licamele, G.: Web metrics report from Fairfax county (2011), http://www.fairfaxcounty.gov/emergency/flooding-090811-metrics.pdf (last visited June 1, 2012)
2. Acar, A., Muraki, Y.: Twitter and natural disasters: Crisis communication lessons from the Japan tsunami. International Journal of Web Based Communities 7(3), 392–402 (2011)
3. MacEachren, A.M., Jaiswal, A.R., Robinson, A.C., Pezanowski, S., Savelyev, A., Mitra, P., Zhang, X., Blanford, J.: SensePlace2: GeoTwitter Analytics for Situational Awareness. In: IEEE Conference on Visual Analytics Science and Technology (VAST 2011), Rhode Island, USA (2011)
4. Li, R., Lei, K., Khadiwala, R., Chang, K.: TEDAS: a Twitter Based Event Detection and Analysis System. In: Proc. of the 28th IEEE International Conference on Data Engineering (ICDE), Washington, USA (2012)
5. Abel, F., Hauff, C., Houben, G.-J., Stronkman, R., Tao, K.: Semantics + Filtering + Search = Twitcident Exploring Information in Social Web Streams. In: 21st International ACM Conference on Hypertext and Hypermedia (HT 2010), Toronto, Canada (2010)
6. Marcus, A., Bernstein, M., Badar, O., Karger, D., Madden, S., Miller, R.: Twitinfo: aggregating and visualizing microblogs for event exploration. In: Proc. of ACM CHI Conference on Human Factors in Computing Systems, pp. 227–236 (2011)
7. Becker, H., Naaman, M., Gravano, L.: Beyond Trending Topics: Real-World Event Identification on Twitter. In: Proc. of the 5th International AAAI Conference on Weblogs and Social Media (ICWSM) (2011)
8. Pohl, D., Bouchachia, A., Hellwagnerr, H.: Automatic Sub-Event Detection in Emergency Management Using Social Media. In: Proc. of the 1st International Workshop on Social Web for Disaster Management (SWDM 2012), pp. 683–686 (2012)
9. Verma, S., Vieweg, S., Corvey, W.J., Palen, L., Martin, J.H., Palmer, M., Schram, A., Anderson, K.M.: Natural Language Processing to the Rescue?: Extracting "Situational Awareness" Tweets During Mass Emergency. In: Proc. of Fifth International AAAI Conference on Weblogs and Social Media (2011)

AdapteR Interoperability ENgine (ARIEN): An approach of Interoperable CDSS for Ubiquitous Healthcare

Wajahat Ali Khan, Maqbool Hussain, Bilal Amin, Asad Masood Khattak,
Muhammad Afzal, and Sungyoung Lee

Department of Computer Engineering
Kyung Hee University
Seocheon-dong, Giheung-gu, Yongin-si, Gyeonggi-do, Republic of Korea, 446-701
{wajahat.alikhan,maqbool.hussain,mbilalamin,
asad.masood,muhammad.afzal,sylee}@oslab.khu.ac.kr

Abstract. Information exchange for interoperability between medical systems and clinical decision support systems (CDSS) is a challenging task to provide personalized healthcare services. Healthcare standards behaves as catalyst for interoperability and plays important role in ubiquitous healthcare. Heterogeneity among these standards creates bottleneck for decision support systems to easily integrate with legacy medical systems. Medical systems and CDSS standards compatibility requires mediation process to ensure seamless information exchange. We propose such mediation system between medical systems and CDSS called AdapteR Interoperability ENgine (ARIEN) to achieve data level interoperability. We consider information flow from smart homes and medical systems in HL7 Clinical Document Architecture (CDA) format with CDSS compliant to Virtual Medical Record (vMR) standard. The responsibility of the proposed system is transformation of smart homes and medical systems compliant standard format information into CDSS compliant standard format for processing of information and vice versa. This work achieves information exchange compatibility among systems for providing better healthcare to patients. It also ensures availability of required information at the specified time for ubiquitous healthcare.

Keywords: CDSS, HL7, HMIS, Interoperability, Ontology.

1 Introduction

Evolution of healthcare standards has contributed in achieving the goal of interoperability among medical systems. Clinical Decision Support System (CDSS) design and development is one of the progressing area to use healthcare standards for ubiquitous healthcare. Standard based CDSS systems exists in the literature that provide benefits like scalability, easy for data sharing and flexibility. One such initiative is taken in our lab [1] that is called as Smart CDSS.

---

[1] http://uclab.khu.ac.kr/

G. Urzaiz et al. (Eds.): UCAmI 2013, LNCS 8276, pp. 247–253, 2013.

Smart CDSS is standard based clinical decision system that provides recommendations to physicians and patients based on the heterogeneous data sources including clinical data, social media data, behavior modeling data and activities and emotion recognition data [5] [4]. Among its different features, interoperability of medical systems and smart homes compliant to different standards with Smart CDSS is a key challenge. This kind of interoperability is considered as data level interoperability, which is the ability to communicate data among systems with the original semantics of the data retained irrespective of its point of access [10]. This challenge can be resolved by resolving heterogeneities between different heterogeneous healthcare standards.

Smart CDSS consumers include systems that are compliant to different healthcare standards (HL7 V3, CDA, openEHR or CEN 13606). Smart CDSS can only process information in Virtual Medical Record (vMR) standard. Therefore, an adapter is required to transform HMIS compliant healthcare standard to Smart CDSS compliant healthcare standard and vice versa. We propose an adapter called Adapter Interoperability Engine (ARIEN) that facilitates Smart CDSS in achieving interoperability with different medical systems and smart homes. Ontology matching technique is used to achieve interoperability between these legacy systems and Smart CDSS.

We are considering HL7 CDA standard for medical systems and smart homes compliancy and developed HL7 CDA and vMR ontologies based on their specifications. Ontology matching techniques are applied to find out appropriate mappings between the two standards. Also, changes can evolve into standards, therefore the proposed system also monitors any changes in the standard to be reflected in the mapping file repository called *Mediation Bridge Ontology (MBO)*. This adds to the accuracy of mappings in the form of continuity of mappings. This leads to removing heterogeneities among standards and allow interoperable communication between systems.

2   Smart CDSS as a Service

Smart CDSS is an initiative taken by our lab, to provide recommendations to physicians and patients based on heterogeneous data sources. The different modules of Smart CDSS as shown in Figure 1 consists of:

- Adaptability Engine, used for obtaining data from different sources and transforming it into standard vMR format.
- Interface Engine, used as a communication medium between Adaptability Engine and Knowledge Inference Engine.
- Knowledge Inference Engine, used to perform reasoning on the input information to provide recommendations.

The different data sources provides information to Smart CDSS through Adaptability Engine. These data sources consists of clinical data, social media data, activities recognition data, and behavior modeling data of the patient.

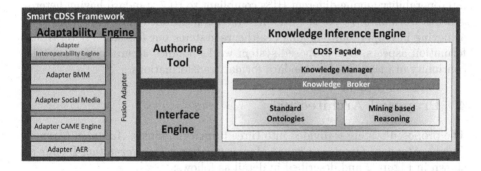

Fig. 1. Architecture of Smart CDSS

Adapter Behavior Modeling Module (BMM) is used for monitoring and obtaining the behavior modeling information of the patient. The Social Media Adapter is used for observing patient social media interaction activities such as twitter. Adapter CAME Engine is used for providing information of patients activities by converting low level sensory information to high level context aware information. Activity and Emotion Recognition (AER) Adapter is used to recognize patient activities and emotions in daily life. Clinical data is handled by ARIEN, that is used for converting one standard format to another, in this case conversion between vMR and CDA. Finally the Fusion Adapter is used to concatenate all the vMR's from different data sources into a single vMR. The proposed system ARIEN is the focus of this paper that provides interoperability services for systems compliant to different standards for using standard based Smart CDSS.

3   Related Work

Existing systems in literature highlights the importance of interoperability for CDSS systems. The role of ontologies becomes more important in the path towards interoperable CDSS. This is highlighted in [1], by describing the role of biomedical ontologies based on healthcare standards to manage knowledge management, data integration and interoperability aspects and their fusion for decision support systems. Another project is SAPHIRE, a multi agent system supported by intelligent decision support system to improve patient lifecare by monitoring their activities. It depends on semantically enriched web services for communicating information to tackle interoperability [3]. Other than decision support systems, there are other systems that work on interoperability aspects among different standards. Prominent work in literature with interoperability as objective among different healthcare standards include: Artemis (semantic mediation between different Health Information Systems (HIS)) [2], PPEPR (resolving heterogeneity between HL7 v2 and v3) [11], LinkEHR (tool used for transformations among standards such as HL7, openEHR and CEN 13606) [8], and Poseacle Converter (CEN 13606 and openEHR standards archetypes and extracts transformation and validation) [9]. Finally, we also have worked on process interoperability among different HISs compliant to HL7 standard having heterogeneous workflows [7]. All the existing systems mentioned above contributed in achieving interoperability among healthcare systems but focuses only on transformation aspects. Our proposed system works handles accuracy of mappings, continuity of mappings for standard format transformations.

4   Proposed Architecture

The proposed system is divided into three primary modules: *Accuracy Mapping Engine*, *Standard Ontology Change Management* and *Transformation Engine* as shown in Figure 2 and described in detail as follows:

4.1   Accuracy Mapping Engine

This component deals with the generation of ontology mappings. CDA and vMR ontologies developed are mapped using ontology matching techniques such as string based, child based, property based and label based matching techniques. These matching techniques are used by our matching system called *System for Parallel Heterogeneity Resolution SPHeRe*[2]. *SPHeRe* takes as input the source and target ontologies for matching and the mappings generated are stored in *MBO*. *MBO* behaves as a mapping file repository for storage of mappings. Another approach that we use for increasing the accuracy of mappings is *Personalized-Detailed Clinical Model (P-DCM)* [6] approach. P-DCM approach uses organizational conformance information to improve accuracy level of the mappings stored in the *MBO.P-DCM* and *Expert Verifications* improves the overall accuracy of the mapping file. Standards can evolve with the passage of time by accommodating new changes, therefore requiring continuity of mappings of *MBO*.

4.2   Standard Ontology Change Management

Standard Ontology Change Management component is responsible for reflecting the changes in the mappings generated that are necessary after change occurs in any or both source and target ontologies. *Change Detector* always listens for any change in the mapping ontologies. The change information is accessed by *Change Collector* once that change is detected by *Change Detector*. This information is then provided to *Change Formulator* for converting the changes into processable format. Matching of only the changes with the target ontology is carried out and reflected in the already stored mappings in the form of updation.

4.3   Transformation Engine

Transformation Engine component performs the conversion of standard formats by communicating with the HMIS. *Communication Content Handler* access information from the HMIS in HL7 CDA format and forwards it to *Conversion*

---

[2] http://uclab.khu.ac.kr/sphere

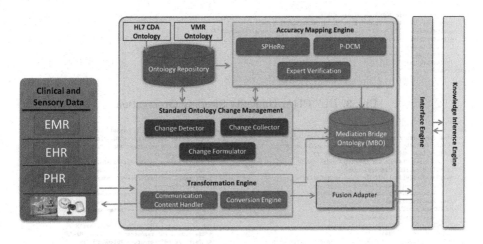

Fig. 2. ARIEN Proposed Architecture

Engine. Conversion Engine uses mappings from *MBO* to convert from HL7 CDA standard format to vMR format for Smart CDSS to process and generate guidelines. In the same way when the guideline are to be provided to HMIS, conversion from vMR to CDA format is performed.

5 Working Scenario

Two steps define the working process of the proposed ARIEN system. Firstly, offline approach includes development of standards ontologies such as CDA and vMR, then generating mappings between them and storing in the *MBO*. Secondly, legacy systems using services of Smart CDSS through ARIEN. This section explains the working model of proposed system.

In this scenario, we assume that smart homes and medical systems are compliant to HL7 CDA standard. Figure 3 shows snippet of HL7 CDA showing patient information from smart home collected using smartphone about his/her sleeping behavior. The information reflects that the patient was having difficulty in sleep as suggested by observation values. Once this information is obtained by ARIEN, Communication Handler passes it to Conversion Engine for conversion into Smart CDSS processable format, vMR.

Conversion Engine access the mapping information from the *MBO* for conversion process to vMR format. Different design patterns are used for alignments creation and storage of mappings in the *MBO*. Classes, properties and values are accessed and their alternative concepts are searched in the *MBO* for translation from one standard format to another. Figure 4 shows the **Overlap Pattern Relationship Model** pattern that has been used for creation of mapping between classes of different ontologies with attribute values. In this case, **Observation** class of HL7 CDA has mandatory attributes such as **classCode** and **moodCode**

```
<observation classCode="OBS" moodCode="EVN">
    <code code="301345002" codeSystem="2.16.840.1.113883.6.96"
    codeSystemName="SNOMED CT" displayName="Difficulty sleeping (finding)"/>
    <effectiveTime xsi:type="IVL_TS">
        <low inclusive="true" value="20080220102200+0300"/>
        <high inclusive="true" value="20080220102200+0300"/>
    </effectiveTime>
</observation>
```

Fig. 3. HL7 CDA: Difficulty Sleeping Observation

```
<rdf:RDF
    xmlns:vmr="http://www.owl-ontologies.com/VMR.owl#"
    xmlns:cda="http://www.owl-ontologies.com/CDA.owl#">
    <owl:Ontology rdf:about="BridgeOntology"/>
    <!-- Defining Classes for Overlap Bridge -->
    <owl:Class rdf:ID="OverlapBridge"/>
    <owl:NamedIndividual rdf:ID="OverlapBridgeInd">
        <rdf:type rdf:resource="#OverlapBridge"/>
        <hasRelationship rdf:resource="#Exact"/>
    </owl:NamedIndividual>
    <owl:Class rdf:ID="Standard1Class"/>
    <owl:Class rdf:ID="Standard2Class"/>
    <owl:Class rdf:ID="MandatoryAttributes"/>
    <owl:Class rdf:ID="Match"/>
    <owl:ObjectProperty rdf:ID="consistMandatoryAttributes">
        <rdfs:domain rdf:resource="#Standard1Class"/>
        <rdfs:range rdf:resource="#MandatoryAttributes"/>
    </owl:ObjectProperty>
    <MandatoryAttributes rdf:ID="classCode">
        <hasValue rdf:datatype="&xsd;string">OBS</hasValue>
    </MandatoryAttributes>
    <MandatoryAttributes rdf:ID="moodCode">
        <hasValue rdf:datatype="&xsd;string">EVN</hasValue>
    </MandatoryAttributes>
    <owl:NamedIndividual rdf:ID="Exact">
        <rdf:type rdf:resource="#Match"/>
    </owl:NamedIndividual>

    <owl:ObjectProperty rdf:ID="hasRelationship">
        <rdfs:domain rdf:resource="#OverlapBridge"/>
        <rdfs:range rdf:resource="#Match"/>
    </owl:ObjectProperty>
    <owl:ObjectProperty rdf:ID="hasSameRelationship">
        <rdfs:domain rdf:resource="#Standard1Class"/>
        <rdfs:range rdf:resource="#Standard2Class"/>
    </owl:ObjectProperty>
    <owl:ObjectProperty rdf:ID="hasSourceClass">
        <rdfs:domain rdf:resource="#OverlapBridge"/>
        <rdfs:range rdf:resource="#Standard1Class"/>
    </owl:ObjectProperty>
    <owl:ObjectProperty rdf:ID="hasTargetClass">
        <rdfs:domain rdf:resource="#OverlapBridge"/>
        <rdfs:range rdf:resource="#Standard2Class"/>
    </owl:ObjectProperty>
    <owl:DatatypeProperty rdf:ID="hasValue">
        <rdfs:domain rdf:resource="#MandatoryAttributes"/>
        <rdfs:range rdf:resource="&xsd;string"/>
    </owl:DatatypeProperty>
    <owl:NamedIndividual rdf:ID="Observation">
        <rdf:type rdf:resource="#Standard1Class"/>
    </owl:NamedIndividual>
    <owl:NamedIndividual rdf:ID="ObservationResult">
        <rdf:type rdf:resource="#Standard2Class"/>
    </owl:NamedIndividual>
</rdf:RDF>
```

Fig. 4. Overlap Pattern Relationship Model

with values **OBS** and **EVN** respectively. Now this information is mapped with **ObservationResult** class of vMR, therefore translation of **ObservationResult** class is performed with **Observation** class with its attributes and values. In the same way, **code** property of **Observation** class in CDA is mapped to **observationFocus** property of **ObservationResult** class in vMR standard as shown in Figure 5 using *Property Matching pattern*. In the same way other ontology matching patterns exists that are used for alignments generation and then used for transformation.

```
<observationResult>
    <observationFocus displayName="Difficulty sleeping (finding)"
    codeSystem="2.16.840.1.113883.6.96" code="301345002"/>
    <observationEventTime
    low=" 20080220102200+0300 " high=" 20080220102200+0300 "/>
</observationResult>
```

Fig. 5. HL7 vMR: Difficulty Sleeping ObservationResult

This converted vMR is passed to Fusion Adapter which forwards it to Knowledge Inference Engine through Interface Engine for processing and recommendation generation. The recommendations generated by Smart CDSS is again communicated through ARIEN with smart home by converting vMR to CDA format using *MBO*.

6   Conclusion

Ubiquitous healthcare requires data interoperability among medical systems and it is a vital factor for success of CDSS. The proposed systems provides the gateway to CDSS for achieving the goal of data interoperability using ontology matching. The two most important factors discussed in this paper for data interoperability are accuracy and continuity of mappings. Accuracy of mappings is dependent on continuity of mappings by handling change management.

Acknowledgement. This research was supported by the MSIP(Ministry of Science, ICT&Future Planning), Korea, under the ITRC(Information Technology Research Center) support program supervised by the NIPA(National IT Industry Promotion Agency)" (NIPA-2013-(H0301-13-2001))

References

1. Bodenreider, O., et al.: Biomedical ontologies in action: role in knowledge management, data integration and decision support. Yearb Med. Inform. 67, 79 (2008)
2. Dogac, A., Laleci, G.B., Kirbas, S., Kabak, Y., Sinir, S.S., Yildiz, A., Gurcan, Y.: Artemis: Deploying semantically enriched web services in the healthcare domain. Information Systems 31(4), 321–339 (2006)
3. Hein, A., Nee, O., Willemsen, D., Scheffold, T., Dogac, A., Laleci, G.B., et al.: Saphire-intelligent healthcare monitoring based on semantic interoperability platform-the homecare scenario. In: 1st European Conference on eHealth (ECEH 2006), Fribourg, Switzerland, pp. 191–202 (2006)
4. Hussain, M., Afzal, M., Khan, W.A., Lee, S.: Clinical decision support service for elderly people in smart home environment. In: 12th International Conference On Control, Automation, Robotics and Vision (ICARCV 2012) (2012)
5. Hussain, M., Khan, W.A., Afzal, M., Lee, S.: Smart CDSS for smart homes. In: Donnelly, M., Paggetti, C., Nugent, C., Mokhtari, M. (eds.) ICOST 2012. LNCS, vol. 7251, pp. 266–269. Springer, Heidelberg (2012)
6. Khan, W.A., Hussain, M., Afzal, M., Amin, M.B., Saleem, M.A., Lee, S.: Personalized-detailed clinical model for data interoperability among clinical standards. Telemedicine and E-Health 19(8), 632–642 (2013)
7. Khan, W.A., Hussain, M., Latif, K., Afzal, M., Ahmad, F., Lee, S.: Process interoperability in healthcare systems with dynamic semantic web services. In: Computing, pp. 1–26 (2013)
8. Maldonado, J.A., Moner, D., Boscá, D., Fernández-Breis, J.T., Angulo, C., Robles, M.: Linkehr-ed: A multi-reference model archetype editor based on formal semantics. International Journal of Medical Informatics 78(8), 559–570 (2009)
9. Martínez Costa, C., Menárguez-Tortosa, M., Fernández-Breis, J.T.: Clinical data interoperability based on archetype transformation. Journal of Biomedical Informatics 44(5), 869–880 (2011)
10. Qamar, R., Rector, A.: Semantic issues in integrating data from different models to achieve data interoperability. Studies in Health Technology and Informatics 129(1), 674 (2007)
11. Sahay, R., Fox, R., Zimmermann, A., Polleres, A., Hauswrith, M.: A methodological approach for ontologising and aligning health level seven (hl7) applications. In: Tjoa, A.M., Quirchmayr, G., You, I., Xu, L. (eds.) ARES 2011. LNCS, vol. 6908, pp. 102–117. Springer, Heidelberg (2011)

Understanding Movement and Interaction: An Ontology for Kinect-Based 3D Depth Sensors

Natalia Díaz Rodríguez[1], Robin Wikström[2], Johan Lilius[1],
Manuel Pegalajar Cuéllar[3], and Miguel Delgado Calvo Flores[3]

[1] Turku Centre for Computer Science (TUCS), Department of IT, Åbo Akademi University, Turku, Finland
[2] IAMSR, Åbo Akademi University, Turku, Finland
{ndiaz,rowikstr,jolilius}@abo.fi
[3] Department of Computer Science and Artificial Intelligence, University of Granada, Spain
{manupc,mdelgado}@decsai.ugr.es

Abstract. Microsoft Kinect has attracted great attention from research communities, resulting in numerous interaction and entertainment applications. However, to the best of our knowledge, there does not exist an ontology for 3D depth sensors. Including automated semantic reasoning in these settings would open the doors for new research, making possible not only to track but also understand what the user is doing. We took a first step towards this new paradigm and developed a 3D depth sensor ontology, modelling different features regarding user movement and object interaction. We believe in the potential of integrating semantics into computer vision. As 3D depth sensors and ontology-based applications improve further, the ontology could be used, for instance, for activity recognition, together with semantic maps for supporting visually impaired people or in assistance technologies, such as remote rehabilitation.

Keywords: Ontology, Kinect, Human Activity Modelling and Recognition, Ubiquitous Computing.

1 Introduction

Recently there has been a spark in developments in the field of smart spaces and ubiquitous computing, especially regarding applications using affordable sensors. One of these sensors is the Microsoft Kinect device, originally intended as an add-on for the Xbox 360 video console, which enables user interaction through movements and voice, instead of using a controller. However, the sensor attracted a lot of interest from the R&D communities, as Kinect can be reprogrammed for other purposes than purely entertainment.

The main goal with ubiquitous spaces is to work towards an ideal environment where humans and surrounding devices interact effortlessly [1]. For this to be realized, context-awareness is key. Semantic technologies have shown to be successful, among other areas, in context representation and reasoning, which can serve

G. Urzaiz et al. (Eds.): UCAmI 2013, LNCS 8276, pp. 254–261, 2013.
© Springer International Publishing Switzerland 2013

in object tracking and scene interpretation [2] and in human activity recognition [3]. We believe that semantic modelling of human movement and interaction could greatly benefit existing data-driven (e.g., computer vision) approaches, increasing context-awareness and potentially, activity recognition rates.

One of the most challenging areas within *UbiComp* is Activity Recognition. Using vision based techniques has substantial disadvantages, as most of them store the images, and become intrusive and privacy compromising. Since 3D depth sensors do not store the image itself, but a skeleton structure, they add an advantage towards traditional data-driven approaches [4] (HMM, SVM, etc.)

To the best of our knowledge, there does not exist any automated semantic reasoning for modelling movement and interaction within computer vision technologies and 3D depth sensors (e.g. Kinect). The rest of the paper is structured as follows. Section 2 presents related work in computer vision and semantic approaches, Section 3 describes our ontology proposal for modelling body movement, and Section 4 exemplifies its usage. Section 5 concludes and gives some future research directions.

2   Related Work

Due to Kinect multimodal features such as gesture and spoken commands, different UbiComp applications have been recently developed. For instance, the combination of Kinect with an airborne robot [5] to enable automatic 3D modelling and mapping of indoor environments.

An interesting initiative in this area is Kinect@Home[1][6], a crowd-sourcing project for large 3D datasets of real environments to help robotics and computer vision researchers, through vast amounts of images, to improve their algorithms. Another project, *Kinect Fusion* [7], allows for real-time 3D reconstruction and interaction using point-based 3D depth sensor data. An application example is touch input enabled arbitrary surfaces.

In the Semantic Web, ontologies represent the main technology for creating interoperability at a semantic level. This is achieved by creating a formal illustration of the data, making it possible to share and reuse the ontology all over the Web. Ontologies formulate and model relationships between concepts in a given domain [8]. The following example illustrates with OWL 2 axioms the activity *TakeMedication*, that can serve to monitor an elder:

$NataliaTakingMedication \equiv isPerformedBy.(Natalia \sqcap performsAction$
$(OpenPillCupboard \sqcap (TakeObject \sqcap actionAppliesTo\ some\ NataliasMedication) \sqcap$
$(TakeObject \sqcap actionAppliesTo\ some\ Glass) \sqcap FillGlassWithWater \sqcap Drink)).$

In [9] ontology-based annotation of images and semantic maps are realized within a framework for semantic spatial information processing. An XML description language for describing the physical realization of behaviours (speech and behaviour) is the Behavior Markup Language (BML) [2], which allows representation of postures and gestures for controlling verbal and nonverbal behavior

---

[1] Kinect@Home http://www.kinectathome.com/

[2] BML: http://www.mindmakers.org/projects/bml-1-0/wiki

of (humanoid) embodied conversational agents (ECAs). However, to the best of our knowledge, there is no current solution integrating the performance power of computer vision technologies, together with a formal semantic representation of the user, its movement and interaction with the environment, to achieve automatic knowledge reasoning. In next section we propose an ontology for combining data-driven and knowledge-based paradigms.

3   An Ontology for Modelling Movement and Interaction with 3D Depth Sensors

We propose an ontology to distinguish among human movement, human-object interaction and human-computer interaction. The Kinect ontology[3] aims at representing 3D depth sensor information generally, but at this stage it is based upon two main Kinect modules. The first and most basic one is Kinect Core, and represents the Natural User Interface (NUI), which is the core of the Kinect for Windows API, and represents the most relevant concepts from Kinect Interaction and Kinect Fusion APIs [10]. The second module of the ontology consists of practical extensions for modelling and recognizing human activity.

3.1   Kinect Core Ontology, Kinect Interaction and Kinect Fusion

The *Kinect Sensor* class represents the camera device, its current location, orientation and frames. A Kinect Sensor associates a *3D Model* with the user' skeleton.

A Kinect 3D *Volume* is characterized through its size and voxel resolution.

Kinect Audio supports a microphone mode, beamforming and source localization (which can be identified through a direction or language). A *Speech* is recognized by a *Speech Recognition Engine*. The latter allows creation of customized grammars for recognition of user commands with a confidence threshold parameter for each grammar.

Kinect Interaction provides several ways to interact with a Kinect-enabled application. The natural gestures, as a way of touch-free user interactions, allow the sensor to operate in a range of 0.4 to 3-4 m. The types of interaction are modelled with gestures (gripping, releasing, pushing and scrolling) (Fig. 1). This class generates interaction streams which are bound to a control, i.e., an action that allows computer interaction. A *Control* is an action performed when an interaction gesture is recognized. The set of interactive controls are classified on video, images or text. An *Interaction Stream* represents the supply of interaction frames as they are generated by a *KinectInteraction*. Each *InteractionFrame* has a timestamp.

Kinect distinguishes among two types of *Tracking Mode*s, *default* or *seated*. Both modes can track 2 out of 6 users, but only one can be active at once.

By using ontology-based modelling, a *SeatingUser* can be defined as:

---

[3] Kinect Ontology: `http://users.abo.fi/rowikstr/KinectOntology/`

Fig. 1. Some available interaction gestures: a) Grip b) Release c) Press

$SeatingUser \equiv User \sqcap isTracked \sqcap (SeatedTrackingMode\,is\,Active)$.
$StandingUser \equiv User \sqcap isTracked \sqcap (DefaultTrackingMode\,is\,Active)$.
$TrackedUser \equiv User \sqcap isTracked \sqcap ((DefaultTrackingMode\,or\,SeatedTrack-ingMode)is\,Active)$.
$InteractingUser \equiv User \sqcap isTracked \sqcap (hasArm\,some\,Arm) \sqcap (hasHand\,some\,Hand) \sqcap (hasInteractionMode\,some\,(GrippingInteractionMode\,or\,ReleasingInter-actionMode\,or\,PressingInteractionMode))$.

Kinect' *Skeleton* class identifies a *User* and is represented with a bone and joint hierarchy, which refers to the ordering of the bones defined by the surrounding joints. Our ontology allows to express relations concerning bones and joints, where the bone rotation is stored in a bone's child joint, e.g., the rotation of the left hip bone is stored in the *HipLeft* joint (See Fig. 2-right)[4]. The skeletal tracking includes rotations of each bone joint and orientations of each bone.

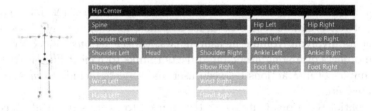

Fig. 2. Left) Skeleton, bones and joints. Right) Joints hierarchy. [10]

The *Hand* class has a set of properties that represent its state, e.g., the user the hand belongs to, whether the hand is primary for that user, whether the hand is interactive, gripping or pressing. *Arms*, in the same way, are provided with an arm state.

3.2 Kinect Extensions Ontology

A set of relevant classes is defined next to make sense on body, objects and actions interactions.

---

[4] Bones are specified by the parent and child joints that enclose the bone and their orientation (x,y,z). For example, the Hip Left bone is enclosed by the Hip Center joint (parent) and the Hip Left joint (child) [10].

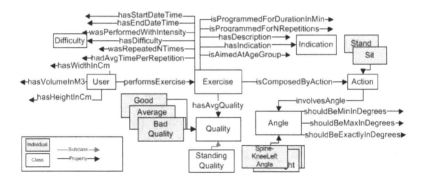

Fig. 3. Exercise & Workout Sub-Ontology

The class *User* identifies the person behind the Skeleton model. A user is modelled with the correspondent arms (and hands) and a set of properties that, e.g., may identify him as *PrimaryUser*[5].

Body Movement mainly represents actions executed with body limbs and articulations. Different kind of movements include to rotate, bend, extend and elevate. These can have a clockwise direction (e.g. *RotateWristClockwise*), a direction (*ElevateFootFront*), a degree or a body part to which they apply (*LeftBodyPart*).

Any physical *Object* and its properties such as dimensions, (partial) colours or number of voxels can be represented, for instance, to recognize activities such as experiments involving volume measurements. *Object actions* model interaction between objects or among users and objects thanks to Kinect Fusion API module. Examples of interactions between user and objects include to *grab, release, touch, click* etc.

The Spatial Relations Ontology [11] is reused to express physical space relations of objects as well as how they are placed or how they interact with each other, e.g. *contains, disjoint, equal and overlaps*.

Elements from NeOn Ontology engineering methodology [12] were used, e.g.: reusing ontology resources, requirements specification, development of required scenarios and dynamic ontology evolution. The main classes, data and object properties of the Kinect Ontology are presented in Table 1.

4 Ontology-Based Human Activity Reasoning

Figure 3 presents the structure of the Exercise & Workout Sub-Ontology, where the goal is to precisely model the specific movements a user performs, e.g., through the exercise duration, repetitions and quality or intensity (*Low, Medium, High*) performed.

---

[5] Kinect Interaction layer decides which of the tracked users is primary and assigns him an ID and a primary hand, although both hands are tracked [10].

Table 1. Kinect Ontology Classes, Data and Object Properties (partial)

OWL Classes	OWL Data Properties and Object Properties
BodyMovement, BodyPart, ObjectAction, Exercise, Angle, (Image, Text, Video-)Control, Exercise(-Difficulty, Frequency, Intensity, Quality) Grammar, HandState, Indication, Location, Object, Orientation, Kinect-(Audio, Interaction, Sensor), Dictation, SpeechRecognitionEngine, TrackingMode, Bone, BoneJoint	*hasStart/EndDateTime, wasRepeatedNTimes, hadAvgTimePerRepetition, shouldBeMin/Max/ExactlyInDegrees, hasDescription, isProgrammedForNRepetitions, IsProgrammedForDurationInMin, hasCoordinateX/Y/Z, hasHeightInCm hasDifficulty, hasIndication, hasAvgQuality, performsExercise, isComposedByAction, involvesAngle, hasOrientation, hasSourceLocation, interactsWith, detectsKinectAudio, hasLoadedGrammar, hasActiveTrackingMode, detectsInteraction/Object, activatesControl, hasBoneHierarchy, isLocatedIn, hasSpatialRelation, hasInteractionMode, hasArm/Hand, hasSpeechRecognition, representsUser*

In order to model human activities and behaviours, the state of environment variables and body postures can be abstracted so that identifying changes of interest is possible. Since existing statistical methods have demonstrated to be robust in activity monitoring [13], the Kinect ontology is intended to support these by adding context-awareness to the end-user application. For instance, long-term queries could be done, since having semantic knowledge adds the capability of integration with other sensor information, allowing for user-customization of the smart environment. Therefore, we focus on representing simple, higher level actions (lay down, washing hands, etc.) and facilitating the finding of longer term changes. Examples of the ontology in use are:

Example 1: Defining basic movement (*Stand, BendDown, TwistRight, MoveObject*, etc.) can be mapped to OWL 2, e.g., the Action *Sitting*, would be of the form:
$performsAction(Natalia, Sit) \land hasStartDatetime(Sit, T)$.

Example 2: When defining an activity, e.g. *Sit_StandExercise* workout, the amount of series done in a given time as well as the exercise quality can be measured. These values can be predefined according to medical parameters, e.g., the difficulty faced when sitting/standing as well as the stretching of the back when standing:

$\forall U, \forall Sit\_StandEx \in Sit\_Stand - Ex, \forall V : performsExercise(User, Sit\_StandEx) \land$
$isComposedByAction(Sit\_StandEx, (Sit \land Stand) \land involvesAngle(Stand, LowerUpper-$
$BackAngle) \land hadAngleValue(LowerUpperBackAngle, V) \land V < 175 \rightarrow$
$hasAvgQuality(Sit\_StandEx, BadQuality)$.

Example 3: Historic analysis can be provided through measurements performed while doing certain activity, to monitor posture quality. E.g., having the back less straight than a year ago could be notified to make the user aware of his posture habits:

$\forall Stand, LowerUpperBackAngle1, LowerUpperBackAngle2, \forall V1, V2, D1, D2 :$
$performsAction(Natalia, Stand) \wedge involvesAngle(Stand, LowerUpperBackAngle1) \wedge$
$hasValue(Lower{-}UpperBackAngle1, V1) \wedge hasDateTime(LowerUpperBackAngle, D1)$
$\wedge involvesAngle(Stand, LowerUpperBackAngle2) \wedge hasValue(LowerUpperBackAngle2,$
$V2) \wedge hasDateTime(LowerUpperBackAngle2, D2) \wedge ((V1{-}V2) > 5) \wedge T2 == (T1{+}(\text{X1-}$
XX-XX}$)) \wedge hasPhone(Natalias, P) \rightarrow SendSMS(P,$"Your back is not as extended as
a year ago").

Example 4: An office worker can be notified when he is not having straight
back and neck:

$\forall Sit, \forall NeckUpperBackAngle, \forall V : isCurrently(Natalia, Sit) \wedge isInLocation(Natalia,$
$NataliasOffice) \wedge involvesAngle(Sit, NeckUpperBackAngle) \wedge hadAngleValue$
$(NeckUpperBackAngle, V) \wedge V < 175 \wedge hasPhone(Natalia, NataliasPhone) \rightarrow$
$SendDoubleVibrationAlarm(NataliasPhone,$"Bad posture!").

Or when he has been sitting for too long:
$\forall T : executesAction(Robin, Sit) \wedge hasEndDateTime(Sit, T) \wedge ((Time.Now - T) >$
$2h) \rightarrow sendSMS(RobinsPhone,$"Stand up and stretch legs!").

The integration with other physiological data such as heart rate, sleep quality
or stress, from sensors such as accelerometers, can be as well integrated for more
complete assessments of every day functions or tasks.

5   Conclusions and Future Work

We developed a OWL 2 ontology ($\mathcal{ALC}$ DL expressivity) composed of 164 classes,
53 object properties, 58 data properties and 93 individuals, based on the Kinect
for Windows API. The structure of the ontology is based on Kinect Natural User
Interface, Kinect Interaction, Fusion and Audio modules.

We believe that ontologies can and should play a vital part in this development
to help abstracting atomic gestures for an incremental, fine, and coarse grained activity recognition. In this way, automatic reasoning for inferring of novel information is facilitated. For instance, the *Exercise & Workout* ontology classes allow the
data integration and registration to follow the evolution of a person's performance
through the quality of the workout or rehabilitation program. We exemplified the
usage of the proposed ontology with different domain examples.

In future work, there is an imminent need to conduct evaluation experiments
with the ontology developed, for validating its modelling accuracy, as well as
its reliability. We are convinced that an appropriate combination of computer
vision algorithms with semantic models of human movement and interaction
can significantly improve context-awareness, recognition accuracy and activity
analysis precision.

Another interesting research direction for the future is the use of fuzzy ontologies, which offer ways for dealing with vague and imprecise data. During the
modelling process of the Kinect ontology, we found features susceptible to be
modelled in an imprecise way. Due to the imprecision inherent to the environment, these features could benefit from being expressed through an extension of

the ontology to Fuzzy OWL 2. This would ease the *looseness* of the model and facilitate user interaction, as linguistic labels can be used for natural language-based customization.

Acknowledgements. The work presented was funded by TUCS (Turku Centre for Computer Science).

References

1. Weiser, M.: The computer for the twenty-first century. Scientific American 165, 94–104 (1991)
2. Gómez-Romero, J., Patricio, M.A., Garcìa, J., Molina, J.M.: Ontology-based context representation and reasoning for object tracking and scene interpretation in video. Expert Systems with Applications 38(6), 7494–7510 (2011)
3. Chen, L., Nugent, C.D.: Ontology-based activity recognition in intelligent pervasive environments. International Journal of Web Information Systems (IJWIS) 5(4), 410–430 (2009)
4. Kim, E., Helal, S., Cook, D.: Human activity recognition and pattern discovery. IEEE Pervasive Computing 9(1), 48–53 (2010)
5. Henry, P., Krainin, M., Herbst, E., Ren, X., Fox, D.: RGB-D mapping: Using Kinect-style depth cameras for dense 3D modeling of indoor environments. The International Journal of Robotics Research 31(5), 647–663 (2012)
6. Kinect@Home Project, KTH, http://www.kinectathome.com (2012)
7. Izadi, S., Kim, D., Hilliges, O., Molyneaux, D., Newcombe, R., Kohli, P., Shotton, J., Hodges, S., Freeman, D., Davison, A., Fitzgibbon, A.: KinectFusion: real-time 3D reconstruction and interaction using a moving depth camera. In: Proceedings of the 24th Annual ACM Symposium on User Interface Software and Technology, UIST 2011, pp. 559–568 (2011)
8. d'Aquin, M., Noy, N.F.: Where to publish and find ontologies? a survey of ontology libraries. Web Semantics: Science, Services and Agents on the World Wide Web 11, 96–111 (2012)
9. Foukarakis, M.: Informational system for managing photos and spatial information using sensors, ontologies and semantic maps. PhD thesis, Technical University of Crete (2009)
10. Kinect for Windows, http://www.microsoft.com/en-us/kinectforwindows/develop/
11. Hudelot, C., Atif, J., Bloch, I.: Fuzzy spatial relation ontology for image interpretation. Fuzzy Sets Syst. 159(15), 1929–1951 (2008)
12. Suárez-Figueroa, M.C.: NeOn Methodology for building ontology networks: specification, scheduling and reuse. PhD thesis, Universidad Politécnica de Madrid (2010)
13. Ismail, A.A., Florea, A.M.: Multimodal indoor tracking of a single elder in an AAL environment. In: 5th International Symposium on Ambient Intelligence, pp. 137–145 (2013)

Ontological Goal Modelling for Proactive Assistive Living in Smart Environments

Joseph Rafferty, Liming Chen, and Chris Nugent

School of Computing and Mathematics, University of Ulster, Northern Ireland
rafferty-j@email.ulster.ac.uk, {l.chen,cd.nugent}@ulster.ac.uk

Abstract. Existing assistive living solutions have traditionally adopted a bottom-up approach involving sensor based monitoring, data analysis to activity recognition and assistance provisioning. This approach, however, suffers from applicability and scalability issues associated with sensor density and variations in performing user activities. In an effort to alleviate these challenges, the current study proposes a goal oriented top-down approach to assistive living which offers a paradigm shift from a sensor centric view to a goal oriented view. The basic concept of the approach is that if a user's goal can be identified, then assistance can be provided proactively through pre-defined or dynamically constructed activity related instructions. The paper first introduces the system architecture for the proposed approach. It then describes an ontological goal model to serve as the basis for such an approach. The utility of the approach is illustrated in a use scenario focused on assisting a user with their activities of daily living.

Keywords: Ontology, Goal Modelling, Assistive Living, Goal Recognition, Smart Environments.

1 Introduction

The worldwide population is aging and as a result it is producing an uneven demographic composition [1, 2]. This is expected to reach a situation where by 2050 over 20% of the population will be aged 65 or over [1, 2]. This growth in aging population is expected to produce an increase in age related illness and will place additional burdens on healthcare provision [2]. In addition, the amount of informal support available will decrease due to a reduction in the ratio of working age people (15-64) to those older than 65 [1].

Ambient Assisted Living (AAL) has been widely viewed as a promising approach to addressing the problems associated with ageing [3, 4]. Within this domain technology supporting independent living can be used to alleviate a portion of these problems, hence offering the potential of enhancing the quality of life of older people. It is possible to create residential environments augmented with this form of technology using the notion of a Smart Home (SH). Typically SHs operate with the following 'bottom-up' process. Sensors monitor an inhabitant's activities/environment. Sensor data is processed to identify Activities of Daily Living (ADL), i.e. the daily tasks

G. Urzaiz et al. (Eds.): UCAmI 2013, LNCS 8276, pp. 262–269, 2013.

required for living, e.g. bathing, preparing a meal, using the telephone. ADLs which are subsequently identified can be monitored to detect difficult progression and to allow assistance to be offered via actuators or other user interfaces within the environment [3–6]. As such, SHs allow older people to live longer independently, with a better quality of life, in their own homes.

The bottom-up approach, whist functional, has issues stemming from its sensor centric nature. Inhabitant privacy is potentially violated by recording activities which are then used as the basis for providing assistive services [3–6]. For efficient operation SHs require a large number of sensors to be placed in the environment which is realistically not feasible for widespread use due to scalability issues related to retrofitting a large number of homes with an appropriate suite of sensors. This retrofitting process may represent a large financial cost and disturbance to inhabitants. In addition, current SHs using this approach cannot flexibly handle variation in activity performance in a satisfactory way. Finally reusability of some of these bottom-up SHs can be reduced as they rely on a record of events that occur within their environment [3–6]. These problems represent a significant barrier to the uptake and adoption of SH technology.

To address these issues we contend a paradigm shift from a sensor centric approach to a 'top-down', goal driven approach can bring additional flexibility whilst simultaneously requiring fewer sensors. In a goal driven approach an inhabitant's goals are the focus of the assistive system. By combining a goal recognition system and an action planning mechanism an assistant system will allow flexible and proactive assessment of an intended inhabitant goal, thus facilitating assistance provision.

The remainder of the paper is organised as follows. Section 2 discusses related work. Section 3 proposes a top-down approach and characterizes SH inhabitant goals. Section 4 provides an overview and description of the ontological goal model which has been developed. Section 5 presents a use case to illustrate the use of goal models for assistive living and Section 6 concludes the paper.

2   Related Work

Current work in the area of SHs is mainly based on the bottom-up approach. While the bottom-up approach follows a general process involving a number of key research areas, central to the approach is activity recognition. A plethora of work relating to activity recognition and SHs currently exists. Additionally, existing literature reviews [3–7] provide coverage of a large number of these works.

In order to realise a goal driven approach to SHs, inhabitant's goals need to be suitably modelled for use by an assistive system. Goal modelling has previously been a focus in areas such as Intelligent Agents (IA) [8, 9].

IAs are software entities which perceive their environments and act towards goals [10]. IAs vary in design paradigm [8–11] which produces differing goal representations. IAs based on the belief, desires and intention (BDI) [11] paradigm have been based on human cognitive models and so provide a suitable basis for modelling inhabitant goals. Traditionally goals in BDI IAs have been modelled implicitly, representing only actions required to achieve a goal. Recent works have added an explicit representation of a goal's objective to allow more flexible deliberation on goal pursuit [8, 9].

In [9] goals are modelled using two aspects, procedural or declarative. Declarative aspects are explicit goal statements, for example *Make coffee*. Procedural aspects are a stepwise instruction of activities which are engaged by an agent for example *(open cupboard) -> (get cup)*. Procedural aspects (action plans) can be combined with declarative aspects to allow advanced reasoning [11]. This combination provides a separation of goal representation and actions allowing deliberation on action plans to achieve a goal, as such this combination is needed to represent inhabitant goals.

Current goal models implicitly provide motivation for a software agent but are not suited for explicitly representing goals of a SH inhabitant. To model the goals of SH inhabitants the goal modelling approach presented in this paper follows the work of Pokahr *et al.* to model declarative and procedural aspects of goals that are pursued by SH inhabitants.

3   Goal Driven Top-Down Approach to Assistive Living

A novel goal driven, top-down, approach to assistive living within SHs is proposed, which is illustrated in Figure 1. The architecture of the approach consists of a number of components, namely a goal repository, a goal recognition component, a specific goal generation mechanism, an activity planning component and an assistance provisioning component. A goal repository is used to store goals, which have been defined by domain knowledge, in an expressive manner. The goal recognition component [12] interprets sensor activations within SHs to recognise which goal in the repository is most likely being pursued by the SH inhabitant. Recognised goals are then passed to the specific goal generation process to be deliberated on and, if required, nominated for assistance. Activity planning determines an action plan to be performed to achieve a nominated goal. An assistive provisioning component uses such action plans to provide stepwise assistance to an inhabitant, e.g. an audio instruction. In order to realize this goal driven paradigm an explicit and expressive goal model is required which is the focus of the remainder of this paper.

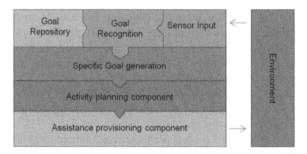

Fig. 1. The proposed generic approach to a goal driven SH

3.1   Goal Characterisation and Conceptual Modelling

ADLs are tasks related to daily living, such as, preparing drinks, preparing a meal and grooming. An ADL is usually composed of a sequence of actions in order to be achieved. For example, preparing a cup of tea involves getting the teapot, a cup, hot water, milk and sugar.

In the presented goal driven top-down SH, goals represent inhabitant intention and are realised by performing actions, similar to realisation of ADLs. Nevertheless, goals are a more abstract representation of activity and so a goal can range from representing many ADLs, one ADL or a simple subset of an activity required to partly achieve an ADL. For example a goal of *GetCup* may be incorporated into a *MakeTea* goal which in turn could be one of multiple goals involved with a *DailyNourishment* goal. Based on how an ADL is performed we can characterise inhabitant's goals in terms of the following dimensions: *types, activation conditions* and *state*.

ADLs have different recurrence characteristics that need to be considered by inhabitant goals. Some ADLs are to achieve something such as making a cup of tea while the others are to maintain a state such as an inhabitant's insulin level. This realisation allows us to characterise inhabitant goals in two categories, namely *Achieve* goals and *Maintain* goals. *Achieve* goals are pursued by inhabitants and are goals that have no set recurrence conditions, e.g. making a cup of coffee. *Maintain* goals represent conditions that an inhabitant must maintain, for example monitoring and controlling blood pressure.

During the performance of an ADL different stages of pursuit are encountered. These are mapped to the lifecycle of a goal through activation conditions. Activation conditions make it possible to model how inhabitants adopt, manage and pursue goals as their attitude to a goal is reflected by its stage in the overall process lifecycle. Examples of these are presented in Table 1. Both goal types have specific conditions to uniquely cater for their use cases.

The stage of a goal lifecycle is determined by which activation conditions have been encountered. For example, a goal is *adopted* when its precondition becomes true; when it is being pursued by an inhabitant. *Adopted* goals can be in one of three states as reflected by encountered activation conditions: *active, suspended* or *assist*. *Active* state represents that the goals is actively pursued by an inhabitant; this is the initial state of an *adopted* goal. *Suspended* state represents that goals are not actively being pursued. *Assist* state represents that goals are in need of assistance.

Achieve goals have an additional achievement condition to determine if a goal has been a success. *Maintain* goals add both an additional *maintain* state and a regular check for a *trigger* condition. In *maintain* goals the *trigger* condition is used to determine if goal maintenance should occur, at this point the goal is in the *maintain* state. When a goal is in a *maintain* state the *assist* condition is eligible and will determine if assistance would be offered. *Maintain* goals do not become achieved; however, they remain active when their precondition is valid. The lifecycles of these goal types are presented in Figure 2.

Using this goal representation and lifecycle it becomes possible to offer assistance for an inhabitant when necessary. This assistance would be realised by use of associated actions plans. These plans are used to determine the current state of goal progress and guide an inhabitant towards goal completion.

An action plan represents a sequence of actions required to produce a plan's effect, for example *Open Cupboard*. These actions contain a description of preconditions required to perform that action, e.g. pouring water into a cup plan requires a precondition and success flag indicating if water has been boiled.

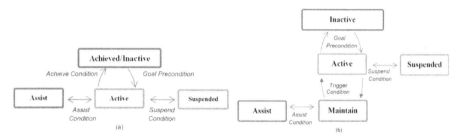

Fig. 2. The lifecycles of achieve (a) and maintain (b) goal types

4   Ontological Goal Modelling

Ontological modelling [13] allows explicit representation of knowledge by structuring it into a hierarchy of concepts and classes which have properties, relationships and restrictions. Ontologies use data properties and object properties to describe a concept. The former models the attributes of a concept such as a goal name using primitive data types, e.g. a string. The latter models interrelationships between concepts, e.g. a goal can be achieved by an action plan, thus an object property *AchievedBy* can link a *Goal* concept with an *ActionPlan* concept. Ontologies have been previously used in [14] to overcome the limitations of knowledge driven activity recognition.

The goals characterised in Section 3.1 have been conceptualised and encoded as ontologies using the Protégé ontology engineering tool. Table 1 presents the properties of the declarative aspect of inhabitant goals. These properties allow an expressive and flexible representation of inhabitant goals.

Table 1. The properties of declarative aspects of a goal

Term	Description	Example
	Base goal	
Name	The name of the Goal	"MakeCoffee"
Description	A description of the Goal	"This goal of making coffee"
Precondition	A property showing when a goal is likely to be considered by an inhabitant	Goal recognition has determined an inhabitant is wishing to make coffee
SuspendCondition	This represents conditions where a goal is considered to be suspended	A representation showing an inhabitant is pursuing an incompatible goal
AssistCondition	This represents a condition where a goal is in need of assistance	Goal progression is occurring in a confused manner
OperationalState	The current state of the goal	"Inactive","Active", "Assist", "Suspended"
PreviousEventTimestamp	Time stamp of a previous goal action	15251628
	Achieve Goal	
AchievementCondition	This condition under which a goal is considered to be achieved	All the actions to complete the goal have been performed
	Maintain Goal	
TargetCondition	The condition to be maintained	An ambient temperature of 19°Celcius
TriggerCondition	The condition specifying the maintain condition should be pursued	Ambient temperature is not below 18° or over 20°Celsius
MaintenanceCheckFrequency	The frequency which the maintain goal is checked (in seconds)	3600

Procedural aspects of goals, also known as action plans, need to be considered. The properties of this aspect are presented in Table 2. In presented ontology, the general class of a Goal has a *hasGoalprofile* object property linking to a *GoalProfile*. The *GoalProfile* entity contains all the common properties for a base goal type. The goal class contains two sub classes to cater for the needs of achieve and maintain goal types. These sub classes contain individual data properties for their goal types. The goal concept is linked by a *hasActionPlan* object property to the *ActionPlan* concept. The *ActionPlan* in turn has a *hasAction* object link which is used to link to the component *AtomicAction* concept. Figure 3 provides two graphical representations of the ontology, a hierarchy of concepts and properties of the modelled goal ontology and a representation of these as modelled in the Protégé tool.

Table 2. The properties of an action plan and atomic actions

Term	Description	Example
Action Plan		
Name	The name of the Action plan	"Make Coffee-Aeropress"
Description	A description of the plan	"Making coffee with an Aeropress"
Atomic Action		
Name	The name of the atomic action	"Open Cupboard", "Reach for coffee"
Precondition	A precondition needed for this action	A representation of the world showing water has been boiled. A value showing that this is the initial action in a sequence.
Effect	How the action is enacted	Moving a cup from storage to a countertop
Action status	The status of this particular action	Complete, incomplete

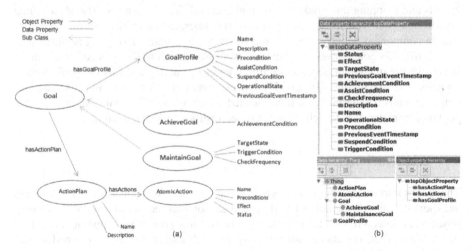

Fig. 3. The goal model ontology classes, object properties and data properties. As shown in a Hierarchy (a) and using the protégé ontology engineering tool (b).

5   Use Scenarios for Assistive Living

In the following we use the EU AAL funded PIA Project[1] as the basis of a scenario to illustrate the suitability of the developed goal model in a top-down, goal-driven SH. PIA aims to provide a system capable of reminding SH inhabitants of steps required to perform an ADL. PIA will provide assistance by affixing NFC[2] tags to items

---

[1] PIA AAL Funded Research Project available at: http://www.pia-project.org/
[2] Near Field Communication – A short range contactless communication technology.

associated with ADLs, e.g attached to a dishwasher. Inhabitants use devices, e.g. smartphones, to interact with these tags. On interaction the device reads identifiers from the tag and references an associated ADL in a database to obtain and display video clips to illustrate how to perform the task. The PIA solution can be extended by employing the top-down approach to create a more capable system with less inhabitant interaction and awareness.

We use an *achieve* goal "making coffee" to illustrate this approach. This goal was given the name *MakeCoffee* and is defined as follows. The precondition of this goal is a symbolic representation of object-sensor activations in the goal recognition component related to making coffee. Depending on the goal recognition approach used this representation can vary [12]. In a similar way, the *suspend* condition of this goal represents an inhabitant concurrently pursing incompatible goals. For illustration, the assist condition is a simple one that triggers assistance if an inhabitant has not acted towards *MakeCoffee* in three minutes. The *achieve* condition is a representation requiring that all actions to complete this goal have been observed by the system. The action plan provides a description of how to achieve this goal.

During the day an inhabitant desires a cup of coffee and acts to achieve this. A goal recognition system monitors object-sensors and by predicting actions from these activations and mapping this prediction to goal preconditions it identifies the *MakeCoffee* goal from a goal repository. This goal is then deliberated on by the specific goal generation component which manages goal lifecycles and states. Every act performed to accomplish this goal causes the previous event timestamp to be updated. While making coffee the inhabitant becomes confused and stops acting towards the goal. After 3 minutes of inactivity the assist condition is encountered. To provide assistance a planning mechanism determines actions needed to complete this goal and then uses a guidance infrastructure to deliver video based instruction to the inhabitant.

6   Conclusion

This paper introduces a top-down, goal driven approach to realising a SH to address the shortcomings of the current widespread sensor-focused paradigm. We have proposed an architecture which can be used to realise this goal driven approach. In a first step towards realising this architecture we have characterised and developed a conceptual model for SH inhabitant goals. This model has been represented in an ontology which has been described. To illustrate this suitability of the developed model for this approach we presented a use scenario extended from the PIA project to show the use of such a system in assistive living. While testing and evaluation await further implementation of this system, we believe the proposed approach and underlying mechanisms are novel. Future work will produce and integrate all system components and will evaluate the overall performance of this approach.

Acknowledgments. This work is conducted in the context of the EU AAL PIA project. The authors gratefully acknowledge the contributions from all members of the PIA consortium.

References

1. United Nation: World Population Ageing 2009 (Population Studies Series) (2010)
2. De Luca, d'Alessandro, E., Bonacci, S., Giraldi, G.: Aging populations: the health and quality of life of the elderly. La Clinica Terapeutica 162, e13 (2011)
3. Cook, D.J., Das, S.K.: How smart are our environments? An updated look at the state of the art. Pervasive and Mobile Computing 3, 53–73 (2007)
4. Chan, M., Estève, D., Escriba, C., Campo, E.: A review of smart homes- present state and future challenges. Computer Methods and Programs in Biomedicine 91, 55–81 (2008)
5. Chen, L., Hoey, J., Nugent, C.D., Cook, D.J., Yu, Z.: Sensor-Based Activity Recognition. IEEE Transactions on Systems, Man, and Cybernetics, Part C (Applications and Reviews), 1–19 (2012)
6. Poland, M.P., Nugent, C.D., Wang, H., Chen, L.: Smart Home Research:Projects and Issues. International Journal of Ambient Computing and Intelligence 1, 32–45 (2009)
7. Chen, L., Nugent, C.: Ontology-based activity recognition in intelligent pervasive environments. International Journal of Web Information Systems 5, 410–430 (2009)
8. Pokahr, A., Braubach, L., Lamersdorf, W.: Jadex: A BDI reasoning engine. Multi-Agent Programming (2005)
9. Riemsdijk, M., Van, D.M., Winikoff, M.: Goals in agent systems: a unifying framework. In: Proceedings of the 7th International Joint Conference on Autonomous Agents and Multiagent Systems, AAMAS 2008 (2008)
10. Wooldridge, M., Jennings, N.R.: Intelligent agents: theory and practice. The Knowledge Engineering Review 10, 115 (2009)
11. Rao, A., Georgeff, M.: Modeling rational agents within a BDI-architecture. Readings in Agents (1997)
12. Sadri, F.: Logic-based approaches to intention recognition. In: Handbook of Research on Ambient Intelligence and Smart Environments: Trends and Perspectives (2010)
13. Chandrasekaran, B., Josephson, J.R., Benjamins, V.R.: What are ontologies, and why do we need them? IEEE Intelligent Systems 14, 20–26 (1999)
14. Chen, L., Nugent, C.D., Wang, H.: A Knowledge-Driven Approach to Activity Recognition in Smart Homes. IEEE Transactions on Knowledge and Data Engineering 24, 961–974 (2012)

A Generic Upper-Level Ontological Model for Context-Aware Applications within Smart Environments

Laura M. McAvoy[*], Liming Chen, and Mark Donnelly

University of Ulster, Jordanstown, UK
McAvoy-L3@email.ulster.ac.uk,
{l.chen,mp.donnelly}@ulster.ac.uk

Abstract. Context modeling has attracted increasing attention due to the prevalence of context-aware applications within smart environments. Whilst upper-level context ontologies exist for use within smart environments, none offer a single generalized model covering all high-level elements that exist across all types of smart environments. This paper presents an upper-level context ontology for smart environments which aims to incorporate all factors deemed important for context in smart environments. Specifically, the proposed model considers key factors that include User, Object, Location, Application, Event, Natural Element and Temporal. The model is able to represent daily routines encompassing both open-world and closed-world activities and this is presented in a short vignette.

Keywords: Smart Environments, Context-awareness, Ontological Context Modeling, Upper-Level Ontology.

1 Introduction

A smart environment can refer to any environment where computer systems and devices interact together to provide an integrated set of services that support the environment's needs [1]. Smart environments exist in both closed and open world settings. Examples of closed-world settings include transport [2] and smart homes [3]. Conversely, open-world settings are used to represent those environments not bound by physical structures. Examples include mobile computing [3] and wireless sensor networks [4]. In order for these environments to offer enhanced levels of monitoring, inference and assistance thereby making them 'smart', they need to be context-aware.

Context is a core concept in smart environments. Dey defines context as: "any information that can be used to characterize the situation of an entity. An entity is a person, place or object that is considered relevant to the interaction between a user and an application, including the user and applications themselves." [5]. Over the last decade, ontological context modeling has emerged as an efficient and extensible approach for representing context information within a smart environment. This context

---

[*] Corresponding author.

G. Urzaiz et al. (Eds.): UCAmI 2013, LNCS 8276, pp. 270–277, 2013.

information is related through classes which are created from a set of concepts, representing context and smart environments.

Various upper-level ontologies have previously been proposed [6—10, 15]. The majority of these ontologies have represented similar entities, such as *Person, Location, Computing Entity* and *Activity* [6-8, 15]. Two pieces of work however, which do not model these similar entities are [9] and [10]. Hervas, Bravo and Fontecha [10] use four individual and related ontologies, rather than an all-encompassing ontology and define the main upper level entities as *Device, Service, User* and *Environment*. Whilst Shih, Narayanan and Kuhn [9] define them as *Place, Action, Time* and *Environment,* with situation domain ontologies being attached as required.

Whilst numerous upper-level ontologies have been created to model context within smart environments, meeting many challenges, a range of challenges still exist. Most upper-level context ontologies that exist are domain specific [6], or have been developed to only apply to a single domain, such as smart homes [7, 8]. Others deal more with factors such as situation awareness [9] or highlight a number of important entities but overlook other factors [10] which are deemed relevant to context based on Dey's definition. Other issues were encountered in our previous work, where a model was created to represent context information across a smart research environment and extended using the Semantic Sensor Network (SSN) model [13]. Consequently it became evident once the extension took place, that there were logical inconsistencies due to the model being convoluted. This paper proposes a single, upper-level context ontology for smart environments, encompassing the important factors for context and smart environments in a logical and consistent manner. The ontology can be used to model context across smart environment domains and platforms with very few, if any, domain ontologies needing to be added. Multiple levels of context information within a smart environment can be modeled in the ontology and the descriptions shall aid in the abstraction level and representation of the context information.

The structure of this paper is as follows: Section two introduces the key elements associated with context and smart environments. Section three presents the methodology undertaken and describes the resulting ontology. Section four describes the context generation in the form of a case study across different environments prior to presenting the conclusions and future work in Section five.

2   Characterization of Context in a Smart Environment

Before an upper-level context ontology for smart environments can be created, the main elements associated with context and smart environments have to be considered. This section details the characterization of context in smart environments, highlighting the elements which form a concept dictionary. These elements are then used to create the ontological context model which is described in Section 3. According to [11] the four key components required to facilitate a 'smart' environment, are the ability to monitor, interpret, infer and feedback. These components are closely interrelated and co-dependent on supporting the services of a smart environment. First it is necessary, on a real-time basis, to monitor the current environment and the behaviour of the systems or occupants within it. The next step is to fuse and interpret the multiple features and signals captured from the previous step. Consequently, by inferring any changes or anomalies in the environment, it becomes possible to provide application specific functions to the systems or occupants within it. As well as the four key components required to make any environment smart, there are also a number of core elements which form smart environments. These core elements can be defined as sensors, objects, natural elements, users, temporal and spatial; where the sensors, objects or users are located and in what proximity to each other. Context also has a number of core elements which can be partitioned into person or user, place, object, application and situation [5]. By combining these elements it is possible to define a concept dictionary, as provided in Table 1. This concept dictionary, once defined, can then be used to create an upper-level ontology, by using the entity names as the main classes within the ontology. The ontology can enable the sharing and reuse throughout different smart environments and by other researchers. What follows is a detailed description of the concept dictionary elements.

Table 1. Concept dictionary linking the elements found in context and smart environments

Entity Name	Entity Description	Examples
User	User involved; may interact with the application or other components.	
Object	Objects found in an environment.	"Door", "chair", "kettle".
Sensors	Sensing Devices existing in smart environments, enabling the key elements in making an environment 'smart'.	"Actuator", "pressure sensor", "contact sensor", "pulse oximeter".
Location	Place, which may be used to characterize the whereabouts of a user, object or situation.	"Meeting room", "car", "kitchen", "N 12° 45.736′, W 98° 20.924′", "mountain".
Natural Element	Natural elements which may be present within a smart environment	"Light", "humidity", "sound", "wind strength".
Application	A user interacts with an application. The application may provide them with information.	"Assistive" – provides user with help with activities of daily living (ADLs).
Event	The situation of an entity (user, object, place and even application).	"Occupied", "Making a cup of tea", "weak".
Temporal	Temporal information; may be denoted as a time point or a series of events.	"12:01:22 16/04/2013"

The *User* entity is central to context and is regarded as the main operator in a smart environment, triggering devices and creating context information which can then be used to provide the user with feedback in real-time, if required. *User* entity subclasses are optional and a user does not just refer to a human-being, but could also refer to a mechanical user. Whilst *User* could be considered a moveable object, it is kept separate in this ontology, to enable easier alignment with other existing ontologies. The *Object* entity is any object found in a smart environment and can be further divided into *fixed*, *moveable* or *sensing devices* as all objects can be categorized by these three subclasses. Fixed objects may include fixtures and fittings, whereas moveable objects are objects which can be moved i.e., household kettle or chair. Sensing devices are explained further in the following sensors section. The reason that the object element has been sub-categorized into fixed, moveable and sensing device is to make it easier for someone to keep track of an entity. A moveable object's location may change, but could be located based on the proximity to fixed objects. Some objects have a transient location, whilst others have a fixed location. The *Sensors* entity is a variety of sensing devices which are located within smart environments and can encompass actuators through to specialist vital signs monitoring equipment. Sensors are used to facilitate the key elements required to make an environment 'smart'. Depending on the types of sensors, a variety of outputs may exist, this should be considered when modeling this element. This leads on to the *Location* class, which has the subclasses *internal* and *external*; these can have a further number of subclasses, making it quite substantial. Due to this being such a vast class, the very high-level modeling of it deals with the subclasses within internal and external locations, where natural elements may be a defining factor in regards to location choice, events and application information required. *Location* refers in this instance to any place or location which may be used to not only characterize the whereabouts of an entity but also which is present within a smart environment.

The *Natural Element* class defines any natural elements which may be found in a smart environment. These elements may be environmental constraints and can affect the location and any event which may be associated with it. The natural elements could also be used to help establish if an event is taking place, i.e., noise levels could be used to establish conversation taking place. The *Application* class has subclasses broken down in to *assistive*, *analytical* and *augmented*, depending on what the application is used for and what information is to be provided. Finally there is the *Event* entity which relates to events or a series of activities forming events which may be taking place. Subclass examples may include *MeetingRoomActivity or TravelActivity*. Fig. 1 below shows the concept taxonomies for these entities.

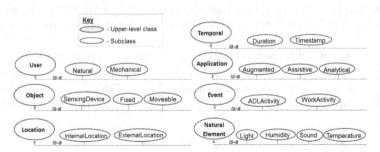

Fig. 1. This figure shows the concept taxonomies for context in a smart environment

To provide some context within which this presented concept can be discussed, two scenarios are considered; a smart home setting and a car commute to work. The smart home would be characterized using *User, Sensor, Object*, multiple *Location*s within it, *Event, Temporal, Application* and some *Natural elements* relating to the applications. These could all be used to provide the occupant with application specific functions pertaining to their activities of daily living. In regards to the second scenario, the user's commute would be tracked via GPS. The characterizing elements would be the same as the first scenario, with the exception of user. *User* would be modeled, but may be connected to a domain ontology which has information relating to the user's preferences. These preferences could be used to regulate the temperature within the car and the sound preferences for the radio. A domain ontology captures domain specific knowledge and whilst context and smart environment domain aspects are covered in the upper-level ontology, aspects such as health are not.

3   Ontological Context Modeling

The conceptual models discussed in Section two were used to create an ontology, adopting a top-down approach that was followed by creating the object and data properties, illustrated below in Fig. 2.

Fig. 2. An illustration of the upper-level ontology as viewed within Protégé [16]; on the left the parent and child classes, top right the data properties and bottom right the object properties

The data and object properties are used to link classes to other classes or instances creating relationships, as shown in Fig. 3 below; the majority of subclasses have been removed from this diagram to create a simplified view. Table 2 shows an example of the relationships with the data and object properties within the upper-level ontology.

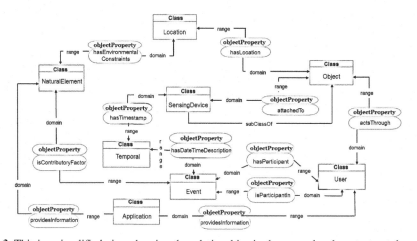

Fig. 3. This is a simplified view showing the relationships in the upper-level context ontology

Table 2. The properties and examples which are associated with each class entity

Class	Properties	Filler Type	Example values
User	actsThrough	Object	Cup/Door/Sensor
	hasLocation	Location	Kitchen/Garden/Car
	isParticipantIn	Event	Eating/Meeting
Object	hasLocation	Location	Office/Corridor
SensingDevice	hasTimestamp	Timestamp	2013-09-05 21:00:09
Event	hasDateTimeDescription	Duration	12:01:00 – 13:15:05
	hasParticipant	User	Staff/Occupant/Machine
Natural Element	isContributoryFactor	Event	Gardening/Dining
	providesInformation	Application	ADLassistance/Calendar
Application	providesInformation	User	Carer/Secretary/Management

Different investigators model context in different ways and even though they may model the same domain [7, 8], the name choices and relationship details may vary; each context model could therefore be regarded as being designer specific. It is hoped that the model presented in this paper has been created in a manner which is intuitive, easy to understand and use by other researchers, due to incorporating the main elements associated with context as defined by Dey. The ontology is currently set up with the instances located within the Smart Environments Research Group at the University of Ulster [14]. The ontology itself is not meant to be exhaustive, but usable in smart environments with the ability to add more information in the form of subclasses, properties or instances, as required. The characteristics from Section two are modeled in an upper-level ontology which can be combined with domain ontologies. The domain ontologies will vary depending on what is being modeled. A domain ontology example which could be connected to the upper-level ontology would be one relating to health. This domain ontology may include vital signs, a user profile, health profile and preferences and could be connected to the *User* element of the upper-level ontology to provide more information relating to the task in hand. The understanding and reuse of this ontology in a clear manner should be enabled due to the key and core elements of context and smart environments being used throughout.

4   Context Generation

The ontological context model discussed in previous sections can be used in the generation of context. For some wider aspects, a domain ontology may need to be attached, but for generic context in smart environments, this is not the case. For instance, it is possible to model a user throughout their daily routine, moving through different environment locations and partaking in different events. If additional information was required though, i.e., their interests or health profiles, then these could be added from domain ontologies relating to these two areas. Sensors within a smart environment when activated capture the details of an activity. These signals are received, stored and then enriched by the ontology which adds semantic metadata to the raw sensor data, generating the potential to obtain high-level context from low-level data.

To illustrate the generation of context and use of the model, the following short vignette outlines a cross-domain example. Sarah lives in a smart home and regularly competes at the weekends. Before leaving the house she puts on an under-garment that has embedded sensors, alongside a watch that is able to receive the sensor activation and monitor her vital signs. Throughout the day, this provides her with feedback which she can use to tailor her training assessments. The information captured is also used to monitor Sarah's temperature and if she is over-heating it initiates a cooling system within the under-garment to keep her at an optimum temperature and enhance her performance throughout the day. Once Sarah has finished competing her watch detects when she is back in her car and heading home, through the use of GPS signals. This information is used by her watch to instruct her home heating system to activate and sets the heating at the ideal temperature for her return home. The upper-level context model can be used to model Sarah, the devices in her house, the location of Sarah or items within the house, and the natural elements such as temperature, lighting and sound. The event related to the radiators can be modeled along with temporal information and application related information which resides in the watch. A domain ontology can be imported into this ontology which may model Sarah's preferences, vital signs, health implications and personal information. Some of this information may include her 'normal' vital signs profile and upper and lower level rates, which could be used to provide the watch with important information. By connecting a domain ontology to the upper-level ontology in this case could maintain a range of users from the same household being modeled for the same activities, but with the applications reacting in different ways based on the extra information. Most of the information from within Sarah's house is low-level data, but with the use of semantic metadata from ontologies, the information can be converted into high-level context enabling understanding, reasoning and inference to take place.

5   Conclusion and Future Work

Smart environments can exist in a large number of settings. The context information within smart environments is used for understanding and providing feedback. This paper proposed an upper-level context ontology for smart environments meeting a range of challenges that were highlighted in Section two. These challenges included creating an upper-level context ontology which covered all the main aspects of smart environments and context, enabling the use across domains and platforms. An ontology was developed which could model context in a smart environment in a way which was concise and logical. The ontology models the main aspects associated with context within smart environments, incorporating multiple levels of context information in an intuitive manner. These multiple levels of context information can be denoted as a situation. The descriptions aid in the level of abstraction and how the context is represented. By using this ontology within our framework [12], the dissemination of data across various platforms, domains, applications and among researchers is possible. Also due to some of the entities matching common entities across previous ontologies, i.e., *Location*, *User* and *Devices*, it should be easier to align this ontology with previously existing ones through the Protégé import tool. This would also ensure all entities relevant to context are included within any past or future ontologies. The future work includes making the upper-level ontology available for other researchers to use and deploying the ontology in a number of real-time scenarios. These scenarios incorporate activities throughout a smart home, intelligent meeting room and offices.

References

1. Weiser, M., Gold, R., Brown, J.S.: The origins of ubiquitous computing research at PARC in the late 1980s. J. IBM Systems 38, 693–696 (1999)
2. Bauer, J.: Identification and Modeling of Contexts for Different Information Scenarios in Air Traffic, Diplomarbeit (2003)
3. Truong, H., Manzoor, A., Dustdar, S.: On modeling, collecting and utilizing context information for disaster responses in pervasive environments. In: Proceedings of the First International Workshop on Context-Aware Software Technology and Applications, pp. 25–28 (2009)
4. Balavalad, K.B., Manvi, S.S., Sutagundar, A.V.: Context-Aware Computing in Wireless Sensor Networks. In: International Conference on Advances in Recent Technologies in Communication and Computing, pp. 514–516. IEEE (2009)
5. Dey, A.K.: Understanding and Using Context. J. Personal and Ubiquitous Computing 5(1), 4–7 (2001)
6. Russomanno, D.J., Kothari, C., Thomas, O.: Sensor Ontologies: From Shallow to Deep Models. In: 37th Southeastern Symposium on System Theory (2005)
7. Hsien-Chou, L., Chien-Chih, T.: A RDF and OWL-Based Temporal Context Reasoning Model for Smart Home. J. Information Technology 6, 1130–1138 (2007)
8. Ni, H., Zhou, X., Yu, Z., Miao, K.: OWL-Based Context-Dependent Task Modeling and Deducing. In: 1st International Workshop on Smart Homes for TeleHealth, pp. 846–851. IEEE, Canada (2007)
9. Shih, F., Narayanan, V., Kuhn, L.: Enabling Semantic Understanding of Situations from Contextual Data in a Privacy-Sensitive Manner. Activity Context Representation 11, 68–73 (2011)
10. Hervás, R., Bravo, J., Fontecha, J.: A context model based on ontological languages: a proposal for information visualization. J. Univers. Comput. Sci. 16(12), 1539–1555 (2010)
11. Chen, L., Nugent, C.D., Wang, H.: A Knowledge-Driven Approach to Activity Recognition in Smart Homes. IEEE Transactions on Knowledge and Data Engineering (2010)
12. McAvoy, L.M., Chen, L., Donnelly, M.: An Ontology-based Context Management System for Smart Environments. In: The Sixth International Conference on Mobile Ubiquitous Computing, Systems, Services and Technologies, pp. 18–23 (2012)
13. W3C Semantic Sensor Network Incubator Group,
   http://www.w3.org/2005/Incubator/ssn/
14. SERG: Smart Environments Research Group,
   http://scm.ulster.ac.uk/~scmresearch/SERG
15. Gu, T., Wang, X.H., Pung, H.K., Zhang, D.Q.: An ontology-based context model in intelligent environments. In: Proceedings of Communication Networks and Distributed Systems Modeling and Simulation Conference, pp. 270–275 (2004)
16. The Protégé Ontology Editor and Knowledge Acquisition System,
   http://protege.stanford.edu/

Improving University Quality of Services through Mobile Devices: The Case of the Technological University of Panama

Alex Sanchez, Lilia Muñoz, and Vladimir Villarreal

Emergent Computational Technologies Research Lab (GITCE)
Technological University of Panama, David, Chiriquí, Panamá
{alex.sanchez1,lilia.munoz,vladimir.villarreal}@utp.ac.pa

Abstract. Society evolves at a rapid pace, integrates the latest everydays life technologies and squeezes the benefits of innovation. At the same time, universities follow these same steps, creating great possibilities by providing better services and formation as the result of this evolution. In this sense, mobile devices have become an instrument that allows a new way of interacting with the university services. This article describes the development of an app-tool called "*UTPMovil*". This tool allows access to the University general information, as well as events, book consultation, schedules and others. "*UTPMovil*" has been developed for the Android platform. This project seeks to be at the forefront of technology hence providing a tool, using mobile devices, for the use of students, teachers and administrators of the Technological University of Panama.

Keywords: web services, software development, human computer interaction, mobile users interfaces design.

1   Introduction

The most profound technologies are those that disappear. They weave themselves into the fabric of everyday life until they are indistinguishable from it, said almost two decades ago, American Computer Scientist Mark Weiser [1]. In this sense, the globalization of the economy and the emergence of new information and communication technologies have change the way that XXI century organizations work. In this regard, higher education should be governed by parameters of social competitiveness: it should convey ideas of quality, organization, planning, and decision, among others, enabling them to staying at the forefront in terms of information technologies and communication.

The understanding of software is changing with the proliferation of applications for mobile devices. University education is beginning to take advantage of the integration of applications for mobile devices in the curriculum and designing their own to cover classroom materials. The potential of applications for mobile devices is being demonstrated in hundreds of projects carried out in institutions of higher education, e.g. at the University of Virginia, where WillowTree apps were selected to develop their own iPhone and Android app [2]. With this app you can search for buildings and

G. Urzaiz et al. (Eds.): UCAmI 2013, LNCS 8276, pp. 278–285, 2013.

other facilities on campus, use GPS to locate their location or use augmented reality to customize maps. It also has very useful components for students that allow them to be updated and interact with campus life at all times: live sport events, curiosities, courses, directories, news, student support, alerts, etc [2]. Access to the University of Panama electronic resources from mobile devices is a necessity. To solve this need in the University's community this project has been proposed and consists of the development of a software application for the University management called "UTPMovil", which allows access to the electronic services from different devices and mobile platforms.

2   Mobile Technologies in Universities

It is a fact that mobile technologies have become an integral part of our lives. The growing demand for mobile devices is a sign that these devices are more immersed in our lives. A few years ago, a cell phone was a dedicated device, only for fulfill the function of making calls, today this function has been relegated to be one application within the smart phone that can hold even thousands of different applications [3]. In other words, mobile devices are being used as a mean of information, entertainment and production, leaving computers running the most complex tasks. In this sense, they are increasingly a reality, offering to the user in a same and reduced device, functions of communication and data processing that do much more than simple phone calls or the execution of basic applications. New mobile technologies have revolutionized human life. This has changed the way in which we learn about the world. Being possible of accomplish tasks tha before were computer exclusive of and now are conducted by mobile devices [4].

Some studies have concluded that integration of tablets in the curriculum has helped increase motivation in students and has improved learning experiences. The real innovation of tablets is how they're used [5], how the user interacts with the device giving it a little touch on the screen, in easy and intuitive requiring no manuals nor instructions. In addition, what makes them so powerful for education is that students already use them outside the classroom to download applications, connect to social networks and immerse themselves in informal learning experiences. These new technologies make possible today to speak of e-learning and m-Learning, providing great benefits for the student.

Currently you can see a great growth in smartphones taken during 2010 with an impressive trend reaching 100 million units in the fourth quarter and with upward trend [6]. There are several factors that have led to this change in such a short period of time. A large sector of the population already does not understand social relations without connectivity based on profiles of users and ongoing dialogue with a certain dose of permanent exhibition the other [7]. According to Rodríguez [5] a mobile device must have the following characteristics: portability, technical aspects (processing, connection, memory), integration (ability to connect to various systems to Web) and Internet without limits (access to Internet via WiFi or 3G, GPS). The way they interact with these computer systems must be completely different from the interaction that we carry out with desktops, and communicate with these new devices with an interaction that we could call natural [8], as we use the voice, fingerprints or eyes. Systems of dialogue for interaction with the devices used in ubiquitous computing are included in an area of growing expansion and, within these, the systems applied to educational environments [9]. Other areas apply an overlay-based solution between elements in the network (mobile phones, desktops, servers, etc.) in order to provide a solid and versatile communications platform [10]. The use of mobile devices in educational environments can provide a high level of performance when interacting with other fixed or ubiquitous systems that can be done in offline mode, not being necessary to keep a communication channel busy. This allows optimizing the concurrent access to the central system in which information resides, as well as to reduce connection costs, since we must bear in mind that the end users of our system will be University students, which will be a decisive factor in the success of the implementation and use.

3   Proposed Software Architecture

3.1   Objective of the Proposal

We developed an application for the University services to be used via mobile devices, specifically Android devices. The development of applications for mobile devices is presented as a new alternative to the current approach in the Technological University of Panama.

3.2   Services Offered by the UTPMovil

- Online Library: this component of the application gives students and teachers information about a book without having to go to the library, and fill out a form to find out that this was the book that they did not want.
- Class Schedule: This component can be one of the most used by students of the University, allowing students to know their class hours.
- Cafeteria: this component provides quick and easy access to the daily cafereria menu.
- Student profile: contains a detailed summary of the academic activity of students during the course of his career at the University.
- Sport and Culture: include informative banners and alerts on the device of students, teachers and administrative personnel.
- Events: also includes a history or log of events in general of the University, including an alerting service to inform students, teachers and administrators about upcoming events.

3.3   Previous Study

A survey was applied to a sample of 110 students. A total of 110 respondents, 96% said that they have cell phones and only 4% said that they do not had a cell phone, which tells of the high percentage of the University population that uses a cell phone. Another of the questions of the survey was what operating systems are used in the cell phones, to this question the results obtained were as follows: 40% used Android operating system, 30% Blackberry, 20% is of unknown type of operating system, 6% used iOS and only 4% use Windows Mobile. As for the type of use of respondents, 53% indicated that they use it to access any information and 47% for quick and simple tasks; these in turn prefer computers to perform more complex tasks. At the end of the analysis of the data collected in the surveys, it has come to the conclusions that the application needed to be developed will be under the Android platform. In the next section will explain the development of this app.

3.4   Development of the Application

The scheme described below was used for the development of the application that will support the University. The University services app, UTPMovil, is more than a simple application installed on a Smartphone. UTPMovil uses a client-server application scheme. GAE and Android SDK have been used for rapid development of UTPMovil. The server side is built and supported by Google App Engine (GAE or AE). GAE offers a development environment on which a Web service can be build locally and then publish to be used immediately. In Figure 1 the three essential elements for the application client-server support are shown.

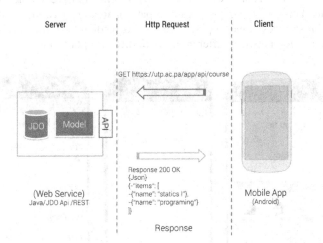

Fig. 1. Model that defines the communication between the mobile device and the central server

- Model: this is probably, between three components, the most important. The model's function defines the behavior of the web service. The model is built using Java Programing Language (JPL) and Java Data Object (JDO) API.
- Database (DB): is an object-oriented or relational database. The database is built based on the model that was previously shown, using annotations for object persistence in java (@).
- API: As well as the Database, the API is built upon the model and persistence objects. The API is responsible for exposing model services to users (client) and persist data that were scored as persistent (@). The API implements a model REST in which available resources are exposed. Through a URI specified for each request to a remote client.

- The http request gives each client access to resources of the Web service. Requests contain the data that is send or remove from the Web service. Data are packaged using JSON (JavaScript Object Notation); it's a lightweight format for data exchange.
- The Client is in charge to make requests to the Web service, as you can see in Figure 1. It has a set of libraries, which are able to speak with the Web service. Libraries make a bridge connection between the Web service and the application that consumes it.

At this point the client is free to persist, use and even destroy, if possible, those resources that the customer wants and in the way most suitable from the point of view of the customer. The most important general characteristic of applications based on the model client/server, is that customers who consume the Web service resources are not tied to a specific platform. The Web service exposes its resources regardless of the technology used by customers. This allows a wide variety of customers using a single application.

The device market is so fragmented that if a development team aims a market goal, the success of its application would be directly related to the success and acceptance that the platform has. That is why most of the developers have adopted this model of development. This new trend has become a pattern among successful developers. This is where Web services come to play their role as mediators of information and allow free communication between different users of different platforms.

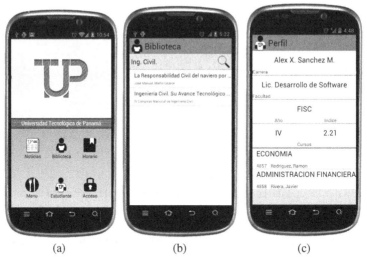

(a)   (b)   (c)

Fig. 2. a. Access to the functions of the application menu, b. library function for book search, c. student profile

The application has the following elements on the main interface (Menu):

- News: access to University news and events.
- Library: provides access to the collection of books that are in the database of the University.
- Schedule: allows students see the schedule of classes.

- Menu: displays the per day menu that will take the University cafeteria.
- Student: allows the access to the student information.
- Access: through this option a user connection to the server is allowed.

The library section, which allows consulting books that currently exist in the database of the library of the University, can be seen in Figure 2b. The student can perform a search for the book of interest and check the book's table of contents. The user pressing the search book button triggers the search sequence. The user presses the button Search to shoot the method (onTouch(View,MotionEvent):boolean). This method is responsible for removing the string entered by the user, packaging the chain within a message and the request sent to the service. Service handler processes the request and asks the service to run a search for books with the string that was extracted from the message. The service executes the search using the string and sends a response to the client, once received the message, the handler informs the customer that received something from the service and executes the method (*loadBookResultSet(ArrayList<ParcelableRow>): void*).

The student can consult class's schedule (Figure 3a). This section shows the subject, the timetable and the classroom location. To make use of all these features, the user must be always registered in the application through a username and password as shown in Figure 3b. The activities of interest of the student and associated career are listed in the activities section (Figure 3 c).

Fig. 3. a. Student agenda, b. the student access to the system, c. news

4   Evaluating the Functionality of the Application

We present an evaluation of the functionality of the developed application. The students use the application and respond some questions about the functionality, usability, design and content. The initial aspects of the evaluation are:

- **Evaluation technique:** a questionnaire was applied where participants complete the specific questions then used the application.

- **Aspects of quality of Access:** We accessed the aspects of content, design and usefulness of the application in end users.
- **Assess of Context:** using the application to review the schedule and others activities.
- **Assess of Population:** the assessment has been applied to 20 people. Undergraduate university population ages range between of 18 to 21.
- **Assess of Time:** the time that the user will take using the application in the defined context. It will take 25 minutes. Then 15 minutes are use to respond to the questionnaire.
- **Scale of Usage:** a Likert Scale from 1 to 5 has been established to evaluate each question, 1 being the lowest evaluation for a question (very much in disagreement) and 5 the highest evaluation (very of agreement).

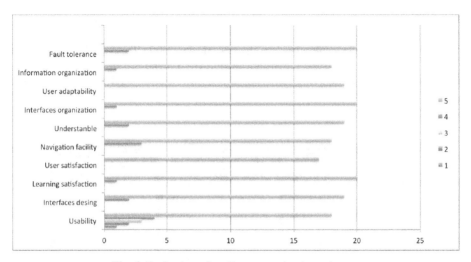

Fig. 4. Evaluation of quality aspects by the end user

5   Conclusions

The generalization of mobile technologies usage in society favours that information reaches a greater number of people and more often; therefore it is presented as an option that increases virtual training. This creates a sense of empowerment in the student, who stands at an important position and activity. The developed application will allow students, teachers and administrative to access information in a more user-friendly and timely manner, contributing to improve the services provided by the University.

Ubiquity and accessibility are very important issues that should be considered, especially when designing new models that can satisfy and improve the experience of our users. These two aspects should be considered for the design of any application. It is important to note that all system oriented to a mobile device, such as a smartphone, should take into account different aspects from traditional application development, and this is due to the technical characteristics of the device. A smartphone is portable, but its ability to data processing, screen resolution does not compare to big computers or laptops. We are currently working on a notes section, a form for teacher's evaluation, and other for academic documents (credits, official notes, plans, studio, etc.).

References

1. Weiser, M.: The Computer of the twenty-first century. Scientific American (1991)
2. Johnson, L., Adams, S., Cummins, M.: The NMC Horizon Report: 2012 Higher Education Edition. Austin, Texas: The New Media Consortium (2012)
3. Fombona, J., Goulão, M., Costales, A.: Using Augmented Reality and m-Learning to Optimize Students Performance in Higher Education. In: 4th World Conference on Educational Sciencies, vol. 46 (2012)
4. Pei-Luen, G., Qin, W., Mei, L.: Using Mobile Communication Techology in High School Education: Motivation. Pressure, and Learning Performance. Computer & Education 50 (2008)
5. Rodríguez, J.: Utilización de dispositivos móviles para la gestión académica de alumnos y docentes de la Universidad de San Martín de Porres (2012)
6. Gimeno., M.: Informe anual sobre el desarrollo de la sociedad de la información en España 2011, 2011 informeeespana (2011),
   http://www.informeeespana.es/docs/eE2011.pdf
7. Morales, E.: La importancia de las redes sociales en la comunicación móvil de los jóvenes españoles en la sociedad de la inmediatez. Revista Prisma Social 8(8) (2012)
8. Abowd, G., Mynatt, E.: Charting Past, "Present and Future Research in Ubiquitous computing". ACM Transactions on Human-Computer Interaction 7(1), 29–58 (2000)
9. Lopez-Cozar, R., Gea, M.: Congreso Interacción Persona Ordenador, Sistema de diálogo ubicuo para entornos educativos (2004)
10. Bravo, J., Villarreal, V., Hervás, R., Urzaiz, G.: Using a Communication Model to Collect Measurement Data through Mobile Devices. Sensors 12, 9253–9272 (2012)

The Internet of Things
to Support Urban Incident Responses

Rodrigo Santos[1], Javier Orozco[1], Sergio F. Ochoa[2], and Roc Meseguer[3]

[1] Department of Electrical Engineering and Computers, IIIE, UNS-CONICET, Argentina
[2] Computer Science Department, Universidad de Chile, Chile
[3] Computer Science Department, Universidad Politécnica de Cataluña, Spain

Abstract. Although the technological components required to implement Internet of Things (IoT) inspired solutions are already available, in most application scenarios it is not clear how to structure and combine them to reach a certain global behavior of a system. This paper proposes an architecture that helps design IoT-based systems that support the first responses during medium-size or large urban incidents. The main components of this architecture are characterized and the interactions between them are also specified. The usefulness of the proposed architecture is illustrated through its hypothetical use in a real urban emergency. The use of this proposal could be extended to other application areas such as security operatives and monitoring of patients at home.

Keywords: Internet of things, human-based wireless sensor networks, emergency response, urban emergencies, ambient intelligence, information sharing.

1   Introduction

Medium and large emergencies affecting urban areas (e.g. train derailments, fires affecting buildings, and accidental or intentional explosions) usually represent a challenging situation for first responders, due the lack of event early detection systems, mechanisms to perform a quick diagnose of the situation, and supporting information to make decisions in a distributed way. The complexity of the urban scenarios usually increases this challenge.

Immediately after an incident occurs, a 911 service receives the emergency calls. The operators receiving these calls has to determine the veracity of the emergency, and then perform a first diagnose of the incident (type, size and complexity), using the information provided by the people [12]. Based on such a diagnosis, the operators dispatch resources (mainly firefighters, police officers, and paramedics) to perform the first response process. The diagnosis and dispatching processes can take several minutes.

The response process involves resources transportation (e.g. fire trucks, ambulances, police vehicles, and first responders) that have to arrive quickly to the emergency place. The reaction time and the efficiency in the first response process are crucial to reduce the number of victims in an emergency [12], [14]. In [3] it is proved that reducing the first response time by 1 minute, correlates to a six percent difference

G. Urzaiz et al. (Eds.): UCAmI 2013, LNCS 8276, pp. 286–293, 2013.
© Springer International Publishing Switzerland 2013

in the number of lives saved in car crashes. These numbers are probably representative of other urban incidents.

The coordination of the emergency response activities represent a major challenge for first responders due to several reasons: (1) civilians usually go to the incident place to see what is happening, obstructing thus the resources transportation and response process, (2) services in the area tends to collapse (e.g. communication and transportation) or they are temporarily suspended for safety reasons (e.g. energy, gas and water), (3) there is little or no supporting information to make decisions and coordinate the efforts among the participants, and (4) the available radio channels used by first responders (e.g. firefighters, police officers, paramedic, and emergency managers) are not enough to coordinate the response activities. Therefore, the regular pattern in these situations is the improvisation of the first response process [10], [11].

This paper shows how regular sensing systems deployed in the affected areas can be used to help improve the efficiency and effectiveness of first response processes after medium-size or large urban incidents. The proposal is based on the Internet of Things (IoT) paradigm [4] and uses a Human-centric Wireless Sensor Network (HWSN) [13] to provide some intelligence to the response process. Particularly, an architecture that integrates information providers and consumers is described, indicating how to support the shared information flow among the participants. The use of the proposed architecture is illustrated analyzing a real first response process, which addressed a train crash happened at the *Once train station*, in Buenos Aires city (Argentina) in February 22nd, 2012. The article analyzes how the proposed architecture could have helped improve the reaction time and response activities after such an incident.

Next section presents and discusses the related work. Section 3 describes the proposed architecture. Section 4 exemplifies, using a real urban emergency situation, how the architecture could have contributed to reduce the incident impact. Section 5 presents the conclusions and the future work.

2   Related Work

The use of mobile devices, wireless sensor networks, and even the use of IoT to support first responses in urban incidents, has been addressed by several researchers. Concerning the incident detection, White et al. [16] proposed an automatic mechanism for traffic accident detection and notification using smart-phones. It delivers early alerts to particular emergency centers and thus accelerates the response process. Similarly, Liu et al. [8] use cyberphysical elements (called intelligent guards) deployed in the physical infrastructure to deliver early alarms when an extreme event affects a certain urban area.

Concerning the support for the first response process, Martin-Campillo et al. [9] propose a RFID-based solution to tag injured people, indicating their health condition before to deliver them to a hospital. Several researchers propose the use of mobile ad hoc networks, usually implemented using Wi-Fi, to provide communications support in disaster areas [1], [11], [15]. Ochoa and Santos [13] go a step forward and introduce the concept of Human-centric Wireless Sensor Networks (HWSN). They also show how HWSN-based solutions can be used to increase the information availability in the affected area.

Zhang et al. [18] describes an IoT-inspired platform, which was designed to support emergency management systems. Although such a proposal is quite general, it allows seeing how the several components participating in the process can interact among them to capture or disseminate shared information.

Yang et al. [17] propose a modified "task-technology fit" approach to help understand how the IoT technology can enhance the urban first response activities. This approach does not indicate how to design IoT solutions to support these operations, but it allows us to realize the role of IoT technology in urban emergencies.

Although the previous proposals are interesting and contribute to improve the effectiveness of the first response process, none of them presents an architecture that indicates the type of components participating in the solution, the role played by each of them, and the way in which the shared information is captured and disseminated using these components. This article proposes an architecture inspired in the IoT paradigms, which uses a HWSN to determine components roles, and also the support required for information dissemination and fusion. Next section describes the proposed architecture, its main components and interactions among them.

3   The IoT-Inspired Architecture

Internet of Things infrastructures allow data and services integration among smart objects (e.g. mobile robots), sensing devices and human beings, using different but interoperable communication protocols [6]. Following this definition, Fig. 1 shows the architecture proposed for systems that support first responders after medium-size or large urban incidents. The architecture involves four layers that implement the separation of concerns: *sensing, communication, information persistence* and *application (i.e. usage)*.

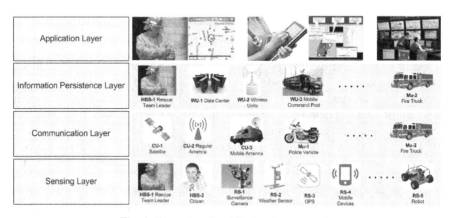

Fig. 1. Hierarchy of architectural components

The *sensing layer* is responsible to capture information from the field, which will be then used to support the decision making and coordination activities. Two types of components contribute to perform this activity: *regular sensors* (RS) and *human-based sensors* (HBS). The first ones (e.g. weather and motion sensors, or video-camera) capture information from the environment and transmit it through a component of the communication layer. The HBS perform the same activity, however these sensors are people that also uses his senses to capture additional the information from the environment. Using such information, and eventually the data given by regular sensors, the HBS produce knowledge that represents the current value of a certain context variable (e.g. the emergency type or size). Although the HBS are not accurate, they represent our best choice when the observed variable is not measurable by a regular sensor.

The HBS uses a mobile device that allows him to share that knowledge with others and also to sense context variables (see the sensing layer in Fig. 1), e.g. the presence of other responders in the area by using an opportunistic network (oppnet). It is assumed that every component participating in this solution has a network interface that allows it to communicate with others through a digital network interface.

The *communication layer* is responsible to provide interaction capability to components participating in the first response process. Because there is not a universal network interface, this layer is implemented as a set of heterogeneous solutions, hopefully linked through communication bridges (Fig. 2a). Typically two types of communication solutions are used in these scenarios: *infrastructure-based* and *ad hoc* networks. The first one uses the regular communication infrastructure (i.e. satellites, cellular antennas and wired networks) and also mobile antennas to communicate the resources in the affected area, with remote components (e.g. emergency offices, data centers, remote experts, government agencies). We call *communication units* (CU) to these components that link resources inside the affected area with those that are outside the emergency place (see Fig. 1). Thus, these CUs allow the remote gathering and analysis of information (e.g. through Internet) that comes from sensors deployed in the emergency area (Fig. 2b).

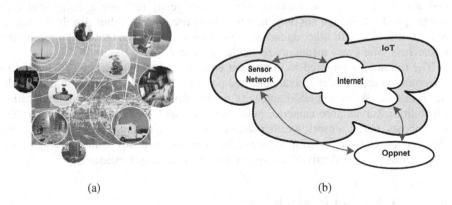

(a)   (b)

Fig. 2. Communication Infrastructure

Concerning the support based on ad hoc networks, its role is to provide and enhance the communication links in the field, increasing thus the information availability in that area and reducing the improvisation during the response process [10], [11], [13]. The use of opportunistic networks (*oppnet*) is highly recommended because they can work although the regular communication infrastructure is not available. An oppnet is a peer-to-peer application-oriented mesh, able to support ad hoc interactions among stationary and mobile units that are physically close; e.g. sensors, human-based sensors and communication units deployed in the affected area. The oppnets are built in the application layer and they use a "store and forward" paradigm for transmitting messages [7]. The nodes participating in these networks can act as gateways bridging oppnets and regular Internet channels, allowing thus services integration and information exchange according to the IoT paradigm.

Provided that oppnets have quite short communication threshold, a special type of mobile node helps connect disjoint networks, allowing thus asynchronous communication among resources in the field. These mobile nodes, known as "mules" (Mu), are typically implemented through computing devices installed on police vehicles, fire trucks and ambulances (see the communication layer in Fig. 1).

The *information persistence layer* is responsible to store and share the supporting information, allowing participants to coordinate their activities and make better and on-time decisions. Several types of components can play this role, for instance the HBS, Mu and Witness Units (WU). The WU are buffers used on-demand by other nodes to store shared information. These WU also act as information gateway, particularly if they are accessible through Internet.

Finally the *application layer* is responsible to provide a direct and useful service to the end-users, e.g. first responders, incident commanders, emergency managers, government agents, hospital personnel and civilians (regular drivers). These applications make use of the services provided by the rest of the proposed architecture.

The role, behavior and services of every component type described in the architecture are clearly delimited. Therefore they can be formalized in a computable language, and then used with several purposes; for instance to evaluate vulnerability of a certain urban area, design response plans during a preparedness or response phase, and also to learn after an incident. Several emergency response agencies can take advantage of it to design not only their own response processes, but also the coordination of activities with other agencies, which is a recurrent limitation reported by the researchers after every medium-size and large incident.

The technology required to implement emergency response solutions adhering to the proposed architecture is available, and part of it is already deployed in many public spaces; i.e. Wi-Fi and GSM antennas, mobile devices with several communication capabilities, surveillance cameras, public speakers and displays, remotely controlled semaphores, traffic sensors, weather sensors, and ad hoc communication and positioning services. Only considering these regular components it is possible to design solutions to make more effective the response process to an urban incident.

4 Application Example

In order to exemplify the usefulness of this proposal, we will analyze some aspects of the response process conducted by first response task forces on February 22nd, 2012, after a train crash at a central station in Buenos Aires, Argentina. After 8:30 AM a train crashed with the end of line at the *Once station*. The accident leave fifty two dead people and over seven hundred injured.

The Once station is the third one in importance in Buenos Aires. It is the head line for a very large rail network that goes to the west of the city. Only 3 km away from the city center, this station is a hub for buses, subway and other train lines. Every day one million people go through this hub for transportation connections (train-bus-subway) or as their final station.

When the accident took place, the diagnose process involved various minutes due the complexity of the physical scenario, and it began when the first firefighters company arrived to the place. Although the accident was recorded by various surveillance cameras (i.e. a regular sensor), neither automatic alarms were delivered nor video records were shared with the emergency centers that could have helped to reduce the reaction time. Analyzing the accident video records it is possible to estimate the size and type of the emergency in approximately one minute. Therefore, sharing this video with the proper emergency center could have allowed triggering a quick response and saving more lives.

Once known the first diagnose and according to the protocol, the emergency center (i.e. the end-user) performed a formal dispatch of emergency resources, particularly firemen and ambulances. At that time the traffic and communication in the area were collapsed, therefore the dispatched resources (many of them can be considered HBS) had several problems to arrive to the emergency place, find the place assigned to park the emergency vehicles (depending on the role played by each resource type), find the incident commander (i.e., a HBS) and the command post, and get basic information about the emergency.

In the response process participated two helicopters, 110 ambulances, 55 police vehicles (over a hundred policemen) and 6 firefighting companies (over three hundred firemen). Fifteen hospitals received the injured people (a total of 676 people according to the official report [5]). The ambulances started transporting these people to the three closest hospitals. Once these hospitals were overcrowded, other options were taken. However, being this situation visible for the ambulances was a complex task that required a considerable time. Therefore, many ambulances tried to leave injured people in more than one hospital until find one able to receive them. The first paramedic (i.e. HBS) arriving to a collapsed hospital could record the hospital status in one or most witness units, and thus other ambulances accessing such an information can know where exactly to transport the people.

After the first 12 hours, no lists of dead and injured people were available. Therefore, relatives and friends of potential victims were asking in different hospitals and at the city morgue for hours, interfering with an already complex response process. The hospital managers (i.e. HBS) could have made public the list of injured people located there, e.g. through a Web portal or in a witness unit, allowing thus that civilians (also HBS) perform their searches quickly and without jeopardizing the response activities.

The search and rescue process took all day, and at the end there was still a missing person, who was found 48 hours later. He was a young man who got into the train 20 minutes before the crash and that was travelling in a compartment were passengers are not allowed to be. The rescuers went over the spot without noticing his presence.

This situation could be overcame due the public transportation system uses a contactless smart card, called SUBE (that stands for Electronic Ticket Unified System, in Spanish), which identifies each user. Making a small extension to the current infrastructure it is possible to know the number of people in the train, and also the identity and location of each passenger. If this information is shared through a witness unit, then it is possible to accelerate the response process, triggering parallel procedures that help reduce the damage. It also would have allowed an early detection of the missing person. An extra support for the people location could also be obtained using localization mechanisms based on cellular phones (with the WAP-OTA protocol).

Concerning communication support in the affected area, there is not clear information in the emergency reports, except that the telephone networks (wired and wireless) collapsed immediately after the incident and that were down for various hours. There is not report of the use of mobile antennas and only VHF radio systems seems to be used to support communication in the field. This situation is aligned with many others large incidents affecting urban areas [9], [11], [15].

The use of sensor networks, for example focused on traffic control, could have helped to change the frequency of the traffic lights when an emergency vehicle is approaching, or route the regular vehicles toward safe areas, where they do not interfere with the response process. Moreover, oppnet-based applications could be used to coordinate the response activities in the field and share valuable information to make local decisions. Although the technology to implement IoT-based solutions that support urban emergency responses is already available, there are no clear guidelines about the role played by each component type, how to integrate them, and how to design the behavior of an integral solution. In that sense, we hope that the proposed architecture and components characterizations contribute to reach such a goal.

5   Conclusions and Future Work

Urban incidents happen frequently in large cities and affect many people. Providing a fast an effective response process is critical to save lives and reduce the impact of these incidents on the civil property. This paper presents an architecture that helps design and implement IoT-based solutions that support first responses in urban areas. The proposal is particularly focused on large response processes, where many information producers and consumers need to be linked, and the information flow should be maximized. The architecture considers heterogeneous participants and communication networks. The example presented in Section 4 allows us to show that IoT-based solutions could play a key role in the improvement of responses to urban incidents.

Provided the role, behavior and services of the components considered in the architecture are clearly delimited, they can be modeled and formalized using a computable language. Thus, several IoT-based solutions adhering to the proposed architecture can be modeled, simulated and evaluated from a theoretical point of view, and then implemented when the designers are sure about the solution capabilities and limitations.

The use of a formal model for integrating the proposed components would also help evaluate vulnerability of urban areas and design coordination protocols between emergency response agencies. The next steps in this initiative are particularly focused on formalizing the architecture components and their interactions using a modeling computable language.

Acknowledgments. This work has been supported by Fondecyt (Chile), Grant No. 1120207 and by Spanish DELFIN grant TIN2010-20140-C03-01.

References

1. Aldunate, R., Ochoa, S.F., Pena-Mora, F., Nussbaum, M.: Robust Mobile Ad-hoc Space for Collaboration to Support Disaster Relief Efforts Involving Critical Physical Infrastructure. ASCE Journal of Computing in Civil Engineering 20(1), 13–27 (2006)
2. Braunstein, B., Trimble, T., Mishra, R., Manoj, B., Lenert, L., Rao, R.: Challenges in Using Distributed Wireless Mesh Networks in Emergency Response. In: Proc. of ISCRAM 2006, NJ, USA, May 13-17 (2006)
3. Evanco, W.: The impact of rapid incident detection on freeway accident fatalities. Technical Report, Center for Information Systems, McLean, Virginia, USA (1996)
4. Feki, M.A., Kawsar, F., Boussard, M., Trappeniers, L.: The Internet of Things: The Next Technological Revolution. IEEE Computer 46(2), 24–25 (2013)
5. Government of the Buenos Aires city. Official Report of the Train Accident in Sarmiento Line,
   http://buenosaires.gob.ar/2012-02-22-accidente-tren-sarmiento (last visit: September 15, 2013) (in Spanish)
6. IoT European Research Cluster. Internet of Things Strategic Research Roadmap. Cluster SRA (2011)
7. Lilien, L., Kamal, Z., Bhuse, V., Gupta, A.: Opportunistic networks: the concept and research challenges in privacy and security. In: Proc. of the Int. Workshop on Research Challenges in Security and Privacy for Mobile and Wireless Networks, Miami, USA (2006)
8. Liu, J.W.S., Chi-Sheng, S., Chu, E.T.-H.: Cyberphysical Elements of Disaster-Prepared Smart Environments. IEEE Computer 46(2), 69–75 (2013)
9. Martin-Campillo, A., Martí, R., Yoneki, E., Crowcroft, J.: Electronic triage tag and opportunistic networks in disasters. In: Proc. of the Special Workshop on Internet and Disasters, pp. 6:1–6:10. ACM Press, New York (2011)
10. Mendonça, D.: Decision Support for Improvisation in Response to Extreme Events: Learning from the Response to the 2001 World Trade Center Attack. In: Decision Support Systems, vol. 43(3), pp. 952–967 (2007)
11. Monares, A., Ochoa, S.F., Pino, J.A., Herskovic, V., Rodriguez-Covili, J., Neyem, A.: Mobile Computing in Urban Emergency Situations: Improving the Support to Firefighters in the Field. Expert Systems with Applications 38(2), 1255–1267 (2011)
12. Monares, A., Ochoa, S.F., Pino, J.A., Herskovic, V.: Improving the Initial Response Process in Urban Emergencies. In: Proc. of the IEEE CSCWD 2012, Wuhan, China, May 23-25 (2012)
13. Ochoa, S.F., Santos, R.: Human-centric Wireless Sensor Networks to Improve Information Availability During Urban Search and Rescue Activities. Inf. Fusion (in Press) (to appear)
14. Ozbay, K., Xiao, W., Jaiswal, G., Bartin, B., Kachroo, P., Baykal-Gursoy, M.: Evaluation of incident management strategies and technologies using an integrated traffic/incident management simulation. World Rev. of Int. Transp. Research 2(2/3), 155–186 (2009)
15. Panitzek, K., Schweizer, I., Bönning, T., Seipel, G., Mühlhäuser, M.: First responder communication in urban environments. Int. J. Mob. Netw. Des. Innov. 4(2), 109–118 (2012)
16. White, J., Thompson, C., Turner, H., Dougherty, B., Schmidt, D.C.: Wreckwatch: Automatic traffic accident detection and notification with smartphones. Mobile Network Applications 16(3), 285–303 (2011)
17. Yang, L., Yang, S., Plotnick, L.: How the internet of things technology enhances emergency response operations. Technol. Forecasting and Social Change (August 2012)
18. Zhang, J., Qi, A.: The application of Internet of things (IoT) in emergency management system in China. In: Proc. of the IEEE Conf. on Technol. for Homeland Security, November 8-10, pp. 139–142 (2010)

Mobile System Surveillance for Vehicular Pollutants Emission, Based on Wi-Fi Ad-Hoc Network

Amadeo José Argüelles Cruz, Mario Matamoros de Luis,
Paulina Elizabeth Moreno Aguilera, and Cornelio Yáñez Márquez

Instituto Politécnico Nacional, Centro de Investigación en Computación
mmatamorosd0700@ipn.mx, {jamadeo,pmoreno_a12,cyanez}@cic.ipn.mx

Abstract. The prototype described in this paper intend to be a tool to correlate different ubiquitous computing devices such as vehicle embedded systems and mobile devices, such as smart phones, to deal with air pollution. This paper presents the results acquired from a prototype based on an embedded system platform and a mobile device using Wi-Fi communication. In general, the objective of the prototype is send data from an automotive gas analyzer to a mobile device by means of an embedded platform based on FPGA, essentially to notify to the vehicle owner about the behavior of the car in terms of pollutant emissions. The results of the masurements are processed and compared with the Mexican Official Standards to finally show them to the user by means of a mobile device. We use a back-end FPGA platform to process data banks from the gas analyzer, and a Wi-Fi IEEE 802.11 compliant module to transmit the results to a front-end Android based smart phone which presents the results to the user. Due to the acquired data and results are handled as in Mexican Official automotive emission test, security and communication protocols are an essential part of this prototype.

Keywords: Wireless communications, mobile devices, automotive emissions, Android OS, air pollution, Wi-Fi, security network, TCP/IP, ad-hoc network, embedded systems, FPGA.

1 Introduction

Many cities around the world are facing multiple and significant challenges regarding pollution, and particularly, air pollution is a special issue that affects importantly urban areas where transportation is a main activity. Around the world, there are diverse initiatives to resolve or to mitigate that situation, for instance, the creation of local environment regulations. In despite of this, some of those regulations are surpassed because of factors such as an accelerated population growth, or simply are being overlooked. Yet more important, uncontrolled air pollution incises not only globally in the environment but also directly in health, causing unsuitable conditions for daily life. As a special case of study, but not the only one, Mexico City has serious concerns about improving air quality; explicitly regarding automotive tailpipe exhaust pollutant emissions [12]. In this city, the vehicle emissions inspection and

G. Urzaiz et al. (Eds.): UCAmI 2013, LNCS 8276, pp. 294–302, 2013.

maintenance program [13] is also called *Verificación Vehicular* (VV) which is based on Mexican Official Standards (NOM) NOM-047-SEMARNAT-1999 and NOM-041-SEMARNAT-2006 [1]. Although the VV applies as an individual test per se, i.e., per vehicle, under several situations the owner is not informed about specific results and statistics that may be useful to take actions related with the vehicle performance.

The presence and use of the information and communication technologies (ICTs) has permeated the way society communicates and share information. On the one hand, the accomplishments in mobile communication in the last decade – with their connectivity, ubiquity and versatility, among other characteristics – provides powerful tools at the front-end, delivering solutions in the monitoring and use of technological resources. On the other hand, ubiquitous technologies such as embedded systems, available in many devices located in houses, offices, manufacturing among other, are the back-end part used for services that require the use of spatially distributed autonomous sensors, for example, for environment care and monitoring applications [19][15]. Nowadays vehicles are an important example of ubiquitous and embedded computing whereas mobile devices, especially smart devices, are also samples of user-machine adaptability, data share and interconnectivity. Indeed, the incorporation and combination of ICTs as a part of complex systems which, for example, aims to urban transportation, can be used as a tool to improve the experience of the user during daily life activities [14][18].

This paper describes the operation of a prototype system used for the transfer of data related with vehicular pollutant emission levels using Wi-Fi wireless communication technology. This prototype aims to the integration of an automotive embedded system and mobile devices to conform an information system for the user/car owner. The transmitted data is shown by means of mobile app which informs about the emission levels of the vehicle using non-technical language. The roles of the computational blocks involved in the development of this prototype are the following: 1) FPGA platform acquire the data from an automotive gas analyzer to process it, 2) Wi-Fi module transmit the results from FPGA and the searches a connection to mobile device, 3) the mobile device receives and compares the data bank with the Mexican Official Standards to finally display the results through an app. The general idea of this prototype is to apply technologies into a specific scenario, automobile-user-smart device, to collaborate with the mitigation of issues like air pollution [20]. Moreover the objective is not only reinforcing the idea toward the creation and maintenance of intelligent infrastructure for Smart Cities [17], but also to enhance the quality of life under ubiquitous computing paradigm as a tool.

This article is organized as follows. In section 2, we review the main idea and its integration with ubiquitous computing; also technical specifications and information related with the development of the prototype. In section 3, we describe the gas measurements with the gas analyzer, the FPGA processing and some results after data transmission. Finally in section 4, we provide considerations in terms of ubiquitous computing and technical specs (databank length, processing, and communication, among others).

2   Materials and Methods

In order to meet the emissions standards demanded by governments around the world, manufacturers of gasoline-propelled vehicles have equipped this units with emission controls systems such as three-way catalyst and exhaust gas sensors [2] [3]. In despite of this, regular maintenance and inspections are required in order to identify and fix problems related to mechanical or electrical components; such maintenance regularly is planned to avoid high exhaust emissions from automobiles as in the case of VV program. As first step, this work intends to integrate an emission test similar to VV but in terms of real driving cycle trough an automotive embedded system. Our prototype uses data from an automotive gas analyzer which take measurements from exhaust tailpipe; this analyzer is totally portable and allows on-road measurements and also determines the concentration of 5 gases: O_2, NO_X, CO, CO_2 and unburned hydrocarbons (HC), as well as the equipment used during VV procedures. The technical specs of the portable gas analyzer exceed the requirements established in NOMs mentioned above. The analyzer is adjusted to take 45-60 minutes of gas-concentration measurements, i.e., a test during a normal (no several traffic problems) travel in Mexico City.

When on-road measurements are ready, a data bank is send to the FPGA platform which process and performs a simple processing routine; this routine involves the evaluation of the average emission levels during the travel, temporally store such values, and configure the Wi-Fi module to transmit such information. The selected FPGA platform is based on Spartan-3A chip, and data processing and peripherals control are achieved by means of *Microblaze* processor. We select this FPGA platform as a part of the prototype because it allows the implementation of a microprocessor, hardware in situ reconfiguration for user specific applications, and also the integration of several communication protocols such as I^2C. The selected Spartan-3A platform lacks wireless connectivity, but its built-in interfaces can be used to extend the reach of platform capabilities through communication protocols; is possible to use a great variety of wireless modules and others peripherals when a communication protocol actuates as an intermediate. The prototype uses a GS1011M module from *GainSpan* as Wi-Fi module; we use as a reference during the development of the prototype this characteristics: is compliant with 802.11b/g/n and meets regulatory and Wi-Fi Alliance requirements, allows easy connection via UART or SPI, the configuration is done through AT commands, has low power consumption, and supports TCP/IP stacks and WPA/WPA2 security which are crucial for exhaust emission data management in terms of Mexican Normativity and user privacy. Another important characteristic is that is possible to use ad-hoc and infrastructure mode, i.e., the Wi-Fi module can communicate directly with other blocks in the network. Particularly, the communication architecture between FPGA platform and mobile device relies on TCP client–server model, where the mobile device (smart phone) is the server, and FPGA platform implements client functions; if the connection is successful, the FPGA platform (client) transmits a processed data bank to the smart phone (server) which displays the vehicle's information to the user. Smart phone run an Android mobile platform based application to work as a server; however, the application is not restricted to a specific platform. [4-9]

Fig. 1. Prototype as a part of ubiquitous computing systems

As mentioned earlier, one of the main aspects of the prototype depends on data transmission and user privacy. In the first case, TCP protocol is used instead UDP because error handling and proper information transmission are priorities, i.e., if the prototype aims to evaluate and display results according to NOMs, proper handling of data is a requirement. In the second case, privacy is a decisive requirement because of the user's comfort and confidence, in other words, vehicle's information is also personal information per se; this is the reason to control the access of the prototype through security protocols. For the last case, the wireless connection between prototype's blocks is achieved by means of implementation of WPA2 (Wi-Fi Protection Access, Version 2) security protocol as a first approximation for user's data security. [10, 11]

The figure 1 shows a general overview of the prototype and its relation with ubiquitous computing common examples explained above. The prototype is not only intended to integrate a specific part of automobile computing (exhaust emissions monitoring), but also as an information system through user's personal data in terms of the vehicle status. The user is not linked to a specific scenario, however, in urban areas where vehicles, traffic and air pollution are closely related as well as communications, several scenarios where user is principal actor appear; in that association of ideas, the prototype considers the user-machine interaction as the main contributor, i.e., the design focuses in user-machine contact as the central source of data sharing, automobile use and air pollution. The user is interested in: vehicle's performance, the contribution to air pollution in terms of exhaust gases when VV is necessary, and the data that is narrowly related with personal information (such as vehicle status).

3   Setup, Experiments and Results

3.1   Setup

The developed Android application provides the configuration for both Wi-Fi module and FPGA platform. The FPGA platform configuration takes at first place the managing of the received information from the gas analyzer, and ultimately the secure connection settings provided by GS1011M module when a server is available. Once the mobile device initiates a TCP server, the next step is data transmission and finally the display of the results from the on-road gas measurements.

The communication process is categorized and divided in two modules. On the one hand, the module which corresponds to FPGA platform module which includes the GainSpan module setup and TCP client software routines, and on the other hand, the mobile device module which includes the configuration for the smart phone, through the android based application, to work as a TCP server. The FPGA communication module comprises a Universal Asynchronous Receiver-Transmitter (UART) to configure and send data to the GainSpan module, a security protocol (WPA) by means of Wi-Fi module, and software routines to halt and shut down the platform. Moreover, the mobile device module is divided in two states, running and stop; if stop condition is present, the FPGA platform will stop and after a specific time it shut down, however, if running condition is present and TCP server is available, on-road measurements routine will execute.

3.2   Experiments

The experimentation process consists in several test and measurements in real driving conditions. The northeast of Mexico City was the field of study. Every test has duration of approximately 49 minutes; we considered that this is the duration of a travel under Mexico City's traffic and specific conditions. The test vehicle is into the category *1990 and earlier* exposed in table 1, indeed, this car has the last VV certificate which indicates that the vehicle can travel in Mexico City.

3.3   Results

After the measurements, the mobile device displays the information to the user by means of a friendly user interface as shown in figure 2. The information that the smart phone shows is the result of the real status of the vehicle in terms of exhaust emissions according to the Mexican normative (NOM). The user interface is comfortable enough to observe if the vehicle is under the maximum emission levels that are described in table 1. The automotive gas analyzer provides not only data about the 5 gases mentioned in section 1 but also an additional element commonly called *lambda factor* which is related to the efficiency of the vehicle in terms of air-fuel ratio; although the user-data stores such information, the user interface only displays if the vehicle is in good conditions to travel in Mexico City.

Table 1. Maximum emission levels of gaseous pollutants from the exhaust of vehicles that use gasoline as fuel. Applicable in Mexico City and its Metropolitan Area.

Model year	HC (ppm)	CO (%VOL)	O_2 (%VOL)	NO_X (ppm)	Dilution (%VOL) $CO + CO_2$		Lambda λ
					Min.	Max.	
1990 and earlier	150	1.5	3.0	2500	13	16.5	1.1
1991 and latter	100	1.0	3.0	1500	13	16.5	1.05

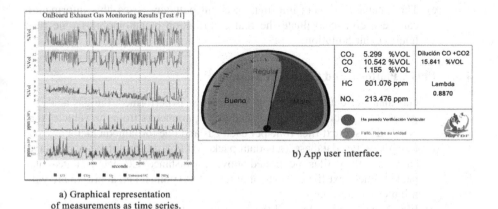

a) Graphical representation
of measurements as time series.

b) App user interface.

Fig. 2. Results from measuremens during real driving cycles

For the experiments described in this article, and according with the NOMs mentioned in section 1, the on-road test applied to the vehicle through our prototype suggest that the vehicle is not passing the VV, i.e., that the test vehicle present problems and should not be used because of the amount of pollutant emissions from its exhaust.

Once the final comparison is done, the mobile device can display the results in different formats; figure 2 shows one of those formats. Whereas figure 2a is a representation of real measurements, figure 2b only shows the definitive result in terms of NOM.

4   Discussion

This section presents some a brief discussion in terms of ubiquitous computing and technical considerations applied to the prototype. The conditions are separated in sections.

4.1   Prototype

(a) Ubiquitous computing in automobiles and smart devices can be used in numerous scenarios such as health care applications, however in this paper the prototype intends to integrate an environmental-care ubiquitous computing. [16]

(b) Is possible to use this kind of actions to create a habit (in terms of air pollution-care) among ubiquitous computing? Observe 4.1c and 4.1.d

(c) Through the mobile application the user can evaluate the vehicle's status and be informed about possible actions to take to avoid the problems, at first glance to pass the VV but in a future to provide regular maintenance.

(d) The information about each test is stored as a record in order to observe the changes in the behavior of the vehicle; these records can be a useful tool to find mechanical or other kind of problems, whose attention eventually contributes with vehicle's performance.

(e) The databases contain information about pollutant gases, this information can be useful to evaluate the real contribution of automobiles (due rush hours) to air pollution.

4.2   FPGA Platform and GS1011M Module

(a) Gas analyzer data base format: When a test is performed, the gas analyzer generates a report for each gas (and other parameters from the vehicle) that is saved in six text files (one per each gas and one for lambda factor).

(b) Length of the database (gas-data-packets): For the prototype a packet is each one of text files mentioned above, for instance, CO data is a gas-data-packet. Each text file consists of at least 2900 points, i.e., approximately 49 minutes of recordings.

(c) FPGA processing: Once all the gas-data-packets are ready, the information is loaded into the FPGA program memory, then, is processed to get the average value of the measurements for each gas. When that process is complete, the results are stored in a reserved memory space, and the temporal buffer is emptied to receive additional data.

(d) Serial communications and UART baud rate: Serial communication between FPGA and GS1011M module is placed in order to configure, drive and manage connection settings of the Wi-Fi module, and also to transmit stored results. We choose an 115200 baud rate to achieve a quicker transmission rate.

(e) GS1011M module auto negotiation and Wi-Fi module connection manager: FPGA control connection settings of the Wi-Fi module such as WPA key or connection ID; however, GS1011M module establish and implements IEEE 802.11 standard, of course if FPGA sends the appropriate command.

4.3   Mobile Device Front-End

(a) Hotspot activity: In order to protect the security aspect of the mobile device and the data, the hotspot is active only for a certain amount of time (approximately 3 minutes) and when the user requires the service, periodic authentication is a requirement.

(b) Communication expiration: to send or to receive the results of a test, the communication between FPGA platform and mobile device must not to exceed 1 minute. Once the connection expires, the hotspot unlinks the selected FPGA platform, and if possible, sends a shut-down signal.

(c) Updates and NOM standards: The mobile device performs the comparison of the obtained results because, if rules (NOM) change, the new standards can be easily integrated into the application.

(d) Complete data verification (sends and receives): If the connections fail, or if the data are corrupted, a data authentication algorithm is not currently supported, however, in future versions of software, this will be a key aspect of the prototype.

(e) According to the experimentation, the volunteer (users) of the application feel comfortable if the security and privacy are main considerations.

5   Conclusions

A general purpose embedded system, based on FPGA technology and coupled with Wi-Fi module communication, was used to generate reports of the amount of pollutants produced by motor vehicles that use gasoline as fuel. Gas sensors, coupled to the automotive exhaust tailpipe, provide evidence of each pollutant to the Spartan-3A Starter Platform for their processing and data format. Wi-Fi module helps to transfer data banks and send them to mobile cellphone for their comparison with the NOM standards and display the results for their analysis. Such system can be modified to handle different configurations that can help to obtain valuable information coming not only from gas exhaust sensors, but also other pertinent parameters like tracking, acceleration, weather data, traffic data, among others.

The method reported in this paper has the objective to be a complementary option to enhance VV, and provide an easy to follow vehicular emission inventory that serves to reduce the impact of pollutants coming from the main source of pollutants emission: gasoline-propelled vehicles. Future versions of this work consider the use of other infraestructures such as WiMAX which support a covering extension greater than Wi-Fi.

Acknowledgements. This work was supported by the Instituto Politécnico Nacional of Mexico (grants no. SIP-20130303 and SIP-20131867) and the Secretaría de Ciencia, Tecnología e Innovación del Distrito Federal (SECITI) (grants no. PIUTE10-77, PICSO10-85, and ICyTDF/325/2011).

References

1. Secretaría del Medio Ambiente Recursos Naturales,
   http://www.ine.gob.mx/calaire-informacion-basica/
   562-calaire-nom-fuentes-moviles1
2. Moos, R.: A Brief Overview on Automotive Exhaust Gas Sensors Based on Electro ceramics. Int. J. Appl. Ceram. Technol. 2(5), 401–413 (2005)
3. Delphi, Planar Oxygen Sensors, http://am.delphi.com/products/parts/
   engine-management-index/sensors/planar-oxygen-sensors/

4. Xilinx, XtremeDSP Starter Kit, http://www.xilinx.com/products/boards-and-kits/DO-SD1800A-DSP-SK-UNI-G.htm
5. GainSpan GS1011M Evaluation Kit, http://www.GainSpan.com/docs2/GS1011M-EVK2-S2W-PB.pdf
6. Nirjon, S., Nicoara, A., Hsu, C.-H., Singh, J., Stankovic, J.: MultiNets: Policy Oriented Real-Time Switching of Wireless Interfaces on Mobile Devices. In: Real-Time and Embedded Technology and Applications Symposium (RTAS), pp. 251–260 (2012)
7. Chen, Y.-S., Tsai, M.-K., Chiang, L.-S., Deng, D.-J.: Adaptive Traffic-Aware Power-Saving Protocol for IEEE 802.11 Ad Hoc Networks. In: Parallel and Distributed Systems (ICPADS), pp. 866–871, 7-9 (2011)
8. Boussen, S., Tabbane, N., Tabbane, S.: Performance Analysis of SCTP Protocol in Wi-Fi Network Computer Sciences and Convergence Information Technology. In: Fourth International Conference on ICCIT 2009, pp. 178–182, 24-26 (2009)
9. Butler, M.: Android: Changing the Mobile Landscape. IEEE Pervasive Computing 10(1), 4–7
10. IEEE Standards Association, http://standards.ieee.org/findstds/standard/802.11i-2004.html
11. Wi-Fi Alliance, https://www.cloudse.com, http://www.Wi-Fi.org/knowledge-center
12. Secretaría del medio ambiete de Distrito Federal, http://www.sma.df.gob.mx/verificentros/
13. United States Environmental Portection Agency, http://www.epa.gov/reg3artd/vehicletran/vehicles/vehicle_emissions_testing.htm
14. Gramaglia, M., Bernardos, C.J., Calderon, M.: Virtual induction loops based on cooperative vehicular communications. Sensors Basel Switzerland 13(2), 1467–1476 (2013)
15. Hwang, J., Shin, C., Yoe, H.: A Wireless Sensor Network-Based Ubiquitous Paprika Growth Management System. Sensors (Peterboroug) 10(12), 11566–11589 (2010)
16. Hii, P.-C., Chung, W.-Y.: A Comprehensive Ubiquitous Healthcare Solution on an AndroidTM Mobile Device. Sensors Basel Switzerland 11(7), 6799–6815 (2011)
17. Resch, B., Mittlboeck, M., Lippautz, M.: Pervasive monitoring–an intelligent sensor pod approach for standardized measurement infrastructures. Sensors Basel Switzerland 10(12), 11440–11467 (2010)
18. Walker, G.H., Stanton, N.A., Young, M.S.: Where Is Computing Driving Cars? International Journal of Human–Computer Interaction 13(2), 203–229 (2001)
19. Hwang, J., Shin, C., Yoe, H.: Study on an Agricultural Environment Monitoring Server System using Wireless Sensor Network. Sensors 10, 1118–1121 (2010)
20. Bagula, A., Zennaro, M., Inggs, G., Scott, S., Gascon, D.: Ubiquitous Sensor Networking for Development (USN4D): An Application to Pollution Monitoring. Sensors 12, 391–414 (2012)

Leveraging the Model-Driven Architecture for Service Choreography in Ubiquitous Systems

Carlos Rodríguez-Domínguez, Tomás Ruiz-López, José Luis Garrido,
Manuel Noguera, and Kawtar Benghazi

University of Granada, Spain,
Escuela Técnica Superior de Ingenierías Informática y Telecomunicación,
C/ Periodista Daniel Saucedo Aranda S/N, 18071, Granada, Spain
{carlosrodriguez,tomruiz,jgarrido,mnoguera,benghazi}@ugr.es

Abstract. In ubiquitous systems, the context information (location, time, networking conditions, etc.) may influence the way of operation or even require to guarantee the availability of particular services at a certain moment. As a consequence, service composition may become more complex from a design viewpoint, due to the need of systematically taking into account all the variations of the contextual information in order to adapt the behavior of the set of involved services. Business Process Model and Notation 2.0 (BPMN 2.0) can be used to specify process choreography, which helps modeling service composition. Even so, the peculiarities of ubiquitous systems make it difficult to actually obtain an executable model that fulfills the mobility, availability and adaptability requirements of these systems. In this paper, it is presented a Model-Driven Architecture (MDA) approach to transform a BPMN choreography model into software templates for specific target platforms. The proposal has been implemented making use of the Eclipse Modeling Framework (EMF).

Keywords: Ubiquitous systems, model-driven architecture, service choreography, software engineering

1 Introduction

Ubiquitous systems incorporate a set of services that provide context dependent functionalities to end users. Those services are usually composed to offer complex, integrated functionalities to realize more complex business process goals [1].

Service composition is a complicated task, specially when dealing with the particular requirements of ubiquitous systems [2], like mobility support and availability. For instance, the availability of a service could be directly related to the system context: networking conditions, user location at a given time, and so on [3]. That way, designing a complex composition scheme for a ubiquitous system may become an arduous and intricate task.

G. Urzaiz et al. (Eds.): UCAmI 2013, LNCS 8276, pp. 303–310, 2013.

Service orchestration and choreography are service composition techniques [4]. The orchestration is a centralized coordination technique in which an *orchestrator* manages the coordination process. In contrast, the choreography is a distributed technique to deal with the coordination of specific interactions between services. Moreover, it is considered that choreography can serve as a generic abstraction that integrates any kind of service composition, including orchestration [5]. As a consequence, the service choreography technique has been increasingly being adopted for service composition.

BPMN 2.0 [6] incorporates a notation for specifying business process choreography to describe the interactions between services in ubiquitous systems. However, the notation needs to be finally translated into a software model implementing those interactions and taking into account the specific requirements of ubiquitous systems.

In this paper, we present a Model-Driven Architecture (MDA) [7] approach to address service choreography in ubiquitous systems. The aim is to facilitate software development by proposing abstractions that avoid taking into account the specific implementation details associated to the orchestration (e.g., underlying technological platforms). For instance, in the approach to be presented, a BPMN choreography diagram is automatically transformed into a UML sequence diagram that specifies the availability and mobility requirements of ubiquitous systems. Also, the sequence diagram can be automatically translated into a software template that implements the described choreography. Finally, the proposal has also been implemented in Eclipse Modeling Framework (EMF), which automatizes the model transformation and code generation.

The remaining of this paper is organized as follows. In Section 2, an overview of some background knowledge related to this research work is given. Section 3 describes the proposed MDA approach. Finally, in Section 4, we summarize the results presented herein and introduce some lines of future work.

2 Background

2.1 Model-Driven Architecture

MDA is an Object Management Group (OMG) standard approach for the development of software systems [7]. In MDA, software is developed on the basis of a forward engineering process, that is, by producing code from abstract models. The general idea is to decouple software design from the technical aspects of its implementation.

MDA is based on two main notions: models and transformations. Models are categorized into three different abstraction levels: (1) The *Computation Independent Model (CIM)* is often referred as a business or domain model, since it uses a vocabulary that is familiar to the subject matter experts (SMEs) and it is independent of the technologies that are going to be used for its implementation; (2) The *Platform Independent Model (PIM)* focuses on the operation of the system, but abstracts out technical details; (3) The *Platform Specific Model*

(PSM) combines the specifications in the PIM with the technical details of a specific platform.

The OMG defines a transformation as *the process of converting one model to another one of the same system* (e.g. PIM to PSM) [7]. Transformations are usually specified using specific transformation languages, like Query/View/Transformation (QVT) OMG standard [8] or Atlas Transformation Language (ATL) (`http://www.eclipse.org/atl`). In this paper, it is used ATL.

2.2   Choreography in BPMN 2.0

BPMN is an OMG standard for modeling business processes using a graphical notation [6]. The focus is to provide a notation that can be easily understood by business stakeholders.

BPMN 2.0 includes a notation for representing the choreography of business processes, that is, the interactions between them. As specified in the standard, the choreography diagrams could be viewed as business contracts between different organizations. An example of a BPMN choreography diagram is depicted in Figure 1.

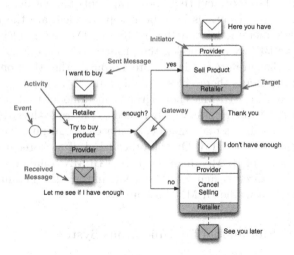

Fig. 1. An example of a BPMN choreography diagram and a summary of its elements

Previous example represents different interactions between a retailer and a provider to buy a product. The notation includes elements that are widely used in BPMN choreography diagrams: activities, participants, messages, events and gateways. An activity is an interaction between two participants and may have sub-activities with different interactions between the participants. A message is an information unit transferred between participants, and it can be communicated in a synchronous or asynchronous mode. A gateway represents a branch or a merge between different activities. Finally, an event is an exceptional occurrence between two activities and/or gateways.

3   An MDA Approach to Service Choreography in Ubiquitous Systems

The models to be introduced in this section offer three perspectives of the choreography, following an MDA approach: (1) The *choreography CIM* is based on the BPMN 2.0 choreography metamodel for specifying service choreography for any business process model; (2) The *choreography PIM* is specifically devised to choreograph services in ubiquitous systems; (3) The *choreography PSM* models the choreography of a ubiquitous system supported by specific platforms (programming languages, operating systems, communication technologies, etc.). Each model is automatically transformed into the corresponding one (from CIM to PIM, and from PIM to PSM) using transformation rules implemented in ATL and defined on the underlying metamodels.

3.1   The CIM Metamodel

The CIM metamodel uses some of the elements devised in the BPMN 2.0 choreography metamodel to represent the choreography of different business processes. In fact, the naming conventions have been kept to facilitate the matching between the BPMN metamodel and the proposed CIM metamodel. However, in contrast with the BPMN metamodel, the proposed CIM metamodel focuses on the abstractions that are present in a choreography, rather than on the notation to represent the elements themselves in a diagram.

All the elements in a BPMN choreography metamodel that do not refer to other kinds of BPMN diagrams can be matched to classes in the CIM metamodel. This way, there is a direct matching between a choreography diagram and the classes represented in the CIM. On the other hand, if a choreography diagram refers to other types of BPMN diagrams (like a BPMN collaboration diagram), it is not possible to directly match the elements in the CIM metamodel with the elements represented in the BPMN diagram.

3.2   The PIM Metamodel for Ubiquitous Systems

The PIM metamodel is equivalent to the UML 2.2 sequence diagram metamodel [9]. The idea, at PIM abstraction level, is to transform an instance of the CIM metamodel into a UML sequence diagram. This way, it is possible to design the choreography of a ubiquitous system through a BPMN choreography diagram, then match the elements in the diagram with the elements in the CIM metamodel to derive a CIM and, finally, to transform the resulting CIM to a UML sequence diagram. Figure 3 exemplifies a transformation between an activity in an instance of the proposed CIM metamodel (represented in XMI) and a set of interactions in a resulting sequence diagram. The sample represents the activity of buying a medicine in a pharmacy by a patient.

The CIM to PIM transformation takes into account the peculiarities of the ubiquitous systems. Particularly, before interacting with a service, it is necessary

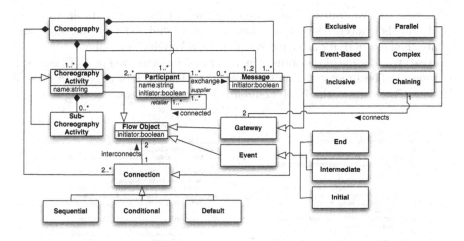

Fig. 2. CIM Metamodel of a Choreography, based on the BPMN 2.0 Choreography Metamodel Specification [6]

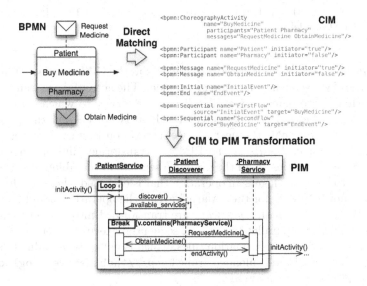

Fig. 3. An example of a transformation from a BPMN choreography diagram into a sequence diagram

to test its availability. This is done through a *discoverer* of nearby services that is automatically included in the sequence diagram for each service. For example, the pharmacy service could only be available when the user were close to the pharmacy.

In order to maintain an interaction ordering in the choreography, services only begin their interactions when they receive an "initActivity" message, and initiate the next activity after receiving an "endActivity" message.

An excerpt of some of the transformation rules, implemented in ATL, is shown in Figure 4. The presented rule transforms an *Activity* into a *Loop* (a type of *CombinedFragment* in the UML standard) in the target sequence diagram.

```
rule ChoreographyActivity2CombinedFragment{
    from activity : BPMN!ChoreographyActivity
    using{
        participants : Sequence(BPMN!Participant) = activity.participants;
        messages : Sequence(BPMN!Message) = activity.messages;
    }
    to
        combinedFragment : UML!CombinedFragment(
            name <- activity.name + 'Loop',
            interactionOperator <- #loop,
            operand <- OrderedSet(oper1, oper2)),
        oper1executionEventOperation : UML!Operation(
            name <- 'discover()'

        oper1executionEventOperationClass : UML!Class(
            name <- participants->first().name + 'Discoverer'),
        oper2 : UML!CombinedFragment(
            name <- activity.name + 'Break',
            operand <- OrderedSet{guardOper, oper3, oper4, oper5}
    continues in the next column >>
```

```
        ...
        guard : UML!InteractionConstraint(specification <- valueSpec),
        valueSpec : UML!OpaqueExpression(
            body <- '[v.contains(' + participants->last().name + 'Service)]'
        ...
        oper3executionEventOperation : UML!Operation(
            name <- messages->first().name,
            class <- oper3executionEventOperationClass),
        oper3executionEventOperationClass : UML!Class(
            name <- participants->last().name + 'Service'
        ...
        oper4executionEventOperation : UML!Operation(
            name <- messages->last().name,
            class <- oper4executionEventOperationClass),
        oper4executionEventOperationClass : UML!Class(
            name <- participants->first().name + 'Service'),
        oper5 : UML!ExecutionOccurrenceSpecification(
            name <- 'initiateActivity',
        ...
```

Fig. 4. An excerpt of the ATL transformation rules to convert the CIM metamodel into the PIM metamodel

The transformation rules convert the elements in the CIM metamodel into elements of the UML sequence diagram metamodel. The activities are transformed into *loops* that try to detect the availability of the service to which transfer the messages. When the service is detected, the loop is *broken* and the messages are transferred. After that, the next service interaction is started by sending a "initService" message. *Events* in the PIM are transformed into a sequence of asynchronous notifications to all the available services in the ubiquitous system. The message to be sent triggers an operation that is executed whenever that specific event is notified (e.g., for the "Alarm" event, the operation would be called "onAlarmTriggered"). Finally, *gateways* are transformed into different kinds of *fragments* (e.g., loops, parallel executions, sequential executions, etc.).

The complete set of transformation rules, which is not presented due to space constraints, but can be downloaded from http://thebluerose.googlecode.com/files/MDAChoreography.zip.

3.3   The PSM Metamodel

The transformation from the proposed PIM to a PSM requires to adopt specific target platforms. The target architecture will consist of the elements in the PIM instantiated by means of the artifacts provided by the adopted platforms. UML profiles [10] could be used for targeting a platform. Additionally, some authors [11] have proposed transformations from sequence diagrams to web services, which could be useful to finally deploy the ubiquitous system resulting from

```
<definitions name="PatientService" ...>          <service name="PatientService">
   <xsd:element="ObtainMedicine"/>                  <documentation>Documentation</documentation>
   ...                                              <port name="ObtainMedicinePort" ...>
   <wsdl:portType name="PatientServicePortType">        <soap:address
      <wsdl:operation name="ObtainMedicine">                location=".../PatientService"/>
      ...                                           </port>
      </wsdl:operation>                             ...
   ...                                           </service>
   </wsdl:portType>                               ...
   <wsdl:binding name="PatientServiceBinding" ...>  <definitions name="PatientDiscoverer" ...>
      <wsdl:operation name="ObtainMedicine">         <wsdl:portType name="PatientDiscovererPortType"/>
         <soap:operation                             <wsdl:binding name="PatientDiscovererBinding".../>
            soapAction=".../ObtainMedicine"/>        <service name="PatientDiscoverer">
      </wsdl:operation>                              ...
   ...                                              </service>
continues in the next column >>                   ...
```

Fig. 5. An excerpt of a WSDL service interface automatically derived from the PIM

applying the approach presented herein in the "cloud". As an example, some transformations have been implemented to produce WSDL interfaces and SOAP messages from the PIM. Figure 5 represents an excerpt of the WDSL interfaces automatically generated from the *Patient* class depicted in Figure 3.

The implementation can be easily extended to produce code in other programming languages. Code generation is implemented using the Acceleo Eclipse plug-in (http://www.eclipse.org/acceleo).

3.4 Implementation of the Proposal Using Eclipse EMF

The proposed metamodels and transformation rules have been implemented using EMF. The implementation aims to create a tool to automatize the transformation from CIM to PIM, and from PIM to PSM. As a consequence, it helps into automatically generating the choreography of a system from its specification as an instance of the CIM metamodel.

The metamodels have been represented in ECORE format in order to be used as inputs for the EMF tools. The transformation rules have been implemented in ATL, as mentioned in previous subsections. The ATLAS plugin for Eclipse takes the source and destination metamodels in ECORE format, the ATL transformation rules and a model in XMI format conforming to the source metamodel as inputs. As an output, it produces another model in XMI format conforming to the destination metamodel. This way, transformations are automatically done.

4 Conclusions and Future Work

This paper presents a model-driven approach for the choreography of services in ubiquitous systems. The CIM metamodel is based on the BPMN choreography metamodel, whereas the PIM metamodel is equivalent to the UML sequence diagram metamodel. CIM instantiations can be automatically transformed into sequence diagrams through a set of transformation rules applied to their metamodels. Then, the PIM can be transformed into a PSM. An example illustrates the transformation of a PIM into web services. The proposal has been implemented in EMF, so as to automate the transformations and the code generation.

As for future work, we plan to explore reverse-engineering techniques that could transform from executable code to the proposed PIM and CIM models. Model checking techniques, like [12], will be explored in order to verify some properties in the generated sequence diagram (like liveness). Finally, the proposal will be integrated in a more extensive MDA method that we are exploring, in order to obtain nearly complete executable codes for ubiquitous systems, on the basis of several CIMs.

Acknowledgements. This research work has been funded by the Ministry of Economy and Competitiveness of the Spanish Government and by the Andalusian Regional Government through the research projects TIN2012-38600 and P10-TIC-6600, respectively.

References

1. Bellavista, P., Corradi, A., Fanelli, M., Foschini, L.: A survey of context data distribution for mobile ubiquitous systems. ACM Comput. Surv. 44(4), 24:1–24:45 (2012)
2. Milner, R.: Theories for the Global Ubiquitous Computer. In: Walukiewicz, I. (ed.) FOSSACS 2004. LNCS, vol. 2987, pp. 5–11. Springer, Heidelberg (2004)
3. Hwang, Y., Lee, K.: Dynamic service composition in ubiquitous environment. In: Proc. 2nd Int. Conf. on Pervasive Tech. Related to Assistive Env., pp. 12:1–12:4 (2009)
4. Peltz, C.: Web services orchestration and choreography. Computer 36(10), 46–52 (2003)
5. Autili, M., Ruscio, D., Inverardi, P., Lockerbie, J., Tivoli, M.: A Development Process for Requirements Based Service Choreography. In: 19th IEEE Requirements Engineering Conference, pp. 59–62 (2011)
6. OMG: BPMN 2.0 (2011), http://www.omg.org/spec/BPMN/2.0/
7. OMG: Model Driven Architecture (2003), http://www.omg.org/mda
8. OMG: Meta Object Facility 2.0 Query/View/Transformation, QVT (2011), http://www.omg.org/spec/QVT
9. OMG: UML 2.2: Superstructure Specification (2009), http://www.omg.org/spec/UML/2.2/Superstructure/PDF
10. Fuentes-Fernández, L., Vallecillo-Moreno, A.: An Introduction to UML Profiles. European Journal for the Informatics Professional 5(2), 6–13 (2004)
11. Bauer, B., Müller, J.P.: MDA Applied: From Sequence Diagrams to Web Service Choreography. In: Koch, N., Fraternali, P., Wirsing, M. (eds.) ICWE 2004. LNCS, vol. 3140, pp. 132–136. Springer, Heidelberg (2004)
12. Benghazi, K., Hurtado, M.V., Hornos, M.J., Rodríguez, M.L., Rodríguez-Domínguez, C., Pelegrina, A.B., Rodríguez-Fórtiz, M.J.: Enabling correct design and formal analysis of Ambient Assisted Living systems. Journal of Systems and Software 85(3), 498–510 (2012)

A Case Study for Validating a Prosumer Framework in Drug Traceability Scenarios

Ramón Alcarria, Diego Martín de Andrés, Tomás Robles, and Augusto Morales

Technical University of Madrid,
Av. Complutense 30, 28040. Madrid, Spain
{ralcarria,dmartin,trobles,amorales}@dit.upm.es

Abstract. Service creation and customization are expensive tasks that require specialized people. In many cases these simple services could be implemented by users without programming skills. In this paper, a framework for creating and adapting services in a drug traceability environment is presented. This framework is able to manage and run services in a hospital pharmacy department as it accesses to the traceability event and alert notification systems. The authors carried out a case study where people with varied experience in technology used the framework for creating and adapting services. This study shows that the framework proposed is very useful for creating services and especially for adapting them and also the quality of services created and adapted are quite high. It is also analyzed the experience necessary by the prosumer for creating and adapting services and how it affects to the services quality.

Keywords: prosumer, case study, mashup, ECA rules, drug traceability.

1 Introduction

Development tools for ambient intelligence (AmI) environments are currently aimed to application designers or developers that must require a high-level of technical expertise. End-user creation tools are currently merging with the motivation that it does not seem possible in AmI environments to deal with all the potential needs of all categories of users and scenarios. In the opinion of some authors it seems much more reasonable to enable end-users, with no technical expertise, to cover these needs by the utilization of appropriate tools for the creation or adaptation of ubiquitous applications and services [1].

The prosumer user (*prosumer* comes from the words *producer* and *consumer*) contributes with content and services to the rest of the community. This concept is currently evolving from "content prosumer", who uses the Internet and other technologies to find information and also to produce content, to "service prosumer", which develop services and make them available to other users. The FIA (Future Internet Assembly) mentions this evolution of Internet users in its roadmap [2], defining prosumer as "a new kind of Internet user, playing both roles consumers of services as well as creators of added value services based on those consumed".

G. Urzaiz et al. (Eds.): UCAmI 2013, LNCS 8276, pp. 311–318, 2013.
© Springer International Publishing Switzerland 2013

Prosumer special requirements are not supported by current creation platforms, which doesn't assist the prosumers (not experts in the user of traditional tools for service development), with the exception of some initiatives for end-users such as iStockphoto, Lego Mindstorms or MIT App Inventor. In this paper we present a prosumer framework, tailored to end-user creation potential and validate its usefulness for service creation and adaptation in drug traceability scenarios.

The structure of the paper is as follows. Section 2 describes related work in service co-creation and frameworks for prosumers. Section 3 describes the design and the implementation of our prosumer framework whereas Section 4 explains our experimental validation by answering some research questions. Finally, Section 5 and 6 explain the results and discussion.

2   Related Work

Some works deal with the concept of prosumer and the difficulty of providing creation tools according to their experience level and adapted to the creation terminal and mobile nature. Among the service creation tools that provide different creation strategies [3] we studied natural language based service composition and other semi-automatic solutions that require additional investment from end-users [4]. We highlight the tools that consist of component interconnection as mashup tools, which facilitate the definition of execution sequences of services by end-users. The Mashup tools Marmite and Yahoo Pipes combine existing Web contents and services from multiple websites and process, filter and direct the information to different sinks, such as databases, map services and web pages. In our approach we combine the benefits of the mashup tools with the flexibility of the ECA (Event, Condition, Action) rules concept [5]. Regarding to domain expert collaboration in the creation of application or services, Context Cloud [6] promotes the collaboration between technical and non-technical users following a situation-driven development methodology, which works in the premise that programmers have context-aware toolkits that can detect user situations and these toolkits can be configured without programming skills.

3   Prosumer Framework

This section describes the prosumer model, as a new development lifecycle that integrates the prosumer user as an expert of a given domain for the development of applications and services. Then, the developed prosumer framework and the creation strategy based on ECA rules are introduced. Finally, the system architecture and the elements that can be used are explained.

3.1   Prosumer Model

Users require tools for providing their own services and consuming services published by others, and thus, transform the network into a collaborative infrastructure, adapted to different areas, such as social, personal and commercial ones. Support of companies to prosumers interested in creating value for themselves and for the company is in the realm of co-creation, which has been tacked in the previous section.

Prosumer users are different from end-users by their producing intentions but also different from service developers by their better engagement with the application domain. Also companies change their role and become service creation framework providers instead of service providers. The provided framework may offer the prosumer different creation strategies, such as service customization, service composition or graphical user interface (GUI) composition.

3.2   A Framework for Creation and Adaptation of Services

The advantage of the prosumer role is found in the deep knowledge of the work environment and in the ability to use tools to create and adapt services and applications. To enact this capability we develop GISAI-Pharma, a Web environment that integrates the service creation and adaptation functions by implementing the strategy of service composition by component interconnection. The prototype was developed in the field of drug management in hospital pharmacy and allows prosumer users (i.e. pharmacy workers, not technology experts) to create, personalize, share and consume location-based services, stock control, notifications and alerts for drugs and other assets present in the pharmacy.

The personalization environment supports service adaptation by considering the modification of adaptable services, which can be personalized in order to generate final executable services. The creation environment supports a creation strategy of mashup composition based on ECA rules. This composition paradigm describes service composition by providing three related components: **Event (E)**, as an occurrence triggering the rule execution; **condition (C)**, logic statement that can be evaluated to "true" or "false"; and **action (A)**, describing the realization of a certain action if the condition is evaluated to true. These requirements are checked for inconsistencies through a validator [5] which is invoked when the user saves the created or adapted service. Rule-based tools facilitate service creation as encode logical knowledge more efficiently and naturally than procedural code-based tools.

3.3   GISAI-Pharma, Framework Architecture and Implementation

The GISAI-Pharma environment is based on a cloud-hosted web solution and accessible from multiple platforms (pc, tablets, and smartphones). The Web server is based on Node.js and communicates via REST and SOAP with environment capabilities. Access to these capabilities is encapsulated in components that are classified as events, conditions and actions. The graphical representations of these components are dragged by the prosumer, dropped in his whiteboard, and connected according to the restrictions of the ECA rules.

The components of type *Event* connect with the traceability event generation and query system through an EPCIS Query Interface Repository, installed in the hospital environment, which provides to the framework information over the medicines crossing some RFID arcs (name of the drug, registration time, expiration date, etc).

The proposed *Conditions* are location-based (acting on the place where the user is executing the service or where events are generated), time-based (specify different time ranges for events) and quantity-based (enable the registration of a certain number of events before invoking an action).

The implemented *Actions* consist of the selection of different communication channels for drug notifications (email, sms, and web notifications).

Fig. 1 describes a service created through the GISAI-Pharma platform, in which components are surrounded by red, amber or green colors, depending on whether they are Event, Conditions or Actions respectively. The service notifies (green) by SMS an RFID event (red) if it occurs in a given time range (amber). The color coding also helps users to assimilate the requirements of the ECA rules, following the traffic light metaphor.

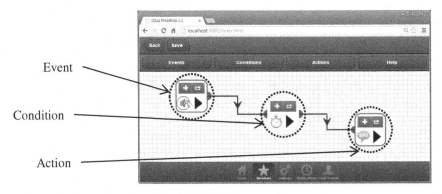

Fig. 1. GISAI-Pharma tool

4   Experimental Validation

In order to define the experimental validation that guides this work, we have proposed the following research questions:

1° What is the usefulness of the prosumer framework for service creation and adaptation?

2° What is the quality of the services created and adapted?

3° What is the experience required to create and adapt services in a prosumer environment?

A case study was carried out in order to address the research questions; it was divided in four phases as shown in Fig. 2. A case study is appropriate to address the previously stated research questions, as they require analyzing a set of events through the application of the prosumer framework in real-life scenarios in order to identify the factors that influence the framework. Moreover, the researchers had little control of the people using the prosumer framework because they had only trained the participants in the prosumer framework and solved their questions during its application. This approach is appropriate to replicate the experiment in similar contexts.

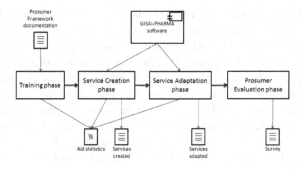

Fig. 2. Case Study plan, inputs and outputs

4.1 Context

The case study was planned, conducted, monitored and evaluated by three experts, all of them with similar research areas in technology, computer science and telecommunications. Ten first year students of telecommunication engineering (hereafter, participants) have participated in the experimentation. The participants created three services to solve three specific problems and then they adapted other three services to solve another three specific problems. The problems were suggested by the experts categorized by easy, medium and hard difficulty.

4.2 Planning

As shown in Fig. 2 the study case was divided in four phases:

-*Training phase*: Participants were trained in prosumer philosophy, the GISAI-Pharma tool, its elements, and the configuration of these elements and operation of the tool. Training sessions consisted of 1h of theory at the beginning of the experimental validation and also personal interviews in order to solve matters related with the prosumer philosophy and specific problems with the use of the framework.

-*Service Creation phase*: The objective of this phase was to create three services by the participants solving three prototypical problems of drug traceability in a hospital pharmacy department using the GISAI-Pharma tool.

-*Service Adaptation phase*: This phase consisted of adapting three sample services to generate new services with the requirements proposed by the experts. The participants used the GISAI-Pharma tool for the adaptation.

4.3 Data Collection

The information collected to address the first research question (*What is the usefulness of the prosumer framework for service creation and adaptation?*) were obtained from two surveys:

In the first survey the participants were asked about the usefulness of each element of the prosumer framework from the standpoint of the creation of services to meet the specific needs of drug traceability in a hospital pharmacy department. In the second one the prosumer framework was analyzed from the standpoint of service adaptation.

The information collected to address the third research question (*What is the quality of the services created and adapted?*) evaluates the quality of the services created in the second phase (Service creation phase) and the services adapted in the third phase (Service adaptation phase). The experts evaluated all the services created and adapted using the following criteria: 5, if the service meets the requirements and is configured properly; 4, if the service meets the requirements but is not configured properly; 3, the service meets most of the requirements; 2, the service meets any of the requirements; 1, the service does not meet any requirement.

Finally, the information collected to address the third research question (*What is the experience required to create and adapt services in a prosumer environment?*) was related to the previous experience of the participants. The participants were asked about their experience, years of experience in service development, experience in software and service development, previous experience with prosumer philosophy, etc.

5   Results

This section presents and discusses the results obtained from the study answering the research questions proposed in this paper.

Usefulness of Prosumer Framework for Service Creation
Table 1 shows a summary of the participants´ usefulness perception of the prosumer framework, in a Likert scale from 1 to 5, by the average score, median and standard deviation (SD). In this subsection we will focus on service creation. We can observe that the perception of the usefulness of the framework for the service creation has been high, 50% of the participants gave the highest score and minimum scores were 3.

Table 1. Summary of usefulness evaluation of prosumer framework

	Average	Median	SD
Usefulness in service creation	4.2	4.5	0.919
Usefulness in service adaptation	4.6	5	0.5164
Usefulness of the environment	4.4063	4.5	1.598

Usefulness of Prosumer Framework for Service Adaptation
This section focuses on the usefulness of the prosumer framework for service adaptation. We have observed that the perception of the usefulness in this case has been considerably higher. 60% of the participants have provided the highest score and the minimum score registered was a 4. Participants were asked about whether they would buy services in a marketplace for using in their smart devices such as smart TVs, home automation systems, cars, etc.; 9 of 10 responded affirmatively.

Quality of the Services Created and Adapted

The overall average quality of all services (created and adapted) is 3.7333, which is a high value. As shown in Fig. 3 the quality is a bit higher for adapted services. That may be because it is easier to adapt an existing service than to create one from scratch. Participants suggested, through surveys and interviews with experts, that it is preferable to start with an already created service, similar to the desired requirements, and adapt it to the specific needs. Easy and medium services obtained higher quality values than hard services. This may be due to two reasons: the experts may have provided extremely difficult requirements for the services or the participants must receive more training in order to create and adapt more complex services.

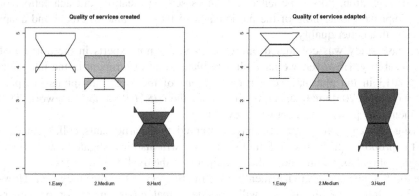

Fig. 3. Quality of services created and adapted

Experience Required to Create and Adapt Services in a Prosumer Environment

We created an experience aggregate for each one of the participants, a distribution with a high SD (1.4944). We tried to find some correlation between the variables that measure the experience and the variables that measure the quality of the services created and adapted, we have not found any conclusive hypothesis. We also tried to fit some linear regression models to predict the quality of services but the results have been unsuccessful. We conclude that it is not necessary to have experience in technology, software development or the use of devices such as smartphones, tablets or computers, in order to create and adapt services in a prosumer environment.

6   Discussion

In this article we present a tool called *GISAI-Pharma* which helps with the creation and adaptation of services in drug traceability scenarios. A case study has been deployed with the participation of 10 people, which were requested to create and adapt various services to solve problems in a hospital pharmacy environment; all of them had varied experience with technology and none of them were specialists on the domain of drug traceability in hospitals, and they only received an hour of training.

The results were very interesting: The perception of the usefulness of the environment was quite high, especially for adaptation of services. Furthermore, participants stated that it would be very interesting to be able to purchase services that solve recurring problems in a marketplace. The quality of created and adapted services was fairly high. The adapted services had better scores than created ones, and the hard services had a lower score on quality. This may be due to the short training received by participants (only one hour). The results in the quality of services were very positive and we were unable to demonstrate that experience improves the quality of services.

The main problem with this validation was the few people who participated in the case study. After such interesting results obtained in this first study, we are designing another experiment with more people involved, and, thus, we will be able to get statistical evidences which help us to know the factors that influence a correct service creation and adaptation, how experience influences service creation and adaptation, or how to improve the training of the participants so they are able to create and adapt services with a better quality.

This case study was conducted on people who are not experts in the domain of drug traceability. However, we have already planned an experiment in the late summer of 2013 in the pharmacy department of one of the largest hospitals in Spain where more than 20 domain experts will validate the *GISAI-Pharma* framework. This experiment may provide new statistical evidences.

During this case study, experts have observed that participants collaborated to solve the proposed problems. In future studies we will also investigate how it affects the degree of collaboration among the participants to the quality of services.

We did not have a real environment for testing the services in the study case. However, for future experiments, we will provide a real environment for prosumers enhance their motivation and to test the usefulness of their services.

References

1. Drossos, N., Mavrommati, I., Kameas, A.D.: Towards ubiquitous computing applications composed from functionally autonomous hybrid artifacts. In: Yuan, F., Kameas, A.D., Mavrommati, I. (eds.) The Disappearing Computer. LNCS, vol. 4500, pp. 161–181. Springer, Heidelberg (2007)
2. Future Internet Assembly Research Roadmap v2.0. Available at the European Future Internet Portal: http://www.future-internet.eu (retrieved: September 14, 2013)
3. Alcarria, R., Valladares, T.R., Morales, A., González-Miranda, S.: New Service Development Method for Prosumer Environments. In: The Sixth International Conference on Digital Society, ICDS 2012, Valencia, Spain, January 30-February 4, pp. 86–91 (2012)
4. Hierro, J.J., Janner, T., Lizcano, D., Reyes, M., Schroth, C., Soriano, J.: Enhancing User-Service Interaction through a Global User-Centric Approach to SOA. In: Fourth International Conference on Networking and Services, ICNS 2008, March 16-21, pp. 194–203 (2008)
5. Alcarria, R., Valladares, T.R., Morales, A., Herrera, E.C.: A Variability Model for Template Personalization in Mobile Prosumer Environments. In: AINA Workshops 2013, pp. 1313–1318 (2013)
6. Martín, D., López-de-Ipiña, D., Alzua-Sorzabal, A., Lamsfus, C., Torres-Manzanera, E.: A Methodology and a Web Platform for the Collaborative Development of Context-Aware Systems. Sensors 13, 6032–6053 (2013)

Plate Location and Recognition
Using Blob Analisys

Armando Aguileta-Mendoza[1] and Jorge Rivera-Rovelo[2]

[1] Carnegie Mellon University
aaguilet@andrew.cmu.edu
[2] Universidad Anahuac Mayab
jorge.rivera@anahuac.mx

Abstract. This work deals with plate location in an image and plate number recognition, which is done by detecting the plate area in the image and then applying a two phase processing: the phase one is to identify the digits (characters) in the plate region, and the second phase is to group them and analyze their properties. We use BLOB analisys for character location and grouping because plate characters have special properties that allows us to identify them from other objects without ambiguity. This (automatic) method can be used in several applications which range from parking or traffic control, to complex security systems.

1 Introduction

Plate Recognition tries to extract the plate number of vehicles from (conventional) images. We can find several comercial solutions, which are implemented using proprietary technologies; therefore such solutions are quite expensive and are like black box solutions. Currently, in the research community, there are several methods for plate detection and plate recognition [1–4]. For the plate detection (extracting the plate area from the image), the methods can be classified according to the data they use to locate it [5]: boundary and edge information, global image information, texture features, color features and character features. Some of them [6–8] achieve a high accuracy, but are mostly used to detect plates with uniform backgrounds and in optimal conditions. Without controlled environments, it is common that plates cannot be identified in the image. This can occur because of changes in the environment, like illumination conditions, confusing textures or similar objects, perspective projection, etc.

In this work, we present a different method for plate detection. First, it searches the image for plate digits directly (as in a 'character features' method), but then it groups them and analyzes the semantic properties derived from its relation with other candidate elements. This is done to determine if they can conform a license plate. The method is easy to implement and it uses only a conventional comercial camera (not a sophisticated one); in addition, it can identify the plate location even when the background of the plate contains some drawings or images which make other methods fail. For the recognition to be accomplished, the method follows two stages: the first one is to identify the plate

G. Urzaiz et al. (Eds.): UCAmI 2013, LNCS 8276, pp. 319–325, 2013.

digits (numbers), and the second one consists in grouping the numbers and then evaluate some properties (cardinality, set or group aspect ratio)

A plate is a generic object, and generally it is defined as a rectangle with a specific aspect ratio, which contains inside a lot of borders, while they decrease in the outside. Methods that deal with plate recognition using this definition ([1, 2]), frequently fails because they get confused with other objects like traffic signs or warnings, which have characteristics that fit this definition and have similar measures.

On the other hand, the plate number, or ID, is a set of characters which can be defined as BLOBS (Binary Large Objects), which have some useful characteristics like location, dimension, aspect ratio, between others.

The plate number determines the relationship between the characters which belong to it. That is, if we are looking for a plate we can know the number of characters in it, measures of a real character as well as its aspect ratio, distance between characters, and some measures can be derived, as a threshold for the distances between characters belonging to the plate.

2   Method

A general scheme of the proposed method is showed in Fig. 1.

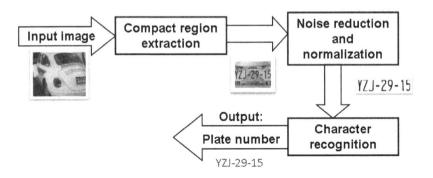

Fig. 1. General Scheme of the proposed method for plate recognition

The procedure for the *compact region* extraction is as follows:

```
Given a RGB image (I) to search for a plate, do:
1. Convert the image to gray scale.
2. Threshold the image gray levels to obtain a binary image.
3. Extract the Binary Objects (BLOBS) in the image.
4. Analyze the properties of the BLOBS.
5. Group BLOBS and select best candidates.
6. Mark the compact region of the plate.
```

The goal in step 2 is the image segmentation, that is, to assign every pixel in the image to a specific group or segment. Given a pixel, we can determine if it belongs to a segment or to other one by comparing its gray value with a threshold. The threshold value in step 2 is calculated in such a way that the resulting value can minimize the variance of every segment, and at the same time maximize the variance between segments [9]; that is, we compute the ratio between the two variances and choose as the threshold the value which maximizes that ratio. The weighted within-class variance is given by Eq. (1), where the the class variances are given by Eq. (2), the class probabilities are given by Eq. (3) and the means are given by Eq. (4). $P(i)$ is the probability of the gray value i.

$$\sigma_w^2(t) = q_1(t)\sigma_1^2(t) + q_2(t)\sigma_2^2(t) \tag{1}$$

$$\sigma_1^2(t) = \sum_{i=1}^{t}[i - \mu_1(t)]^2 \frac{P(i)}{q_1(t)} \qquad \sigma_2^2(t) = \sum_{i=t+1}^{I}[i - \mu_2(t)]^2 \frac{P(i)}{q_2(t)} \tag{2}$$

$$q_1(t) = \sum_{i=1}^{t} P(i) \qquad q_1(t) = \sum_{i=t+1}^{I} P(i) \tag{3}$$

$$\mu_1(t) = \sum_{i=1}^{t} \frac{iP(i)}{q_1(t)} \qquad \mu_2(t) = \sum_{i=t+1}^{I} \frac{iP(i)}{q_2(t)} \tag{4}$$

The goal of the analysis of the BLOBS is to eliminate the non-useful BLOBS considering some properties, like aspect ratio, neighborhoods, or characteristics of the neighborhood. After that, we can group the BLOBS with similar characteristics; that is, given the blobs A and B, we group them if and only if they accomplish Eq. (5) to (8).

$$A_{y_{min}} - \frac{A_{y_{min}}}{C_1} < B_{y_{min}} < A_{y_{min}} + \frac{A_{y_{min}}}{C_1} \tag{5}$$

$$A_{y_{max}} - \frac{A_{y_{max}}}{C_1} < B_{y_{max}} < A_{y_{max}} + \frac{A_{y_{max}}}{C_1} \tag{6}$$

$$B_{x_{min}} < A_{x_{min}} - C_3(A_{x_{max}} - A_{x_{min}}) \tag{7}$$

$$B_{x_{max}} < A_{x_{max}} + C_3(A_{x_{max}} - A_{x_{min}}) \tag{8}$$

where subscript x or y indicates the horizontal or vertical position, respectively; and min and max indicates the minimum and maximum value, respectively. C_1 and C_3 are constants (we use $C_1 = 8$ and $C_3 = 9$).

In step 6 we obtain the coordinates of the compact region, we copy such region of the original image and we proceed to normalize and to eliminate noise in such a region. In this step, we compute the width R_w, height R_h and maximum position of the horizontal and vertical axis ($R_{x_{max}}$ and $R_{y_{max}}$),for the compact region. Once we have the compact region coordinates, we proceed to save the resulting image for the next step in processing.

For the normalization and noise elimination in the compact region we do the following:

1. Threshold the image
2. Apply the erosion method to avoid noise, computing a local minimum in the area covered by a 3x3 pixel kernel, for each pixel in the image
3. Compute the BLOBS inside the compact region and select those which have the aspect ratio and size required (minimum).
4. Save the resulting image.

Once we have the image of the plate characters, we proceed to the character recognition phase. To recognize the characters we are using Tesseract 2.04; an Open Source Optical Character Recognition (OCR) library, which performs a connected component analysis, word segmentation and a two-pass recognition process using an adaptive classifier [10]. As a result, we obtain a character vector containing the ASCII characters in the image of the compact region.

3   Experimental Results

The proposed method was applied to a set of 68 images with different characteristics (different lighting conditions, brightness, plate size, environment of the car (on the road, at the parking, near vegetation, in the city)). As a result, the region of interest (plate region) was successfully identified in 92.64% of the tests. Figure 2 shows the percentage of correct and incorrect detection of plates and character recognition for the set of images.

Fig. 2. Results for plate area detection and for character recognition using a set of 68 images under diferent illumination conditions and background images in the plate area

If we compare the method we propose with others without considering the context, it would seem to be less accurate by a 4-7 percent. Nevertheless it is important to consider the following factors:

– Most of the methods with highest accuracy [6–8] are designed for, and tested with, license plates with a solid background while the method we propose is designed to account for plates with background images and other decorations within the plate.

Fig. 3. Image of diferent cars in diferent conditions; the identification of the plate region obtained with the proposed method, and results from compact plate region normalization

– The pictures used to test this method represent mostly non-optimal environments, as can be seen in Fig. 3.

The character recognition was successfull in 76.5% of the tests; in other words, we recognize correctly 344 of the 455 characters in the test set (see Fig. 2). The average time in the recognition stage was 5 seconds with images of 5Mpx.

Figure 3 shows examples of successful compact region identification using the method described, even in the case of distortions, noise, different plate colors and a non-uniform background in the plate region.

4   Conclusion

The method described in this paper gives better results than traditional methods when applied to find plate numbers in *problematic* images, like those with a lot of borders or plates with background images and other decorations within the plate; for example, images of a car in an environment full of vegetation, or plates with background like the mexican plates. The main disadvantage of the method is that it consumes a lot of memory. That is because it requires to maintain reference to every BLOB in order to compute the comparisons and analysis.

Now we will adjust the presented method in order to do all the process remotely (cloud computing), in order to make it available for mobile devices with a camera, but with limited resources. This can also be implemented at the University access and parking services, as part of the security system.

Acknowledgment. The authors would like to thank to Universidad Anahuac-Mayab for supporting this work.

References

1. Evans-Pughe, C.: Road watch (automatic number plate recognition system). Engineering and Technology 1(4), 36–39 (2006)
2. Shaaban, Z.: An Intelligent License Plate Recognition System. International Journal of Computer Science and Network Security 11(7) (July 2011)
3. Kulkarni, P., Khatri, A., Banga, P., Shah, K.: Automatic Number Plate Recognition (ANPR) System for Indian conditions. In: 19th International Conference Radioelektronika (2009)
4. Shen-Zheng, W., Hsi-Jian, L.: A Cascade Framework for a Real-Time Statistical Plate Recognition System. IEEE Transactions on Information Forensics and Security 2(2) (2007)
5. Du, S., Shehata, M., Badawy, W.: Automatic License Plate Recognition (ALPR): A State of the Art Review. IEEE Transactions on Circuits and Systems for Video Technology, 23(2) (February 2013)
6. Bai, H., Liu, C.: A hybrid license plate extraction method based on edge statistics and morphology. In: Proceedings of the International Conference in Pattern Recognition, vol. 2, pp. 831–834 (2004)

7. Guo, J.-M., Liu, Y.-F.: License plate localization and character segmentation with feedback self-learning and hybrid binarization techniques. IEEE Transactions on Vehicular Technology 57(3), 1417–1424 (2008)
8. Anagnostopoulos, C., Alexandropoulos, T., Loumos, V., Kayafas, E.: Intelligent traffic management through MPEG-7 vehicle flow surveillance. In: Proceedings of IEEE International Symposium on Modern Computing, pp. 202–207 (October 2006)
9. Otsu, N.: A Threshold Selection Method from Gray-Level Histograms. IEEE Transactions on System, Man, and Cybernetics. SMC 9(1) (1979)
10. Smith, R.: An Overview of the Tesseract OCR Engine. In: Proceedings of the International Conference on Document Analysis and Recognition, Curitiba, Brazil (September 2007)

Applying Ambient Intelligence
to Improve Public Road Transport

Gabino Padrón, Carmelo R. García, Alexis Quesada-Arencibia,
Francisco Alayón, and Ricardo Pérez

Institute for Cybernetic Science and Technology
University of Las Palmas de Gran Canaria
{rgarcia,gpadron,aquesada,falayon,rperez}@dis.ulpgc.es

Abstract. This paper described the smart system that is executed on board the vehicles of the fleet of a public transport company whose mission is to help the regulating authorities to control, verify and enhance the public transport service. This system is autonomous and does not interfere in the operations carried out by the vehicle; it provides useful data obtained transparently from drivers and passengers, using different sensors installed in the vehicle. The system has been used in several vehicles of the public transport fleet's in real operational conditions and some of the results obtained are presented here.

Keywords: ambient intelligence, ubiquitous computing, ubiquitous data management, intelligent transport systems.

1   Introduction

The people responsible for regulating public passenger road transport need data that will enable them to verify that services [1] and itineraries are being completed as planned. For this reason, these agencies constantly request data from the companies charged with offering this service in regard of each vehicle. The data requested include: the time the vehicle sets out, the time it reaches each stop, the frequency and journeys carried out. These data are often difficult to supply because the companies lack the necessary technology to obtain them, which obliges them to gather the data manually. The authorities request such data not only to supervise the offered services, but also to enhance operational planning, for example: optimizing frequencies, fine-tuning the times the vehicles reach each stop in line with reality, and designing the public transport network infrastructure by changing the location of stops, enhancing the infrastructure of stops depending on the use made of them by passengers, etc. We will here describe a system that aims to provide a smart environment to supervise the activity that takes place in the vehicle based on installing various devices and sensors in the vehicle. This also enables useful information to be obtained that enables the public transport service to be enhanced, improving the punctuality of the vehicle at the various stops, the frequency of the routes depending on demand, and security, by making the drivers' task easier.

G. Urzaiz et al. (Eds.): UCAmI 2013, LNCS 8276, pp. 326–333, 2013.
© Springer International Publishing Switzerland 2013

The objectives of the proposed system will be explained in the next section. Subsequently, the main aspects of the system are presented, the following section offers some results and the last sets forth the main conclusions.

2   Related Works

In the bibliography, there are several references about on board data processing in public transport to improve quality service. Some of these works are based on Automatic Vehicle Location System (AVLS), for example the contributions of Furth [1], [2] and García [3]. Other authors, such as Dell'Olio [4] and Zaho [5], try to achieve this goal by the optimization of cost functions based on a set of parameters. Finally, another approach to this problem is the development of systems for and automatic generation of scheduling and timetables, being a case of this kind of system the Dynamic Timetable Generator proposed by Okunieff [6] that is based on traditional clustering techniques.

3   System Goals

The system we will describe provides an intelligent environment on board a public transport vehicle. The system has four objectives, all of which are very important in this sector. The first is to control the quality of the service in order to ensure that it goes according to plan. The second consists of improving planning, bringing it in line with passengers' needs, for example Furth [7] uses localization data of public transport vehicle to improve the reliability of the services analysing the waiting time of the passengers. The third objective is to share a vehicle's information with the infrastructure of urban areas in order to facilitate the enhancing of the quality of life in cities and urban areas, for example Kon [8] describes a system that using different kind of sensors provides real-time information about the traffic of the metropolitan area of Shanghai. The fourth objective consists of making driving safer by providing the driver with useful information of automating tasks so that the driver can concentrate on driving the vehicle. In order to achieve these four objectives, the system has to integrate the various elements (devices and sensors) that provide the data to these ends. This integration should not interfere in the normal operation of the vehicle, in the tasks carried out on board or affect the performance of the infrastructure of the vehicle itself (both hardware and software) and it must be transparent to the driver and the passengers on board. Coughlin [9] proposes a system, named AwareCar, based on ambient intelligence and pervasive technology for detecting driver states (stress, fatigue and inattention). Doshy [10] describes a pervasive system to enhance the driver safety detecting in real-time on-road line-change-intent.

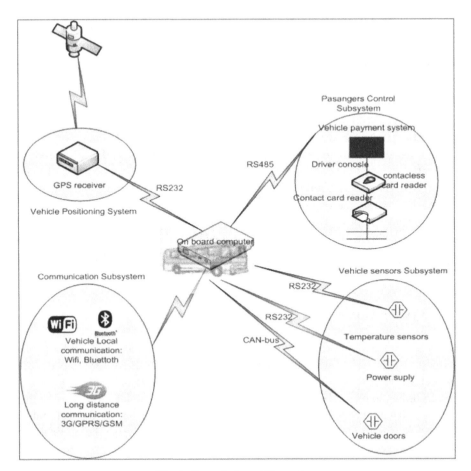

Fig. 1. General view of the system

According to Furth [2], two models of systems have been developed to attain the objectives laid out: Automatic Vehicle Location Systems, which, as its name indicates, they are based on obtaining ongoing data regarding the exact position of the vehicle and from these data, partially reaching the above-mentioned objectives. The other kind of system is the Automatic Passenger Counting System, which registers the passengers that get on and off the vehicle. These systems also enable the objectives to be partially met. The system we propose in this paper uses not only information regarding the position of the vehicle and passenger registration, but also data provided by sensors and by executing artificial intelligence techniques, generating a smart system on board. This approach is coherent with the proposal of Dias Camacho [11], this author uses the pervasive technology in public transport in order to enhance the quality and the customer satisfaction. A case of intelligent system for public transport, using a similar architecture to that proposed in this work, is Mobi+ [12] that improves the disabled people accessibly.

4   System Description

The developed system is functionally structured in four subsystems (Fig. 1). The Vehicle positioning subsystem provides location data in order to be able to reference all the vehicle's activity in space and time. The device currently used is a GPS receiver that provides the spatial coordinates of latitude, longitude and height and a reliable time reference that is common to the whole fleet. The Passenger Control Subsystem enables us to know how many passengers are on board at all times and where exactly they get on and off the vehicle. In order to obtain these data, this subsystem uses the payment devices (ticket sale terminal and contact-free ticket terminal). The Sensor Subsystem provides data regarding certain states of the vehicle and the prevailing environmental conditions. More specifically, the devices used are the sensors that detect open doors, temperature and the state of the batteries. The On-board Computer is responsible for obtaining, processing and storing all the relevant data provided by the above-mentioned subsystems. This computer is capable of operating in adverse environmental conditions (both in terms of temperature and vibrations), is small in size and has sufficient computer and storage capacity to execute all the processes needed in this intelligent environment. Lastly, the Communications Subsystem enables the On-board Computer to communicate both with the various on-board subsystems using different communication standard protocols (RS232, RS485 and CAN-bus) and with other external systems using wireless communication infrastructure: GPRS/GSM, Wifi and Bluetooth.

4.1   System Data

From the point of view of data handling, the system proposed represents a case of an ubiquitous massive data management system. According to Perich [13], this type of system characteristically has four properties. Firstly, its capacity to operate in environments where the number of data spaces and applications that access these data spaces is dynamic. Secondly, its capacity to operate with different data catalogues and schemas. The high risk of inconsistency in data found in ubiquitous environments, resulting from the spontaneity of the connections and disconnections of the applications accessing them, gives rise to the third property, which consists of the provision of mechanisms to solve any such possible inconsistencies. The fourth property is that, in order to facilitate access to the data, the system must include collaboration mechanisms among the applications.

In our case, these challenges have been solved by using a collaborative model of agents that obtain the data provided by the various sensors and devices of the above-mentioned subsystems. The conceptual model and its implementation in the form of a database have been described in García [3]. Basically, all relevant events that take place in the vehicle are represented in a set of data produced by the sensors or devices; the number of data and structure of this set is variable and depends on the type of event represented. In order to guarantee the interoperability between databases, an ontology that is implemented by means of a catalogue and a data schema called interoperability database is used. All data are referenced in time and space (geo-referenced), so that the following coordinates make it possible to reproduce and infer everything that occurs in the vehicle:

- Universal Time Coordinate (UTC)
- Dynamic Vehicle Coordinates (Latitude, Longitude, height, speed)

The obtained data represent relevant events in the vehicle's operations. This record can be taken periodically, or not. An example of a datum obtained periodically is the position of the vehicle provided by the location subsystem; this datum is obtained each second. An example of a datum obtained non-periodically is the boarding or disembarkation of a passenger, or the opening of one of the vehicle's doors.

Fig. 2. Point at which a vehicle stops

5   An Example of the System in Use

In 2009, the Gran Canaria Transport Agency, within the framework of which all this study has taken place, installed the necessary technological equipment to set up the described system in all its public road transport service on the island of Gran Canaria. A common problem in locating vehicles is to determine, given the specific position of the vehicle in question, exactly which point of the journey it is at. If it is moving, we can assume that it is passing between two spots on the route it is covering in a specific direction. If it has stopped, it may be in situations like the one we can see in Fig. 2, where the vehicle has stopped not at a programmed stop on the route but at traffic lights, or where it does not have right of way and therefore stops often. The identification and detection of this type of points is important since these spots on the route may, depending on the traffic conditions, affect the time it takes to get from one stop to the next, and therefore it helps to determine if the scheduled operations are satisfied. Due to the fact that the proposed system enables us to differentiate between situations in which the vehicle has had to stop at traffic lights, as we can see in Fig. 2, or at a programmed stop, it is possible to improve the data model of the transport network by including points that, not being elements of the transport infrastructure (such as stops and stations), should be taken into consideration when establishing the arriving time of the vehicles to the programmed stops. Moreover, since traffic conditions are dynamic, the time taken to reach those stops will vary depending on the time of day, whether the journey is undertaken on a weekday or at the weekend and also due to possible changes in traffic signs. The proposed system can identify and detect these types of conditions.

The identification of these types of spots could be carried out using the data provided by the open doors sensors, but not all vehicles carry these sensors and, sometimes, the signals issued by the sensors may not be accessible. Hence, the method used by the system only considers the data provided by the vehicle location system, specifically its location coordinates (latitude, longitude, height, speed).

Firstly, our method records the vehicle's dynamic coordinates over a significant period of time. Secondly, once the journey covered has been established, i.e. the set of geographic points through which the vehicle will pass, it applies a data mining method based on the K-means algorithm. The goal is to identify patterns of the vehicle positioning associated with different situations: bus stop, traffic congestion, traffic signal, etc. The method uses the location of the stops along the journey as an initial approximation.

The result of applying the method to all the measurements available on the journey produces three clearly identifiable types of clusters, each of which has a different meaning:

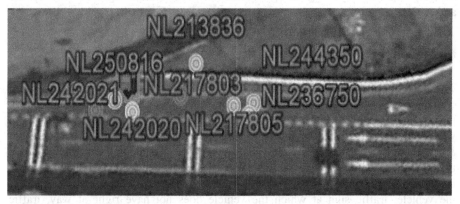

Fig. 3. Point of the route where the vehicle does not have right of way and so it is frequently forced to stop. The orange circles represent vehicle positions at zero speed, the text in green are the labels of these positions (image obtained from GoogleMaps).

- Case 1: A cluster with just one programmed stop, whose centroid is very close to that stop. This case corresponds to a normal stop made by the vehicle at a point on the journey, and represents the most common case in our study.
- Case 2: A cluster of non programmed stop. The second case corresponds to those places on the journey where the vehicle does not have right of way and so it is forced to stop (Fig. 2). However, the specific spot at which it stops does not

appear among the points on the network so a similar result to case 1 is not obtained. In this case, the position of the centroid of the cluster corresponds to the location of the traffic sign that constrains the passage of the vehicle (give way, stop, traffic lights or a narrowing of the road, Fig. 3).

- Case 3: A cluster with more than one programmed stop on the line. This case corresponds to urban journeys on which the stops are relatively close to one another and also tend to feature traffic sign that do not give the vehicle right of way.

For the type 3 clusters, the method executes a new iteration, i.e. the K-means algorithm is applied once again, this time restricted to the points assigned to the cluster in the first iteration, taking as an initial approximation for the second and following iterations, the stops in the network present in the cluster and the centroid obtained in the first stage. Thus, the points come together in new centroids, each located around the network stops that are in the cluster and around the signs where the vehicle does not enjoy right of way. The operation has to be reiterated until a result is obtained. In this case the points form clusters that are close to the centroids of their group associated with just one stop in the network or with a traffic sign where the vehicle does not enjoy right of way. Thus, the system enables these signs to be automatically located and to be included in the network, or points to the possibility of studying the viability of granting public transport vehicles right of way by the authorities.

6   Conclusions

This paper has described the case of a system that, using different elements (on-board computer, sensors, location-determining devices, payment devices and network infrastructure) installed in a transport vehicle, produces an intelligent environment in which the on-board system is able to identify and automatically handle elements that affect operations carried out by the vehicle. We have presented an example of a case in which the system is able to identify the causes by which a public transport vehicle is stopped during an expedition: programmed stop at which passengers get on or off the vehicle, traffic sign at which the vehicle does not have right of way, traffic congestion, etc. Based on this information, it is possible to check whether or not the vehicle arrives at the programmed stops on time in order to determine the extent to which it complies with the envisaged quality of service to the passenger. These data give the public transport agencies information that is closer to reality and enables them to make decisions from an enhanced perspective. A further capacity offered by the model presented here is that of detecting and identifying new situations given the dynamic character of the factors that affect traffic and influence the vehicles' operation, making it possible to detect and identify what is happening without needing to go out onto the road.

References

1. Furth, P., et al.: Data Analysis for Bus Planning and Monitoring. Transit Cooperative Research Program, Synthesis 34, 1–71 (2000)
2. Furth, P.G., Muller, T.H.J., Strathman, J.G., Hemily, B.: Uses of Archived AVL-APC Data to Improve Transit Management and Performance: Review and Potential. TCRP Web Document 23, Project H-28 (2003)
3. García, C.R., Padrón, G., Quesada-Arencibia, A., Alayón, F., Pérez, R.: Ubiquitous Data Management in Public Transport. In: Bravo, J., López-de-Ipiña, D., Moya, F. (eds.) UCAmI 2012. LNCS, vol. 7656, pp. 342–349. Springer, Heidelberg (2012)
4. Dell'Olio, L., Moura, J.L., Ibeas, A.: A bi-level mathematical programming model to locate bus stops and optimise frequencies. In: TRB 85th Annual Meeting and Transportation Research Record, Washington (2006)
5. Zhao, F.: Large Scale Transit Network Optimization by Minimizing User Cost and Transfers. Journal of Public Transportation 9(2) (2006)
6. Okunieff, P.: Dynamic Timetable Generator, Transit Cooperative Research Program, Transit IDEA Project 39, Final Report (2006)
7. Furth, P.G., Muller, T.H.J.: Services Reliability and Hidden Waiting Time: Insights from AVL Data. Transportation Research Record, 1–21 (2006)
8. Kong, Q., Chen, Y., Liu, Y.: A Fusion-Based System for Road-Network Traffic Satate Surveillance: A Case Study of Shanghai. IEEE Intelligent Transport Systems Magazine 3(2), 37–42 (2009)
9. Coughlin, J.F., Reimer, B., Mehler, B.: Monitoring, Managing, and Motivating Driver Safety and Well-Being. IEEE Pervasive Computing 10(3), 14–21 (2011)
10. Doshi, A., Morris, B.T., Trivedi, M.M.: On-Road Prediction of Driver's Intent with Multimodal Sensory Cues. IEEE Pervasive Computing 10(3), 22–34 (2011)
11. Dias Camacho, T., Foth, M., Rakotonirainy, A.: Pervasive Technology and Public Transport: Opportunities beyond Telematics. IEEE Pervasive Computing 12(1), 18–25 (2013)
12. Zou, H., Hou, K., Li, J.: Intelligent Urban Public Transportation for Accessibility Dedicated to People with Disabilities. Sensors 12, 10678–10692 (2012)
13. Perich, F., et al.: On Data Management in Pervasive Computing Environments. IEEE Transaction on Knowledge and Data Engineering 16(5), 621–663 (2004)

Towards a Train-to-Ground and Intra-wagon Communications Solution Capable of Providing on Trip Customized Digital Services for Passengers

Itziar Salaberria[1,*], Asier Perallos[1], Leire Azpilicueta[2], Francisco Falcone[2], Roberto Carballedo[1], Ignacio Angulo[1], Pilar Elejoste[1], José Javier Astráin[3], and Jesús Villadangos[3]

[1] Deusto Institute of Technology (DeustoTech), University of Deusto, 48007 Bilbao, Spain
{itziar.salaberria,perallos,roberto.carballedo,
ignacio.angulo,pilar.elejoste}@deusto.es
[2] Electrical and Electronic Engineering Department,
Universidad Pública de Navarra, 31006 Pamplona, Spain
{leyre.azpilicueta,francisco.falcone}@unavarra.es
[3] Mathematics and Computer Engineering Department,
Universidad Pública de Navarra, 31006 Pamplona, Spain
{josej.astrain,jesusv}@unavarra.es

Abstract. The widespread adoption of Smartphone by citizens represents a great opportunity to integrate such nomadic devices inside vehicles in order to provide new on trip personalized digital services for passengers. In this paper a proposal of communication architecture to provide the ubiquitous connectivity needed to enhance the concept of smart train is presented and preliminarily tested. It combines an intra-wagon communication system based on nomadic devices connected through a Bluetooth Piconet Network with a highly innovative train-to-ground communication system.

Keywords: smart train, ubiquitous communications, bluetooth piconet network, train-to-ground communication, context-aware services.

1   Introduction

The widespread use of wireless and Internet technologies in transport systems enables the provision of a large number of new intelligent services. Moreover, the presence of ubiquitous connected vehicles (trains, undergrounds, buses or cars), including intra and inter vehicular communications, as well as continuous connectivity with their traffic control centers, is a key factor for the new generations of Intelligent Transportations Systems (ITS). On the other hand, the rise of Smartphone adoption by citizens represents a great opportunity to integrate such nomadic devices inside vehicles in order to improve the services and quality of information provided to the passengers.

In railway industry, where our work is focused on, wired networks (such as Ethernet) for intra-train communications are commonly adopted. These networks are

---

* Corrresponding author.

G. Urzaiz et al. (Eds.): UCAmI 2013, LNCS 8276, pp. 334–341, 2013.
© Springer International Publishing Switzerland 2013

mainly used by safety and control systems hosted inside the train. The innovation of this work is to enhance the concept of ubiquitous connected smart train by contributing with advances in train-to-ground wireless communication systems [1] and taking advantage of the communication and interaction possibilities of Smartphones for communications inside the train. The combination of these two challenges, an intra-train communication system based on nomadic devices and a highly innovative train-to-ground communication system, will be able to improve the experience of passengers who could be provided with more customized information.

The rest of the paper is organized as follows. First, the current network architecture of the train where our proposed solution is being tested is described. Second, the train-to-ground communications design. Third, intra-wagon communications are proposed including several simulation results. Finally, the conclusions and future work.

2   Related Work

Nowadays the use of wireless and Internet technologies is increasing in the railway industry enabling bidirectional train-to-ground communications [2]. However these kinds of communications applied to this environment have to respond to several challenges related to aspects like coverage, bandwidth, communication disruptions, multiple network interfaces for communications and different priorities in the data transmission, responding at the same time to Quality of Service (QoS) [3] demanded by applications.

There are multiple works regarding communications optimization, including traffic prioritization and QoS control. However, these works are usually focused on networks instead of applications or services that use these networks [4]. In addition, there are industrial solutions designed to respond to these detected communications needs and challenges in transportation systems [1, 5]. But neither of these projects establishes a communication system that prioritize data transmissions dynamically, making at the same time a QoS control based on bandwidth availability. The solution proposed on this paper includes a train-to-ground communication system designed to respond to all these challenges.

3   Architecture of the Ubiquitous Connected Train

The proposed solution establishes a communication system that enables intra-train and train-to-ground connectivity. This work has been deployed in a train manufactured by CAF (one of the largest train manufacturers in the world). Concerning integration issues, trains connectivity architecture is one of the most important aspects of the work. Specifically, the train used to carry out our tests has two networks that connect all devices that are deployed on the train.

On the one hand, it is the control network known as Train Communication Network (TCN). This network was the result of the work of the most important railway manufacturers (mainly Bombardier and Siemens) and its architecture is based on IEC 61375 standard [6]. TCN is used to control and exchange of information among the most important elements of the train; basically those responsible for the movement and braking.

On the other hand, there is the Added-Value Network (AVN). This network architecture is very similar to a local area network. It is usually based on the Ethernet

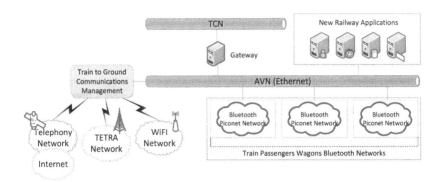

Fig. 1. Network architecture of the ubiquitous connected train

standard. The objective of this second network is the connection of the devices that support other essential components of the train, such as: people counting systems, air conditioning systems, infotainment systems.

Taking into account this train network architecture (Fig. 1), firstly, the solution presented in this paper proposes the creation of a Bluetooth Piconet Network (BPN) [7] inside each passenger wagon. These BPN enable to share and distribute information and contents with passengers' devices, allowing the establishment of ad-hoc operation between dynamic users, which can change along a variable time-span within the proposed scenario. Individual dongles could also be employed, which in principle would not modify the results in radioelectric terms. Secondly, in our approach a reliable train-to-ground communication system is developed which integrates the on-board communication network, GSM radio links, TETRA network and Internet technologies. It becomes the key element to offer ubiquitous remote access to on-board equipment and distribute applications from transportation ground systems.

So, this solution deploys a BPN on each wagon. BPNs are interconnected each other through train Ethernet network (AVN), which enables an information channel along the train. AVN is also integrated with the train-to-ground communication system in order to achieve external connectivity.

This approach will allow the railways companies to exchange information with their trains and distribute contents and information to the users. Thus, this kind of communications enables the development of new on trip personalized digital services for passengers (e.g. trip information, weather forecast or train connections in destination).

4   Train-to-Ground Communications

In order to respond to train-to-ground communications challenges, we propose a communication middleware that aims to enable several physical network links between train and ground system (3G, WiFi, etc.). It chooses the network link considered as the best at every moment according to the bandwidth availability.

This middleware has been designed to respond to several requirements:

1. *Dynamic and efficient communication request management:* this system prioritizes train-to-ground communications requests taking into account communication urgency criteria, as well as previous performance logs.
2. *The best bandwidth:* the system always selects the physical link considered as the best taking into account the bandwidth in order to respond to final applications communication requirements.
3. *Quality of Service:* this solution aims to make a service quality management too. Therefore it is necessary to know the bandwidth availability offered by the network link which is active at every moment, as well as the bandwidth offered by the rest of communications links (although they are not being used). At this point it is essential to establish a set of connection procedures which enable to reserve a certain bandwidth for a particular communication.

This middleware is composed of two software elements (Fig. 2); one in the terrestrial side (Ground Communication Manager, GCM), and the other boarded in trains (Train Communication Manager, TCM). The former manages terrestrial aspects of the architecture and the latter train-side issues. They interact with each other in order to control and manage train-to-ground communications. In addition, this system includes a Bandwidth Measurement Service (BMS) that notifies available links bandwidth values to the GCM at every moment.

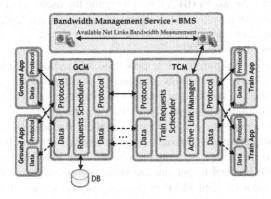

Fig. 2. Train-to-ground communication middleware architecture

In order to establish train-to-ground communications, TCM and GCM can communicate through different communications network physical links. The TCM is who selects the active link considered most favourable for communications based on available links bandwidth measurements notified by BMS, and then establishes active link connection with GCM. Two kinds of flows are involved in these communications: data and control. Thus, GCM and TCM on each train communicate each other and exchange commands in order to establish active links and manage the prioritization of train and ground final applications requests. These priorities are managed using specific queue scheduling techniques. The control protocol is defined using XML messages where information is exchanged via TCP/IP sockets.

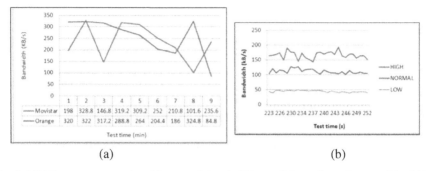

(a)   (b)

Fig. 3. Middleware tests results: (a) network bandwidth conditions along the test, (b) middleware communications management performance applying different request priorities

At this moment, all these abilities are being successfully tested through preconfigured scenarios which includes a set of known communication requests (generated both on ground side and on trains) and network conditions.

5   Intra-wagon Communications

Our approach proposes an intra-wagon communications network establishment based on Bluetooth Piconet Networks (BPN), which enable the users' ubiquitous interaction with the train information systems. So, Bluetooth devices are organized in small networks (piconets) with one device acting as the master and up to seven others acting as active slaves, at any given time [7].

Piconet [8] is a general-purpose, low-power ad hoc radio network that provides a base level of connectivity to even the simplest of sensing and computing objects. It provides a broad range of mobile and embedded computing objects with the ability to exploit an awareness of, and connectivity to, their environment.

Sensors can use piconet to relay information about the state of the local environment or of a particular device. Personal connectivity is improved because the multitude of mobile and fixed devices commonly used by an individual can be connected by piconet; it might be used to personalize things nearby or allow two devices near each other to interoperate. Embedded networking is also suitable for smart information services: active diaries, alarms, information points, and electronic business cards, for example. The proximate connectivity that piconet provides means these applications can be context-aware [9].

Therefore, the proposed solution applies intra-wagon communications creating a BPN inside each passenger train wagon. The tests have been based on three devices, one master unit and two slaves. The master unit device is collocated just below the ceiling in the central part of the wagon, and the two slaves are just above the seats, emulating a real person who is sitting in the wagon sending information with a mobile device.

In addition, simulations have been made using the indoor wagon passenger train as scenario. The wagon has been modeled as a metallic cube, with rows of seats with a polycarbonate base. Simulations are based on the deterministic method of a 3D beam source, with the aid of an in-house developed ray launching code [9-11] to analyze the complex scenario of the indoor wagon passenger train. This approach is based in

Geometrical Optics and Uniform Geometrical Theory of Diffraction. It is important to emphasize that the topology and morphology of the indoor section of the vehicle have a significant impact in the response of the system. Reflection, refraction and diffraction phenomena have been taken into account, as well as all the material parameters (given by dielectric constant values as well as conductivity values at the operational frequency of the system). The passenger seats are made of polycarbonate, the floors and walls of aluminum and the windows of glass. Simulation parameters are shown in Table 1. The cuboids resolution and the number of reflections have been set to 10cm and 5, respectively, to balance accuracy with simulation time.

Table 1. Parameters in the ray launching simulation

Frequency	2.4GHz
Vertical plane angle resolution $\Delta\theta$	1°
Horizontal plane angle resolution $\Delta\varphi$	1°
Reflections	5
Transmitter Power	0dBm
Cuboids resolution	10cm

Fig. 4 shows the power distribution inside the wagon for a height of 1.5meters. As it can be seen, morphology as well as topology of the considered scenario has a noticeable impact on radio wave propagation.

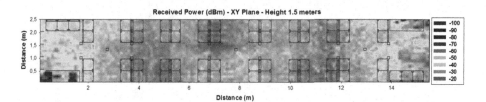

Fig. 4. Estimation of received power (dBm) on the indoor passenger wagon train for a height of 1.5m, obtained by full 3D Ray Launching algorithm

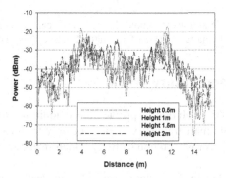

Fig. 5. Estimation of radials of received power (dBm) along the X-axis for Y=1.25m along the indoor passenger wagon train

Fig. 5 depicts the radials of power along the wagon train (X-axis) for a fixed value of Y, which is Y=1.25m, for different heights. It is observed that the distribution of power has a lot of variability due mainly to the strong influence of multipath components.

As stated above, in this type of environment, the fundamental radioelectric phenomenon is given by multipath propagation. To illustrate this fact, the power delay profile for the passenger wagon in a central location has been obtained and is shown in Fig. 6 for each transmitter of the BPN. As it is observed, there are a large number of echoes in the scenario due to this behavior of multipath channel.

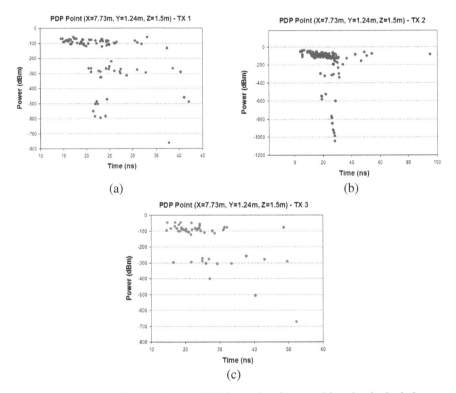

(a)   (b)

(c)

Fig. 6. Power Delay Profile at a given cuboid, located at the central location in the indoor wagon train (a) Transmitter 1 (master unit) (b) Transmitter 2 (slave 1) (c) Transmitter 3 (slave 3)

6   Conclusion and Future Work

This paper has proposed a solution to provide the ubiquitous connectivity needed to enhance the concept of smart train. It includes not only train-to-ground communication systems, but also intra-wagon connectivity which integrates passengers' devices in the environment.

Regarding the last challenge, results of several radioelectric simulations have been presented in order to analyze the viability of the applications of Bluetooth Piconet Networks inside train wagons, using an indoor wagon passenger train as test scenario.

On the other hand, a research work focused on the development of a train-to-ground communication middleware designed to respond to communication requirements demanded by railway applications was presented. It manages aspects related to QoS, uses multiple radio and mobile interfaces (GPRS, UMTS, WLAN, etc.) and adopts an "always best connected" approach to enhance communications availability and obtain the best bandwidth capabilities, by selecting always the most favorable network link. Finally, future work relative to the exploitation of this communication system by the development of on trip customized added value services for passengers will be explored.

Acknowledgments. This work has been funded by the Ministry of Science and Innovation of Spain under INNPACTO funding program (RailTrace project, IPT-370000-2010-036). Special thanks to Eusko Trenbideak - Ferrocarriles Vascos S.A. for their support.

References

1. Salaberria, I., Carballedo, R., Perallos, A.: Wireless Technologies in the Railway: Train-to-Earth Wireless Communications. Wireless Communications and Networks - Recent Advances, 469–492 (2012) ISBN: 978-953-51-0189-5
2. Qi, L.: Research on Intelligent Transportation System Technologies and Applications. In: Workshop on Power Electronics and Intelligent Transportation System, pp. 529–531 (2008)
3. Marrero, D., Macías, E.M., Suárez, A.: An admission control and traffic regulation mechanism for infrastructure WiFi networks. IAENG International Journal of Computer Science 35(1), 154–160 (2008) ISSN: 1819-656X
4. Martínez, I.: Contribuciones a Modelos de Tráfico y Control de QoS en los Nuevos Servicios Sanitarios Basados en Telemedicina. Tesis Doctoral (2006)
5. Boss: On Board Wireless Secured Video Surveillance (2012), http://celtic-boss.mik.bme.hu/
6. Schifers, C., Hans, G.: IEC 61375-1 and UIC 556-international standards for train communication. In: IEEE 51st Vehicular Technology Conference Proceedings (VTC), Spring Tokyo, vol. 2, p. 1581 (2010)
7. Bluetooth SIG, Specification of the Bluetooth System – Architecture & Terminology Overview. Version 1.2 1 (2003)
8. Bennett, F., et al.: Piconet: embedded mobile networking. IEEE Personal Communications 4 (1997) ISSN 1070-9916
9. Azpilicueta, L., Falcone, F., Astráin, J.J., Villadangos, J., García Zuazola, I.J., Landaluce, H., Angulo, I., Perallos, A.: Measurement and modeling of a UHF-RFID system in a metallic closed vehicle. Microwave and Optical Technology Letters 54(9), 2126–2130 (2012)
10. Nazábal, J.A., Iturri López, P., Azpilicueta, L., Falcone, F., Fernández-Valdivielso, C.: Performance Analysis of IEEE 802.15.4 Compliant Wireless Devices for Heterogeneous Indoor Home Automation Environments. International Journal of Antennas and Propagation (2012)
11. Aguirre, E., Arpón, J., Azpilicueta, L., de Miguel, S., Ramos, V., Falcone, F.: Evaluation of electromagnetic dosimetry of wireless systems in complex indoor scenarios with human body interaction. Progress in Electromagnetics Research B 43, 189–209 (2012)

Reducing Drivers' Distractions in Phone-Based Navigation Assistants Using Landmarks

Gioconda Tarqui[1], Luis A. Castro[2], and Jesus Favela[1]

[1] Centro de Investigación Científica y de Educación Superior de Ensenada (CICESE)
[2] Instituto Tecnológico de Sonora (ITSON), Mexico
gtarqui@cicese.edu.mx, luis.castro@acm.org, favela@cicese.mx

Abstract. Distracted driving can pose serious risks of injuries to car occupants as well as other drivers and pedestrians. Although increasingly in use, GPS units have been found to distract drivers. In this work, we examine the use of landmarks for wayfinding aimed at reducing distracted driving by making the technology 'disappear' from drivers' attention. In this paper, we present SOL, a mobile phone application to provide navigation instructions in a more human-like way by using landmarks. We conducted an in-situ evaluation comparing SOL with Google Maps for wayfinding. Preliminary results suggest that the use of landmarks helped the drivers occupy their attention in driving rather than on the mobile phone, thus avoiding distractions that could be dangerous while driving.

Keywords: GPS wayfinding, distracted driving, landmark-based wayfinding.

1 Introduction

Our ability to estimate location, has given rise to in-vehicle location-based systems. These days, GPS-based navigation systems (hereinafter referred to as GPS) are almost ubiquitous in some regions. Most GPS systems provide turn-by-turn spoken instructions or visual feedback (i.e., maps). Those who do not own a GPS unit usually use mobile phones apps for navigation (e.g., Google Maps), which may involve a prolonged use while driving (i.e., distracted driving). This behavior can pose serious risks of injuries to car occupants as well as other drivers and pedestrians. This has generated calls in some countries to ban the use of GPS devices while driving. Thus, in the terms of Mark Weiser's vision, 'disappearing' the phone while driving can be essential for road safety by minimizing distraction.

One of the reasons why GPS units (or phones for that matter) have not been successful in disappearing is that they place extra cognitive load on the user: maps distract users, more than just spoken instructions [1]. Also, GPS-provided instructions (i.e., turn-by-turn) usually do not resemble the way humans do so, thus many drivers do not follow their instructions [2, 3]. For instance, when asking directions to a friend, they generally provide detailed accounts of features (e.g., buildings, business, roads, etc.), which often are easier to remember and make more sense to a human.

G. Urzaiz et al. (Eds.): UCAmI 2013, LNCS 8276, pp. 342–349, 2013.

For example, "The Chinese restaurant you are looking for is located behind Wal-Mart on Fresno Avenue", where the retail company and the avenue are the landmarks.

Wayfinding is the process of determining and following a path between origin and destination [4]. For successful travel, it is necessary to identify origin and destination. Human wayfinding is a purposive activity; it involves memory-based spatial knowledge to move around and find their way to their destination. In some cases, choosing a route over another is related to subjective decisions (e.g., fondness for the area, safety or familiarity with the place), and not a matter of optimizing driving time or fuel consumption, as most GPS unit do i.e., GPS units calculate routes that "have qualities that make it a dis-preferred route by a human driver" [2]. This route selection process is particularly true when driving around a familiar area, where a few hints will be enough to get to an unknown destination. For example, after looking at a map, we just realize that our destination is two blocks away from a place we know, and so our sense of orientation becomes relative to that known location.

In this paper, we examine the use of landmarks in wayfinding instructions. We first determine a prominent or known location, close to the final destination, and we provide the navigation instructions from there as a departure point. In doing so, we disregard unessential instructions that might be making the system 'appear' before the user, adding extra cognitive load on the user. With this, we aim at providing presumably simpler instructions on how to get to the destination and therefore minimizing drivers' attention devoted to interacting with the mobile phone. In this paper, we present SOL, a mobile phone application using landmark-based navigation instructions. SOL was evaluated in situ with users driving their cars around a city. During the evaluation, we focused mainly on comparing SOL with Google Maps in terms of distracted driving and user experience.

2   GPS and Landmarks for Wayfinding

A recent report by the World Health Organization (WHO) states that, in high-income countries, around 7 in 10 drivers reported having used their mobile phones while driving [5]. They also report that drivers who use a mobile phone while driving (i.e., distracted driving) have a higher crash risk than those who do not. In addition to the mobile phone use while driving, it is also important to account for the length of use that impacts on risk i.e., the longer the use, the greater the risk.

The penetration of GPS devices and mobile phones for wayfinding has made it an important aspect to study, not only for the navigation problem itself, but for the implications that errors, misunderstandings, and distractions can have on road safety. In [2], the authors highlight a series of common 'troubles' by users when interacting with the GPS. Among them, not having an exact destination, preferred routes, and timing of the instructions are part of what makes turn-by-turn instructions kind of problematic for users with good sense of orientation. GPS based instructions can be meaningful for users with a poor sense of orientation, people with difficulties reading a map, or people in unfamiliar areas (e.g., tourists). Some users apparently blindly follow the instructions provided by the GPS, which can be devastating. For example,

Sabine Morea, 67, drove for two days instead of the actual two hour trip[1]; other cases have been fatal[2]. On the other hand, for drivers with a good sense of orientation or in familiar areas, the GPS instructions can be cumbersome [6].

The use of landmarks for wayfinding has been suggested in previous research [7, 8]. Many works have been devoted to studying the use of landmarks, mainly for pedestrian wayfinding [9-12]. In [10], the authors compare different modalities in which they present the instructions. One of the modalities involved the use of spoken vs. visual instructions, as well as comparison between different media. Similarly, in [9], the authors find some evidence that the use of landmarks is good for user orientation. In natural environments, the use of landmarks has also proven to be useful [11]. In [12], they used photos to augment the routing instructions provided in pedestrian navigation. In many of these projects, the use of actual photos of landmarks has yielded two main problems that confused users: photos taken from different angles and photos taken at a different season or time of the day (e.g., with snow, at night). Finally, it is also important to remark that photos can distract drivers since s/he needs to look at the display for some time before making sense of the photo.

3   Requirements of a Wayfinding Mobile Application

Aside from distracted driving, much debate around the use of GPS is about the potential changes that these navigation systems can have on humans [6, 13], for spatial experience somehow changes brain structures. In [14], it was found that taxi drivers in London, when compared to bus drivers, had a much larger gray matter in the hippocampal area, the area of the brain where spatial memories are integrated. Thus, finding your way around, keeping track of your whereabouts and building a cognitive map is part of challenging, complex brain processes involving the recall of landmarks, calculating distances, remembering details, or spatial and semantic relationships.

In some way, these processes are less problematic in familiar areas where driving can become automatized, thus the working-memory use is reduced [15]. In addition, the cognitive load on drivers can be further reduced by including landmarks in directions as they are usually part of basic human navigational strategies [7, 9]. What's more, easier recognition of features while driving could have significant impacts on distracted driving by reducing the number of times a drivers looks at the mobile phone. Some of the main requirements for a landmark-based wayfinding system are:

— Reduced number of instructions: The number of landmark-based instructions had to be minimal to avoid distraction.
— Instructions in human-like language: The instructions were provided in a more natural way, resembling the way humans provide directions. This could minimize cognitive load on the user, reducing the need to re-read instructions.

---

[1] http://gizmodo.com/5975787/woman-drives-for-900-miles-instead-of-90-thanks-to-gps-error
[2] http://gizmodo.com/5655527/man-drowns-after-gps -guides-him-into-a-lake

4   SOL: A Mobile Application for Wayfinding Using Landmarks

The architecture of SOL is next described:

— Mobile device. Users can use SOL on a mobile device (Android 2.2+).
— Client. It provides information for place finding; it posts and retrieves data to and from the servers.
— SOL server. It handles requests from the Client; It provides information related to the weighting of each landmark.
— External servers. They are used to retrieve information: Google Places, Google Maps, and Foursquare.

SOL was implemented for the Android OS. It uses data from Google Places and Foursquare, through their Application Programming Interfaces (API). When the user types in the place s/he is looking for (e.g., an address, business), the application searches on Google Places for location information (e.g., coordinates). Then, the application retrieves the coordinates of the destination, and also requests nearby places using Foursquare. The application then checks if the user has previously visited one of those places through the check-in data. Then, the retrieved places are compared to the ranking of landmarks in the SOL server i.e., identifying which of those places are relevant. Finally, a list of the five most relevant places (i.e., the highest weighting) is shown to the user. She or he must select one of those places, and the directions are then shown relative to that place using human-like instructions (see Figure 1).

The relevance is computed using three landmark features: visibility, diversity, and instances. Visibility is the degree to which a landmark is visible to a human observer or the area it spans across. For example, a skyscraper is highly visible; a convenience store is not. Diversity is the degree to which a place congregates different kind of people. For instance, a bar is highly diverse; a household is not. Finally, instances represent the number of branches or instances there are in the city. Unique landmarks were rated higher than landmarks with multiple instances.

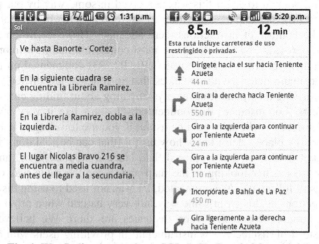

Fig. 1. Wayfinding instructions: SOL (left); Google Maps (right)

5   In-situ Evaluation of SOL

An in-situ evaluation, mainly aimed the effects of landmarks in distracted driving, was designed with users driving a car to different locations within the city. The evaluation was within-subjects, meaning that the users used both SOL and Google Maps for directions. For road safety, our participants were instructed to pull over whenever they needed to check anything on the mobile phone.

Given the complexity of evaluating Ubicomp systems [16], we used a procedure inspired in the naturalistic enactment technique [17]. Apart from videotaping the evaluation sessions and user activity logging, we took detailed notes regarding our participants' interaction with the mobile device. In particular, we collected the initial time to read the instructions, the number of times that the user used the mobile device (even quick glances), and the length of use of the mobile device. After the driving session, we conducted in-depth interviews aimed at collecting qualitative data on user experience.

During the evaluation, having a common departure point, each participant had to drive to three different unknown locations within the city, meaning that the session consisted of a route with 3 stopovers. The routes were composed of route segments, in which participants were supposed to use either SOL or Google Maps. The order was controlled to minimize threats to validity. All routes comprised the same locations, but there were two routes (R1, R2) depending on the first stopover.

We recruited 7 graduate students (Female=3, Male=4) from two local universities. Participants were 27.9 years old (SD=2.27), ranging from 25 to 31 years old. Given the reduced number of participants, we considered that the participants' homogeneity in terms of age could be positive to the analysis of the data. All of them were users of smartphones. Our informants had been living in the city for 11.5 years (SD=11.4), and most were used to drive around the city more than once a day.

5.1   Perceived Number of Instructions

Given that one of the design principles of our application was a reduced number of instructions, we wanted to see if this was perceived in some way by our participants. With regard to this, participants had little to say about SOL. In general most commented that the number of instructions were adequate. However, when asked about the instructions provided by Google Maps, most commented on how impractical they can be due to their 'bulkiness'. Some users (P1, P2, P3) commented on how Google Maps uses too many details with distances that in practice are difficult to measure since you are driving a car, and it never says anything about finding clues on the way but street names. For instance, P1 commented: "I don´t like it very much when it gives you kilometers. Well, that could be useful if you are traveling to a distant place, but if it is a nearby place I don't know how useful [that can be]… I don't know if it is because I'm not used to it, but I ignored that, since it was useless… and about the instructions, I was rather looking at the map and, since the route was colored, that [feature] helps to follow it." As commented, P1 was not used to using distances when following directions as this is, in some way, not very natural when providing instructions among humans, especially when distances are short. We believe that using landmarks instead of distances was instrumental in providing users with a perception that instructions were adequate.

5.2   Mobile Phone Use While Driving

We measured how often and for how long the participants used the mobile phone during our evaluation (Table 1). The average number of glances at the mobile phone per route was 15 for our application and 24.17 for Google Maps. Also, the average number of glances per participant was 12.86 for our application and 20.71 for Google Maps. Thus, participants looked at the mobile phones fewer times while driving (t=2.695, df=6, p=.01, one-tailed), meaning that SOL had a real effect.

Table 1. Number of glances at the mobile phone (Google Maps data are in bold)

	Route 1			Route 2		
	RS1	RS	RS3	RS1	RS2	RS3
P1	18	**11**	5	-	-	-
P2	**14**	15	0	-	-	-
P3	-	-	-	6	1	**13**
P4	-	-	-	7	**8**	1
P5	2	**14**	5	-	-	-
P6	**37**	12	9	-	-	-
P7	-	-	-	14	1	**21**

The number of times a driver looks at her mobile phone while driving is important, but perhaps even more important is knowing how long those glances are i.e., occupying their attention while driving. The average total time spent per participant looking at the mobile phones was 2:29m for SOL, and 4:51m for Google Maps. The difference between these means is 2:22m, which is almost twice for Google Maps. The average glimpse was 9.1s for SOL and 13.5s for Google Maps, meaning that on average our participants' glances while driving took longer on Google Maps (~1.5x). However, a t-test showed no statistical significance (t=1.206, df=6, p=.13, one-tailed).

It is also important to characterize the situations wherein our participants looked at the mobile phone, while driving. Fig. 2 shows the types of situations in which our participants were looking at their mobile phones. We can observe that using the mobile phone while the car was on the move was almost 3x for Google Maps (82) than for SOL (30). However, when the car was fully stopped, as in a traffic light or parked, the number of glances were very similar using both Google Maps and SOL.

The post-evaluation interviews suggested that this difference was due to the complexity of following instructions not anchored to the urban infrastructure. At least in the case of the city where the evaluation took place, as in other cities in developing regions, street names signs are uncommon and so are noticeable house numbers, which is the main form of reference used by Google Maps. On the other hand, in the case of SOL, local landmarks were being used, which could have contributed to a reduced cognitive load on the driver. This can be the case of recognition vs. recall, in which participants needed less time using our application for they might have been recognizing the landmarks in their memory, rather than recalling what landmarks are around that area (using a map) in order to get to their destination.

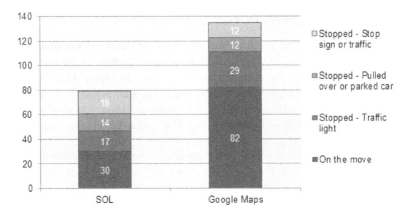

Fig. 2. Situations in which our participants were looking at the mobile phone while driving

6   Conclusions

We presented SOL, an application using landmarks for wayfinding in familiar settings aimed at reducing distracted driving by making the phone 'disappear' from drivers' attention. The results of the evaluation suggest that the use of landmarks helped our participants occupy their attention on driving rather than on the mobile phone.

Future work includes studying what comprises 'good/bad' directions for humans, including how detailed instructions should be. That is, estimating an appropriate number of instructions for each user. Also, In addition to those aspects, further studies are needed to investigate the way people name landmarks, as they generally name places and ascribe meanings such that makes sense to them, but doing so through intelligent systems is still an ongoing challenge [18].

References

1. Kun, A.L., et al.: Glancing at personal navigation devices can affect driving: experimental results and design implications. In: Proc. of the 1st International Conference on Automotive User Interfaces and Interactive Vehicular Applications (AutomotiveUI 2009), pp. 129–136. ACM, Essen (2009)
2. Brown, B., Laurier, E.: The normal natural troubles of driving with GPS. In: Proc. of CHI 2012, pp. 1621–1630. ACM Press, Austin (2012)
3. Hipp, M., et al.: Interaction weaknesses of personal navigation devices. In: Proc. of the 2nd International Conference on Automotive User Interfaces and Interactive Vehicular Applications (AutomotiveUI 2010), pp. 129–136. ACM, Pittsburgh (2010)
4. Golledge, R.G.: Human Wayfinding and Cognitive Maps. In: Golledge, R.G. (ed.) Wayfinding Behavior: Cognitive Mapping and Other Spatial Processes. The John Hopkins University Press, Baltimore (1999)
5. Mobile phone use: a growing problem of driver distraction. World Health Organization, Geneva (2011)

6. Leshed, G., et al.: In-car gps navigation: engagement with and disengagement from the environment. In: Proc. of CHI 2008, pp. 1675–1684. ACM, Florence (2008)
7. Burnett, G.E.: "Turn right at the traffic lights": The requirement for landmarks in vehicle navigation systems. The Journal of Navigation 53(3), 499–510 (2000)
8. Hile, H., et al.: Landmark-Based Pedestrian Navigation from Collections of Geotagged Photos. In: Proc. of the 7th International Conference on Mobile and Ubiquitous Multimedia (MUM 2008), pp. 145–152. ACM Press, Umeå (2008)
9. Aslan, I., et al.: Acquisition of spatial knowledge in location aware mobile pedestrian navigation systems. In: Proc. of MobileHCI 2006, pp. 105–108. ACM, Helsinki (2006)
10. Krüger, A., Aslan, I., Zimmer, H.: The effects of Mobile Pedestrian Navigation Systems on the Concurrent Acquisition of Route and Survey Knowledge. In: Brewster, S., Dunlop, M.D. (eds.) Mobile HCI 2004. LNCS, vol. 3160, pp. 446–450. Springer, Heidelberg (2004)
11. Snowdon, C., Kray, C.: Exploring the use of landmarks for mobile navigation support in natural environments. In: Proc. MobileHCI 2009, pp. 1–10. ACM, Bonn (2009)
12. Beeharee, A.K., Steed, A.: A natural wayfinding exploiting photos in pedestrian navigation systems. In: Proc. MobileHCI 2006, pp. 81–88. ACM, Helsinki (2006)
13. Burnett, G.E., Lee, K.: The effect of vehicle navigation systems on the formation of cognitive maps. In: Underwood, G. (ed.) Traffic and Transport Psychology: Theory and Application, pp. 407–418. Elsevier, St Louis (2005)
14. Maguire, E.A., Woollett, K., Spiers, H.J.: London Taxi Drivers and Bus Drivers: A Structural MRI and Neuropsychological Analysis. Hippocampus 16(12), 1091–1101 (2006)
15. Montello, D.R., Sas, C.: Human Factors of Wayfinding in Navigation. In: Karwowski, W. (ed.) International Encyclopedia of Ergonomics and Human Factors, pp. 2003–2008. CRC Press/Taylor & Francis, Ltd. (2006)
16. Carter, S., et al.: Exiting the Cleanroom: On Ecological Validity and Ubiquitous Computing. Human-Computer Interaction 23(1), 47–99
17. Castro, L.A., Favela, J., Garcia-Peña, C.: Naturalistic enactment to stimulate user experience for the evaluation of a mobile elderly care application. In: Proc. of MobileHCI 2011, pp. 371–380. ACM, Stockholm (2011)
18. Lin, J., et al.: Modeling people's place naming preferences in location sharing. In: Proc. of the 12th ACM International Conference on Ubiquitous Computing (Ubicomp 2010), pp. 75–84. ACM, Copenhagen (2010)

Pervasive System for the Local Tow-Truck Service

Eduardo Martín-Pulido, Alexis Quesada-Arencibia, and Carmelo R. García

Dept. of Computer Science and Institute for Cybernetics,
University of Las Palmas de Gran Canaria
E35017, Las Palmas, Spain
emartinpulido@gmail.com, {aquesada,rgarcia}@dis.ulpgc.es

Abstract. This paper presents the development of a pervasive system prototype for the Local Tow-Truck service. This system makes it possible to video, process, store and transfer each service carried out by the company with any of the tow-trucks in its fleet. The data are administered by the tow-truck operators by means of mobile devices and are temporarily stored in a system on board the tow-truck in question. On arrival at their base, these data are automatically transferred to a common repository, which can be accessed from the offices of the central municipal vehicle pound. The aim of this system is to enable the Local Tow-Truck Service to certify the quality and safety of each transfer and guarantee the state of the transported vehicle at all times, and thereby to respond to any potential claims.

Keywords: pervasive systems, intelligent transport systems.

1   Introduction

Video surveillance has offered an increasingly common technical safety solution in recent years, used in office blocks, external structures, schools, shops, supermarkets, hotels and even on city streets [1]. Currently, the most advanced video surveillance systems integrate technologies such as video and audio surveillance, wireless sensor networks, distributed intelligence and awareness, architecture and middleware, and mobile robots [2]. Its importance lies in the feeling of security people get when they are in protected areas and the deterrent effect it has on potential vandals. Moreover, the speed with which authorities can then act in these types of cases should be borne in mind. Should any such incident occur, the corresponding investigation can use the video recording, which constitutes solid proof for the case and enables the legal procedures to run more smoothly and quickly, based on a more accurate account of events [3].

In the evolution of these systems, specifically in the transport sector (of both people and goods), specific technical solutions are being sought that offer added requisites to the standard repertoire for this type of system [4, 5]. Obtaining the most relevant data automatically is one of the most noteworthy, as well as the capacity to withstand vibrations, bumps, damp and changes in temperature while continuing to work normally.

G. Urzaiz et al. (Eds.): UCAmI 2013, LNCS 8276, pp. 350–357, 2013.

The system presented in this paper provides relevant information of diferent type (video, image and textual), that has been acquired in an automatic way, in order to improve the quality and security of a local tow-truck service. This information describes how a towing away service has been carried out. Vehicles may need towing away because they have been involved in an offence, been stolen, abandoned or been involved in an accident. Traditionally, the process the truck driver follows to tow the vehicle away basically consists of:

1. Arriving at the exact spot where the vehicle is located
2. Loading it onto the tow-trailer
3. Transporting it to the vehicle pound and parking it there

The tow-truck operator will register manually all the documents that describe these operations. The developed system allows the company to obtain and transfer automatically information regarding all these operations. With this information, it can be certified that the whole process has taken place without any damage being done to the vehicle that has been towed away. This enables the company to supervise the transfer of the vehicle and, should a complaint be lodged, see what actually happened during the process with reliable information.

This project is part of the development of an integral management system of the municipal vehicle pound commissioned by the City Council of Las Palmas de Gran Canaria and encharged to the Municipal Parking and Urban Management Company (Sociedad Municipal de Aparcamientos y Gestión Urbanística [SAGULPA[1]]). The system as a whole is co-funded by the Spanish Ministry for Industry, Tourism and Trade, as part of the 2008-2011 National Plan for Scientific Research, Development and Technological Innovation, under project reference number TSI-050100-2009-6, and also co-funded by the European Social Fund. SAGULPA, the University Institute for Cybernetic Science and Technology (IUCTC) and the Scientific Technological Park Fund signed a collaboration agreement to develop the system presented here.

2   Objectives

The main objective of this project was to build a video-survillance system that would make it possible to generate automatically information in the tow-truck regarding each time the truck towed a vehicle away. This information constitutes documentary evidence that the necessary quality and safety was adhered to during the transfer process, ensure the safety of the tow-truck driver as well as the state of the vehicle that is towed away. The following requirements and restraints were taken into consideration in the design phase:

- The capacity to obtain information when the tow-truck driver desires so.
- To create an interface adapted to the company's PDAs.

---

[1] www.sagulpa.com. Contact person: César García García (cesargarcia@sagulpa.com), Organization and operation coordinator.

- A system that is independent from others on which the company is currently working.
- The system must be easy to assemble and disassemble cheaply and quickly.
- The system must be protected from adverse weather conditions, acts of vandalism, vibrations and bumps. It must also be able to cope with possible fluctuations in the electricity supply.
- The system should be capable of gaining information in adverse conditions, for example, raining, low illumination condition, with an automatic activation of the operation mode.
- The information must be identified by a file number and the date on which it is generated, and it must be accessible from a common repository.

3   Architecture Overview

3.1   Hardware Components

The architecture of this system has a distributed nature integrating different types of devices and technologies. Its task is a complex one involving people, management procedures, and technology. Like PRISMATICA system [6], on-line surveillance system for metropolitan railway environments, it aplyes ambient intelligent principles.

Camera
The selected camera is certified with a protection level of IP66. This means that it is protected against dust and strong water jets in all directions. In terms of night vision capacity, it has infrared lighting with 23 leds that illuminate up to 20 metres, thereby perfectly covering the length of a tow-truck and the full tow-truck including the towed vehicle. It has a fixed optic of 3.6 mm, with sufficient angle of vision to see the car that requires towing and all the movements carried out in each manoeuvre. The gain control is automatic, as well as the brightness and clarity adjustments. The images obtained by the camera show how the removaling, transporting and depositing operations of vehicles have been performed. Aditionally, useful vehicle information, such as dimensions and existing damage, can be obtained.

Personal Digital Assistant (PDA) - Motorola MC5574
This device has a 3.5 inch screen, 320×240 pixels, a 520 MHz processor, the Windows Mobile 6.1 operating system and an expandable RAM memory of 128 MB. It also has a 2MP auto-focus camera with flash. It can communicate via Wi-Fi, Bluetooth and USB interfaces. Besides it has a GPS receptor. In our case, the functionalities that we will use are the possibility of creating an Ad-Hoc network with the embedded system and the possibility of using the web browser to access the system's web interface. Using the GPS receptor, the operations of removaling, transporting and depositing can be georeferenced in order to record from where the vehicle has been removed, to select the best route to transport the vehicle to the vehicle pound and to obtain a reliable time reference of all these operations.

On Board Computer
The small selected computer (11.5 x10.1 x2.7 cm) has a CPU that works at 2 GHZ, and 2GB DDR2 memory. Electricity consumption does not exceed 10W and its working temperature fluctuates between 0 and 70°. It weighs just under 330 g. The supply voltage can fluctuate between 8 and 14 V, as in the case of the camera we have chosen. Thus, the electricity supply system is simplified, since the two devices require the same voltage. A further characteristic is the possibility of an automatic start-up when a difference in voltage from 0 to 12 V is detected. Finally, we should underline the Wi-Fi communication interface it includes and its four USB 2.0 ports. A 64 GB 2.5" compatible solid state hard drive (SSD) has been added to this computer. The decision to opt for a solid state hard drive is based on the vibrations in the environment to which the equipment is exposed, and also aims to minimise as far as possible the temperature of the system. All the multimedia data related to the removing, transporting and depositing operations of vehicles are temporally stored in this device.

Image Capturer
The selected image capturer is compatible by default with the Linux kernel from version 2.6.36 on. It enables us to obtain high quality images from an analog camera at 25 frames per second, by means of a USB interface. In order to reduce the space required to store the frames, the image quality can be configured.

An Uninterrupted Power System
This device has been incorporated into the system to ensure that the computer and camera have a stable power supply. Therefore, the system will continue working normally even if a drop in voltage occurs, at least for 3 hours. It also prevents micro power cuts when the tow truck is started up, as well as any possible voltage peaks. In order to power this element, a 12V-20V converter has had to be incorporated. Thus, the tow-truck's battery feeds the converter, which, in turn, feeds the UPS. The UPS issues 12V current to feed both the camera and the computer by means of an associated switch.

Wireless Controller
The system uses two wireless controllers. A Wifi adaptor is used to establish the communication between the on board computer and the system housed in the municipal vehicle pound so that all the multimedia information could be transferred. A second wireless controller is used to connect the PDA with the on board computer by an Ad-Hoc network. Currently this connection can be made by Wifi or Bluetooth.

3.2   Software System

The software solution that we are presenting in this paper has been implemented in a Xubuntu distribution, specifically in its version 11.04. Broadly speaking, and as we can see in Fig. 1, it is based on a server that deals with internal requests made through the web server by sockets. This Apache web server deals with requests from the web interface, designed in PHP, operated by the truck driver using the PDA linked to the truck. This is achieved by means of an Ad-Hoc network that enables these two devices to communicate with each other.

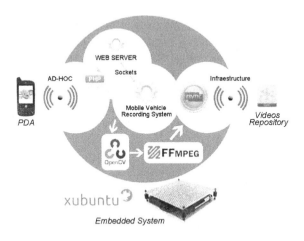

Fig. 1. Overview of the system

The creation and transmission of a video of a tow-truck service is the most critical functionality. This functionality goes through three clearly differentiated stages. The first starts when the recording is activated by the interface, initiating a communication with the OpenCV library in order to start generating the video. Once it is time to stop this recording, the web interface is used and a similar process to the one just described takes place.

Subsequently, a second phase automatically kicks in, in which compression takes place thanks to a call to the FFMPEG library, which compresses the video following the specifications stored in the configuration file.

The default setting for the compression comprises the following parameters: 25 fps at a resolution of 640x480 pixels. Once the process has finished, the video is prepared and the third phase starts.

The final phase consists of transferring the recorded video to the central video repository. This process is carried out through the RSYNC application, in charge of synchronizing the repository of temporary video folders in the tow-truck computer with the corresponding folder in the central data repository, in accordance with the configured parameters. In order to carry out this process, the tow-truck has to be near to one of the connection points of the Wi-Fi infrastructure located in the vehicle pound in order to ensure connection and data transmission.

To safeguard against any possible system failures and as a safety precaution, a local back-up copy is also generated in the embedded computer. This copy is stored for seven days, although this option can also be programmed for a different length of time. Logfiles are also created to indicate both, the state of the on-board computer over time and the generation of videos and a record of the results of the application. Fig. 1 shows the whole process as we have explained and the various components involved in each of the phases.

3.3 Communication Interfaces

Throughout the process described above, communication was established through wireless mesh network [7]. On one hand, the link established between the PDA mobile unit and the on-board computer and on the other, the channel by which the on-board computer communicates with the computer that acts as the data repository in the vehicle pound. Both channels are based on wireless communication, the difference lying in the way it is established. The first channel is configured Ad-Hoc, while the second is configured in an infrastructure mode and the two devices communicate by means of a communication router with wireless capacity.

Fig. 2. Shot of one of the towing services carried out and recorded with the system

4   Results

The deleloped system has been tested by the company SAGULPA which gives the local tow-truck service at Las Palmas de Gran Canaria at the moment (Canary Islands, Spain). The verification test of the hardware consisted of checking the installation of all hardware components of the prototype. The different component parts were physically put in place and the lay-out of the leads needed for a definitive installation was established. On one hand, an energy supply point from the battery to the on-board system and on the other, the electricity supply and analog video signal from the camera to the same point. Moreover, the camera was fixed to the tow-truck chassis. The software system verification consisted of real tests on the road. These tests were successful. Therefor, we are now in a position to implant the project in the whole tow-truck fleet, together with the necessary infrastructure in the municipal vehicle pounds to ensure the transfer of files to the central repository.

Fig. 2 shows a shot of one of the videos generated in one of the tests. This image is part of the video generated after compression at a resolution of 640x480 pixels. As we have already mentioned, these compression parameters can easily be adjusted. These parameters include frames per second, the resolution of the image and the compression format. Although compressing the image reduces its quality, it has been proved to be both useful and an indispensable requirement since it significantly reduces the size of the files. The average time it takes to tow away a vehicle in the city of Las Palmas de Gran Canaria is 20 minutes. The videos generated in this time occupy approximately 1.5 GB, and after compression, they weigh around 37 MB. It should be borne in mind that these videos then have to be transferred by a wireless link in the shortest possible period of time since the tow-trucks spend just a few minutes in the actual unloading area. The end result of the implantation of this system can be seen in Fig. 3. This image was taken in the municipal vehicle pound, where the vehicles that have been towed away are left until they are picked up by their owners.

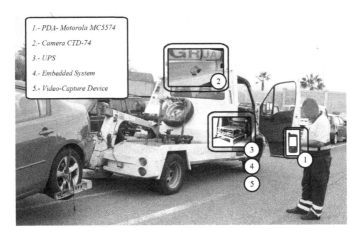

Fig. 3. Implantation of the system

5   Conclusions and Future Work

In this paper, a pervasive system for obtaining relevant information of the operations of a local tow-truck service has been described. The system is capable of registering all relevant information regarding the towing away service of a vehicle. At the moment, the system manages information related to identification data of each service (vehicle identification data and place where the vehicle was taken away) that are manually process by the operator by means of a PDA and a video that record all the manoeuvre of towing away, transporting and parking of the vehicle.

As future works, we are working on the automatic recovering of all data that are manually inserted at this moment. One of this data is the plate number of the vehicle, which can be obtained from an image of the plate number of the vehicle through a character-recognizing module. Another data is the place where the tow-truck towed away the vehicle, using the GPS receptor of the PDA so that the cartographic information could be obtained by means of a geographic information system.

Acknowledgments. We would like to thank the employees of SAGULPA for their willingness to participate and collaboration at all times, both in the analysis and design meetings and during the assembly and testing stages of the prototype. We are also grateful for the project management work carried out by the Technological Scientific Park Foundation at the University de Las Palmas de Gran Canaria.

References

1. Koskela, H.: The gaze without eyes': video-surveillance and the changingnature of urban space. Progress in Human Geography 24(2), 243–265 (2000)
2. Räty, T.D.: Survey on Contemporary Remote Surveillance Systems for Public Safety. IEEE Transactions on Systems, Man and Cybernetics 35(1), 164–182 (2005)
3. Vu, V., et al.: Audio-video event recognition system for public transport security. In: International Conference on Crime Detection and Prevention (ICDP 2006), London, pp. 1–6 (2006)
4. Bigdeli, A., Lovell, B.C., Sanderson, C., Shan, T., Chen, S.: Vision Processing in Intelligent CCTV for Mass Transport Security. In: IEEE Workshop on Signal Processing Applications for Public Security and Forensics (SAFE 2007), Washington, DC, pp. 1–4 (2007)
5. Ahmad, I., Habibi, D.: High Utility Video Surveillance System on Public Transport Using WiMAX Technology. In: IEEE Wireless Communications and Networking Conference (WCNC), Sydney, pp. 1–5 (2010)
6. Velastin, S.A., Boghossian, B.A., Lo, B.P.L., Sun, J., Vicencio-Silva, M.A.: PRISMATICA: toward ambient intelligence in public transport environments. IEEE Transactions on Systems, Man and Cybernetics 3(1), 164–182 (2005)
7. Yarali, A., Ahsant, B., Rahman, S.: Wireless Mesh Networking: A Key Solution for Emergency & Rural Applications. In: Second International Conference on Advances in Mesh Networks (MESH 2009), Athens, pp. 143–149 (2009)

Early Vehicle Accident Detection and Notification Based on Smartphone Technology

Roberto G. Aldunate[1], Oriel A. Herrera[2], and Juan Pablo Cordero[2]

[1] College of Applied Health Sciences, University of Illinois at Urbana-Champaign, USA
aldunate@illinois.edu
[2] Engineering Informatics School, Catholic University of Temuco, Chile
{oherrera,jcordero}@inf.uct.cl

Abstract. Prompt assistance to people involved in vehicle accidents could make a significant difference on the consequences of such accidents. Some vehicle manufacturers include technology embedded into the vehicles they build to detect and communicate crash vehicle events to emergency agencies. Nevertheless, this approach adds cost to the vehicles, and as it is only present at a small proportion of vehicles in most urban settings. Nowadays, most cell phones are equipped with a diversity of sensors, including accelerometers, GPS units, microphones, among others, which present an opportunity for these devices to be used, while carried by people, as both sensors for vehicle accidents and remote notification of such events. By means of simulations, this article presents encouraging results regarding using smartphones for vehicle crash detection. The main conclusion presented is that a model for early detection of vehicle accidents has been elaborated and preliminary proved.

Keywords: Sensors, Vehicle Accident, Smartphone.

1 Introduction

The rate of accidents in highways and in urban contexts requires that the different stakeholders involved with these events search and elaborate on solutions to mitigate the big economic and social impact that these events have on the population [1]. One research and development venue to cope with this problem focuses on early detection and notification of these events. Examples of these approaches are OnStar, in USA [2-3], and e-Call and Saferider in Europe [4-5]. All these solutions are based on technology embedded in the vehicle's infrastructure [11-13]. On the other hand, today we witness technology advances in many fields, but specially in mobile platforms such as cell phones, which are equipped with powerful sensory capabilities while being broadly used by the population [6][10]. Given the varied sensory capability, e.g.; accelerometers, electronic compass, microphone, video camera, etc, and the processing power that we can encounter in several cell phones already widespread in the population in urban contexts, the question whether this technology can be used or not to complement and improve early detection and notification of vehicle accidents emerges naturally. This question is precisely the driving interrogant for this research

G. Urzaiz et al. (Eds.): UCAmI 2013, LNCS 8276, pp. 358–365, 2013.

and exploration effort. This article describes the starting point of a research that aims to generate a solution to the problem mentioned before based on current Smartphone platforms.

2   Related Work

In addition to the vehicle crash support systems mentioned in the Introduction, which are embedded in vehicles by vehicle manufacturers and are not broadly available to the population [11], today there are several software applications for Smartphone platforms, which operate under the same principle; to become aware of an accident, then send an "S.O.S" message to either an emergency agency or some of the contacts the user defined previously. Some examples of these Smartphone applications are SOS my Car, SOS Alarm, and SOS Friendly. SOS my Car continuously tracks the vehicle's speed so when it detects a sudden change of the speed of the vehicle it activates an alarm. Shall the user not deactivate the alarm, the application will send an E-mail, including the location in a map, to a pre-defined list of contacts. SOS Alarm will generate a similar action, a text message with coordinates of the event, but based on the force applied to the Smartphone, which is classified as 1G, 2G, and 3G, to represent low, medium, and high intensity events, respectively. Finally, SOS Friendly will send an SMS (Short Message Service) message including the lat/long coordinates to a list of pre-defined contacts if it does not detect movement for a given period of time and the user oes not deactivate this process once the application is in such stage.

The literature review reveals that current approaches to determine vehicle accidents by Smartphone are based on speed and acceleration changes. The algorithms utilized for this type of objective are called "Droid pedometer" [7]. Nevertheless, this approach has several drawbacks. First, there is no guarantee the GPS system will work in a reliable manner in urban contexts[14]. Smartphone may also use tri-lateration with cell phone towers and already know Wi-Fi spots location in such case, but these methods are also prone to highly inaccurate position measurements in cluttered contexts [15]. Second, acceleration by itself will not determine the user is a vehicle which has been involved in an accident.

This research effort proposes an approach to improve current developments on vehicle accident detection based on an integrative model to reduce the number of false positive vehicle detection instances. This model is based on the concept of error reduction based on independent, but related to the same event, data aggregation.

3   Vehicle Accident Detection Model

The key element of the model proposed in this research effort is the integration of data gathered by the sensors available at the Smartphone platforms. In this work, a simple linear model is proposed to improve estimations of vehicle crashes based on the sensory capability of a Smartphone. The model presented below establishes the detection of a vehicle crash as a variable which is a function of a weighted aggregation of the data sensed by every pertinent sensor from the available ones at the Smartphone.

$$\text{Mcrash} = \sum \alpha i * Mi \qquad (1)$$

Where,

      Mcrash is crash value resulting from collective sensing
      αi is the specific weight for sensor i, with $\sum \alpha i = 1$
      Mi is the sensor data output in a standardized scale, e.g., [0-1].

The model proposed above sets immediately to questions; how do we calibrate the model, given differences will likely exist between sensors in different Smartphones and given we do not know what are the weights for what conditions in the detection process, and how do we validate the model once calibrated. Some fo these questions will be addressed in the rest of this article.

$$\text{Mcrash} = \text{Maccelerometer} + \text{Mmicrophone} \qquad (2)$$

The model presented in (1) was instantiated with the accelerometer and the microphone sensors. Both sensors were equaly weighted as we had no preliminary information on which sensor would be more relevant for what type of accident. In this research the GPS sensors was not used for crash detection, given the coarse granularity of this sensor, and the non-real-time refresh rates, but for notification purposes through SMS and/or E-mail services.

4   Sensors Calibration and Metrics

This research effort used 3 different Smartphones, from different vendors (Samsung, Erickson, HTC), on Android 2.3.3 Smartphone to determine values and thresholds for the model presented before. The values and thresholds obtained have a more qualitative than quantitative value, given there are expected variations in the sensing capabilities for same sensors in different devices, and for similar sensor types in different devices as well. The objective of this research effort is not to provide a comprehensive and accurate value for the parameters of the model, i.e.; very precise values for normal driving and crash situations, but to find gross values that allow us to articulate on a mechanism for early vehicle accident detection and notification.

The tests conducted on the sensors focused on two variables; a) data gathering refresh rate, and b) the actual value obtained from the sensor representing the magnitude of the feature, i.e., acceleration and sound, being measured. The variance for data gathered was consistently lower than 3%. For the development of a prototype to gather data from the Smartphone's sensors and notify remote contacts through SMS or E-mail, the Eclipse IDE and Android SDK were used, with Java and PHP as programming languages, under an open-source and Enriched Client Applications approach [8]. In addition, for the data analysis determining a signature for the audio signal, Fourier transforms were applied on the microphone data to determine the salient dominant frequency using MATLAB.

4.1   Accelerometer Calibration

To determine acceleration values indicating a vehicle crash, a simple experiment involving a frontal crash in a physics laboratory was conducted. For this experiment, we reproduce a uniformly decelerated movement. A dynamic cart weighing 0.29 Kg was used to represent a vehicle that would crash against an object of similar mass such that it represents a real life situation at a speed of 70km/h. The Smartphone, weighing 0.12 Kg, is mounted on the moving object. The application running on the Android Smartphone gathers data during the experiments with the higher possible rate. At the time of the crash the tri-axial accelerometer comes to getting a module peek 16.5 m/s² which corresponds to an increase of 5.5 times the acceleration in its normal state.

4.2   Microphone Calibration

For the audio signature from a vehicle accident this research effort choose to use the dominant frequency from the audio data gathered instead of the decibels. The reason for this is that the variability of types of microphones used in Smartphones is large and their capability to determine decibels may fluctuate significantly, based in preliminary observations conducted by this research team. It has also been observed preliminarily by this research team that, still a qualitative assessment though, a signature in the domain of frequencies for audio signal are significantly different between normal urban driving conditions and vehicle crash situations, as it will be presented in the following pages.

To analyze the feasibility of using the microphone sensor a test was conducted on data from LATIN NCAP crash tests [9] available online. These tests are conducted to test structural performance of cars in laboratory conditions. For this calibration process, this work utilized the judgment of a subject matter expert to set the volume from the online material to a level that re-creates real-world vehicle accidents conditions. This test considered several crashes each showed the same graph frequency v/s time. The sensor in the Smartphone platform was able to capture the noise range and the predominant frequencies were consistently in the range between 7-30 kHz.

5   Results

To test the capability of the model to detect vehicle crashes this work has focused first in eliminating the occurrence of false positives. Real life crash conditions testing will be part of further research. Thus, the Smartphone has been subjected to real life conditions when a vehicle comes to a rest position after the driver sharply applies the brakes. For this purpose, a 2001 Ford F150 pickup truck with a 4200cc V6 engine, was used. The ABS brakes prevents wheel locks and thus prevents slippage, thus giving us an almost ideal sharp deceleration process.

This part of the experimentation consisted on the vehicle for 500 meters, accelerating from rest, reaching a speed of 60 km / h, then braking sharply to come to rest again. After several tests, the maximum acceleration reaches about 12 m/s2, while the maximum deceleration reaches about 10 m/s2, as shown in Figure 1.a, which are significantly lower than the corresponding values obtained during calibration. Clearly the model using the calibration parameters presented in the previous section will not consider sharp braking as vehicle crashes.

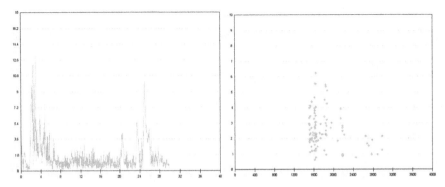

Fig. 1. Acceleration and frecuency for sharp braking: (a) acceleration per time 3-axis accelerometer readings; (b) predominant frequencies (acceleration magnitude v/s frequency)

As the detection model is based on a threshold-based mechanism which the researchers of this work anticipate is positively related with the magnitude of the data gathered by the sensors; i.e., crashes at higher speed will generate higher acceleration/deceleration and noise signatures, finding already above normal data signatures for speeds of 60 km/h makes it unnecessary to go at higher speeds.

For the microphone testing it was necessary, first, to understand the magnitude of the environmental noise for daily life urban conditions. Given the assumption this research team holds on that vehicle crashes will generate higher noise frequencies, based on simple preliminary observations, the measurement of predominant frequencies is conducted during sharp braking testing, which were conducted simultaneously with the acceleration testing described in the previous section. Results of part of the experiment are shown in Figure 1.b, which plots the magnitude of the predominant frequency for the audio data signal related to sharp braking, on the frequency domain.

Figure 1.b shows a predominant frequency of about 1.6 KHz with a magnitude of 6.21, while the vehicle was sharply braking. These values are significantly lower than the values obtained for the model during the calibration phase, described in the previous section, which confirms at least that the model will not issue a crash detection event for sharp braking situations.

Next, this applied research effort focused on testing the system with online video material captured from inside of vehicles during collisions. This material is broadly available at online video streaming repositories such as YouTube, Yahoo, etc. A sample of such video clips were selected and subjected to the judgment of a subject matter expert for sample validation rigor. The material resulting was classified as material related to crashes between cars and crashes involving a car, from which the audio sample was obtained, and a truck. The graphs for predominant frequencies for both types of crashes are shown in Figure 2.

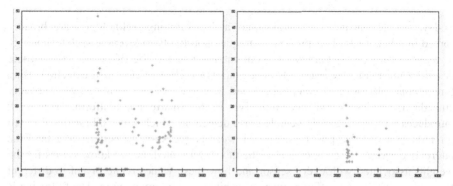

Fig. 2. Predominant frequency for two types of crashes: a) car-and-car, b) car-and-truck (acceleration magnitude v/s frecuency)

The graphs presented in Figure 2 shows that for the collision of two cars we could find predominant frequencies around 1.5 kHz with magnitudes around 48, while for the case of a collision between a car and a truck we could expect to find predominant frequencies around 2 KHz, with magnitudes around 20. Magnitudes of the sounds studied are very sensitive to volumes used when reproducing the sample material. For the purpose of this research, the relevant measurements are the predominant frequencies related to the events, which consistently seem to become a signature for sounds originating from vehicle crashes.

6   Discussion

Preliminary results are both encouraging and challenging. Progress is needed on actual real life crash situations, analyzing the performance of each of the sensors, and incorporating as many variables as possible. As real vehicle crash experiments need to be conducted, contact with the local authorities has been established to evaluate how to exercise this possibility.

Different factors are present during vehicle accidents. There may be other sensors that can help improve accurate vehicle crash detection processes, such as electronic compasses which could help understand abnormal vehicle rotations for certain types of accidents. Failures in sensors at the time of the accident can significantly influence the detection capability. Also, the types of accidents are varied, for example, a stopped vehicle that falls above a truck load, have a normal behavior for the accelerometer. In this sense, Wahlberg [16], for example, studied low speed crashes of public transport buses, creating a taxonomy that considers 17 variables in their classification.

7   Conclusions and Future Work

Today, mobile sensing, communications and positioning technologies are broadly spread in urban areas. This presents a unique opportunity to leverage such technology to reduce problems that impact the community and the life of people. This article describes an applied research effort to improve early vehicle crash detection using Smartphone platform, to complement and leverage existing technology   currently embedded in vehicles and other initiatives in the Smartphone platform. This work introduces a model for early vehicle crash detection, which was calibrated and tested for reduction of false positives. Further work is necessary to better understand the interplay between the components of the model presented, i.e., to know values for the weights associated with every sensor and how these values relate or not to different types of accidents that different types of vehicles can be involved in. The following is a list of the key findings this research effort produced.

Key findings:

The range of sensors including Smartphones today opened many doors to the development of various applications. In particular, in the area which focuses this research has achieved proof of concept that leads to promising results in the detection solution crashes. High availability and the large computing power of these devices leads to the assumption that the lines of development in this area will continue along the path marked in this research.

The performance of the sensors in terms of sensitivity and response time is appropriate, which is of utmost importance when it comes to applications where life is at stake people.

This article corresponds to the first step on validationg the model presented, which focused on reducing the occurrence of false positives while qualitatively calibrating the model with broadly used Smartphones. This is achieved by considering the contribution of multiple sensors in the determination of the crash. Thus, not only just a sudden change in acceleration, or just a loud noise, but that the combination of these sensors, and other make detection as reliable. This will be part of further research.

References

1. Peden, R., Scurfield, R.: World Health Organization. World Report on road Traffic Injury Prevention (2004)
2. Bretz, E.A.: The car: Just a web browser with tires. Spectrum, IEEE38.1, 92–94 (2001)
3. Farris, P.: General Motors OnStar (2008)
4. Bekiaris, E.D., Spadoni, A., Nikolaou, S.I.: SAFERIDER Project: new safety and comfort in Powered Two Wheelers. In: 2nd Conference on Human System Interactions, HSI 2009. IEEE (2009)
5. Montanari, R., Borin, A., Spadoni, A.: SAFERIDER: results from Yamaha test site on advanced rider assistance system. In: Proceedings of the 9th ACM SIGCHI Italian Chapter International Conference on Computer-Human Interaction: Facing Complexity, pp. 132–138. ACM, New York (2011)
6. Smith, A.: 46% of American adults are smartphone owners. Pew Internet & American Life Project (2012),
   http://www.pewinternet.org/Reports/2012/
   Smartphone-Update-2012/Findings.aspx (accessed April 27, 2012)
7. Fan, Y., Chen, Q., Liao, C.F., Douma, F.: UbiActive: Smartphone-Based Tool for Trip Detection and Travel-Related Physical Activity Assessment. Submitted for Presentation at the Transportation Research Board 92nd Annual Meeting (2012)
8. McAffer, J., Lemieux, J., Aniszczyk, C.: Eclipse rich client platform. Addison-Wesley Professional (2010)
9. Lee, S., Diez, E.: A Comparative Analysis of Latin NCAP to Global NCAPs. In: Transportation Research Board 92nd Annual Meeting. No. 13-1397 (2013)
10. Mohan, P., Padmanabhan, V.N., Ramjee, R.: Nericell: rich monitoring of road and traffic conditions using mobile smartphones. In: Proceedings of the 6th ACM Conference on Embedded Network Sensor Systems. ACM (2008)
11. Martinez, F.J., Toh, C.K., Cano, J.C., Calafate, C.T., Manzoni, P.: Emergency services in future intelligent transportation systems based on vehicular communication networks. IEEE Intelligent Transportation Systems Magazine 2(2), 6–20 (2010)
12. Fogue, M., Garrido, P., Martinez, F.J., Cano, J.C., Calafate, C.T., Manzoni, P., Sanchez, M.: Prototyping an automatic notification scheme for traffic accidents in vehicular networks. In: 2011 IFIP Wireless Days (WD). IEEE (2011)
13. Barba, C.T., Mateos, M.A., Soto, P.R., Mezher, A.M., Igartua, M.A.: Smart city for VANETs using warning messages, traffic statistics and intelligent traffic lights. In: Intelligent Vehicles Symposium (IV). IEEE (2012)
14. Borriello, G., Chalmers, M., LaMarca, A., Nixon, P.: Delivering real-world ubiquitous location systems. Communications of the ACM 48(3), 36–41 (2005)
15. Aldunate, R., Nussbaum, M., Pena-Mora, F.: An Empirical Wi-Fi Based Location Mechanism for Urban Search and Rescue Operations. In: Langendoerfer, P., Liu, M., Matta, I., Tsaoussidis, V. (eds.) WWIC 2004. LNCS, vol. 2957, pp. 48–61. Springer, Heidelberg (2004)
16. af Wåhlberg, A. E.: Characteristics of low speed accidents with buses in public transport. Accident Analysis & Prevention 34(5), 637–647 (2002)

An Ontology-Driven Framework
for Resource-Efficient Collaborative Sensing

Brayan Luna-Nuñez[1], Rolando Menchaca-Mendez[1], and Jesus Favela[2]

[1] Instituto Politécnico Nacional
bluna_b12@sagitario.cic.ipn.mx, rmen@cic.ipn.mx
[2] Centro de Investigación Científica y de Educación Superior de Ensenada
favela@cicese.mx

Abstract. The massive adoption of smartphones that incorporate wireless connectivity and a growing set of embedded sensors is leveraging the emergence of personal and community-scale sensing applications. In these applications, the smartphones act as a cloud of sensors that move around with their human users and hence, are capable of gathering a rich variety of data from their users and from their environments. However, in order to realize their full potential, the designers of these applications face a set of technical challenges related with the limited resources available to mobile devices, their heterogeneity, and the dynamics of the scenarios where they are deployed. In this paper we introduce an ontology-driven framework aimed at efficiently supporting collaborative opportunistic sensing tasks. The proposed framework is composed of a set of local and distributed algorithms that support the establishment and coordination of sensing tasks by performing in-network processing to locate the devices that are most fit to perform the task and by establishing routes that can be used to exchange information among relevant devices. We present theorems that prove that the proposed algorithms are correct.

Keywords: Collaborative sensing, distributed algorithms, ontology.

1 Introduction

Smartphones that incorporate wireless connectivity and a variety of sensors, such as GPS, accelerometer, gyroscope, camera and microphones are becoming ubiquitous. This has given rise to the field of mobile sensing, namely, the use of mobile devices to gather data from its users. The data sensed might include information about the users' level of physical activity, the places they visit and their patterns of on-line communication. In the context of the smart cities, the information gathered from many users can also be used to characterize the state of complex urban systems such as road networks and public transportation systems[1]. This information can be further used to develop models that describe such systems [2]. Research in this area has motivated the development of mobile sensing platforms such as CRN Toolbox [3], Funf [4], and InCense [5].

The demands that continuous opportunistic sensing poses on mobile devices have also motivated the development of collaborative sensing strategies, were

G. Urzaiz et al. (Eds.): UCAmI 2013, LNCS 8276, pp. 366–369, 2013.

two or more mobile devices divide the sensing, processing or communication load to save resources [6]. For instance, if the sensing application can infer that two users are traveling together in a car, sensing location information from only the car's GPS might be sufficient and the GPS sensors of the two smartphones can be turned off, preserving battery.

In this paper we introduce an ontology-driven framework aimed at efficiently supporting collaborative opportunistic sensing tasks. For a given sensing task, the proposed framework is capable of selecting the devices currently in the environment that are most fit to perform the task based on their sensing capabilities and their level and consumption of bandwidth, energy and storage.

2 Opportunistic Collaborative Sensing

The proposed framework is composed of a *request dissemination protocol*, a *converge-cast protocol*, and a *distributed ambient ontology*. The request dissemination protocol shown in Fig. 1(a) is in charge of finding the set of nodes that can fulfill a request issued by a node and of establishing a breadth-first search tree that is further used to deliver the replies back from the sensors to the requesting node. Fig. 1(b) illustrates the previous idea. In Fig. 1(b), node x issues a request (CSReq) to the network looking for a given sensing service. The request is disseminated up to a threshold R that is application-dependent and can be defined in a number of ways such as maximum allowed-delay, distance in hops or euclidean distance. As the request is disseminated, it establishes parent-children relations that define a breadth-first search tree. In Fig. 1(b), these relations are denoted by solid-black arrows.

The converge-cast protocol also shown in Fig. 1(a) performs in-network processing to identify the best sensor currently available. It works by contracting the breadth-first search tree from leaves to the root relaying the best option seen so far. A sensor is considered better than another sensor if the semantic distance between the requested service and the service provided by the sensor is smaller, or if the path connecting the two nodes is more efficient in terms of energy, bandwidth, congestion and contention. This way, the node issuing the request receives only the information regarding the best sensor. Alternatively, the network can deliver not only the best sensor but a set of sensors that can perform a collaborative sensing task. In this latter mode, the node issuing the request acts as the leader of the group and uses the breadth-first search tree to deliver coordination information to the sensors. For instance, it can compute and deliver sensing schedules to the set of sensors so that they can turn-off their radios or sensing hardware to preserve energy and bandwidth. Request and reply messages have the following formats $CSReq = \{requesterId, service, disThreshold, cost, maxAllowedCost, seqNum\}$, $CSRsp = \{requesterId, providerId, service, providedService, cost, seqNum\}$.

In the proposed framework, every node stores a fraction of a *sensing-services ontology* that describes the services the node is capable of providing. As shown in Fig. 1(c), the instantaneous ambient ontology is the union of the ontology

```
1 Algorithm: Requester node i
2 define provider //initially null;
3 define pendingResponses //initially empty;
4 define routingTable //global and initally empty;
5 define seqNum // global and initially 0;
6 define status = finding | consuming | noProvider;
7 status := finding;
8 responses := null;
9 pendingResponses := getNeighborhood();
10 seqNum := seqNum + 1;
11 send CSReq{i, service, j, 0, k, seqNum};
12 while status == finding do
13   if pendingResponses != null then
14     ∀j ∈ pendingResponses | j ∉ getNeighborhood()
15       delete j from pendingResponses;
16   end
17   if receive CSRsp{i, j, service, providedService, k, l} then
18     add CSRsp to responses;
19     delete sender from pendingResponses;
20     update routingTable adding sender as a path to j;
21   end
22   if pendingResponses == null then
23     provider := getBestFit(CSReq, responses);
24     if provider == null then
25       status := noProvider;
26     else
27       status := consuming;
28     end
29   end
30 end
```

```
1 Algorithm: Non requester node j
2 define contactCapacity //actual contact capacity;
3 define seenRequests //list of already seen request;
4 define providedService // initially null;
5 while true do
6   if pendingResponses != null then
7     ∀p ∈ pendingResponses | p ∉ getNeighborhood()
8       delete p from pendingResponses;
9   end
10   if receive CSReq{i, service, k, l, m, n} & CSReq ∉ seenRequests then
11     update CSReq cost;
12     update routingTable adding sender as a path to i;
13     if m >= l then
14       add CSRsp{i, j, service, getService(service), l, seqNum} to i's
         responses;
15       seqNum := seqNum + 1;
16     else if m > l & l isIn k then
17       send CSReq{i, service, k, l, m, n};
18       i's pendingResponses := getNeighborhood();
19     end
20     add CSReq to seenRequests;
21   end
22   if receive CSRsp{i, k, service, providedService, l, m} then
23     add CSRsp to i's responses;
24     delete sender from i's pendingResponses;
25   end
26   ∀ i | i's pendingResponses == null
27     provider := getBestFit(CSReq, responses);
28     send provider as a CSRsp to i;
29     empty i's responses;
30 end
```

(a)

(b)   (c)

Fig. 1. (a) Distributed algorithm. (b) Instantaneous topology of an ad hoc network. (c) Instantaneous ambient ontology that describes the services provided by the network.

fragments of the sensors currently in the environment (Fig 1(b)). This ontology can grow or shrink as new sensing nodes arrive and leave the environment. When a sensing request arrives to a node, it computes the semantic distance between the service requested and the services it is able to provide. We use a very simple semantic distance that equals 0 if the requested concept (service) is an ancestor of the service provided by the sensor, and the hop distance otherwise.

2.1   Analysis

For the following theorems we assume that packets sent in unicast mode are reliably delivered and that nodes know the constituency of their one-hop neighborhood through a call to function $getNeighborhood()$.

Theorem 1. *When the algorithm of Fig. 1(a) terminates, the value of **provider** equals the identifier of the node of minimum cost located in the BFS-tree induced by the dissemination of the request (CSReq).*

Proof. (*Sketch*) By contradiction. Assume that $provider = j$ and j is not the identifier of the node (i) of minimum cost. Since unicast messages are reliable, nodes either leave the network or report the best node known to their parent in the BFS-tree. Therefore, an inner node in the BFS-tree (it may be the root) should have selected j over i. This contradicts line 23 of the requester node or line 27 of non requester nodes where the best known node is selected.   □

Theorem 2. *The algorithm of Fig. 1(a) terminates.*

Proof. (*Sketch*) By contradiction. Assume that there is at least one branch of the BFS-tree that is not contracted up to the root. Let node i be a leaf node of such branch. Since it is a leaf, the condition of line 16 has to be false and it should have sent a CSRsp back to its parent. The latter should have removed i from the tree.   □

3   Conclusions and Future Work

We presented a new ontology-driven framework for resource-efficient opportunistic collaborative sensing. Given a request for a sensing service, the algorithms that compose the framework perform in network processing to find the set of nodes that more closely match the request and which are able to provide the service in the most efficient way. At the same time, the algorithms establish routes that sensor and requesting nodes can use to communicate and coordinate among themselves. We are currently designing a series of simulation-based performance experiments where we intend to use precision, recall, consumed energy, end-to-end delay, success ratio and network overhead as our performance metrics.

Acknowledgments. This work was sponsored in part by CONACyT and by the ICyT-DF.

References

1. Lane, N.D., Miluzzo, E., Lu, H., Peebles, D., Choudhury, T., Campbell, A.T.: A survey of mobile phone sensing. IEEE Communications Magazine 48(9), 140–150 (2010)
2. Cuff, D., Hansen, M., Kang, J.: Urban sensing: out of the woods. Communications of the ACM 51(3), 24–33 (2008)
3. Bannach, D., Lukowicz, P., Amft, O.: Rapid prototyping of activity recognition applications. IEEE Pervasive Computing 7(2), 22–31 (2008)
4. Aharony, N., Pan, W., Ip, C., Khayal, I., Pentland, A.: Social fmri: Investigating and shaping social mechanisms in the real world. Pervasive and Mobile Computing 7(6), 643–659 (2011)
5. Perez, M., Castro, L., Favela, J.: Incense: A research kit to facilitate behavioral data gathering from populations of mobile phone users. In: Proc. of UCAmI, Cancun, Mexico, pp. 25–34 (2011)
6. Sheng, X., Tang, J., Zhang, W.: Energy-efficient collaborative sensing with mobile phones. In: Proceedings IEEE INFOCOM 2012, pp. 1916–1924. IEEE (2012)

Enabling Citizen-Empowered Apps over Linked Data

Diego López-de-Ipiña[1], Sacha Vanhecke[2], Oscar Peña[1], and Erik Mannnens[2]

[1] Deusto Institute of Technology, DeustoTech, University of Deusto, Avda.
Universidades 24, 48007 Bilbao, Spain
[2] Ghent University – iMinds – Multimedia Lab, Gent, Belgium
{dipina,oscar.pena}@deusto.es,
{sacha.vanhecke,erik.mannens}@ugent.be

Abstract. Smarter cities can be achieved by leveraging already available infrastructure such as Open Government Data and deployed sensor networks in cities, and, very importantly, citizens' participation through apps in their smartphones. This work contributes a platform, namely IES CITIES, with a two-fold aim: a) to facilitate the generation of citizen-centric apps that exploit urban data in different domains and b) to enable user supplied data to complement, enrich and enhance existing datasets about a city.

Keywords: Smart City, Linked Data, Apps, provenance, trust, JSON.

1 Introduction

Smart cities aim to increase citizens' quality of life and improve the efficiency and quality of the services provided by governing entities and businesses. The IES Cities project is defined to promote user-centric mobile micro-services that exploit open data and generate user-supplied data. Its main contribution is to define an open Linked Data apps-enabling technological solution. Such platform will be deployed in different cities across Europe, allowing the citizens to produce and consume Internet-based services (apps) based on their own and external open data related to the cities.

Something especially remarkable about IES Cities is that users may help on improving, extending and enriching the open data in which micro-services, i.e. urban apps, are usually based. The main stakeholders of the resulting urban apps ecosystem by our envisaged smart city-enabling platform are mainly the citizens, but also the SMEs and public administration of different cities.

2 Related Work

Users may enrich a given city's datasets by contributing with data through urban apps execution in their smartphones. However, the quality of such data may significantly vary from a given citizen to another. It is important to be able to assess and qualify the provided data, thus promoting valuable and trustable information and decrementing and eventually discarding lower quality data. In order to address this, the W3C

G. Urzaiz et al. (Eds.): UCAmI 2013, LNCS 8276, pp. 370–373, 2013.

has created the PROV Data Model [**¡Error! No se encuentra el origen de la referencia.**][1] for provenance interchange on the web.

Human Computation [1] enables to leverage human intelligence to carry out tasks that otherwise would be difficult to accomplish by a machine, e.g. identifying the names of people present in photographs [2] [3].

This work fosters the generation of provenance-based trusted Linked Data through citizen contribution, inspired by other works such as [4]. Users' data contributions are mediated by the IES CITIES-enabled mobile apps that leverage the back-end provenance support. Furthermore, this work proposes the use of JSON schema[2] and query languages[3] to facilitate urban apps development, since structured and non-structured data in the form of RDF, CSV or even HTML pages can be easily mapped into JSON.

3   A Platform for Urban and Participatory Linked Data Apps

The client/server architecture of the IES CITIES platform is shown in Fig. 1. The role of the *server* is to enable the retrieval and the storage of data provided by both users and public infrastructures. Independent developers create new services and register them; new datasets are also published and registered with the platform by public administrations. In order to track both the registered IES Cities services and users, the server manages their related information and current location and location scope, respectively. Thus, the server allows users to find and access services based on a degree of relevancy. The *client* app installed on the user's mobile device serves as the communication portal to browse and run services.

All information about services and users of the IES Cities platform is persisted in a PostgreSQL database and all the open datasets provided by city councils are registered and accessible through CKAN[4] for structured RDF datasets and TheDataTank[5] for semi-structured and unstructured data. The server accesses them whenever a dataset is requested by an IES CITIES app. A Virtuoso RDF store was also installed in order to handle linked datasets and user-provided RDF data managed by the platform.

Open data is fetched by defining a generic JSON-formatted query and sending it to the server's RESTful "/data/" interface, together with the requested dataset's name. This query consists of key/value pairs to specify required fields and optionally some parameters. The server side resolves the location of the requested dataset from the publication engines, after which it transforms the JSON query into the query language specific to the nature of the data's resolved endpoint. Currently, a query mapper has been implemented for both SPARQL, the query language for RDF, and SPECTQL, the query language used by TheDataTank[6].

---

[1] http://www.w3.org/TR/2013/NOTE-prov-primer-20130430/
[2] http://json-schema.org/latest/json-schema-core.html
[3] http://www.jsoniq.org/
[4] http://ckan.org
[5] http://thedatatank.com
[6] http://thedatatank.com/

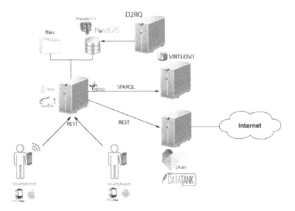

Fig. 1. Deployment of IES CITIES platform

The client application, the IES Cities Player, was developed using PhoneGap[7]. The GUI of the player was completely written in HTML5 and CSS3, using the JavaScript libraries jQuery and jQuery Mobile. Using AJAX, simple HTTP requests are sent to the RESTful "/service/" interface of the IES Cities server. This interface returns information in JSON format.

Fig. 2. 311 Bilbao IES CITIES service

4   An IES CITIES-Enabled App: 311 Bilbao

The 311 Bilbao (Fig. 2) is an IES CITIES-enabled app that uses Linked Open Data to get an overview of reports of faults in public infrastructure. It demonstrates how a developer can create a complex mobile app relying on semantic data, without

---

[7] http://phonegap.com/

technical knowledge of the query language SPARQL. A query using JSON sent to the IES Cities platform's RESTful "/data/" interface is only needed.

During initialization, the service queries for reported faults, and displays the result on a map (Fig. 2a). Using the filter functionality on the second tab (Fig. 2b), a user can choose to see reports of only a certain type. By clicking on the marker of a particular report, the ID and the underlying nature of the reported fault is displayed. When the user decides to inspect the report an information page (Fig. 2c) is shown. On this page, users can read the full description of the report and watch an app snapshot. Notably, here, they are also able to vote the credibility of the report up or down, clue which is used to register and recalculate in the server the credibility score of such report. Finally, they can create their own reports (Fig. 2d).

5   Conclusion

The IES CITIES platform can be used to facilitate the use of open data from heterogeneous formats; all of it through a simple JSON query language. Moreover, citizens' involvement in the management of a city can be increased by allowing them to actively participate in the creation and validation of new data. The IES Cities platform helps councils to easily publish their open data in different non-proprietary formats, while making them accessible as common machine-readable formats through uniform REST interfaces, easily consumable by developers.

References

1. Bozzon, B., Galli, L., Fraternali, P., Karam, R.: Modeling CrowdSourcing scenarios in Socially-Enabled Human Computation Applications. Journal on Dada Semantics (Springer)
2. von Ahn, L.: Games with a Purpose. IEEE Computer 39(6), 92–94 (2006)
3. Celino, I., Contessa, S., Corubolo, M., Dell'Aglio, D., Della Valle, E., Fumeo, S., Krüger, T.: Linking Smart Cities Datasets with Human Computation – the case of UrbanMatch. In: Cudré-Mauroux, P., et al. (eds.) ISWC 2012, Part II. LNCS, vol. 7650, pp. 34–49. Springer, Heidelberg (2012)
4. Celino, I., Cerizza, D., Contessa, S., Corubolo, M., Dell'Aglio, D., Della Valle, E., Fumeo, S.: Urbanopoly – a Social and Location-based Game with a Purpose to Crowdsource your Urban Data. In: Proceedings of the 4th IEEE SocialCom, Workshop on Social Media for Human Computation, pp. 910–913 (2012), doi:10.1109/SocialCom-PASSAT.2012.138
5. Heath, T., Bizer, C.: Linked Data: Evolving the Web into a Global Data Space, Synthesis Lectures on the Semantic Web, 1st edn. Morgan & Claypool Publishers (2011)
6. Lebo, T., Sahoo, S., McGuinness, D. (eds.): Prov-o: The prov ontology (2013), http://www.w3.org/TR/2013/REC-prov-o-20130430/ (last accessed: May 10, 2013)
7. Braun, M., Scherp, A., Staab, S.: Collaborative Semantic Points of Interests. In: Aroyo, L., Antoniou, G., Hyvönen, E., ten Teije, A., Stuckenschmidt, H., Cabral, L., Tudorache, T. (eds.) ESWC 2010, Part II. LNCS, vol. 6089, pp. 365–369. Springer, Heidelberg (2010)
8. Halpin, H.: Provenance: The missing component of the semantic web for privacy and trust. In: SPOT 2009, Workshop of ESWC (2009)
9. Magliacane, S.: Reconstructing provenance. In: Cudré-Mauroux, P., et al. (eds.) ISWC 2012, Part II. LNCS, vol. 7650, pp. 399–406. Springer, Heidelberg (2012)
10. Ceolin, D., Groth, P.T., van Hage, W.R., Nottamkandath, A., Fokkink, W.: Trust Evaluation through User Reputation and Provenance Analysis. In: URSW, pp. 15–26 (2012)

The Citizen Road Watcher – Identifying Roadway Surface Disruptions Based on Accelerometer Patterns

Luis Carlos González-Gurrola, Fernando Martínez-Reyes,
and Manuel Ricardo Carlos-Loya

Universidad Autónoma de Chihuahua, Facultad de Ingeniería, 31125, Chihuahua, MX
{lcgonzalez,fmartine,p168786}@uach.mx

Abstract. Roadway surface disruptions present multiple challenges for both individuals and governmental agencies; knowing the exact number and location of road imperfections in a specific area could help save lives, freight and money to citizens, companies and authorities. This work presents earlier results of a tool being proposed to report the existence of road's disruptions by enabling citizens' cars as road watchers. Using Android-based devices situated on the copilot floor side of a car 5 Mbytes of road information has been collected. We run a series of experiments aiming to observe changes in the acceleration patterns when vehicles pass over potholes, speed bumps and metal humps. Currently, the classification of disruptions is being experimented with techniques from the field of Machine Learning (ML). Our vision for such a tool is to offer an accurate and automated system that can report the presence of road imperfections to a web-based information system.

Keywords: Road surface disruptions, RSD, mobile computing, mobile sensing, machine learning algorithms.

1 Introduction

Potholes, speed bumps, speed humps, expansion joints, manhole covers, storm drains and railway crossings are among the most common roadway surface disruptions (RSDs). The random presence of potholes represents a challenge for drivers. Speed bumps and humps, in developing countries, are often not clearly signaled which represent a danger for both the car and the driver. Even worst, one can find that citizens install their own traffic calming measures, which regularly do not follow regulations and might be poorly placed and marked. Therefore, these road features present multiple challenges for individuals, industry and governmental agencies. Damaged cars can affect the individual's economy. For a company, in addition, road disruptions can alter delivery routes affecting its service reputation. For the agencies in charge of roads, finding and repairing potholes in the many kilometers of roads under their jurisdiction can be complicated and very costly.

Car technology could help inform peers and government agencies about the location and nature of RSDs. GPS and accelerometer technology could help monitoring and tagging roadway surface disruptions. The availability of databases containing the location of RSDs could lead to driving assisting technologies warning drivers of

G. Urzaiz et al. (Eds.): UCAmI 2013, LNCS 8276, pp. 374–377, 2013.

potential traveling disruptions. This information could also help municipalities since they can improve the planning tasks of maintenance and signaling, and the removing of unauthorized speed bumps. In this paper we present our work towards building a system that can automatically identify and report RSDs so that citizens can contribute to an urban information system.

The order of the paper is as follows. Section two reviews other authors' contributions in the identification of RSDs. Section three describes our ongoing work with an automated strategy using machine-learning algorithms. Finally, conclusions and future directions for this work are given.

2   Related Work

Accelerometers have been among the most popular sensors used to address the problem of detecting irregularities in roads. Accelerometers have been tried out for instance, in the shaft of a wheel, inside the glove box, windshields, dashboards, and the car's trunk. The aim has been to get understanding of acceleration data generated by a car when driving on roads with potholes, bumps, humps and rail crossings. The "Pothole" [1] and the "Roadroid" [2] systems, for example, use a 380 Hz and a 512 Hz accelerometer, respectively, to collect road data and to identify potholes out from other road anomalies. New mobile platforms, like smartphones and tablets, have provided easier and cheaper alternatives to carry on studies that focus not only on the identification of road irregularities but also on the identification and labeling of road traffic. In the "Nericell" project [3], wireless enabled 310 Hz accelerometers were communicated to smartphone devices to collect road data. Accelerometer data was processed to differentiate bumps and potholes from the rest of the road anomalies. To collect information of traffic jams the authors used the smartphone's microphone to record the use of the honk. Together with GPS information and honks the labeling of chaotic routes was made. Similarly, in the second development phase of "Roadroid", Android-based devices with a 100 Hz accelerometer were used to monitor and to inform about the quality of roads. A web-portal was made available with information regarding four road categories: "Good", "Ok", "Poor" and "Bad". Other work has extended previous experiences by exploring additional factors such as device orientation, sampling frequency and speed [4], which seemed to affect the identification of road imperfections. In the UNIquALroad [5] project, a mobile device with a 5Hz accelerometer and a tablet with a 100 Hz accelerometer were used to collect road data and to identify potholes and bumps. Although the algorithm used in this project was not affecting the detection of bumps regarding potholes, a 65% of effectiveness was reached. Recently, researchers have been looking for a more natural way to collect information of mobile devices accelerometers. Due to the fact that mobile phones are part of the lifestyle, the mobile phone carried by drivers can be the means by which to collect acceleration data [6]. For instance, The "SWAS" system [7] collected information from an accelerometer of a smartphone that is in the driver's pant pocket. That road data was used to classify humps and bumps. A server is used to share information of unknown and improperly signed speed breakers. In most of these experiences, the common approach for the identification of irregularities on roads is based on setting fixed thresholds, which were figured out from a sensor characterization process.

In our work, Android-based mobile devices with a 15Hz sampling frequency were used to collect road data of some low and high traffic streets in Chihuahua, Mexico. Two different cars were used in two different experiments, and so far we have collected >5MB of data. Applying a machine learning approach we are exploring to what extent it could be possible to increase the accuracy of the classification of potholes, bumps and humps as reported by previous work. Collected data is available and free to use at https://sites.google.com/site/luiscarlosgonzalezgurrola/datasets.

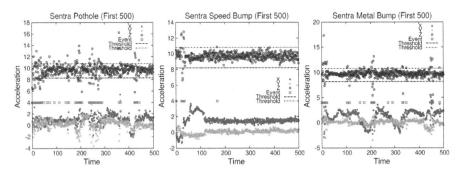

Fig. 1. The acceleration patterns in the x (red), y (green) and z (blue) axes identified for the Nissan Sentra car. The evenness zone is indicated by the minimum and maximum threshold values. The pink data points are useful to pinpoint events of interest.

3   Identifying Roadway Disruptions

In our first attempt a principal component analysis was used to reduce dimensionality. This first analysis (data not shown) suggests, among other things, that metal and speed bumps are not easy to discriminate from each other solely based on the variance of their acceleration values. This clearly represents a challenge to any algorithm trying to uniquely identify one class from the other. Based on this premise, in our second experiment we started using a more sophisticated approach. We used a machine-learning approach to classify potholes, speed and metal bumps out from road data. We arbitrarily chose 500 data points to run our set of computational experiments. 250 events were used for training and the other half was used for validation and testing. Fig. 1 shows the patterns in the acceleration data for the x, y and z axes for each event recorded by a Nissan Sentra car. By visual inspection we manually labeled the data points belonging to an event. Since there is noise affecting the ground value for each axis, we made two assumptions: (i) we decided to take as an event indicator the z axis, since a road disruption always cause vertical acceleration; and (ii) we set minimum and maximum threshold limits so that any data point with its z-axis value falling in this zone would be deemed road evenness, otherwise an event of interest. For the classification task we selected the very well-known Multi-layer perceptron (MLP). We decided to create different datasets for the experimental section. In the first stage, we applied the MLP over datasets containing two classes: evenness and one kind of road disruption, therefore there were six different experiments, three for each car (pothole, speed bump and metal bump). Afterwards, we mixed all the events identified on each car and run the MLP over this dataset. Finally, we mixed all events from the two cars on the same dataset and run the MLP. Table 1 presents the results of the MLP over these datasets.

Table 1. Classification accuracy percentage of the MLP

Car	Pothole	Speed Bump	Metal Bump	Overall	Final
Sentra	98.4%	99.2%	97.6%	92.7%	87.7%
Tsuru	96.7%	98.4%	96.8%	92.36%	

4   Conclusions and Future Work

This paper describes our ongoing work with the application of a machine learning technique for the identification of roadway surface disruptions (RSD). Using two different cars and an Android-based mobile phone placed on the cars' floor we collected data from different roads in Chihuahua, Mexico. The applied multi-layer perceptron provided a very high accuracy when two classes are present within a given dataset. Even when different events are mixed within the same car, the accuracy of the MLP is pretty competitive with state of the art approaches. The challenge comes when all events from different cars are used. In order to improve final accuracy we plan to apply frequency-based filters to reduce noisy data, and we would like to experiment with other classifiers such as decision trees and support vector machines.

References

1. Forslöf, L.: Roadroid smartphone road quality monitoring. In: 19th ITS World Congress (October 2012)
2. Astarita, V., Caruso, M.V., Danieli, G., Festa, D.C., Giofré, V.P., Iuele, T., Vaiana, R.: A mobile application for road surface quality control: Uniqualroad. Procedia-Social and Behavioral Sciences 54, 1135–1144 (2012)
3. Mohan, P., Padmanabhan, V.N., Ramjee, R.: Nericell: rich monitoring of road and track conditions using mobile smartphones. In: Proceedings of the 6th ACM Conference on Embedded Network Sensor Systems, pp. 323–336. ACM (2008)
4. Eriksson, J., Girod, L., Hull, B., Newton, R., Madden, S., Balakrishnan, H.: The pothole patrol: using a mobile sensor network for road surface monitoring. In: MobiSys 2008 (2008)
5. Jain, M., Singh, A.P., Bali, S., Kaul, S.: Speed-breaker early warning system (2012)
6. Mednis, A., Strazdins, G., Zviedris, R., Kanonirs, G., Selavo, L.: Real time pothole detection using android smartphones with accelerometers. In: Distributed Computing in Sensor Systems and Workshops (DCOSS) 2011, pp. 1–6. IEEE (2011)
7. Sinharay, A., Bilal, S., Pal, A., Sinha, A.: Low computational approach for road condition monitoring using smartphones

Participatory Sensing for Improving Urban Mobility

Miguel Angel Ylizaliturri-Salcedo, Saul Delgadillo-Rodriguez,
J. Antonio Garcia-Macias, and Monica Tentori

Departamento de Ciencias de la Computación
Centro de Investigación Científica y de Educación Superior de Ensenada
Carretera Ensenada-Tijuana No. 3918,
Zona Playitas, C.P. 22860, Ensenada, B.C. México
{mylizali,sdelgadi,jagm,mtentori}@cicese.edu.mx

Abstract. Urban computing leverages mobile participatory and opportunistic sensing to monitor and provide continuous awareness of urban cities. CICESE Research Center offers students and staff an intra-campus transportation service called *CICEMóvil* to help them get around campus. However this service lacks of formality as trips are constantly being cancelled without previous notification and it's hard to discover when the vehicle is going to be available for the next trip. We present the design and development of a mobile augmented reality system using participatory and opportunistic sensing to empower users to track and share the location and status of *CICEMóvil* via their smartphones. We concluded discussing directions for future work, as we aim to study how participatory sensing could be used to promote self-reflection at a collective level through the design and evaluation of mobile sensing campaigns in public transportation.

Keywords: urban sensing, participatory sensing, smartphones, supervision, transportation, mobile applications.

1   Introduction

Participatory sensing has its origin in sensor networks showing how sensing has evolved from a paradigm centered in technologies to a one centered in people. Increasingly, individuals are using mobile devices to create "sensing campaigns" gathering, analyzing, and sharing knowledge. These campaigns empower individuals to reveal and share personal data about their lifestyle or environment status [1]. The deployment of sensing campaigns in urban areas, proving feasible the use of pervasive computing [2], enables the collective gathering of data and uses it as a monitoring tool to provide awareness and support decision-making at individual and collective levels.

An interesting area to study participatory sensing as a reflection tool in cities is the monitoring of public transportation. In [3] authors describe a combination of data from cell towers and GPS devices installed in buses and taxis to represent urban mobility captured in real-time. Urban mobility metrics include road congestion and pedestrian movement in Rome.

G. Urzaiz et al. (Eds.): UCAmI 2013, LNCS 8276, pp. 378–381, 2013.

As identifying bus arrival time is a concern from urban citizens, in [4] authors describe the use of smartphones passengers data to identify the location of cell towers and discover the routes of public transportation. This information is used to predict the waiting time for other users querying the system using their smartphones. Although, sensing campaigns have been widely used for monitoring road conditions (e.g., [5,6,7]) or providing continuous awareness [3,8] of "big data", little has been said about how individuals could use this data to reflect on their habits and change behavior at a collective level. In contrast with the literature in this area, in this paper we study how participatory sensing could be used to promote self-reflection in a concrete scenario of public transportation.

2   System Design and Implementation

The research center CICESE implemented a local transportation service called *CICEMóvil* consist in a small shuttle van with 7 passenger seats, working every weekday from 8:00 to 15:00 hrs, transporting students and staff around campus. However, there isn't a formal schedule and it is very hard to plan trips with this service. The driver usually takes long breaks and suspends the service without public notification. This system aims to supervise the driver's behavior, but more importantly to make the driver aware on his data and promote behavior change trough reflection.

Following an interactive user-centered design methodology we iteratively designed several low-fidelity prototypes and design scenarios envisioning how participatory sensing could help to both monitor *CICEMóvil* and promote self-reflection.

2.1   Architecture

The system has an architecture similar to [4] composed by three elements (Figure 1). One of the advantages of our approach is the simplicity of implementation, allowing to instrument vehicles at a low cost.

- **Monitor.** This is a mobile application for Android smartphones that allows sensing location and speed of the *CICEMóvil* trough GPS, and its proximity to known Wi-Fi hotspots placed throughout the campus, sending data to a cloud server. Monitor shows a map of the campus and the current location of *CICEMóvil* (Figure 2 a), and also offers the option of sending an "away" notification (Figure 2 b).
- **Visor.** This augmented reality application for Android smartphones shows the information about prominent landmarks within the campus, and other available services, like transportation (Figure 2 c). When requested, a screen with more details and a request service button are presented (Figure 2 d)
- **Application Server.** This server application has been deployed and hosted in the Heroku cloud. It offers a RESTful representation of the resources (*i.e.,* location of the vehicle, driver notifications and users requests of service), working as a proxy between both smartphone applications.

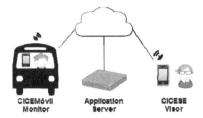

Fig. 1. System components

2.2   Use Scenario

Luis is the driver of the *CICEMóvil*. When he starts his journey, the Monitor starts running in a smartphone. As he gets into the vehicle, the application shows a map with the current location of *CICEMóvil*, making him aware of what data is being shared. Later, after driving for two hours, Luis needs to take a break, and decides to stop the vehicle. He then selects the notification icon on top of the map, and a screen for publishing an "away" notification appears. He announces that the service is suspended for 15 minutes. After 20 minutes, Rosa, a student using the augmented reality visor application searches for the *CICEMóvil* and identifies its location, noticing that the vehicle is already late; that's why she announces her request of service pressing a Request Stop button in the application. Luis gets a notification and he realizes that he's already late because there are some students waiting for transportation and gets back to work.

3   Future Work

We conducted a proof of concept using both applications touring the circuit as a passenger inside the *CICEMóvil*. This prototype is going to be scaled into production, following some technical adaptations. This Visor augmented reality application works well but it's limited to Android devices, in consequence a mobile website is also going to be deployed. More interesting it's to explore how this community campaign could promote a change behavior in the driver as the users employing their own smartphones are empowered to demand availability change in the quality of the transportation service.

More important to remark, this work is also our first approach to monitoring transport services. Our investigation is aimed to include a service with multiple vehicles, willing to detect which are the habits of a driver that can be sensed, in consequence the driver's application is going to get more important as it can work as a window into collective data (i.e. the statistics of the other drivers and their personal behaviors) in order to reinforce and to promote the adoption of better driving practices.

Fig. 2. From left to rigth: a) Monitor showing the location of CICEMóvil, b) Monitor screen for sending away notifications, c) Visor main screen showing the augmented reality view and d) Visor screen for details about CICEMóvil

4   Conclusions

A system composed by two Android smartphone applications and a web server has been developed and tested as concept. Our approach shows a simple and economic way to monitor vehicles in confined environments. More important, it's the precedent for our future investigation in exploring ways to employ participatory sensing as a tool for improving urban mobility and how to persuade and promote better driving behaviors. Our future work aims to reach an evaluation in a public transportation system and to use the produced data as constructs of the pulse of the city.

References

1. Burke, J.A., Estrin, D., Hansen, M., Parker, A., Ramanathan, N., Reddy, S., Srivastava, M.B.: Participatory sensing (May 2006)
2. Cuff, D., Hansen, M., Kang, J.: Urban sensing. Communications of the ACM 51(3), 24–33 (2008)
3. Calabrese, F., Colonna, M., Lovisolo, P., Parata, D., Ratti, C.: Real-Time Urban Monitoring Using Cell Phones: A Case Study in Rome. IEEE Transactions on Intelligent Transportation System 12(1), 141–151 (2011)
4. Zhou, P., Zheng, Y., Li, M.: How long to wait? In: Proceedings of the 10th International Conference on Mobile Systems, Applications, and Services, MobiSys 2012, p. 379 (2012)
5. Mohan, P., Padmanabhan, V.N., Ramjee, R.: Nericell. In: Proceedings of the 6th ACM Conference on Embedded Network Sensor Systems, SenSys 2008, p. 323 (2008)
6. Bhoraskar, R., Vankadhara, N., Raman, B., Kulkarni, P.: Wolverine: Traffic and road condition estimation using smartphone sensors. In: 2012 Fourth International Conference on Communication Systems and Networks (COMSNETS 2012), pp. 1–6 (January 2012)
7. Yoon, J., Noble, B., Liu, M.: Surface street traffic estimation. In: Proceedings of the 5th International Conference on Mobile Systems, Applications and Services, MobiSys 2007, p. 220 (2007)
8. Zheng, Y., Liu, Y., Yuan, J., Xie, X.: Urban computing with taxicabs. In: Proceedings of the 13th International Conference on Ubiquitous Computing, UbiComp 2011, p. 89 (2011)

Risky Driving Detection through Urban Mobility Traces: A Preliminary Approach

Luis C. Cruz, Adrián Macías, Manuel Domitsu, Luis A. Castro,
and Luis-Felipe Rodríguez

Depto. de Computación y Diseño, Instituto Tecnológico de Sonora (ITSON)
luiscruz.2908@gmail.com,
{adrian.macias,manuel.domitsu,luis.caztro,
luis.rodriguez}@itson.edu.mx

Abstract. In Mexico, car accidents are the leading cause of death among young people. Thus, the identification of drivers that can be potentially involved in car accidents is of particular interest. There are certain risky driving behaviors that are highly correlated to car accidents, including speeding, overtaking, and tailgating. In this work, we present a preliminary approach for automated detection of risky driving in urban environments. The system, Tracko, makes use of GPS data to compute mobility traces, which are used to preliminarily characterize driving behaviors. This work presents the design of the system as well as preliminary data to be used for automated identification of risky driving behaviors.

1 Introduction

In Mexico, car accidents are the leading cause of death among people under 30. According to the National Institute of Statistics and Geography (INEGI), in 2011 there were 387,185 car accidents in Mexico, from which around 95% were ascribed to human factors (e.g., distracted, drowsy, and drunk driving). Mobility traces of motor vehicles can be used to identify risky driving. In particular, mobile technology provides an appropriate framework for the development of computer systems capable of collecting data regarding mobility traces of motor vehicles useful for identifying behaviors related to risky driving. Importantly, this technology-based approach can address the limitations of questionnaire-based studies, conducted by researchers in the field of Medical and Health sciences, as drivers' behavior is analyzed based on data collected in their daily lives and, if desired, without awareness of the drivers [1, 2].

Many applications aiming at enhancing urban life have been devised in the domain of urban computing. In the case of road safety, some systems have been created for reducing risks while driving. For example, CarSafe is an app that uses the front and rear cameras of a smartphone to provide alerts of risky driving behaviors such as drowsy driving or tailgating [3].. DriveDiagnostics [4] is an in-vehicle data recorder used to monitor and analyze driver behavior. This system capture mobility traces that help determine overall trip safety and risky driving behavior by identifying and classifying a series of maneuver types.

G. Urzaiz et al. (Eds.): UCAmI 2013, LNCS 8276, pp. 382–385, 2013.

In this paper, we present Tracko, a system based on mobile technology for collecting mobility traces of vehicles in urban settings. This collection of traces is used to detect risky driving behaviors such as aggressive driving and breaking speed limits. Detecting these behaviors is essential for identifying risky drivers and for developing strategies to reduce accidents. In contrast to previous works, Tracko takes advantage of the data collected only from GPS-enabled devices to detect risky driving.

2   Detecting Risky Driving with Tracko

There are several patterns of driving behavior that can be considered risky and that can be associated with traffic accidents such as going through red lights and stop signals, overtaking, and tailgating. Detecting and analyzing such behaviors becomes important mainly for road safety purposes. Data collected from GPS devices allow the monitoring and analysis of risky driving. Commercial GPS devices generally provide geographic coordinates as well as visual information about current locations. Most GPS-enabled smartphones can also provide these types of data. Moreover, through the Application Programming Interface (API) provided by the mobiles' OS, traces of GPS data along with speed, error, and timestamp can be usually obtained. Some aspects of risky driving behavior can be analyzed on the basis of such data. Nevertheless, risky driving behavior that can be identified using only GPS data is limited.

Table 1. Risky driving identification through GPS data only

Behavior	Identification method
Aggressive driving	Speed data can be obtained from GPS data. Acceleration data can be computed
Breaking speed limits	Using geo-fences or marks on maps
Going through a stop sign	Placing points of interest at stop signs (i.e., geo fences) and determining a speed threshold at that particular spot.

Table 1 presents examples of risky driving behavior and indicates how they can be identified using GPS data. Other risky behaviors such as going through red lights, changing lines, overtaking, and tailgating are not considered since their identification requires additional information from other types of sensors. We devised Tracko for the identification of risky driving, a system that could be scalable, flexible and that can work in heterogeneous environments. Tracko consists of three main elements:

- Web client: It is represented by the web client nodes, using a browser with JavaScript VM enabled. It comprises two components: browser and Javascript VM.
- Server: The server node stores and processes data collected through mobile devices using HTTP methods. The system is deployed using Glassfish Java Application Server, which is composed of a web Server and a business server. It mainly comprises three components: Web application, business logic and a database.
- Mobile device: A mobile node where GPS data are collected. The mobile device can be any device capable of making HTTP requests, including Arduino devices.

3   Preliminary Detection of Risky Driving

Our experimental testbed was deployed in public transport in two mid-size cities in northwest Mexico. To facilitate the collection of samples, we designed a mobile app for a Nokia Lumia 710 running Windows Phone 7.8. The app collects samples every 5 meters. We collected 12,477 samples corresponding to three local routes of public transport in the aforementioned cities. For testing purposes, a heuristic (i.e., thresholds) was devised to determine when a driver was externalizing risky behaviors. Particularly, speed was computed from successive GPS readings and acceleration was computed by subtracting starting velocity from final velocity divided by time used.

3.1   Aggressive Driving

Aggressive driving is when a driver accelerates the vehicle too rapidly or presses the brakes too sharply. Avoiding aggressive driving behavior can save around 25 liters of diesel per day [5]. In their study, [5] reported that fuel consumption increased 67% for acceleration increase in the range of 0.5 m/s^2 to 1.5 m/s^2. In our study, the max acceleration detected was 1.66 m/s^2. This is important not only for fuel optimization but also for passenger safety. In our experiment, the min acceleration detected was -2.76 m/s^2, meaning that at some points the driver braked sharply.

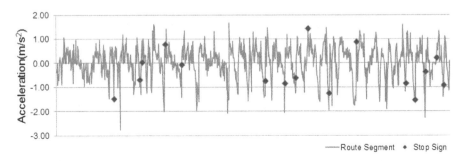

Fig. 1. Vehicle acceleration during a 30min window for one driver

Following Figure 1, we can observe the acceleration/deceleration at stop signs. In general, for this segment, the average acceleration was 0.5 m/s^2, which is reasonable since an average sport car takes around 6s to reach 0.100 km/h at around 4 m/s^2. In Figure 1, it can be seen that the driver decelerates before stop signs in 11 times. However, there are two times in particular when the acceleration rate is really high at stop signs. For deceleration, the average was -0.53 m/s^2 for this timeframe.

3.2   Breaking Speed Limits

According to the World Health Organization (WHO), speed control is one of various interventions likely to reduce road casualties. This is one of the reasons why is important to identify such behavior. From our analysis, perhaps not very surprising, speed is mainly decreased at stop signs. However, at only one stop sign, the driver seemed to have completely stopped (speed below 10 km/h). In this particular 30min window, the average speed was 32 km/h, and the max speed was 68km/h. In addition, the driver seems to break the speed limits in two occasions.

3.3   Going through a Stop Sign

Going through a stop sign can be detected using geo-fencing, placing points of interest where speed or acceleration can be computed in those regions. There are 16 stop signs in the 30min window shown (Figure 1), in which the driver does not seem to make a full stop at stop signs, as required by law. Instead, the driver seemed to have made semi-stops by reducing the overall speed of the vehicle. Two possible explanations arise. First, the driver actually did not stop at most stop signs, which can be worrisome as passenger and road safety must be paramount. On the other hand, GPS readings could have yielded these results. More experiments must be carried out adding sensors to fully determine when a vehicle makes a full stop.

4   Closing Remarks

In this work, we presented preliminary results toward detection of risky driving using only GPS data. We carried out an experiment to determine the feasibility of detecting such behaviors. Future work includes combining the results from analyzing risky driving with other kind of information such as drivers' background and driver affective condition when exhibiting risky driving behavior (using additional sensors) as well as machine learning techniques for automated detection. This may help to understand the relation of people's background or mood and their driving habits. Thus, this can lead to strategies for improving people driving behavior and increasing road safety through persuasive techniques or incentives.

References

1. Ivers, R., et al.: Novice Drivers' Risky Driving Behavior, Risk Perception, and Crash Risk: Findings From the DRIVE Study. American Journal of Public Health 99(9), 1638–1644 (2009)
2. Blows, S., et al.: Risky driving habits and motor vehicle driver injury. Accident Analysis and Prevention 37(4), 619–624 (2005)
3. You, C.-W., et al.: CarSafe App: Alerting Drowsy and Distracted Drivers using Dual Cameras on Smartphones. In: 11th International Conference on Mobile Systems, Applications and Services (MobiSys 2013). ACM, Taipei (2013)
4. Toledo, T., Lotan, T.: In-Vehicle Data Recorder for Evaluation of Driving Behavior and Safety. Transportation Research Record 1953, 112–119 (2006)
5. Rohani, M.M.: Bus Driving Behaviour and Fuel Consumption, in School of Civil Engineering and the Environment. University of Southampton, Southampton (2012)

Ambient Urban Games for Reducing the Stress of Commuters Crossing the Mexico-US Border

Marcela D. Rodríguez and Cecilia M. Curlango Rosas

School of Engineering, Universidad Autonoma de Baja California, Mexicali, Mexico 21280
{marcerod,curlango}@uabc.edu.mx

Abstract. The long waits that commuters, going from Mexico to the United States (US), face every day to cross the border affects their health in several ways. Commuters express boredom, stress and feeling that they are wasting time, which they could otherwise employ to a better end. In this paper, we hypothesize that using ambient urban games is an appropriate strategy that will help commuters to reduce the level of stress that they feel while waiting.

Keywords: Urban games, smart cities, stress.

1 Introduction

The border between Mexico and the United States (US) is one of the most heavily used in the world. The high volume of traffic brings with it a series of issues that range from urban congestion and pollution to health problems. Those problems, though they are most prevalent when crossing northward from Mexico to the US, are also present to a lesser degree when crossing from the US into Mexico. They are caused by the long lines of cars that are created by border crossers as they await their turn for inspection in order to gain access into the US. These waits can range from one and half to four hours, depending on the time of day and season, and at times due to other events, for example the attacks on 9-11 caused a significant increase in the time required to cross due to more thorough inspections [1].

The long waits that commuters face every day when they cross the border affects their health in several ways [2]. Commuters express boredom, stress and feeling that they are wasting time which they could otherwise employ to a better end; however, they are not aware that continual high stress levels have a detrimental effect on health and well being [2,3]. Others express feelings of frustration and powerlessness while waiting to cross. Coupled with these feelings is the health impact that is caused by inhaling pollutants spewed from the hundreds of cars that are idling. While reducing waiting times at the border would provide an ideal solution to these problems, that is out of the scope of our research. Instead we seek to propose strategies that will ameliorate conditions for border crossers, in the sense that their emotional well being is increased by reducing the level of stress that they feel while waiting. To this end, we will explore the use of games to achieve this goal. Game playing has been found to decrease stress levels significantly [3]. While this is true, the type of games to propose

G. Urzaiz et al. (Eds.): UCAmI 2013, LNCS 8276, pp. 386–389, 2013.
© Springer International Publishing Switzerland 2013

must meet strict criteria so as not to endanger the lives and well being of the persons playing as well as that of fellow commuters, that is the activities must not cause drivers to become distracted, as this could lead them to crash or spark a risky situation if they fail to advance in the line promptly. Therefore, we hypothesized that ambient urban games are appropriate applications that will help commuters to cope with their stress while they are waiting in line. Urban games are location-based applications that seek to move computer gaming out from behind the PC and into the "real world" of cities, streets, parks, and other locations [4]; to this end, they may include ambient intelligence characteristics.

2   Related Work

Several location-based games have been developed to enable users to experience nature and urban life, while socializing and making scavenger hunt activities. For instance, Geocaching is a GPS- enabled treasure hunt. Players known as geocachers, hide physical containers with a paper logbook and record the GPS coordinates on the Geocaching Web site; other geocachers then use this information to find the containers [4]. Similarly, Floracaching is a serious game that helps collect scientific data of specific plants, which serve as the site of virtual caches (implemented with QR codes). These data is then used to study topics such as the effects of climate change and the dissemination of allergens [5]. Mystery Spaces is an urban game that encourages users to explore and discover the mystery of abandoned public infrastructure. To reach this end, the game implements geo-caching activities by using Augmented Reality (AR) [6]. Finally, Urbanopoly is a location-based game similar to the monopoly board game. The player is a landlord whose aim is to create a rich portfolio of venues, which are real places in the surroundings of the Urbanopoly user, like shops, restaurants, and monuments [7].

The aforementioned games, provide evidence that for developing urban games, designers may consider aspects, such as the physical organization of the space, the accessible services and events (functional city), and define the narrative of the game, which should be appropriate to the context of use of the game [8]. To obtain a preliminary understanding of the context of use, we carried out the following study to comprehend the border crossers' perception of how they spend time crossing to the US, and how it affects their mental and emotional state.

3   Characterizing Border Crossers

The number of participants of our study was 31 (17 female and 14 male) who work at our organization. Most of them (29) said they cross the border once a month at least, from which 8 cross the border once every fifteen days and 7 once a week. Just 9 of the 29 indicated they go to US with no company. The top three reasons mentioned by the participants, for crossing into the US were related with shopping: shopping for food (9 respondents), shopping for clothing (8 respondents), shopping for other items (6 respondents). By using a Likert scale with 5 choices, participants rated how often they felt certain emotions while waiting in line, such as upset, stress, angry, and bored. As presented in table I, most of them stated that they have never or almost never felt upset (24), stress (21), or angry (26); and 19 stated that they have felt bored (from some-times to very frequently). As emphasized in parenthesis in Table I, bored is experienced more frequently in most of the 9 who go to US alone. Crossers do some actions to avoid or cope with these emotional states. It is not surprising that the most mentioned action is listening to music, which was mentioned by 22 participants. And reading was the second one, which was mentioned by 11 participants, including 4 that cross alone. This is evidence that border crossers likes to do simple activities that can explicitly interrupt while they are in their cars waiting in the line.

Table 1. Emotions feel by border crossers

Emotion	Never	Almost never	Some-times	Fre-quently	Very Fre-quently	Total of Participants
Upset	10 (4)	14 (3)	3 (1)	1 (1)	3 (0)	31(9)
Stressed	14 (4)	7 (2)	7 (2)	2 (1)	1 (0)	31(9)
Angry	15 (6)	11 (2)	1 (0)	1 (1)	3 (0)	31(9)
Bored	7 (2)	5 (1)	13 (4)	3 (2)	3 (0)	31(9)

The domain problem understanding gained so far, enabled us to identify some of the open questions associated with our hypothesis, such as:

-       How does the slowed vehicular mobility and the physical space of the queue influence the design of an ambient urban game?

-       What design characteristics should be incorporated into the ambient game design to contribute to the user's pleasure and reduce his/her stress?

In order to address these questions, the following section presents a preliminary analysis of the design features we envision that ambient urban games should include to cope with the border crossers' issues.

4   Design Requirements

We are aware that our application should satisfy some design requirements of location-based games, such as scalability (regarding time, and number of players) [4] and promote a pleasurable social experience [O'Hara]. However, some of these design requirements should be adapted to satisfy the specific context of use, in addition to we identified new ones:

-   *Location-based,* in the sense that i) the game should be only accessible when players are waiting in line, and ii) provide activities based on their specific position in the line.

- *Aware of drivers' behavior* in order to: i) control the life cycle of the game without disturbing users' main activity (driving); i.e. the game will be initiated (if the driver arrives at the line), interrupted (if the driver moves ahead or changes lanes), resumed (when the driver stops in the lane), and stopped (when the driver finally crosses the border).
- *Provide simple activities* that drivers can explicitly interrupt and resume when desired, i.e. activities that do not demand their attention continuously.
- *Provide awareness and maintain records of waiting times*, which can be implemented by registering the duration of the game's life cycle since it represents the time spent crossing the border. Enabling crossers to access this information could be used for purposes such as determining the best time of day to cross the border or the best days to cross.

5   Conclusions and Future Work

We propose that ambient location-based games are an appropriate approach for enabling commuters to reduce the stress generated when crossing the Mexico-US border. The study we presented provides evidence that border crossers may present emotional states associated with stress, such as feeling upset and bored. However, we need to carry out further studies to understand the characteristics of commuters, who are the most frequent border crossers (i.e. they cross for business purposes every day). In particular, we plan to carry out studies that enable us to inform the design of urban games, which will include focus group and participatory design sessions.

References

1. Cordova, J.: Crossing the World's Busiest Border: Transborder Commuters, Performance, Culture and Supercion. Master's Thesis, Univ. of California, San Diego (January 1, 2010)
2. http://suite101.com/article/delays-when-entering-the-us-from-mexico-by-car-a121783
3. Russoniello, C.V., O'Brien, K., Parks, J.M.: The effectiveness of casual video games in improving mood and decreasing stress. J. of Cyber Therapy & Rehabilitation 2, 53–66 (2009)
4. Neustaedter, C., Tang, A., Judge, T.K.: Creating scalable location-based games: lessons from Geocaching. Personal Ubiquitous Comput. 17(2) (2013)
5. Graham, E.A.: BudBurst Mobile and the Floracaching game. In: AGU Fall Meeting Abstracts vol. 1, p.2 (December 2011)
6. Zarzycki, A.: Urban games: application of augmented reality. In: SIGGRAPH Asia 2012 Symposium on Apps (SA 2012), Article 8, 1 pages. ACM Press, New York (2012)
7. Celino, I., Cerizza, D., Contessa, S., Corubolo, M., Dell'Aglio, D., Della Valle, E., Piccinini, F., Urbanopoly, F.: Collection and Quality Assessment of Geo-spatial Linked Data via a Human Computation Game. In: Finalist to the 10th Semantic Web Challenge (2012)
8. Gentes, A., Guyot-Mbodji, A., Demeure, I.: Gaming on the move: urban experience as a new paradigm for mobile pervasive game design. In: International Conference on Entertainment and Media in the Ubiquitous Era (MindTrek 2008), pp. 23–28. ACM, New York (2008)

User Statistics and Traffic Analysis of Public Internet Access in Buses

César Cárdenas and Fernando Camacho

Tecnológico de Monterrey – Campus Querétaro
Epigmenio González 500, Fracc. San Pablo, C.P. 76130, Santiago de Querétaro, México
ccardena@itesm.mx, A00888663@itesm.mx

Abstract. Internet-based transportation systems are becoming widespread due to advances in Internet, computing, geospatial information system (GIS) and intelligent sensor technologies. They are essential to enable Smart City concepts. Traffic analysis and user statistics are very important to improve Quality of Service (QoS) provisioning in Internet networks. In this paper, we present the first user statistics and traffic analysis of the *Qronectate* project, a government initiative that offers public Internet access in buses. Results shown that the number of users has not achieved its momentum. Therefore, common statistics such as average users age, number of days used per week, time spend on bus and more visited Webpages were identified and confirmed by applying a survey. To the authors knowledge this is the first work to analyze such networks.

Keywords: Intelligent Transportation Systems, Smart City, Internet on Buses.

1   Introduction

In recent years, urban studies have attracted a lot of attention from the ICT research community and industry. This is mainly due to social changes but also because the evolution of ICT beyond its legacy applications. Smart City concepts take into account such convergence. One of the first concepts proposed was Intelligent Transport Systems (ITS). ITS aim to provide advanced transport services to users so they can become better informed and can make better transport decisions [1]. Transport systems are also living environments due to the time the users spend on them, especially in megacities. As such, having a good telecommunications infrastructure in these systems ensure good service provisioning and traffic analysis and user statistics are important procedures to determine if such systems are meeting its requirements. Traffic engineers use this information to better design and configure the networks, and to ensure the QoS demands by the users.

Buses are the most used transportation systems around the world. There are few projects providing public Internet access during bus travels. In the city of Santiago de Querétaro, México, a recent project has been implemented with the intention to

G. Urzaiz et al. (Eds.): UCAmI 2013, LNCS 8276, pp. 390–393, 2013.

provide public Internet access in buses; the project has the name of *Qronectate*[1]. In this paper we present first user statistics and traffic analysis of this project. The paper is organized as follows. First we present some projects related to public Internet access in buses. Second, we present the *Qronectate* project. Third, we present user statistics and traffic analysis. Last, we present some conclusions and future work.

2 Public Internet Access in Buses

Public Internet access has been offered since the 90's. Municipalities worldwide offer public Internet access to provide services to citizens. The terms Municipal WiFi, Muni Wi-Fi or Muni-Fi have been assigned to such services. Public Internet access has been extended to transportation systems such as vehicles and buses; in the following we will describe the main projects up to date and related to buses.

In Australia. Adelaide administration tested an Internet-enabled bus program. The program provide real-time passenger information through 2 LCD screens, including accurate estimated time to arrival to the next stop, real-time news feeds, community information, etc. [2]. In San Francisco, the Alamenda-Contra Costa Transit Agency introduced free Internet connectivity on its Transbay bus fleet. The project was named NetBus. The service allows passengers to use WiFi enabled portable devices to access Internet and extend technology to their work commute trip. The NetBus concept utilizes a mix of Wireless Wide Area Network (WWAN) and Wireless Local Area Network (WLAN) technologies. The basic idea behind the NetBus service is to take a 3G, mobile modem, which connects to a mobile carrier's cellular infrastructure and share the connection between users via WiFi [3]. In [4], authors proposed a system using a variety of sensors (GPS, RFID, temperature sensors, and Bluetooth) to collect information, and transmitting it to a comprehensive information processing platform by GPRS networks. The platform completes information storage, analysis and real-time update. By login a WEB interface of the platform by a mobile phone, users can obtain some specific information of the bus which they wish to take. In [5], authors proposed a system allowing public transportation users to find routes and buses between pairs of origin and destination addresses. The methodology is intended to be easily accessible and available through standard Web browsers on the client machine and be interoperable. To demonstrate some of the features and capabilities of the methodology, a prototype of the methodology, called iBus, was also proposed.

In México, the first city to provide public Internet access was the Obregón City in 2007[2]. This network provides city coverage of 62 Km^2 of wireless connectivity. It was intended to provide public, private and academic, services and contents. Among other things, police cars are equipped with on-board computers, they can consult information in real-time or control cameras installed around the city. Fixed electronic kiosks have been also considered. Bus access for long transportation routes were also

---

[1] http://www.municipiodequeretaro.gob.mx/
listadocontenidos.aspx?q=vsaUTHVrpb55Ed/
xFWSAJcufNGgZ54QUEhsjEnAaze4=

[2] http://www.sonorasoft.com.mx/ss_conozcaelpts_3_situacion.swf

considered as well as ambulance services. WiMAX/WiFi technology is used. The second city in México to promote intensive public Internet services was Guadalajara with the project named Jalisco Digital. Jalisco intends to achieve 70% of coverage at the end of the current administration. Other cities around México then started to promote their public Internet access projects. In the city of Querétaro, the first project was proposed in 2009 by a startup named Transcell. It offers real time information regarding the public transit system upon request of the user. It provides a control system to companies operating within the public transit system. It allows the user, using the internet or a cellular messaging system, to request the location and the estimated time a public transit unit will take to arrive at his/her place, thereby allowing the person to use his/her time more effectively and be able to choose between several transit options[3]. In the next section we will present in detail the *Qronectate* project, a municipality initiative focused on providing public Internet access in buses.

3   Analysis of the *Qronectate* Project

The *Qronectate* project was proposed by the Municipality of Santiago de Querétaro in México. It has similar architecture as the NetBus project in San Francisco. In the first stage it was tested in parks, gardens and one bus. In the second stage the coverage was extended to main bus transit avenues and 100 buses with 32 different routes. Third stage will extend the service to more administrative offices and buses. Bus fee is not modified and buses with the service were marked with stamps.

3.1   Informal Sources of Information

Based on online forums, 69% of the people in Querétaro use the bus in a frequent manner. Users report excellent Internet speed access. It was also reported that once on the bus, 5 pages were accessed simultaneously without feeling speed degradation. Squares have good access quality, in 4 months they were visited by 80 users per day in average. Gardens were visited by 833 users per day in average. Main streets were visited by 907 users per day in average. Buses were used by 37 users per day in average. The Websites more visited were: Twitter, Facebook, Youtube and Google search. There is a web link where users can make complains to the service. Despite this official information is interesting, it cannot be used to dimension the network.

3.2   Secondary Source of Information

We took into account formal qualitative methods (secondary sources) to get estimation on some parameters. Mainly, the data provided by the National Institute of Statistics and Geography (INEGI)[4]. Main results associated to global population are: 58% of Internet users send emails. 3.5% have Internet service in their business, 2.6% execute bank transactions, 35.7% use Internet for educational activities and 28.1% use it to read. Again, this cannot be used for network design.

---

[3] http://parquetecnologico.campusqueretaro.net/en/transcell
[4] http://www.inegi.org.mx/

3.3   Primary Source of Information

A questionnaire was applied to users in 5 important crossroads of the 32 routes with the service. From 40 questionnaire respondents, 92% use smartphones while 8% use laptop. The average ranges of ages were: 28%, between 18 and 25, 42%, between 26 to 35, 28%, between 36 and 45, 0%, between 46 and 60, and 3% above 60. 14% use the bus all weekdays, 64% use them 5 days a week, 21% use them 3 days a week. 3% of them spend 5 to 10 minutes in bus, 37% spend 10 to 20 and the same quantity spend 21 to 30, 23% spend 30 to 40 minutes and none of them spend above one hour. 39% of the questionnaire respondents used the service. Facebook, Twitter, Google Search and E-mail were the Webpages more consulted.

3.4   Traffic Analysis

To better understand network use, we performed a first traffic analysis review. We used the Wireshark^{TM} tool, a free and open-source network protocol analyzer. We acquired information from the 3 most important routes during a transit time around 15 minutes in different weekdays. The percentage of TCP packets was 96.53%, 92.33% and 93.85% respectively, and finally UDP packets was 3.47%, 7.67% and 6.15% respectively. These results follow normal Internet traffic behavior.

4   Conclusions and Future Work

This is the first study to understand buses with access to Internet on the move. The executed work is very important to design and configure networks for QoS provisioning. In the context of a Smart City concept they are required to understand citizen needs and to execute citizen service (application) design. Formal and informal user statistics were presented, identified and confirmed. From the traffic analysis, we draw that the number of network users needs to be increased. In the future we will extend our survey to a wide population and for traffic analysis, we will wait more time. We also foresee coverage, WEB mining studies and urban application development.

References

1. Ghosh, S.: Intelligent Transportation Systems: Smart and Green Infrastructure Design, 2nd edn. CRC Press (2012)
2. Branko, M.: Roads and Transport: Internet Bus Online in Adelaide. Government News 29(9) (October 2009)
3. Twichell, J., Minoofar, C.: The "Netbus" WiFi Project: Delivering Internet Access to AC Transit Bus Riders. In: Proceedings of the 13th ITS World Congress, London, October 8-12 (2006)
4. Wang, Y.-K., et al.: A Bus Information Query System Based on the Internet of Things. Electronic Science and Technology 25(10), 32 (2012)
5. Karimi, H., et al.: Finding Optimal Bus Service Routes: Internet-based Methodology to Serve Transit Patrons. Journal of Computing in Civil Engineering 18(2) (2004)

Sentiment Characterization of an Urban Environment via Twitter

Víctor Martínez and Víctor M. Gonzílez

Department of Computer Science,
Instituto Tecnologico Autonomo de Mexico,
Rio Hondo #1, Progreso Tizapan, Del. Alvaro Obregon 01080
Mexico City, Mexico
{victor.gonzalez}@itam.mx

Abstract. We propose a statistical study of sentiment produced in an urban environment by collecting tweets submitted in a certain timeframe. Each tweet was processed using our own sentiment classifier and assigned either a positive or a negative label. By calculating the average mood, we were able to run a Mann-Withney's U test to evaluate differences in the calculated mood per day of week. We found that all days of the week had significantly different medians. We also found positive correlations between Mondays and the rest of the week.

1 Introduction

Twitter, the most popular microblogging platform of our time, allows users to broadcast brief text updates to a public or selected group of contacts [1]. By analyzing this publicly available broadcast of information is possible to infer population attitudes in a similar manner as those obtained by pollsters [1, 2]. Several studies have been able to use Twitter obtained data to explain and predict outcomes in social, cultural, economical and political data [1–3].

Our aim is to use these attitudes portrayed in the Twitter-sphere as a way to estimate the collective mood of an urban environment.

1.1 Related Work

Most of the related work was done by Bollen, Pepe and Mao who found out that political and economical events influence the quality and quantity of messages submitted to Twitter [1]. In a continuation of the study, they were able to predict stock market changes [4]. O'Connor and Balasubramanyan were able to correlate tweets to political opinion over the 2008 U.S. presidential election [2].

2 Results

2.1 Data and Methodology

We obtained a collection of public tweets recorded from June 15th to July 19th, 2013 (1,226,981 tweets from 1,805 distinct locations around Mexico City).

G. Urzaiz et al. (Eds.): UCAmI 2013, LNCS 8276, pp. 394–397, 2013.

For each captured tweet, we stored an unique identifier, date-time of submission (GMT-6), coordinates of submission and place identifier, alongside with the text of the tweet. Unfortunately, The Twitter API explicitly prohibit us of providing user demographics such as gender or age.

Using a previously trained Naive Bayes Classifier[1] we assigned each tweet to either a positive or a negative mood. We then obtained an average mood score $m_{d,t}$ for tweets submitted on day $d \in \{Monday, Tuesday, \ldots, Sunday\}$ and time $t \in \{5z : z \in \mathbb{N}\}$ as described by equation 1

$$m_{d,t} = \frac{\sum_{w \in T_{d,t}} \mathbb{1}(w)}{||T_{d,t}||} \tag{1}$$

where $T_{d,t}$ denotes the set of captured tweets from day d and time $[t - 5, t]$ and $\mathbb{1}(w)$ is the characteristic function for positiveness in tweet w.

Each $m_{d,t}$ represents a percentage of positive tweets with respect of the total tweets captured at the time. Grouping by day of week yields seven 24-hour time-series with values ranging from 0 (no positive tweets at the time) to 1 (no negative tweets at the time).

2.2   Mood Analysis

In a typical day, the day starts with an aggregated score of 80% which slowly downgrades to 45% - 50% on weekdays by 7 am until 8:30 am (begin of labor). The mood starts climbing from 9:30 am reaching its peak (85% - 90%) around Mexican lunch hour (1 pm - 2 pm) from where it goes down again (post-meal work hours) finishing the day around 70% - 75%. Fig. 1 shows the aggregated mood for each day of the week.

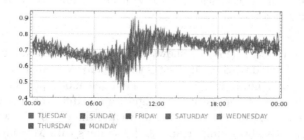

Fig. 1. Evolution of the aggregated mood score as a function of time. Typical days start around 80% positiveness and end close to 70%.

We decided to investigate further this progression by color coding the range of possible moods ($m_{d,t} \in [0, 1]$) with extreme values taking colors red (RGB:

---

[1] With 145,520 features (unigrams and bigrams, basic stopwords, without stemming) using a automatically labeled [5] dataset of 118,092 positive and 77,265 negative examples.

255 0 0) and green (RGB: 0 255 0) for negative and positive moods respectively. Following this idea, a neutral mood appears with a color resembling olive (RGB: 127.5 127.5 0). Fig. 2 exemplifies this idea. It can be noticed that even when all days tend to follow a similar pattern, weekdays (with the exception of Friday) are more likely to end in a neutral mood whereas Fridays, Saturdays and Sundays end with a positive feeling.

Fig. 2. By color coding the range of possible moods we are able to identify the way the mood change in a certain week

Descriptive statistics (Fig. 3) shows that the worst day for inhabitants of Mexico City is Thursday while the best is the Sunday. We ran a Mann-Withney's U test to evaluate the difference in the calculated mood per day of week. We found that all days of the week have significantly different medians. We also found positive correlations between Mondays and the rest of the week (meaning that a good start is always important) and Tuesdays with Monday, Wednesday, Thursday and Friday. A multivariate regression analysis shows that Sunday's mood depends on the values from the week (adj. $R^2 = 0.6121$, $F(2, 281) = 76.47 \, p < 0.001$) with all days except Saturday ($p > 0.1$) having significant effect. In contrast, Thursday's mood can be explained by mood changes in the week (adj. $R^2 = 0.6578$, $F(6, 281) = 92.94 \, p < 0.001$) with only Wednesday ($\beta = 0.3181 \, p < 0.001$), Saturdays ($\beta = 0.2405 \, p < 0.001$) and Sundays ($\beta = 0.4068 \, p < 0.001$) being of significant importance.

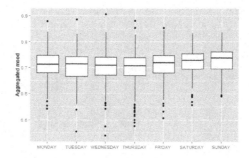

Fig. 3. Descriptive statistics for each time series. For Mexico City, the worst day was Thursday while the best was Sunday.

3   Conclusion

In this work, we propose the usage of the sentiment portrayed by tweets, submitted within city boundaries, as a way of characterizing the collective mood of an urban environment. By studying a dataset of over 1 million tweets from Mexico City, we found statistical differences in the way Mexico City's inhabitants feel about the weekdays. We also found linear relations between certain days and the rest of the week. Finally, by mapping moods to a gradient of colors we were able to visualize the progression of mood swings in different days.

Acknowledgments. We would like to thank everyone involved during the course of this study and to the Asociacion Mexicana de Cultura A.C. for all their support.

References

1. Bollen, J., Mao, H., Pepe, A.: Modeling public mood and emotion: Twitter sentiment and socio-economic phenomena. In: ICWSM (2011)
2. O'Connor, B., Balasubramanyan, R., Routledge, B.R., Smith, N.A.: From tweets to polls: Linking text sentiment to public opinion time series. ICWSM 11, 122–129 (2010)
3. Diakopoulos, N.A., Shamma, D.A.: Characterizing debate performance via aggregated twitter sentiment. In: Proceedings of the SIGCHI Conference on Human Factors in Computing Systems, pp. 1195–1198. ACM (2010)
4. Bollen, J., Mao, H., Zeng, X.: Twitter mood predicts the stock market. Journal of Computational Science 2(1), 1–8 (2011)
5. Go, A., Bhayani, R., Huang, L.: Twitter sentiment classification using distant supervision. CS224N Project Report, Stanford, 1–12 (2009)

Author Index